MW01484764

Palgrave Studies in Economic History

Series Editor
Kent Deng, London School of Economics, London, UK

Palgrave Studies in Economic History is designed to illuminate and enrich our understanding of economies and economic phenomena of the past. The series covers a vast range of topics including financial history, labour history, development economics, commercialisation, urbanisation, industrialisation, modernisation, globalisation, and changes in world economic orders.

Rossella Del Prete

The Neapolitan Creative Economy

The Growth of the Music Market and Creative
Sector in Naples, 17th–19th Centuries

Rossella Del Prete
Department of Economics
University of Sannio
Benevento, Italy

ISSN 2662-6497   ISSN 2662-6500 (electronic)
Palgrave Studies in Economic History
ISBN 978-3-031-55902-0   ISBN 978-3-031-55903-7 (eBook)
https://doi.org/10.1007/978-3-031-55903-7

The translation was done with the help of an artificial intelligence machine translation tool. A subsequent human revision was done primarily in terms of content.
Translation from the Italian language edition: "Le forme sonore di un'economia creativa: Il mercato musicale a Napoli in età moderna (secc. XVII-XIX)" by Rossella Del Prete, © Kinetès Edizioni 2022. Published by Kinetès Edizioni. All Rights Reserved.

Cover illustration: Universal Images Group North America LLC/Alamy Stock Photo

This Palgrave Macmillan imprint is published by the registered company Springer Nature Switzerland AG
The registered company address is: Gewerbestrasse 11, 6330 Cham, Switzerland

Paper in this product is recyclable.

Do what you feel in your heart to be right—for you'll be criticized anyway. You'll be damned if you do, and damned if you don't.

—*Eleanor Roosevelt*

FOREWORD

The unique cultures of early and late modern Naples have generated more than three centuries of inquiry, whether, historical, social, political, or artistic (to name only a few of the myriad disciplinary areas). A subtle, even imperceptible thread (albeit of significant impact) interwoven within these broad sectors and one too often unnoticed has been the role of the Neapolitan cultural economy. In this case, its role as a mechanism for economic and social development as well as promoting innovation and a broader societal cohesion, the latter often transcending politics, religion, and the contemporary social hierarchy and unrest. The dense artistic nexus of culture within early and late modern Naples, despite the often fluid and ever-changing political contexts, disclosed tightly intertwined economic networks that not only promoted the creative and cultural sectors but also imparted an imprimatur of commodification. Perhaps nowhere else did this phenomenon of economy and culture take root in such profound manners than the Neapolitan conservatories, whose bearing and legacy transcended their role within contemporary musical practices.

The establishment of the four local conservatories initially reflected the social initiatives of the Catholic Church. Naples, as in other large European cities, witnessed a significant rise in immigration in the early modern period. And like other urban centers, the city remained ill-equipped to accommodate the influx of new arrivals; it had neither crafted social policy regarding the welfare of new residents, nor addressed the significant and rising issue of endemic poverty. There were, however, clearly articulated views on the civic nature of poverty and its impact on contemporary society. As early as 1586, a royal edict distinguished the "honest poor" from the "idle vagabond;" a dichotomy aimed clearly at the preservation of social order. Given the dearth of political policy (beyond this simple bifurcation), the Catholic Church increasingly filled the void of assistance to address the rising number of residents in poverty. A substantial number of entities devoted to the poor emerged in early modern Naples, including *ospedali*, congregations, confraternities, religious orders, and many others in addition to the burgeoning conservatories.

The shared charism of faith and charity professed by these groups extended to and often overlapped in their ultimate objective, one clearly economic: the provision of the means to acquire a living in the future, through the acquisition of a trade or a skill. The coalescence around this central aim was progressive as it inherently focused on the future generation, specifically children. Nevertheless, the administrative oversight of the conservatories remained in the hands of a secular entity and these individuals viewed the institutions as elements within the larger economy of the city as well as the trade imparted, in this case music, as a commodity. As such, each institution was entrusted to a "president" and a board of six governors, appointed annually (although often serving multiple terms), who were nominated by the districts in which each conservatory was located. The office of the Viceroy (either Spanish or Austrian) and later the Bourbon court confirmed their positions. The individual governors focused on all areas of management, including physical infrastructure (maintenance, repair, construction), economic resources (revenue, investments, donations), and legal issues (individual or collective relating to the State). This framework posited inherent threads of continuity among creativity and culture, economy and art, and social and political order.

Rossella Del Prete's study *The Neapolitan Creative Economy. The Grow of the Music Market and Creative Sector in Naples, 17ᵗʰ—19ᵗʰ Centuries,* represents an unprecedented inquiry into this evolving sector of contemporary scholarship. Although past scholarship has emphasized the pedagogical innovations of the conservatories and their larger impact on the European Continent, Del Prete's sheds new light on the larger economic, creative, and social resonances of these institutions. Her careful scholarship emphasizes the notion and definition of a "creative economy" and the resultant productive systems established. The insightful analysis of the musical "market" specifically in early modern Naples creates not only context but also how the broader culture of the capital city had created both civic and social institutions geared toward and deeply embedded within the attendant creative economy. Given the European renown of the Neapolitan conservatories, often a favored topic of inquiry for contemporary travelers and travelogs on the Grand Tour, Del Prete addresses the undiscussed nature of institutional life for the *musici*, not solely that artistic and pedagogical, but especially their role as human capital within an economic entity of considerable impact. Del Prete's access to the remaining corpus of primary sources regarding the Pietà dei Turchini Conservatory (associated with many of the most famous alumni of the Neapolitan school) grounds her perspective and enlarges the breadth of analysis. The tangible outcomes, most prominently creative and economic, are traced through the diverse channels within the history of this venerable institution, allowing an understanding of its administration, musical and social activities, but also postulating a *modus operandi* for the other three Neapolitan conservatories, whose present-day understandings lack the existence of such rich documentation. Of particular merit is the analysis of financial resources, namely bequests and legacies, as well as the extensive administrative apparatus of the Turchini, which remained inherently complex, yet articulated in often modern, progressive manners. Del Prete's study concludes with the onset of the late modern period, a watershed for contemporary Europe, socially, politically, and of course economically. The transformation of long-standing artistic institutions such as the conservatory and related sectors of theater and cultural life indelibly altered the rapport between music and economy. The unification of the Italian peninsula as a single entity and its profound, often detrimental impact on the former capital city, are lain bare in Del Prete's insightful utilization of existing data.

Rossella Del Prete's manifold achievements in *The Neapolitan Creative Economy (17th—19th Centuries)* bridge disciplinary borders to illustrate the role of the creative sector in forming then nourishing economic structures marked by innovation. Equally important is the multiform demonstration within her analyses of how culture contributes to community building, cohesion, and social development. This monograph represents a valuable achievement and a model for scholars working in the disciplines of music, economics, the social sciences, and multiple related areas.

January 2024   Anthony R. DelDonna, Ph.D.
                                                              Thosmas E. Caestecker
                                                                 Professor of Music
                                                              Georgetown University
                                                              Washington, DC, USA

PREFACE

The debate on the relationship between creativity, culture, economics, and technology, or the ability to create and circulate intellectual capital capable of generating income, new jobs, and promoting social inclusion, cultural diversity, and human development, is increasingly global and more and more interesting.

Today we know that creativity and innovation are forces that can transform the world and that countries that invest more consciously in these two resources will increase their economies, producing higher profits and more employment.

This is what happened in Naples, one of the major capitals of European culture, between the modern and contemporary ages, which, by indulging the typical behavior and traditions of the Neapolitans, known as "festaioli," lovers of music, the sea and food, strengthened a typical Neapolitan creative economy, the one produced in artisan and harmony workshops, in copy shops and printing houses, in music conservatories and chapels, in theaters and private drawing rooms; in urban spaces and by the sea, in all the viceroyal and popular festivals: a triumph of creativity, of productive and financial initiative, of travel and cultural exchange, of inclusion and participation at various social levels.

The social, political, and artistic conditions of the city of Naples stimulated a significant growth of music, musicians, and culture in the Kingdom of Naples from the beginning of the seventeenth century.

In particular, the music of early modern Naples and its renowned artistic traditions remained a fertile field for eighteenth-century scholars (cf. L. Bianconi, A. Del Donna, G. Olivieri, P. Maione, and other).

This book investigates the Neapolitan creative and cultural economy, which was generated by an informal system of historical inclusion, cultural diversity, and human development that turned into a formalized production system of knowledge and circular economy. Decisive for the creation and professional development of Neapolitan music and theaters was the birth of four ancient music conservatories, founded as assistance institutes for abandoned children and transformed, in the mid-seventeenth century, into four "music workshops," the first centers of mass musical instruction and the first centers of musical production closely linked to the territory, the theaters, and the copy shops and harmonic workshops present in Naples at that time.

Those first music schools inherited from the European *renfermement* practice the principle of social inclusion, using the art of music as a lever for the construction of a creative economy based on the increasingly professional training of a human capital made up of musicians, singers, and instrumentalists, but also luthiers, copyists, theatrical extras, etc., and on the production of musical and theatrical services as well as musical compositions distributed and performed in increasingly broad musical and theatrical contexts.

The research conducted on the four ancient Music Conservatories of Naples took into account the various agents that contributed to the transformation and innovation of those ancient institutions analyzed as productive systems of knowledge, know-how, and skills.

The reconstruction of the functioning mechanisms of the Conservatorio della Pietà dei Turchini, taken as a model for Neapolitan music education institutions, allows, through the examination of its financing and expenditure flows, to analyze various problems. Among these is the question of whether there is continuity or rupture with the more traditional welfare structure. In reality, the music conservatory fully fits into it, both in its patrimonial configuration and in its intervention policy. It was born as a foundling hospital based on an educational program aimed at education and learning a trade and manages the "patrimony of the poor" like many other contemporary charitable institutions, but what is most surprising in its functioning is the setting of a singular educational agency, which, while referring to welfare models common to the practice of *renfermement*, aims at the maintenance of poor and abandoned children through a music school with a continuous exchange of tasks and functions. Music, in fact, did not respond to a simple need for image but, in addition to being a means of exalting faith, the institution, and the city, increased the participation in religious functions, procuring a greater number of supporters and introducing, on the market, musicians and musical productions of various kinds, both sacred and profane.

Between the seventeenth and eighteenth centuries, Italian and French opera productions were vying for supremacy in the international cultural market. In the first half of the eighteenth century, Naples became one of the most lively and attractive cities in Italy for both musicians and composers, with is much-admired music school and facilities and venues for music and opera lovers. It's renowned as a "musical city," and its Royal Theatre, the biggest in Europe, granted it a special place in the European tourist market (see among many studies, Robinson 1972; and Del Donna, 2012, 2020; Van Damme, De Munck and Miles, 2018).

The reason for this blossoming has little to do with the conditions of the material economy. Indeed, the image of Naples as a hub of intellectual and cultural creativity is in a sharp contrast to its representation as a "parasitic" city, as affirmed in traditional historiography. This contradiction was nicely expressed by one of the best-known historians of the Italian "Mezzogiorno" in his description of the relationship between the capital city and the provinces in the eighteenth century (Galasso, 1978).

That does not mean we should replace the parasitic with the creative image of the city by reproducing a mythical view of the city itself as a subject with its own agency. Indeed, we should historicize the matter of creativity by recognizing that its role in the production and redistribution of wealth had a relevant impact in the old regime of urban economic and social balances and played an important role in the promotion of creative industries.

To avoid the risk of anachronism, we define theatrical and musical production as cultural industries in a broad sense as those that produce goods and services with a symbolic rather than instrumental value (Thorsby, 2001). Therefore, the now dominant idea of creative industries as those based on the generation and exploitation of intellectual property and on the individual ability to generate something new (Howkins, 2001) does not fit the historical context we are dealing with, to the extent that there was not any clear legal definition of intellectual property regarding music and operas: indeed, the first legal definition of the author's property rights on music and operas was introduced in 1811 (Maione and Seller, 1994). Moreover, the individualist notion of creativity is not useful for really understanding its social genesis. The blossoming of the musical and theatrical industry cannot be understood if not in relation to the specific city. Here we will try to highlight the following: 1) the formation of human capital as the result of the peculiar institutional urban welfare system that generated a musical industry by also promoting the international image of Naples as a "musical city"; 2) the role of cultural consumption, specifically of the demand for musical services and theatrical entertainment, as it evolved from a mainly religious matter toward the shaping of a proper cultural market; and 3) the role that central power played in attaching a prestige value to theatrical enjoinment by stimulating in this way its broader consumption and the private investment in theatrical business.

Creativity and culture are now key recognized sectors for global recovery: they contribute to dialogue and understanding of people, and at the same time, they are fertile areas for innovation and for inclusive and sustainable growth (Report *Creativity, Culture & Capital—Impact investing in the global creative economy*, January 2021).

Words like "creativity at work" and "impact capital connection" seem highly anachronistic for the topic we are about to address in this book, but absolutely necessary to give value to an experience that, six centuries ago, starting from similar words and principles, such as assistance, education, work, art, creations, profit and non-profit, modeled a "spontaneously" creative economy, more inclusive and sustainable.

That was the beginning of the care experience aimed at so-called "irregular childhood" for which an educational offer was created based on artistic and professional preparation within the many shelters that have arisen for minors in difficulty, either because they are orphans or because they are naughty. And, focusing on what we define today "urban and social redevelopment, sharing, inclusion and participation," many of those charitable-welfare institutions built a professional training system which, responding to a very strong social demand—for hospitality, education, survival—and starting from putting into practice an idea that used practical education and the introduction to "arts and crafts," contributed to diversifying the market, to strengthen it and make it increasingly "regulated" and "inclusive."

Some of these institutes, "social enterprises" themselves, created real manufacturing businesses, others founded healthcare service businesses and "hospitals"; in only two cases, Venice and Naples, our Conservatories founded in the sixteenth century dedicated themselves to a form of creative economy, training musicians, producing music products, selling music services. That was the birth of today's Third Sector.

In Naples, in particular, a party city with a strong attitude to theatricality, four ancient boys' Conservatories, focusing on social impact as well as financial, took back the reins of human capital being neglected and often abandoned to a fate of hardship, ignorance, and marginality.

The young people welcomed into those institutions experimented with different forms of creativity, from craftsmanship, to textile production, to silk socks and felt caps, to the manufacturing of the typical "riggiole," the Neapolitan majolica, to that of the more or less artistic workmanship of wood or iron, to the point of exercising forms of harmonious apprenticeship in the field of violin making or musical copy making and finally in the practice of musical performance, an indispensable ingredient for any occasion of celebration. Thus, a real music market and, more generally, a live entertainment one was born.

Today we know that the creation of a "cultural" market is not necessarily the bearer of economic development, if not within the limits of the internal economies of these markets (often, however, very modest). We have to acknowledge that culture is actually capable of creating economies and therefore a significant employment effect, but only under certain conditions: a city, to be a city of art and culture, must live from culture, analyzing an appropriate model of local development which cannot ignore real entrepreneurial ability and an original and intense creative effort.

It is necessary to create a context of accessible experiences that enable to give value and meaning to "cultural heritage" in its broadest sense. Cultural actions, especially if political and institutional, will have to allow the individuals to understand and appreciate their own cultural heritage. Without creating the conditions for the accumulation of intangible resources (human capital) that trigger the synergistic interaction of supply and demand, no partial or unilateral intervention may have an appreciable effect.

The governance applied to the four ancient musical conservatories of Naples (the approach of the Venetians was different) had the ability to reconcile economic, cultural, and social value of that undertaking. The adoption of entrepreneurial logics in the management of those institutions and the turning point in music schools, constituted the first basic keystone for the system, to be declined on the approaches of both operators and public decision-makers.

Without considering the formal corporate aspects, the structures, and the purpose of profit or charity, let's look at some simple and linear concepts: objectives, management of resources and results, and a profit logic that does not consist only in the economic return (which those first businesses cultural and creative social groups also produced), but also, and above all, in maximizing the socio-cultural impact of an activity, composed by much more heterogeneous indexes than the economic equivalent.

And it was in those original "music factories" that an *ante literam* model of cultural and creative industry—reaped results extraordinary,—was born, in the name of that necessary inclusion, of creative work to be regulated, of a creative economy to be strengthened.

The effects have never ended: over the centuries, they have only changed names and forms. The experience of teaching and practicing music established in Spanish Naples was revived over the 1970s in Venezuela, before returning to Naples in the Rione Sanità, with another name: the "Abreu method" applied to create and run Italian children's and youth orchestras. It remained the experience of the sense of social reintegration through music and the trait of cultural enterprise is better defined. The UN today encourages and finances creative projects involving children and adolescents "at risk," while the reform of the Third Sector, in Italy, supports inclusion and cohesion projects aimed at fostering the development of sub-urban and peripheral neighborhoods with the implementation of cultural, creative, innovative projects, and the creation of social and community enterprises.

The connection between an experience of the past—which belongs to the history of people, the Neapolitans, that became a model of education followed throughout Europe and which laid the foundations for a highly original creative economy, in the capital of the Kingdom of Naples—and the current reality of cultural and creative enterprises, as with the reform of the Third Sector in Italy, it is too strong to not to be mentioned at the beginning of our discussion.

The fascinating world of live entertainment expresses, today, like in the past, a heterogeneous, composite, and very complex reality, in which extremely different souls, vocations, and stories coexist. It is exactly this complexity, belonging mostly to the sphere of the ephemeral that makes it more difficult to define its institutional, training, legislative, financial, and organizational.

The world of art, always inserted into a broader economic-productive system, like any other production sector undergoes and defines the dynamics of a particular market space, in which supply and demand intersect. Making art also means production and distribution activities, operating and planning space, promotion, training, dissemination, or support and service to artistic initiatives. It is all this that makes art a "productive sector" like the others, but it is its essence that diversifies it and, in some ways, its ability or inability to keep an eye on the world, trying to understand it, interpret it, and represent it.

The case of Naples illustrates a complex example of interaction between political and market dynamics. The flourishing of a creative economy in the eighteenth century was certainly also the result of a political invest-ment (Maione and Seller, 2000) fostered by the cosmopolitan stimuli of the cultural market and motivated by a project of social control. Its success was due both to the presence of an already established musical and theatrical tradition and the rise of a theatrical public market which enhanced the already existing musical capital. Yet the rise of a theatrical market was, in fact, an unintended consequence of the political will. That immaterial production and performing arts could have an economic value was not the main idea of eighteenth-century politicians and intel-lectuals. During the seventeenth-century, theater had been part of the religious welfare system, and with the advent of an absolute monarchy, it became *instrumentum regni* and a tool for social control; this func-tion serves to explain why theater was a matter for the central and not the local authorities. The Royal Theatre S. Carlo, though managed by private impresarios, was a political and cultural success, but not a well-run enterprise per se: the few and often messy accounts left in the Neapolitan archives show a fatal tendency to financial losses, due to the consider-able expenses incurred by the staging of spectacles suited to the greatness of the king and court, and to the frequent arrearage of season tickets by indebted nobles (Robinson 1990). Yet the economic relevance of the public investment cannot be measured merely by the profitability of S. Carlo as an enterprise. By producing 4 operas per year, with a minimum of 70 reruns, it had several effects on urban creativity: firstly, as already mentioned, it consecrated public consumption of theatrical works; secondly, it attracted artists and professional figures who often circu-lated among commercial theaters too (librettists, composers, musicians, and skilled laborers) (Yamada 2004; Stiffoni 2001; Tufano 2009; Glixon 2017 and Gjerdingen 2020). Indeed, theaters had a huge "multiplier" effect on the urban economy: they not only gave work opportunities to a varied local workforce (musicians, stage designers, light designers, choir members, carpenters, tailors, painters, printers) but they also created a spin-off in the service sector (hotels, inns, taverns, casinos), as the trademark of Naples as a musical city was the main attraction for grand tour visitors. Finally, theaters were also music trendsetters, as public spectacles were reproduced in the private salons, fueling the private demand for musicians, music teachers, and music hand-copyists. They also had an impact on the value of the urban real estate and, generally speaking, theaters were more profitable as a real estate investment than as an artistic enterprise, as the property stayed in the same hands for centuries (Traversier 2009b).

Our overview of the creative industries in early modern Naples began by pointing out the contradiction between the positive image of Naples as a cultural capital and its negative image as a city based on parasitic revenue. Indeed, the effervescence of creative industries, based on the production of intangible goods related to the sphere of symbolic consumption, was somehow the flipside of the weakness of its material economy and its very unequal social order. Cultural consumption was a tool of distinction for the upper classes, strongly encouraged by the royal consecration of theater, whereas it was also an opportunity for employment and social ascent for the lower classes. The music labor market was indeed a by-product of the urban social assistance system, from whence it gradually became emancipated in parallel with the consolidation of a broader market for music services, linked to an expanding entertainment industry. Conservatories not only produced musicians but also promoted the image of Naples as a musical city attracting composers and musicians from abroad. The "creative class" of musicians, composers, and actors was the result of a rising creative economy rather than its premise, as argued by contemporary sociology (Florida 2000). Indeed, the transformation of the conservatories into music factories during the seventeenth century was the answer to a growing demand for music, which created the conditions for the enhancement of their talents. Later, the lure of Naples for foreign musicians and composers was based on its existing reputation as a "musical city."

It would seem obvious to consider Naples' creativity as one aspect of the broader intellectual flourishing of Naples, since it was one of the capitals of the European Enlightenment (Rao 2009). Although the tendency toward change is considered one of the general conditions that historically seems to have enabled the emergence of a creative economy (Borsay 2008), the concentration of intellectual or human capital does not automatically lead to the flourishing of creative industries, just as creativity doesn't automatically result in widespread innovation. In the particular case of eighteenth-century Naples, Anna Maria Rao (2009) stressed the general frustration of the intellectual class about the absence of significant job opportunities in the urban setting. The rise of the music and theatrical industry, on the contrary, represented an important exception, since it promoted an expanding "creative" labor market. In this regard, the role of central power was prominent.

In the view of the central rulers, theater had a strong political significance, both inside, as a tool of social control, and outside as a means of symbolic international competition. They used the theater as the physical and mythical image of power itself, thus stimulating its development and the private investment in theatrical enterprise, despite its low economic profitability; this is certainly one of the reasons why the music and theatrical industry underwent a much greater development than other sectors of the cultural economy (such as the publishing industry), despite the existence of intellectual capital. Finally, we can say that creativity was the result of a complex entanglement of favorable conditions on the demand and supply side, both of human capital and of cultural goods; yet, it was also the result of a central policy which aimed at centralizing and fostering a cultural industry with a relevant political, symbolic, and social function.

The research was conducted on archival documents available from two principal Italian public institutions: the Conservatory of music "San Pietro a Majella" and the Italian National Archive of Naples.

A very interesting relationship was established, ten years ago, with the study conducted by Gillian Arrighi and Victor Emeljanov (2014), *Entertaining Children: the participation of Youth in the Entertainment industry*, Palgrave. The "children," accepted and trained in the four Neapolitan conservatories, began to feed an entertainment industry that even in Naples posed a demand for musical performances required both by churches and liturgical services and by private individuals and popular festivals.

A few years later, Van Damme, De Munck, and Miles published the volume *Cities and Creativity from the Renaissance to the Present*, Routledge (2018). Even then, the expression of creativity in the city of Naples was mainly through music, theaters, water festivals, and all the other entertainment occasions of the viceroy court and the minute people.

But this study also relates to the current debates on *The Economics of Spectacle. The Financing of Ephemeral Arts in Early Modern Europe*. The Studium. Institute for Advanced Studies. Tours, June 2023, which reaffirmed that there is a gap in the economic management of the performing arts during the early modern period.

Our book aims to contribute in some way to filling that gap. Indeed, we should historicize the matter of creativity by recognizing that its role in the production and redistribution of wealth had a relevant impact in the old regime of urban economic and social balances and that urban and political actors were well aware of that, as they played an important role in the promotion of creative industries.

The nineteenth century also brought about a radical change in the structures of cultural production in Naples under the old regime, as in the rest of Europe: the author traces the transformations that simultaneously affected urban spaces and the scenic spaces of music, also in the light of the measures for culture that animated the agenda of the post-unification governments, not always recognizing the specifics of the Neapolitan musical culture, sometimes humiliated to a caricature and mannered dimension. Finally, this stimulating fresco on musical institutions and their protagonists in Naples between the modern and contemporary ages has the merit of drawing the attention of scholars to numerous research paths, with reference both to a polymorphic and inexhaustible reality such as that of the Southern Capital and to numerous possible comparisons and cross-readings with other major European realities.

Benevento, Italy   Rossella Del Prete
January 2024

About This Book

The debate about the relationship between creativity, culture, economics, and technology; the ability to create and circulate intellectual capital that can generate income, new jobs, and promote social inclusion, cultural diversity, and human development is becoming more global and increasingly interesting, but it needs to be connected to history. Creativity and innovation are forces that can transform the world, and the countries that focus their efforts on these two resources will be the ones able to expand their economies the most, creating more investment, more profits, and more jobs.

This is what happened in Naples, one of the greatest capitals of European culture, between the modern and contemporary ages, with the enhancement of the typical Neapolitan creative economy, the one produced in artisanal and harmonic workshops, in copy shops and print shops, in music conservatories and chapels, in theaters and private halls, in urban spaces and the sea, in all the viceregal and popular festive occasions: a triumph of creativity, of productive and financial resourcefulness, of travel and cultural comparisons, of inclusion and participation at multiple social levels.

CONTENTS

ABOUT THE AUTHOR

Rossella Del Prete, Ph.D. is Professor of Economic History at the University of Sannio, Italy. She is an expert in Cultural Heritage governance and works in Public History and Economics of Art and Culture, and also in Labor History and Cultural and Creative Industries. She founded the cultural enterprise Kinetès-Arte.Cultura.Ricerca.Impresa as a Unisannio academic spin-off, of which she is Scientific and Editorial Manager. She is Editor-in-Chief of the Journals "Il Giornale di Kinetès" and "O.S. Opificio della Storia." She is Regional Delegate for Campania of the Italian Society for Tourism Sciences (Sistur) and a Member of the "UNESCO Heritage Cities" R. I. Commission District 2101—Italy. She is the author of numerous publications, most recent monograph includes *Il Teatro Comunale di Benevento (1852–2022)*, Kinetès Editions 2024.

ABBREVIATIONS

APG	Archivio Storico del Conservatorio dei Poveri di Gesù Cristo
APM	Archivio del Conservatorio S. Pietro a Majella di Napoli
APT	Archivio del Conservatorio della Pietà dei Turchini
ARC	Archivio Storico del Real Collegio di San Sebastiano
ASBN	Archivio Storico del Banco di Napoli
ASCCIAA	NA Archivio Storico della Camera di Commercio di Napoli
ASML	Archivio Storico del Conservatorio di Santa Maria di Loreto
ASN	Archivio di Stato di Napoli
ASOC	Archivio Storico del Conservatorio di Sant'Onofrio a Capuana
BNN	Biblioteca Nazionale di Napoli

LIST OF TABLES

Chapter 5

CHAPTER 1

Creative Economy and Production Systems

1 CREATIVE ENTERPRISE

2021 has been declared by the UN as the year of creative economy for sustainable development. Creativity and culture are now recognized as key sectors for global recovery: they contribute to dialogue and understanding among peoples and at the same time are fertile areas for innovation as well as inclusive and sustainable growth.[1]

Words such as "creativity at work" and "connection of impact capital" seem highly anachronistic for the topic we are about to address in this book, but absolutely necessary to lend value to an experience that six centuries ago, starting with similar words and principles such as care, education, labor, art, creations, profit and non-profit, modeled—certainly unaware of how much GDP and the global economy could grow—a "spontaneously" creative, more inclusive, and sustainable economy.

Thus began the welfare experience aimed at the so-called "irregular infancy," for which an educational offer made up of art and vocational preparation was created within the many shelters that had sprung up for minors in difficulty, either because they were orphans or because they were naughty.[2] And, focusing on what we now call "urban and social redevelopment, sharing, inclusion, and participation," many of those charitable institutions built a system of vocational training that, responding to a very strong social demand—for shelter, education, and

R. Del Prete, *The Neapolitan Creative Economy*, Palgrave Studies in Economic History, https://doi.org/10.1007/978-3-031-55903-7_1

survival—and starting by putting into practice an idea that used practical education and initiation into the "arts and crafts," they contributed
to diversifying the market, empowering it, and making it increasingly
"regular" and "inclusive."

Some of these Institutes, "social enterprises" themselves, created real
manufacturing enterprises; others founded health service enterprises and
"hospital companies"; in just two cases, one in Venice and one in Naples,
four Conservatories dating from the sixteenth-century devoted themselves to a form of creative economy, training musicians, producing
musical products, and selling musical services. What Italian jurisprudence
today calls the Third Sector was then born.

In Naples, in particular, a festive city with a marked aptitude for theatricality, four ancient male Conservatories, focusing on social as well as
financial impact, took back the reins of a neglected human capital often
abandoned to a fate of hardship, ignorance, and marginality.

The youngsters accepted in those institutions experimented with
different forms of creativity ranging from craftsmanship, textile production, silk socks, and felt caps, to working with the typical *riggiòle*, made
of Neapolitan majolica, from working, more or less artistically, with wood
or iron, to exercising forms of harmonic apprenticeship in the field of
violin making or musical copying and finally in the practice of musical
performance, an indispensable ingredient for any festive occasion. Thus
a veritable market for music and, more generally, live entertainment was
born.

Today we know that the creation of a "cultural" market does not
necessarily bring about economic development, except within the limits
of the economies within these markets (which are often, moreover, very
modest). In order for real economies to arise within the local system, there
must be a *widespread* ability to attribute meaning and value to cultural
experiences. We must become aware of the fact that culture is indeed
capable of creating economies and thus significant employment, but only
under certain conditions: a city, to be a city of art and culture, must
"live of culture," analyzing an appropriate model of local development
that cannot be separated from real entrepreneurial ability and original and
intense creative effort.

There is a need to *create a context of accessible experiences* that allow
for the value and meaning of "cultural heritage" in its broadest sense.
Cultural actions, especially if political and institutional, must therefore enable individuals to understand and appreciate their own cultural

heritage. Without creating the conditions for the accumulation of intangible resources (the human capital) that trigger the synergistic interaction of supply and demand, no partial or unilateral intervention will be able to have any appreciable effect.

The *governance* applied to the four ancient music Conservatories in Naples (the approach of the Venetian ones was different) had the ability (now a requirement for Creative and Cultural Industries) to reconcile the economic value, cultural value and social value of that venture.

The adoption of entrepreneurial logics in the management of those institutes and the transformation in music schools, constituted the first milestone for the system, to be developed and adapted to the approaches of both the operators and the public decision-maker. Without considering the formal corporate aspects, arrangements, profit, or charitable purpose, we go to some simple and linear concepts: objectives, resource management and results, and a logic of profit that doesn't consist only of the economic return (which those first cultural and creative social enterprises produced, too), but also, and above all, of the maximization of the socio-cultural impact of an activity, that is made up of indices far more heterogeneous than economic consideration.

Thus it was that, in those original "music factories," an *ante litteram* model of cultural and creative industry was defined that obtained extraordinary results, in the name of that necessary inclusion, a creative labor to be regulated, and a creative economy to be empowered.

The effects have never worn off: over the centuries, they have only changed names and forms. The experience of musical education and practice developed in Spanish Naples, was revived in the 1970s in Venezuela, and then returned to Naples, in the Sanità district, with another name, that is, the Abreu method that led to the foundation of Italian children's and youth orchestras.[3] The sense of social reintegration through music has remained alive and the trait of the cultural enterprise has been better defined. Today, the UN encourages and finances creative projects involving children and adolescents "at risk," while the reform of the Third Sector, in Italy, wholeheartedly supports inclusion and cohesion projects that redevelop urban and peripheral neighborhoods with the activation of cultural, creative, innovative projects, and the creation of social and community enterprises.

The connection between an experience of the past belonging to the history of the Neapolitan people, which became a model of education followed throughout Europe and which laid the foundations for a highly original and creative economy in the capital of the Kingdom of Naples, is too strong not to be mentioned in the opening of our discussion.

The neologism *creative economy*, coined in 2001 by John Howkins, refers to "a type of economy in which imagination and ingenuity determine what people want to make and produce. And what they want to buy."[4] Three basic conditions are needed for such an economy to produce effective development actions:

- each individual is born creative, with his or her own imagination, and intends to flaunt it.
- the creative person needs a certain kind of freedom.
- creative people must have the opportunity to be able to establish clear and efficient relationships.

Building on these three assumptions, Howkins credits the creative economy (that of ideas used to make money), with playing a key role in contributing to community growth.

Only three years after the publication of his book, the creative economy has become part of the UN's global economic and development agenda. The exponential growth of the creative industries has now reached 3% of global GDP; thanks to enterprises in the performing arts, publishing, advertising, architecture, arts and crafts, design, fashion, film, video, photography, music, research and development, software, computer games, electronic publishing, TV, and radio. This is a rapidly increasing percentage (growing annually by 9% and 12% in developing countries) and establishes the creative economy as one of the fastest-growing sectors of the world economy (expected to reach about 10% of global GDP in the next few years).[5]

Howkins analyzes the unprecedented relationship between individual creativity and market economy, pointing out how industries interested in the production of services or goods through the use of the creative capacities of its workforce (as for the sectors of performing and visual arts, fashion, music, film, television and, more generally, for all those sectors that require innovation as a necessary productive requirement) could have provided the new economic systems of the third millennium with greater guarantees of development and welfare diffusion than the traditional "repetitive" economies of manufacturing and assembly.

The debate about the relationship between creativity, culture, economics, and technology —the ability to create and circulate intellectual capital that can generate income, new jobs, and promote social inclusion, cultural diversity, and human development—is becoming more global and increasingly interesting. Creativity and innovation are forces that can transform the world, and countries that focus their efforts on these two resources are the ones that will be able to expand their economies the most, creating more investment, more profits, and more jobs.[6]

This is what happened in Naples, between the seventeenth and nineteenth centuries, with the strengthening of the typical Parthenopean creative economy, the one produced in artisanal and harmonic workshops, in copy shops and print shops, in theaters and private halls, in musical conservatories and chapels, and in all the viceregal and popular festive occasions: a triumph of creativity, of productive and financial enterprise, of travel and cultural exchange, of inclusion and participation at multiple social levels.

Today we know very well that Italy does not possess oil fields, does not produce gas for the world, but has always produced men and women, minds and art, that is, other forms of energy, and all of them "renewable." Our ambassadors in the world, the great promoters of Italy, are still Raffaello Sanzio, Leonardo da Vinci, and Michelangelo Buonarroti, but also Giuseppe Verdi, Enrico Caruso, and Salvatore Di Giacomo. Our cultural heritage, tangible and intangible—from the monuments to live entertainment, from the art market to the cultural and creative industry, from UNESCO heritage sites to the landscape—is our true *made in Italy*, but we need precise and decisive moves to enhance it, starting with investment in historical research, the only one capable of reconstructing cultural paths and development processes related to art and culture. It is impossible to promote and enhance what is not thoroughly known: historical research thus becomes indispensable and must be placed at the top of the "culture chain."[7]

It was also in Italy that the first structured form of theatrical company was born, that is, the first managerial form of entertainment, and it was Cavour who first called opera theater "a real and great industry with ramifications all over the world," entrusted then to agents and impresarios of great skill and today to new professional figures, such as the *manager*, who has the task of managing a very ancient art form, often, however, knowing little about it because it is not always supported by history.

The management of art and culture today should ensure, for example, the survival of live performance companies, bringing the right audience to the right show, disseminating art, but without *selling it out*, without *belittling it*, as it happens, unfortunately, when it is inserted into trivial and instrumental commercial circuits that, if they pay in terms of profit, have little or no impact on real social growth and the *renewable energies of art*.

The fascinating world of live performance expresses, today as in the past, a heterogeneous, composite, and very complex reality, in which extremely different souls, vocations, and histories coexist. It is precisely this complexity, belonging mostly to the sphere of the ephemeral that makes it more difficult to define its institutional, training, legislative, financial, and organizational structure. The art world, which has always been embedded in a broader economic-productive system, like any other production sector, undergoes and defines the dynamics of a particular market space, where demand and supply intersect. *Making art* also implies activities of production and distribution, operating and programming a space, promotion, training, dissemination, or support and service to artistic initiatives. It is all of this that makes art a "production sector" on par with others, but it is its essence that diversifies it and, in some ways, its ability or inability to *maintain a view of the world*, attempting to understand it, interpret it, and represent it.

2   ART, CULTURE, ECONOMY

Half a century has passed since Francis Haskell with his *Patrons and Painters* (1963) pioneered the study of patronage in seventeenth-century Rome and formulated his pioneering idea of a possible synthesis between different subjects—history, economic history, and art history—to describe that multidimensional phenomenon of *collecting*, linked to social and economic principles that regulate a market and produce conscious consumption.[8]

Recent research from a social–historical perspective has proposed a new interdisciplinary approach to the study of cultural consumption and in particular art consumption, placing them in relation to their material, social, and economic context, with the intention of once again highlighting the lack of an established historiographic tradition and shared interpretive paradigms among historians of different specializations.[9]

One of the most important and innovative contributions is undoubtedly that of Goldthwaite, who described the great Italian artistic tradition of the Renaissance as an important economic phenomenon, placing art at the origins of modern consumer society: among the main expenditures of the wealthy classes of the modern age were those destined to the construction and furnishing of private palaces and the collection of works of art.[10] A type of consumption that already in renaissance society expressed a new cultural code: the noble *elite* defined and showed off their identity through architecture and decoration, in the construction of palaces and the furnishing of interior spaces. Paintings and furnishings became sought-after objects, and the higher and more refined they were, the more they assured the owner a particular identity in the public sphere. And the more the potential buyer (the *demand*), assigned to such objects symbolic values and content, with a cultural value, the more the artists did their best to refine the technique, rendering, and overall quality of the product, inventing and re-inventing it over and over again, so that, not only did it meet the needs of the applicant, but even educated the buyer to the characteristics of the object.

The direct relationship that was established between the general increase in demand and the overall increase in painterly and artistic production in general appears evident. The painter (the *supply*), in the continuous act of responding to increasingly specific and diversified needs expressed by patrons and buyers (*demand*), sought to organize himself, devising new modes of production, aimed at the increase, diversification, and specialization of his work (*product*).[11] In a more recent essay, the American scholar proposes some programmatic lines of research for economic historians, considering the different parameters with which to approach the study of the economics of art.[12]

Sticking to a basic explanatory scheme within which to trace the essential structure of the art market, on the one hand, there is the demand, or consumer, driven by needs and taste, and on the other hand, there is the producer, or artist, driven by the artistic impulse. Goldthwaite therefore invites economic historians to analyze the art market from at least three points:

1. production, meaning technology, labor organization, product type, and characteristics;

2. the market in its most immediate form of art sales or prices as measures for judging the qualitative performance of production in general;
3. demand, i.e., the most problematic aspect to be considered.[13]

But Goldthwaite's analysis, like Haskell's or Gombricht's, or that of other art historians or economic historians,[14] continues to talk about the art market and cultural consumption by privileging only one of the four main subject areas of the field of *cultural economics*: that of the so-called *visual art*, which includes painting and sculpture, with the addition of that relating to *fine art*, which turns its attention to products such as furniture, antiques, jewelry, watches, and more generally to collectibles. That is, an art market based on the trading of material and "tangible" objects, even with the difficulty of defining their prices.

On the other hand, with regard to the music market, which falls within the broad field of *performing arts* (instrumental and operatic music, ballet, theater...), examples of the application of historical-economic research are even more reduced and, except for the exemplary case of the English John Rosselli,[15] and the more recent one by Stefano Baia Curioni (with a more corporatist slant),[16] we would not know which names to recall, except, with a hint of immodesty, our own and those of so many fellow historians of music and theater.[17]

3   THE PERFORMING ARTS SECTOR

In 2010, the European Commission published, as part of the European Digital Agenda for Culture, *The Green Paper on cultural and creative industries* (the original title was *Unlocking the potential of cultural and creative industries*). The "general" definition of Cultural and Creative Industries (CCI) finally seemed to be the definitive one: by "cultural industries," the Green Paper meant those that produce and distribute goods or services that, when conceived, are considered to possess a specific character, use or purpose, that incorporate or convey cultural expressions, whatever their commercial value. In addition to the traditional arts sectors (performing arts, visual arts, cultural assets—including the public sector), these goods and services would also include film, DVD, video, television and radio, video games, new media, music, books, and printed media.[18]

It all seemed clear, and yet, in the same year, another study was prepared for the European Commission: *The entrepreneurial dimension of the cultural and creative industries* by the Hogeschool vor de Kunsten, Utrecht. Here cultural enterprises are those that produce and distribute goods or services related to a specific form of cultural expression. They therefore include more traditional sectors such as visual and performing arts, but also film, TV, radio, new media, publishing, and printed media. Creative industries, on the other hand, are those that use culture as an *input*, but whose products have a distinct function. Therefore, this classification also includes design, fashion, advertising, and architecture. The sequence of business sectors in which CCIs operate is also proposed: advertising, architecture, printing and publishing, design, fashion, film, music, performing arts, visual arts, radio and television, and ICT.

The so-called *core* sphere of *the arts, the* focus of our historical and economic survey, includes, according to that classification, the sectors of visual arts (visual *arts*), *performing arts (performing arts)*, and artistic and historical heritage (*cultural heritage*), including museums, libraries, archives, monuments, and archeological sites.

That is, the *core of the arts* encompasses an immense cultural heritage, both tangible and intangible. The distinction of the other spheres, all indicated by the noun *industries*, decidedly more communicative in economic terms, is evident. The *core* thus seems confined to the sphere of the ephemeral, the one that is perhaps most important but most difficult to quantify through a price (Table 1).

According to a more recent definition, companies that fall within the *performing arts* sector, that is, what we call in Italy «*spettacolo dal vivo*» (aka live performances), devote their productive efforts to satisfying "entertainment needs through the production and distribution of individual or organized events within stable structures."[19] Forms of live performances range from theatrical, choreographic, and musical performances, to acrobatic and sports performances, to circus performances, and finally to many other occasions of "live" cultural production such as lectures, readings, *vernissage*, and more.

The field, often referred to as the ephemeral, is characterized by certain peculiarities:

- first, because of the coincidence of the time of production of the show with the time of its distribution (unlike, for example, film, radio, and television productions);

Table 1   European classification of cultural and creative industries

Spheres	Sectors	Sub-sectors
Creative industries	Design Architecture Advertisement	Interior design, graphic design, fashion, product design
Cultural industries	Movies and videos Television and radio Video games Music Books and printing	Recorded music market Live musical performances Publishing Magazines and newspapers
Arts core	Visual arts Live performance Historical and artistic heritage	Crafts, painting Sculpture, photography Theater, dance, circus, festivals Museums, libraries, archives, archaeological sites
Related industries	Computer and digital player manufacturing, industry of mobile telephony, etc.	–

Source Eurobarometer, European Cultural Values, The European Commission, 2007

- for the intangibility of the product (as is the case for most service enterprises);
- for unrepeatability and heterogeneity (no representation will ever be identical to another);
- for non-durability (its products are ephemeral, impossible to "store");
- for the contextual participation of the public in the delivery/production phase.[20]

Market competition among cultural and creative enterprises is very strong. Their profits—very difficult to standardize, especially in a long-term data set—depend on the tastes of a fickle public, which is subject to strong psychological and social conditioning in its cultural consumption and which must be attracted and involved at the right times, those that people are able to allocate to so-called leisure, to time free from work and the worries of everyday life. Precisely for this reason, the so-called *entertainment industry* must strive to produce a product with a high degree of involvement, originality and uniqueness, and high symbolic and emotional value, leaving its customers/viewers with something worth "buying" not only with their own money (by paying, for example, an entrance fee to the show) but also with their own time and attention, otherwise their preferences will go to other activities.

If, as mentioned in the previous section, in the *visual arts*, some of the main research directions have now been clarified, in the *performing arts* there is still much to be done. Even if the three basic points suggested by Goldthwaith for the analysis of the art market are to be considered still applicable, it is necessary to remember that a musical performance, a ballet, or a theatrical performance, are not products produced by a single "hand," but are the result of a very complex and articulated cooperation, in which disparate components and forces are at work, each capable of weighing on the final result in a different, but significant way. Opera, for example, is not a libretto or a score (the value of which, moreover, can be measured within the publishing industry), it is not vocality or set design, choreography, or dramaturgy: it is a combination of these and many other interdependent and interacting factors all affecting the finished product. Moreover, an opera performance in any case involves a considerable economic and organizational effort and the involvement of numerous and disparate workforces, each with its own specific technical expertise.

Any form of live performance (concert, theatrical performance, ballet, …) is intended for a kind of enjoyment with different social motivations or distinctions; it is promoted by individuals or groups with interests ranging from self-celebration to profit; it is carried out by occasional performers or by specialized professionals.[21]

All *performing arts* share the same prerogative: they are unique and unrepeatable because they take place in a given place, at a given time, and in the presence of a given audience. The *context* in which the performance takes place is decisive in establishing an emotional relationship, an exchange, a *barter* with the audience; because we can talk about barter when the *offer of* a performance changes with the changing of the audience and the context in which it takes place. The live performance *offer* operates in a qualitative-quantitative *context*, which is constantly evolving, which defines and influences its market space. It may be demographic (quantity, type…), economic (per capita income, prevailing production activities…), political-institutional (laws, forces in the field…), socio-cultural (social fabric, level of education…), organizational (competing infrastructure….), but it will always exert its influence on the production and even more so on the representation of the spectacle.

In general, studies in *cultural economics* have pointed to a number of basic principles for the study of the economic aspects of the arts, arguing in particular that art, like other products, is subject to constraints of scarcity and that the making and consumption of a work of art is the result of an individual behavior.[22] In the wake of these interpretations, what we will try to do in this space of our reflection, will be to look at the development of a music market and its production system in one of the main European capitals of art, Naples, a city of theaters par excellence and a privileged destination first of the *Grand Tour*, then of tourism *tout court*.

The varied musical background that was defined during the seventeenth century, and which preceded the birth of Opera Houses in Italian cities, laid the foundations for the creation of a creative industry that over time diversified its cultural offers in spaces and modes of realization, supporting even the subsequent changes in the demand occurred in the passage from *Grand Tour* to *cultural tourism*, to the point of defining a more specific form of *musical tourism*. There is now a vast and articulate literature of reference: from Charles Burney (1726–1814), musical traveler par excellence, who, with his diaries and epistolary, preparatory to the writing of a history of music, provided insights into musical repertoires, institutions, musicians,[23] to Bizzarini (2018), who analyzes cultural tastes and habits from a new angle[24]; to the various studies on the *Grand Tour* as an occasion of knowledge and taste formation in the seventeenth century (Fabris et al., 2015),[25] XVIII (Rice, 2013; Dubowy, 2016),[26] and XIX (Calella, 2012)[27]; up to the interesting multidisciplinary experience realized in Cremona by the Research Group of the Catholic University of the Sacred Heart of Milan (UCSC) coordinated by Rosa Cafiero, professor of History of Music, and Guido Lucarno, professor of Geography at the Catholic University of the Sacred Heart of Milan, on *Musical Tourism: history, geography, didactics.*[28]

4   For an Economic History of Art and Culture

If *economists* have identified and now widely accepted the important link between art and economics, to the point that the Economics of Cultural Heritage and Activities is now a recognized course in the Italian university system in the area of Political Economics, *economic historians* still struggle to recognize the *scientific character* and *relevance of* the topic with respect to their disciplinary field. And if, for their part, art historians have also long been concerned with the production, commissioning, and market of art, historians of economics, by privileging their interest in economic quantitative disciplines, continue to neglect a field that today, as in the past, is embedded in an articulated global system of cultural and economic exchanges.[29]

Thus, there appear to be very limited case studies of the economic history of art and culture, perhaps because of the difficulty of integrating quantitative and serial analyses with qualitative ones linked to other historiographic categories, judged to be too humanistic.[30] Nevertheless, it is a fact that economic historians are in-between Economics and History, with the former being perched between the bastions of the exact sciences, destoricized and dehumanized, and the latter, a humanistic discipline par excellence, forced to mediate between two cultures and two ways of thinking that, unfortunately even today, often continue to remain foreign to each other.[31] Nevertheless, it was precisely one of the founding fathers of Italian Economic History, Carlo M. Cipolla, to suggest how to resolve that basic irreconcilable dualism (*quantity vs. quality*), inviting us to go "behind the scenes" of the economic historian's work, to follow his or her sourcing and critique of sources, and his or her *creative* effort in the reconstruction phase. The metaphor used well fits our frame of reference:

A play is normally watched from the audience: and then (if things go well) it is all lights and glitter and the audience is all absorbed in the unfolding of the story or the succession of musical notes or both at once. But a play can also be seen from behind the scenes: and then things look quite different. The acted or set to music affair is no longer of interest. What is of interest is the production effort and the way it is carried out. One sees ropes, electric cables, reflectors, machinery, actors just coming off stage with the signs of the complete effort and makeup dripping along with sweat, other actors ready to go on stage putting on the finishing touches and preparing the facial expression required by the role, a silent bustle of actors, extras, administrators whispering phrases to each other or making unintelligible nods, all in an appearance of great confusion. The historian's work is normally followed by the audience from the point of view of the audience, and the audience is invited to immerse themselves in the historical event being narrated, without worrying about everything behind the scenes, that is, everything behind the historical narrative: the materials that the historian has collected, how he has collected them, and how he has recomposed them in the interpretation of that great puzzle [...] that is history....[32]

The reference to the words of C. M. Cipolla explains our historical-economic approach to art and culture and seems to us all the more necessary today when, in academia, the *Economics of Art and Culture* has now gained scientific recognition and autonomy as a discipline, while the *Economic History of Art and Culture* is still seeking its affirmation.[33]

On the other hand, the debate on the role of artistic and cultural assets as exclusive public goods, for which the adoption of efficient management principles is or is not necessary, or, on the contrary, as assets that, only through management based on innovative tools, can be properly enhanced and protected is still a live and burning issue today.

In 1990, Luigi De Rosa summarized the stages that had brought economic history from the uncertainties of its beginnings to the then state of research and recalled, among others, that of financial history, which he called "deficient sector [...] as far as it pertains to both revenues and expenditures, both central and local finance, and public debt policy" and added, "if some attempts had [been] made recently with the reconstruction of a few large urban centers, one was still enormously backward as far as it pertained to knowledge of the history of public services".[34] Theater is a *public service*.[35]

In another passage of his volume, he asked "what do we know about the economic history of communication systems, that of the post office, the telegraph [...] radio and now television? [...] or of the economic history of cinema, variety shows, theater, publishing?" He then recalled John Rosselli's studies on theatrical impresarios and suggested:

> certainly, John Rosselli failed to extend the investigation into the operation and impresario structure of opera houses beyond the age of Verdi. But the theory that the growth of wealth and the bourgeoisie was always accompanied, between the end of the eighteenth century and the eve of World War I, by the expansion of the opera house, should also be tested for the later period. Even with the change in theatrical taste, it should be ascertained whether it holds true, as Rosselli argues, that the success of the opera house, or any other kind of performance, was always a function of the favorable economic situation.[36]

Well, we have always been convinced of this, and that is why over the years we have continued to look with special interest at the diverse world of live entertainment (theater, music, opera, dance) as a central element of a *cultural industry* whose history is yet to be retraced because yet to be invented is its most appropriate field of study: the economic and financial history of art and culture, precisely.

The world of art, literature, and culture has never been far from the world of economics and finance. Yet most economists of the past, while not considering culture—seen as a sector of economic activity that produces cultural goods and services—deserving of specific study, neither the political economy nor the business economics, "accidentally" mentioned it, to argue, however, that the categories of economic analysis could not be applied to the sector.

Today, we know that this is not the case! The best-known case is that of J. M. Keynes:

> our experience has clearly shown that such activities cannot be carried out if they depend on the motive of profit and financial success. The exploitation and eventual destruction of the divine gift of the showman being prostituted to the goal of financial gain is one of the worst crimes of today's capitalism.[37]

Reading further into Keynes' statements, one can deduce that his criticism is directed to the idea that public intervention should be subjected to purely financial valuation criteria, thus favoring expenditures that are "productive" at first sight over those that are "unproductive," at first sight but in reality are related to the creation of values outside the market, and which for that very reason the market is unable to appreciate (in the sense of assigning a price to them).

Even according to Adam Smith, cultural work is unproductive work, which does not contribute to the creation of surplus:

> their [unproductive workers'] labor, like the actor's declamation, the orator's eloquence or the musician's chords, vanishes the very moment it is produced.[38]

However, Smith recognizes the peculiarities of cultural work, and especially the long and costly investment required to produce cultural goods and services, which will have to be reflected in remuneration: "the monetary remuneration of painters, sculptors, law and medicine people will therefore have to be sufficiently high".[39] He also expresses himself on the desirability of an active role for the state, both in promoting performing arts activities and for erect and preserve those public institutions and public works which, though extremely useful to a large society, are nevertheless of such nature that profit could never reimburse the expense of them to an individual or a small number of individuals who could erect or preserve them. Fulfilling this duty requires very different levels of expenditure at different stages of society.[40]

For Smith, therefore, the production and/or preservation of these goods not only cannot be regulated by the "invisible hand" since it requires independent spending by the state but the share of this spending must increase as the nation's wealth increases.

One aspect of cultural goods that has interested classical economists and has yet to find a satisfactory solution is the identification of the rules that determine their "value," or price. For some, it is essentially an "erratic" value, unrelated to any economic law capable of determining it, for others, "unpredictable" fluctuations in the prices of art works are explained by resorting three factors: portfolio choices, the irreproducibility of works, and the existence of monopoly forms. W. Baumol argues that "on the basis of a priori considerations and the analysis of several hundred price data [...] in the visual arts market, particularly in that of the works of the great artists no longer living, there may be no equilibrium value, so that the price of these art objects may be said, in the classical sense, to be strictly 'non-natural'".[41]

The interest of economic analysis in the cultural sector increases significantly from the 1960s, in correspondence with the growth of cultural consumption. There are several reasons for this. First, there is the growing role played by the demand for and production of cultural goods and activities in more advanced economies. This growth is also connected to the use of cultural goods and activities as means of production of other market and nonmarket goods (production of information, entertainment, audiovisual items, content for the multimedia industry, inputs for education and training processes; resources of tourist attractiveness, etc.). Second, the cultural sector is, in whole or in part, a beneficiary of public spending, and thus, as it has grown, it has become relevant in terms of collective choices. The cultural sector, like other sectors of the public economy, has thus become an experimental laboratory for the introduction of constraints on effectiveness, efficiency, and equity in welfare spending, while at the same time, the need has grown to document and quantify, wherever possible, the extent of the economic and social benefits that justify collective regulatory apparatuses for these goods.[42] Starting from a dual definition of the cultural sector, which, "in the narrow sense," includes cultural heritage (protection, preservation, restoration, enhancement, management), libraries, archives, museums, live entertainment (theater, music, opera dance), production and distribution of contemporary art (in the visual, scenic, musical, literary, architectural arts, etc.), and, "in a broad sense," in addition to the activities already mentioned also extends to the "cultural industries" (publishing, information, cinema, discography), here we will focus our attention on live entertainment, the one in part already investigated by John Rosselli[43] and then by Fiamma Nicolodi,[44] but which presents, still today, especially for Southern Italy, numerous shadow zones.

Theatrical agents and impresarios represent the cornerstones of a world in which a number of not untalented business leaders stand out. To them we owe, in addition to the theatrical and operatic activity, the publication of a number of agency journals which, although within a commercial and business logic, provide valuable and first-hand information, not only on the life and productive activity of many artists and their companies but also on the destinies of many dramatic texts, another cultural product on which relevant investments were made.

The starting point of any study of the economic and financial history of art and culture will have to be the cities, of course, the richest and liveliest: Naples, for example, but also Venice, Rome, and Milan. We will meet not only with the portraits of prominent operators who in addition to being managers in economy of theaters were also real projectors of an idea of entertainment but also with the different forms of public and private financing from which live entertainment has benefited over the centuries. In short, the goal is to offer further reflection on a cultural industry that has its deepest roots in the construction of a music market that intersected with the theatrical market from the very beginning. We will thus try to reconstruct the birth and evolution of an enterprise, the theatrical-musical enterprise, which has ancient roots and found its most prosperous season in the first half of the nineteenth century. It began with the commedia dell'arte and continued with opera buffa to find the apex of its cultural, political, and economic evolution in melodrama. In a multiform and plural production context, products, producers, and distributors were defined, on which it is necessary today to channel the energies of historical-economic research.

How was the supply and demand for music defined in the period from the seventeenth century to the Risorgimento? What was the geography of Italian music venues? What professional and productive roles were defined in its market? What was the role of the state in the development of a musical culture? How much did artists earn in the modern age and how much did those living in Italy earn in the long nineteenth century? What kind of strategies did they use to secure important commissions? How and to what extent precise stylistic choices influenced their careers in different periods? How much did a stage set cost?

We will try to answer some of these questions starting from the birth of an Italian music market and from two particular urban contexts: the Neapolitan one, first of all, and the Milanese one, profoundly different for institutional and political reasons, but very similar in the ways they approached the art market, especially in the nineteenth century. We will try to cast a few more brushstrokes on the fresco of Italian musicians, on the many men and women who "lived by art" and helped to produce income, consumption, and purchases and that, amidst pomp and debts, changed the socio-economic structure of a society that found its symbolic representation in the theater.[45]

NOTES

1. This is according to the report published on the platform "Creativity, Culture, and Capital"—which brings together international stakeholders in the culture and creativity industry—titled *Impact investing in the global creative economy*, January 2021. The report explains how investment in the sector will be crucial to major global challenges and refers to the resolution passed on December 19, 2019, by the 74th United Nations General Assembly and supported by more than 81 countries, declaring 2021 the international year of the creative economy for sustainable development.
2. See, among a multitude of published works on abandoned child care the work of colleagues C. Cenedella, G. Fumi (eds.), *Oltre l'assistenza. Lavoro e formazione professionale negli istituti per l'infanzia irregolare in Italia tra Sette e Novecento*, Vita e Pensiero, Milan 2015.
3. R. Del Prete, *La musica come rinnovamento sociale e professionale: dagli antichi Conservatori italiani ai Nuclei de El Sistema Abreu*, in A. Carbone (ed.), *Popolazione, famiglia e società in età moderna*,

Scritti in onore di Giovanna Da Molin, Cacucci, Bari 2017, pp. 173–192.

4. J. Kowkins, *The Creative Economy: How People Make Money from Ideas*, Penguin Books Ltd, 2013.

5. Symbola, *Io sono Cultura*, 2019 Report.

6. It is the topic of the knowledge economy that I recently addressed: *Istruzione, sviluppo economico e capitale umano: l'economia della conoscenza in Italia nei secc. XIX–XXI*, in R. Del Prete (ed.), *Saperi, parole e mondi. La scuola italiana tra permanenze e mutazioni (secc. XIX–XXI)*, Kinetès edizioni, Benevento 2020, pp. 607–674.

7. We have dwelt on this topic on several occasions: see, among others, R. Del Prete, *L'industria creativa: creazione, regolazione e dinamiche del mercato musicale a Napoli, nel Seicento*, in F. Cotticelli, P. Maione (eds.), *Storia della Musica e dello Spettacolo a Napoli*, Tomo II, *Il Seicento*, Turchini Edizioni, Naples 2019, pp. 1715–1766; R. Del Prete, *Le imprese culturali e creative in Italia: un settore produttivo in crescita, tra occupazione e sistemi di governance*, in M. Vetis Zaganelli, L. Síveres, M. C. da Silva Gonçalves, R. Del Prete, (Organizadores), *GESTÃO PÚBLICA: responsabilidades e desafios contemporâneos—estudos interdisciplinares*, CENBEC-FINOM, Paracatu 2018, pp. 22–47; R. Del Prete, A. Leone, C. Nardone (eds.), *La Bellezza del Paesaggio Rurale. Sostenibilità e buone prassi per la valorizzazione delle infrastruttre rurali*, Napoli, Regione Campania, 2018; R. Del Prete, A. Clemente, *Cultural Creativity and Symboli Economy in Early Modern Naples: Music and Theatre as Cultural Industries*, in I. Van Damme, B. De Munck, A. Miles (eds.), *Cities and Creativity from Renaissance to the Present*, Routledge, Taylor & Francis, New York and London 2017, pp. 107–126; R. Del Prete, *Gli archivi storici locali come strumento di promozione territoriale. L'Archivio dell'Istituto "San Filippo Neri" di Benevento (secc. XVII–XX)*, in C. Cenedella (ed.), *Istituti di assistenza, biblioteche e archivi: un trinomio caratteristico, virtuoso e previdente. Conservare e promuovere*, Vita e Pensiero, Milan 2015, pp. 3–39; R. Del Prete, *Arts & Business: Cultural Institutions and Artistic Market in the Italian History in Support of Cultural Tourism*, in A. Morvillo (ed.), *Competition and Innovation in Tourism: New Challenges in an Uncertain Environment*, Morvillo, Naples 2012, pp. 521–539;

R. Del Prete, *Il Teatro nell'industria culturale e creative italiana*, "Amaltea. Quarterly of Online Culture—Year VII", 3 (2012).

8. F. Haskell, *Mecenati e Pittori: studio sui rapport tra arte e società italiana nell'età barocca*, Sansoni, Florence 1966. On these issues see also L. Spezzaferro (ed.), *Mercanti di quadri*, «Quaderni storici», 116 (2) (2004), monographic issue, pp. 327–532.

9. R. Ago, O. Raggio (eds.), *Consumi culturali nell'Italia moderna*, «Quaderni storici», 115 (1) (2004), monographic issue; P. Coen, *Il mercato dei quadri a Roma nel sec. XVIII. La domanda, l'offerta e la circolazione delle opere in un grande centro artistico europeo*, L. Olschki, Florence 2010.

10. R. A. Goldthwaite, *Ricchezza e domanda d'arte in Italia dal Trecento al Seicento. La cultura materiale e le origini del consumismo*, Unicopli, Milan 1995.

11. Ibid., pp. 254–261.

12. R. A. Goldthwaite, *Economic Parameters of the Italian Art Maker (15th–17th Centuries)*, in M. Fantoni, L. Matthews-Grieco, S. F. Matthews-Grieco, *The Art Market in Italy (15th–17th Centuries)*, Panini, Modena 2003, pp. 423–444.

13. Ibid., 425–426.

14. Among Italian economic historians who have dealt with the art market, we remember Enrico Stumpo and Renata Ago, and those of the new generation, Guido Guerzoni, Valeria Pinchera, Isabella Cecchini, and Daniela Manetti.

15. Absolutely pioneering was John Rosselli's historical-economic approach in his studies of musical theaters and their operators (singers, impresarios, musicists...). He argued that the growth of wealth and the bourgeoisie was always accompanied, between the late eighteenth century and the eve of World War I, by the expansion of the opera house.

16. Stefano Baia Curioni is an expert in cultural enterprise and devotes his research to understanding the processes of transformation of modern and contemporary artistic production systems. He has dealt with music publishing in *Mercanti dell'Opera. Storie di Casa Ricordi*, Il Saggiatore, Milano 2011.

17. Paolo Maione and Francesco Cotticelli, to whom we owe the research and coordination of study groups on economic and accounting sources, such as the bank policies consulted and surveyed for the years 1726–1737 and 1776–1785 at the Historical

Archives of the Bank of Naples. An impressive research project that flowed into three volumes of *Studi Pergolesiani/Pergolesi Studies* [IV (2000); V (2006); IX (2015)] and the *Proceedings of the 2001 Aversa Conference on Domenico Cimarosa* (Lucca, LIM, 2004); but also Francesca Seller with her studies on Neapolitan music publishing and musical instrument makers, Rosa Cafiero who has continued to study music education in Naples in the seventeenth–nineteenth centuries and music production in Milan and Lombardy, and also Cesare Corsi, Pierpaolo De Martino, Tiziana Grande, and Bianca Maria Antolini who was the first to study music publishing.

18. R. Del Prete, *Le imprese culturali e creative in Italia*, cited, pp. 22–47.
19. P. Dubini, *Economia delle aziende culturali*, Etas, Milan 1999.
20. V. A. Zeithaml, M. J. Bitner, *Il marketing dei servizi*, McGraw-Hill, Milan 2000.
21. A milestone in Italian historiography on these issues is volume IV of the Storia dell'Opera Italiana, *Il sistema produttivo e le sue competenze*, edited by L. Bianconi, G. Pestelli, EdT, Turin 1987, which includes a body of essays signed by Franco Piperno, John Rosselli, Fiamma Nicolodi, Fabrizio Della Seta, Elvidio Surian, and Sergio Durante—all of which are of great interest to an economic historian who wants to deal with music and theater.
22. B. Frey, W. W. Pommerehne, *Muse e Mercati. Indagine sull'economia dell'arte*, Il Mulino, Bologna 1991.
23. C. Burney, *The Present State of music in France and Italy, or The Journal of a Tour Through Those Countries, Undertaken to Collect Materials for a General History of Music*, T. Becket and Co., London 1771, p. 7.
24. M. Bizzarini, *La versione di Burney. Modalità esecutiva della musica sacra in Italia al tempo di Mozart*, in R. Cafiero et al. (eds.), *«La nostra musica di chiesa è assai differente...». Mozart e la musica sacra italiana*, Proceedings of the International Study Conference (Pavia, Collegio Ghislieri, October 9–10, 2015), Società Editrice di Musicologia, Rome 2018, pp. 9–23.
25. D. Fabris, *Italian Soundscapes: Souvenirs from the Grand Tour*, in D. Fabris, M. Murata (eds.), *Passaggio in Italia. Music on the Grand Tour in the Seventeenth Century*, Brepols, Turnhout 2015, pp. 23–32.

26. J. A. Rice, *Music and the Grand Tour in the Eighteenth Century*, Hollander Distinguished Lecture in Musicology, Michigan State University, March 15, 2013, https://sites.google.com/site/joh naricecv/music-and-the-grand-tour (date u.c.: 10.07.2020); N. Dubowy N., *Musician Travels. Sources of Musicians' Tours and Migrations in the Seventeenth and Eighteenth Centuries*, in G. zur Nieden, B, Over (eds.), *Musicians' Mobilities and Music Migrations in Early Modern Europe. Biographical Patterns and Cultural Exchanges*, transcript Verlag, Bielefeld 2016 (Mainz Historical Cultural Sciences, 33), pp. 207–226.

27. M. Calella, *Musik und imaginative Geographie: Franz Liszts Années de pèlerinage und die kulturelle Konstruktion der Schweiz*, «Die Musikforschung», 65, pp. 211–230.

28. R. Cafiero, G. Lucarno, R. G. Rizzo, G. Onorato, (eds.), *Turismo musicale: storia, geografia, didattica*, Pàtron Editore, Bologna 2020.

29. R. Moulin, *Mercato dell'arte contemporanea e globalizzazione*, «Economia della Cultura», X (3) (2000), pp. 273–284; p. 277; A. Esch, *Prolusione. Economia ed arte: la dinamica del rapporto nella prospettiva dello storico*, in *Economia e Arte secc. XIII–XVIII*, edited by S. Cavaciocchi, Proceedings of the «Trentaseiesima Settimana di Studi», April 30–May 4, 2001, Florence 2002, pp. 21–49; F. Codignola, *Globalizzazione e mercato dell'arte culturale*, «Tafter Journal», 24 (June 2010), www.tafterjournal.it.

30. V. Pinchera, *Arte ed Economia. Una lettura interdisciplinare*, «Rivista di Storia economica», Il Mulino, 2 (August 2006), pp. 241–266; p. 246.

31. C. M. Cipolla, *Tra due Culture. Introduzione alla Storia economica*, Il Mulino, Bologna 2003.

32. Ibid.

33. On this issue see V. Pinchera, *Arte ed Economia. Una lettura interdisciplinare*, cit.

34. L. De Rosa, *L'avventura della storia economica in Italia*, Laterza, Roma-Bari 1990, pp. 218–219.

35. On the concept of theater as a public service see P. Grassi, *Teatro, pubblico servizio*, in «Avanti!», April 25, 1946; C. Merli, *Il teatro a iniziativa pubblica*, Led-edizioni, Milan 2007.

36. De Rosa, *L'avventura della storia economica*, cit. p. 219.

37. J. M. Keynes, *Art and State*, in "The Listener", August 26, 1936, in G. Pennella, M. Trimarchi, *Stato e mercato nel settore culturale*, in *Quaderni di Problemi di Amministrazione Pubblica*, Il Mulino, Bologna 1993, p. 27.

38. J. A. Smith, *An Inquiry into the Nature and Causes of the Wealth of Nations*, 1776, Book II, ch. 3, edited by R. H. Campbell and A. S. Skinner, William B. Todd, Textual Editor.

39. A. Smith, *An Inquiry into the Nature*, cit., book I, ch. 10.

40. Ibid., p. 714.

41. W. J. Baumol, W. G. Bowen, *Performing Arts: The Economic Dilemma*, Twentieth Century Fund, New York 1966.

42. P. Leon, *Beni Culturali: il dilemma fra Stato e merkato*, «Economia della Cultura», 1, 1991.

43. John Rosselli's thoroughly pioneering approach is attested by a bulky bibliography: J. Rosselli, *The Castrati as a Professional Group and a Social Phenomenon, 1550–1850*, Brighton 1980; Id., *Governi, appaltatori e giochi d'azzardo nell'Italia napoleonica*, «Rivista Storica Italiana» (1981); Id., *Agenti teatrali nel mondo dell'opera lirica italiana dell'Ottocento*, Olschki, Florence 1982; Id., *The Opera Industry in Italy from Cimarosa to Verdi: The Role of the Impresario*, Cambridge University Press 1984; Id., *L'apprendistato del cantante italiano: i rapporti contrattuali fra allievi e insegnanti dal '500 al '900*, Olschky, Florence 1989; Id., *Music & Musicians in Nineteenth-Century Italy*, Batsford 1991; Id., *Elenco provvisorio degli impresari e agenti teatrali italiani dal 1770 al 1890*, 1983; Id., *From Princely Service to the Open Market: Singers of Italian Opera and Their Patrons: 1600–1850*, 1988; *Sulle ali dorate: il mondo musicale italiano dell'Ottocento*, Il Mulino, Bologna 1992; *La musica sul palcoscenico*, in V. Castronovo (ed.), *Il trionfo della borghesia*, Electa, Milan 1992; Id. *Il cantante d'opera: storia di una professione (1600–1990)*, Il Mulino, Bologna 1993.

44. F. Nicolodi, *Il sistema produttivo dall'Unità a oggi*, in L. Bianconi, G. Pestelli (eds.), *Storia dell'Opera italiana*, EDT, Turin 1987, pp. 167–229; Ead., *Il teatro lirico e il suo pubblico*, in S. Soldani, G. Turi (eds.), *Fare gli Italiani. Scuola e cultura nell'Italia contemporanea*, vol. 1, *La nascita dello Stato nazionale*, il Mulino, Bologna 1993, pp. 257–304.

45. These issues have been addressed by, among others: P. Besutti, *Note e Monete. Strategie economiche di musicisti nella prima Età moderna*, in Raffaella Morselli (ed.), *Vivere d'arte. Carriere e finanze nell'Italia moderna*, Carocci, Rome 2007, pp. 167–204; and Neapolitan scholars Paologiovanni Maione and Francesca Seller: F. Seller, *L'editoria musicale a Napoli*, in F. Cotticelli-P. Maione (ed.), *Storia della musica e dello spettacolo a Napoli. Il Seicento*, tomo II, Turchini edizioni, Naples 2019, pp. 1815–1824; P. Maione, F. Seller, *Domenico Barbaja a Napoli (1809–1840): meccanismi di gestione teatrale*, in P. Fabbri (ed.), *Gioachino Rossini. Il testo e la scena*, Urbino, Fondazione Rossini Pesaro, 1994, pp. 403–429; P. Maione, F. Seller, *Da Napoli a Vienna: Barbaja e l'esportazione di un nuovo modello impresariale*, «Römische Historische Mitterlungen», 44 (2002), pp. 493–508; F. Seller, *Editoria verdiana a Napoli nell'Ottocento*, «Studi verdiani», 18 (2004), pp. 148–230; P. Maione, F. Seller, *Le fabbriche di pianoforti nel regno delle due Sicilie*, «Napoli Nobilissima», VII (I–II) (January–April 2006), pp. 47–56; F. Seller, *I pianoforti a Napoli nell'Ottocento*, «Fonti Musicali Italiane», 14 (2009), pp. 171–199; P. Maione, F. Seller, *Artigiani e mercanti: l'industria degli strumenti musicali a Napoli nell'Ottocento*, in M. Vaccarini, M. G. Sità, A. Estero (eds.), *Musica come pensiero e come azione. Studi in onore di Guido Salvetti*, Lim, Lucca 2015, pp. 363–401.

CHAPTER 2

Creation, Adjustment, and Dynamics of the Music Market in Naples in the Seventeenth Century

1 THE ART OF ENTERTAINMENT: PARTIES, GAMES, CUCKOLDING, AND SHOWS

The socio-economic evolution of the city of Naples between the sixteenth and eighteenth centuries is described as a continuous and inescapable decadence, in contrast to its growing cultural vibrancy, which saw it rise to the status of a cultural capital, especially in the fields of music and theater.[1] This contradiction stems again from a stereotypical and unfortunately established separation between cultural history and economic history, the latter of which, as noted above, has so far been very little interest in analyzing the economic processes underlying artistic and cultural activities. As noted above, economic history still struggles to recognize the existence of creative industry and "alternative" forms of enterprises.[2] On the contrary, the new season of urban studies and economics applied to art and culture looks at the evolutionary history and economics of cities from a multiplicity of visual angles, contemplating a variety of factors, material and immaterial practices, social customs, rules, and production processes, in which the distinction between economic and cultural essence is never distinguishable, avoiding rigid hierarchical models of structure/superstructure.[3]

Politically and economically negative factors contributed to characterize the Spanish phase (1504–1707) of the city of Naples. First, an extraordinary increase in population, which had already grown steadily

© The Author(s), under exclusive license to Springer Nature Switzerland AG 2024
R. Del Prete, *The Neapolitan Creative Economy*, Palgrave Studies in Economic History, https://doi.org/10.1007/978-3-031-55903-7_2

throughout the sixteenth century and accelerated in the first half of the seventeenth century[4] when, on the eve of the plague of 1656, the population reached 400,000. This exceptional population increase was compounded by a decidedly negative economic situation due to the sclerotization of parasitic classes linked to the occupant, but ready to pay tribute to others in order to keep their power intact. The well-known insurrections of Masaniello, in 1647, and of Messina, in 1674, did not help to shake the political immobility and crystallization of social imbalances of this period. The city authorities and the central government were faced with two major problems: public order and social control and the conditions of habitability of the increasingly built-up and urbanized city space to accommodate the demand for housing posed by an increasingly and steadily growing population. This socio-economic situation was countered by an unquestionable cultural vivacity that would emerge in seventeenth-century Naples: the city produces culture, which, in turn, creates identity and rents of position, key elements for its development and competitiveness. If this is true today, for every city, it was even more so in the past, even in the absence of refined instruments of economic investigation and territorial promotion.

Culture has always been an indispensable element of development and growth, and artistic and cultural heritage constitutes the *brand* that can distinguish one city from another. The role that culture can play in urban development is extraordinarily important not only because of its magnitude but especially because of its continuity and interweaving with the territorial and anthropic context. The relationship between cultural heritage (tangible and intangible) and territorial economic development is a complex and strategic issue: cultures, identities, knowledge, innovations, and creativity are relevant factors of socio-economic progress and poverty reduction processes.

In such a perspective, authenticity, cultural vitality, and the ability to innovate characterized the cultural and productive life of Naples between the modern and contemporary ages leading up, in the first half of the twentieth century, to the *boom* of "Neapolitan song," which, by enhancing the truest cultural identity of the Neapolitan people, succeeded in reinvigorating the urban economy, unexpectedly projecting the city of Naples on the international scene and, even today, constitutes its most main feature and the most saleable *product* in the tourist offer.[5] Looking back at that period of great transformations, we will meet not only a series operators, who in addition to running the theaters were also real designers of an idea of entertainment, but we will also see different forms of public and private financing from which live entertainment benefited over the centuries and the imponent economic and commercial spin-off that animated city life.

The aim is, therefore, to offer a further reflection on a *cultural industry* that retains its deepest roots in the construction of a music market that, having developed in seemingly opposing environments, the religious and the secular, the aristocratic and the popular, from the very beginning intersected with the theatrical one. This was the broad sector of the *performing arts* (instrumental and operatic music, ballet, theater...) generated by the system of *festivity* and civil and religious *apparades* that, especially between the sixteenth and seventeenth centuries, created an increasingly urgent and substantial demand for true *loisir* professionals, as well as a whole universe of workers, performers, suppliers of goods and services, including the army of musicians, singers, actors, comedians, jugglers, and acrobats of all sorts.[6]

It is no coincidence that, among tourism scholars, there has been a growing focus on the sociability of Italian and foreign visitors to cities, especially around places of entertainment. Italian and European cities have experienced important transformations in relation to the culture and leisure sector, development sectors subject to market dynamics as well as political discourse and action; focal points for both local business and city *governance*. But while European capitals were marked by the expansion of their theatrical spaces during the nineteenth century,[7] in Naples, the expansion of "performance" spaces began as early as the seventeenth century and was not a mechanical response to the increased demand for entertainment by an expanding urban society; rather, it was an intense process driven by political, social, and commercial issues. The spaces of stage performance were diverse: they could be indoors (theaters, churches, conservatories, halls, drawing rooms) or outdoors (squares, gardens or courtyards, paths, natural settings such as the Bay of Naples where boat rides with musical entertainment took place) and could have secular or exquisitely religious connotations.[8] By the end of the seventeenth century, in Naples, there were more than five hundred churches, mostly linked to monasteries, pews, conservatories, or other institutions, while the number of secular orders that had sprung up and were active in the capital had multiplied by leaps and bounds. It is evident that one of the most powerful means at the disposal of religious institutions to make themselves competitive in the face of the widespread supply of devotional practices was stage sets (large figurative works of art, processions, wedding ceremonies, funeral ceremonies, etc.) and especially musical events.[9]

The metropolitan life of Naples, therefore, wasn't short of artistic and cultural activities but, rather, of the large commercial and financial operations that, in the absence of a leading and entrepreneurial bourgeoisie, and thus administrators of the kingdom's economy, remained in the hands of the large international merchants. Naples was an indispensable base for the kingdom's economy, but it lacked the autonomy of an economic and financial body. On the contrary, a large number of academies, circles, and salons animated an intense and constant cultural and artistic debate. Performance occasions were numerous, and a significant civil and religious patronage maintained and attracted outstanding artists.[10] Musicians, singers and canterers, dancers, acrobats, and jugglers: there were so many men, women, and children who "lived by art," contributing with their "professional" jobs to produce income, consumption, purchases, and modifying, between pomp and debt, the socio-economic structure of a society that found its symbolic representation in the theater.[11]

The image remains vivid of a *festive* people which, apparently devoid of daily worries about basic needs, "dissipate and induce to dissipate huge financial means in episodes of artificial euphoria that, after a few hours and a few days of events—in most cases little different from each other—dissolve like the foam on the wave without leaving any beneficial trace."[12] The secret aspiration of the Neapolitans to live off the ephemeral and to be, at the same time, actors and spectators in any performance, especially if animated by words, sounds, and colors, might suffice to give us a first, hasty explanation of their propensity to organize and participate in festivities of various kinds. "Naples lacked many things (wheat and bread, urban planning and building control, the economic and financial autonomy of its commerce...), but [...] it never lacked the luster of culture and art."[13] As a reminder of the social, religious, political, and financial value of the ancient tradition of live entertainment, it will suffice to mention the Baroque festivals, the water festivals of the Viceroy of Onãtte, and even the historical cuccagna tree mounted in the Piazza del Plebiscito.[14] The information that can be gleaned from the handwritten *notices,* with which announcers, *leafleters,* or *gazetteers* spread the news, laying the foundations of modern-day journalism, describes the many public occasions for making music. Several were the occasions for *partying* in Naples: sacred music, for example, responded to a demand sustained by the numerous Neapolitan churches, oratories, congregations, and academies; then there was the music played in the houses for the parties, weddings, or baptisms; sacred drama and opera theater; music intended for celebratory occasions of political power, religious festivals, and much more.[15]

Cuccagne, spectacular machines, festivals accompanied by sound and gunfire, jugglers, menageries, and acrobats of all kinds, characterized the often frantic and uncontrolled vibrancy of a city animated by a pro-fond theatrical vocation. *Sea, music,* and *festivity* have, since time immemorial, been the defining elements of the city myth of one of the most frequented European capitals of the time and, from a vast and heterogeneous archival record, it emerges an increasingly clear awareness that the foundations of the late sixteenth- and seventeenth-century Neapolitan economy rested on other foundations, the ephemeral and evanescent essence of which has long escaped historical-economic interpretation. On that foundation was also born the *entertainment industry*, over which the central power always tried to exert control, in an attempt to convey contents and behaviors functional to the management of consensus. However, attracting artists and intellectuals from all over Europe, that unusual productive activity inserted the city of Naples into the international circuits of exchange of ideas, goods, and cultural practices, characterizing it as a city of *loisir,* a privileged destination of the *Grand Tour,* and contributing to the consolidation of a cultural economy in which theater, music, luxury manufactures, and monumental construction became symbolic means of production of consensus, grandeur, and, at one point, even national identity. Gradually, Naples built up its own live performance system, perhaps realizing—thanks to the continuous cultural exchanges with the other Italian city, Venice, founded on the same elements (*sea, music,* and *festivity*)—that, with the birth of the first Italian paying theater, the way of *making* music and the way of *consuming it* had radically *changed.*[16]

2 *Maestranze,* Musicians, and *Sonatori:* Early Aggregations of Crafts

Social rank and family of origin were factors of considerable importance to many aspects of Neapolitan musical life in the modern age.

By the end of the sixteenth century, the distinction between the two fundamental components for the transmission and survival of *music* was well understood: *education* and *instruction.* Studying, knowing, and playing music for pleasure and high recreation, rather than profession-ally, was again considered a nonsecondary aspect of a man's formative process. Thus, *music education*, intended for the scions of the emerging classes, was developed, whereas the *music instruction* taught in chapels to train and nurture the "placement" of professionalists, composers, and performers, was better defined. Having a chapel became a sign of distinction: in courts and cathedrals, monarchs and bishops competed to hire the service of singers skilled in the new compositional techniques and imposing musical ensembles, which benefited the splendor of the prince and the concentration and absoluteness of his power.[17]

In addition to the viceregal chapel, those of the Duomo, the Tesoro di San Gennaro, the Holy House of the Annunziata, the Hospital of the Incurables or the Pio Monte della Misericordia were all active in Naples.[18]

Thus, alongside a more aristocratic musical practice, a more public musical performance space was defined, hosted by the public and religious institutions. In fact, alongside a new generation of aristocratic musicians, a reserved and elitist musical practice arose, which, at first was the exclusive prerogative of the Neapolitan nobility and of few other families interested in music, but that later spread, at several levels and pervaded the musical life of the city.[19] The propaganda and representative use of music contributed, thanks to the patronage of some noble families, to the professional consolidation of the composer's activity, which, from intellectual *otium* of high-ranking literati and clergymen, became paid work at major ecclesiastic institutions and court chapels.

Non-aristocratic musicians were distinguished into *sonatori* and *musici*, two very different categories in terms of culture and lifestyle. The former were simple performers, often instrumentalists, belonging to the plebs (convicts, itinerant musicians, or paid players of trumpet, fife, and drum); the latter could be both composers and performers and belonged to the people.[20]

The social connotation of Neapolitan musicians underwent a profound and surprising transformation in the seventeenth century when aristocratic musicians were replaced by a plethora of new composers from the middle class or from a lower social background. The most useful explanation for the purposes of our treatment is to be found in the process of consolidation of particular educational structures, the four music conservatories, which being autonomous from the chapels and musical institutions that had flourished in the previous centuries, were soon able to produce "specialized labor." The demand for music became more and more oriented toward secular uses (musical theater and concerts), and the phenomenon gradually influenced the chapels as well, which began to welcome performers (singers and instrumentalists) who were no longer trained in-house but in the new "music schools." The experience of the only Italian case of the transformation of four Neapolitan conservatories that went from men's charitable institutions for the poor and abandoned children to professional training centers for musicians turns out to be of enormous interest,[21] on various levels of analysis. Being the result of a process ruled essentially by economic principles, it determined the advent of a music market and gave birth to the *Neapolitan School of Music*.[22]

The Christian world recovered the concept of *music education*, but on a different basis: music was no longer a source of corruption and lasciviousness for the young but, with the new liturgy, it even became an instrument of salvation and elevation. The aristocratic world, for its part, perhaps in the wake of the musical apprenticeship offered to the sons of the people and of the plebs and the growing operatic production that ensued, gradually went back to consider music as a servile activity to be enjoyed only passively.

A new cultural fashion, which was very widespread during the seventeenth century, contributed to the social transformation of the family in terms of consumption, but also in terms of the management of parental relations. The "craft" of musicianship was often handed down from father to son. The first technical notions were imparted to the musician mostly within the family (if someone was already practicing the musical profession) or by the local cathedral's chapel master according to the principle of artisan transmission of the craft between master and pupil. In Naples, the massification of musical education intensified, in different forms, the relationships between the artisan class and musicians.

In this context, the varied associative experience of Neapolitan musicians, with whom the harmonic craft began to be defended as early as the sixteenth century, is not surprising. Over the centuries, the category presents itself as numerous, versatile, and above all very active. Various were the associations through which Neapolitan musicians sought to protect their professional interests, but above all to guarantee mutual aid to those who chose the path of associationism and mutual aid, sometimes undertaking original forms of aggregation.[23]

The guild organization was generally of a uniform type and was organized in three three grades: bondsmen, laborers, and masters. To move from one grade to the other it was necessary to complete a certain amount of service, education, and apprenticeship time. The "garzonato" was the first step of the process. The new garzone, aged between eight and twelve, sought out a master in the craft he wanted to follow and placed himself at his service. Of paramount importance was that such a master, in addition to being capable, should be of good morals and good life, of patient character, and should be under the direct control of the Art, which, constantly, verified the qualities required for the delicate function of educator. Under the dependence and service of the master, the apprentice would acquire the first notions of the trade he was about to undertake, following the teachings and initiatives regulated by the Artisan Corporation. After a given time, the apprentice would become a worker, that is, he or she could be considered as a companion of the master, assisting him or her in the work and finally receiving a wage. After completing the minimum time envisaged by some arts for the advancement to the rank of maestro, the worker was required to pass an examination, pay the relevant taxes, and prove to be capable of exercising the trade in his own name and with his own responsibility. Once he had risen to the role of maestro, he would then be able to compete in the elections of the various members of the guild, to make judgments on the various matters inherent in the trade, and to enjoy all assistance. Each guild, which moreover had to maintain relationships with the political authority, decided its own juridical *status*, establishing its own rules and statutes. The purposes were first and foremost economic, then social, moral, and political: the guild represented the defense of the professional interests of its affiliates and was jealous of the prosperity and honor of the trade, principles it applied in controlling production and sale.

A constant feature of the guilds was the solidarity of its members in any manifestation of guild activity: in cases of misery, the needy member was relieved with common money; in cases of illness, he received medical and spiritual assistance; in cases of death, his body was surrounded by the affection of his fellow members. Besides this kind of social assistance, there was also moral and religious assistance: chapel institutions, guild festivals, foundations of monasteries for the "daughters of the Art," maritages, that is to say, all the things that gave the artisan the security for himself and his own family, allowed him to do his job with less worry.[24]

3   The Five Congregations
of Neapolitan Musicians

In the second half of the seventeenth century, at least five congregations or guilds of musicians sprang up in Naples, sharply divided by categories:

1644—*Congregation of the musicians erected in St. Bridget's under the title and protection of the Most Holy Pontiffs Gregory the Great and Leo, and of St. Cecilia V. et M*.[25];
1649—*Congregation and Mount of Musicians in S. Giorgio Maggiore of the Pious Workers Fathers*[26];
1653—*Lute strings* (new capitulations in 1685)[27];
1667—*Congregation of St. Mary of the Angels, players of strings and music, dances, trumpets, and shawms, erected in the Church of St. Nicholas of Charity at the Royal Customs House* (statute reformed in 1681)[28];
1676—*Congregation of St. Cecilia,* receipts and payments.[29]

The statutes retrace the typologies adopted by those of other trades and, at least in their general approach, they all appear very similar to each other: they protect the profession, calling for higher artistic quality, rationalization of work, and early distribution mechanisms. The various chapters contain details about the various roles of the musicians, their different needs, and also about the new typologies emerging in different eras.

A congregation for musicians was founded, in 1649, in S. Giorgio Maggiore by Father Domenico Cenatiempo (uncle of the famous Celano). The statute provided that only those who

sono Musici, cioè Maestri di cappella cantanti e quelli che sonano d'Istromenti purché esercitino con decoro nobilmente et honoratamente la loro professione [...]; Tutti quelli che vorranno esser del Monte et godere delli suffragij di quello dovranno prima essere ammessi et ascritti alla nostra Congreagat.ne, nè potranno essere ammessi nel monte se prima non sono di detta Congregatione [...] et haveranno da pagare nel loro ingresso docati tre, li quali se qualcuno per impotenza non potesse pagarli più una sola volta habbia dilatione di pagarli almeno fra mesi quattro, e se fusse tanto impotente che neanco potesse pagarli fra d.ti quattro mesi, volemo che sia in arbitrio delli Governatori di poterli dare dilatione per due altri mesi, e non più, oltre delli d.ti docati tre per l'ingresso haverà anco da pagare due altri carlini per ciascuno mese incominciando dal giorno che si fece scrivere nel Monte.[30]

The Statute envisaged the various obligations and related benefits. These included the subsidies, aids and suffrages guaranteed by the Mount:

Al fratello scritto nel Monte e che haverà pagato docati tre nel suo ingresso
et per lo spatio d'un anno continuo havarà seguitato a pagare due carlini
per ciascuno mese, e seguitarà a pagare, di modo che non sia contumace
per non aver pagato tre mesi, se starà infermo con febbre se li diano carlini
5 per ciascuno giorno per il spatio d'un mese purché tanto duri la febbre,
o tanti giorni meno d'un mese, quanti giorni meno d'un mese durerà la
febbre. Ma se la febbre passasse un mese, se lo daranno per ciascuno giorno
solamente carlini 3 purché non passi un altro mese, ma se la febbre ancora
durasse più di detti due mesi se li darà solamente uno carlino il giorno
per tutto quello tempo che durerà la febbre purché non ecceda un anno,
includendosi li detti due mesi, e passato l'anno et la febbre ancora durasse
se li daranno docati 18 l'anno solamente et si pagheranno in tre volte,
cioè docati 6 ogni 4 mesi e così s'osserverà per sempre mentre dura detta
febbre, et anco se li darà Medico stando ammalato in Napoli.[31]

It also stipulated, with great precision, the mode of governance of
Mount:

Il Monte dovrà essere governato da 5 Governatori e questi istessi
governaranno la congregatione di detti musici [...], qual Gestione di
Governatori si farà una volta l'anno nel mese di Gennaro congregandosi
tutti li Musici ascritti al Monte non contumaci del Monte e da quelli riti-
ratisi in disparte li cinque Governatori vecchi. In presenza del Padre della
Congregatione determineranno cinque musici del Monte delli più esem-
plari e di buona vita e che ciascheduno almeno s'habbia anni 25 di età non
contumaci del Monte, facendosi di questa determinatione, per la maggior
parte de" voti di detta Consulta, né si debbiano eliggere per Governatori
due fratelli, né Padre e figlio. In uno stesso tempo e fra detto numero di 5
musici che s'havranno da proponere per Governatori, volemo che vi siano
tre almeno della Cappella Reale di Palazzo, e gli altri due al più possano
essere eletti, benché non di detta Reale Cappella e fatta questa determi-
nazione si ritornerà al Pubblico la Consulta et in preferenza di tutti li
Musici che vi si troveranno si proponeranno li cinque eletti per Governatori [...]. Dopo questo, tutti gli altri Musici daranno li loro voti secreti et
in scriptis a chi delli 5 proposti dalla Consulta meglio li parerà per primo
Governatore, li quali voti si pigliaranno dal secretario e si leggeranno in
pubblico in preferenza del P.re e delli Governatori, contandosi prima le
cartelle se si confrontano col numero de Musici, che hanno dato li voti e
quello delli 5 musici proposti che haverà più voti purché creda la mità de'
voti sarà il primo Governatore, e quello che haverà più voti appresso del
primo sarà il secondo e così via [...] I quali haveranno amplissima potestà
di governare et amministrare l'Intrate et effetti di detto Monte e possano

stipulare, cassare Istromenti et obliganze, quietar debitori, firmar polize de banchi et altre scritture tanto publiche quanto private e che le cose fatte da essi vagliano come se fussero fatte da tutti li Musici.[32]

Also important was the "way of storing money":

Il danaro del Monte si debbia conservare al banco in fede di credito in facce a tutti li Governatori e conforme va venendo il dinaro ponerlo sotto la fede. Volemo che in potere del primo Gov.re vi debbiano stare sempre ducati 10 de contanti per qualche bisogno urgente. Nel detto banco vi debbiano sempre stare almeno docati duecento de contanti e tutto quello c'avanzasse purché ascenda alla summa de docati 100 se ne habbi a far compra sopra beni stabili con parere delli officiali maggiori e 5 deputati elgendi del modo detto di sopra.[33]

Curious, finally, is the chapter devoted to Benefactors:

persone quanto più nobili e qualificati si potranno havere [...] Il Bene-fattore pagarà almeno ducati 6 nel suo ingresso nel Monte e seguiterà a pagare carlini tre per ciascun mese e per un anno non goderci suffragio alcuno se moriva se non che un funerale per la sua anima, la sepultura gratis et officio in Congregatione. [...] Quando starà in fermo qualche benefattore s'anderà a visitarlo e parendo così bene alli Gov.ri del Monte se li potrà fare qualche regalo in una o più volte purché non ecceda in tutto ducati tre e se l'infermo dimostrasse havere a caro d'essere consolato con qualche canzonetta spirituale, di peso dell'istessi Gover.ri di farlo o almeno deputare altri fratelli che meglio li parerà che vadino a far questo caritativo officio e questo non una sola volta, ma più conforme durante l'infermità.[34]

Later on, string musicians, wind musicians, and cantors with their own constitutions and rules joined in. And in 1667, the association of the "Mastri Sonatori di Corde assentati sotto il titolo della Venera-bile Cappella di S. Maria degli Angeli" was founded. The statutes were perfected in 1681, when the distinction from the wind musicians was firmly reaffirmed. Members of the congregation of musicians paid 2 carlins in monthly dues: the wind players, the half. The musicians of the viceroy's chapel—the choicest group—held congregation in the church of Santa Maria di Montesanto.[35]

The first attempt to come together as a congregation of the "men of the art of making lute strings," dates back to 1653, to oppose the clear symptoms of crisis in the deteriorating sector of that art. The lute was certainly still important and widespread in the city, even if it was not officially part of the Royal Chapel's roster. The statute of the congregation of master string makers consists of twenty points (among which particularly striking was the clarification on the role of women, removed in no uncertain terms "for being said to be the art of men and not of women") that traced without significant novelty the usual pattern of similar constituent acts.[36] Corporative regulation marked the first necessary distinction between educated and corporately recognized musicians and wanderers, mendicants, homeless, and unemployed musicians. One of the first rules set by the musician guilds was the absolute prohibition of "posturing," that is, making music in taverns and masquerades, begging, and questing after festivals. The ban was aimed at protecting the "craft" of the musician, exalting the "professionals" and marginalizing the "wanderers." Later on, the members of the guilds added a further differentiation: that between musicians and sonators. The former included chapel masters, composers, and singers whereas the latter included all instrumentalists. Other sub-differentiations were included in these two macrocategories that distinguished wind players from string players, and so on.

By guaranteeing assistance and charity (marriages, infirmity, or death), the various statutory chapters regulated the spiritual and working life of the various members. The main objective for a musician or any other craftsman was to guarantee his livelihood during periods of inactivity, illness, calamity, and old age, because the wages received for the various services rendered, even if accumulated, guaranteed neither ease nor economic security. The congregation thus took on the role of welfare institution but was also an ideal link between the parties, inviting new and probable working relationships or alliances, acquaintanceships, and connections.

The vastness of the Neapolitan musical phenomenon and the creation of a market imposed, therefore, in the mid-seventeenth century, a necessary regularization of it, which prompted the musicians to unite in guilds: the desire to acquire greater contractual strength led to the formulation of increasingly specialized and professional requirements, and it was necessary, as for the other trades, to guarantee economic subsidies for assistance, infirmity, and death. By reconstructing the histories of the five congregations of musicians active in Naples in the second half of the seventeenth century, the *musician*'s state of precariousness and economic hardship emerges clearly. The variety of roles, characters, and vocations makes it difficult to assemble in a single associative structure the many musicians affiliated with the congregations, among whom we find the recurring names (Tommaso Persico, Filippo Coppola, Giovan Battista Pergolesi, Andrea Murino...) of masters well established in the emerging musical circuits of the city of Naples, some teachers working at the four Conservatories, as well as other chapel masters working at the highest places of sacred music: the Royal Palace Chapel, the Chapel of the Treasure of S. Gennaro, and the Chapel of the Annunziata.

The myriad of job opportunities was matched by the growth of the musical offer and its use so much so that many of those artists found stable employment in the various city institutions. Looking at the distribution of jobs, a similar hierarchy of roles and compensation emerges in the different institutions, whether they were chapels, monasteries, or conservatories. In the first place there were the chapel masters, with the second masters and organists, followed by the singers—and first among these were sopranos—then the instrumentalists, a prominent positing being reserved to the violins, while the woodwinds were in the lowest position. Wages varied according to the person, his or her notoriety, age, and continuity of service; over the years the average wages increased, respecting the increases in living costs, but also a growing recognition of the qualification of the profession. The custom of paying musicians with food or guaranteeing—in addition to the fee—a full-board accommodation, tends to be abandoned with the passage of time.

On the criteria adopted for the hiring of the various musicians we have already reasoned: certainly one of the basic requirements for employment was the notoriety of the artist that grew, acquiring new prestige, depending on the institution to which he or she was able to affiliate. For this reason, many musicians, in order to hold an authoritative position, were ready to accept it even in a supernumerary role and without any pay. There was no lack, of course, of a system of recommendations run by powerful patrons, maecenas, guarantors, and public admirers, who were in the habit of "signaling" their pupils to the various institutions.

However, one fact seems recurring and certain: the destitute state of some musicians was sometimes declared by the same institution offering employment. The monthly wages were thus inadequate to guarantee a decent standard of living or to ensure a decent old age, and not even with the accumulation of jobs did the musicians, more or less prestigious, achieve a real state of economic well-being. This state of affairs, although never really curbed, provoked a psychological attitude tending toward the preservation of laboriously acquired rights.[37]

The market's consideration of musicians remains to be scrutinized: despite the unquestionable placement of music among the liberal arts, they continued to be considered lenders rather than artists.

4   THEATRICAL AND MUSICAL OFFER

The offer of music in the early seventeenth century was being stimulated by an articulated and ever-increasing demand, which was also fed by the four male conservatories founded at the end of the sixteenth century and which in the first half of the new century, gradually transformed into schools of music and, starting from the bottom, contributed on the one hand to structuring an educational system that became a model of European music education, and on the other hand, posed themselves as the result of a widespread and increasingly structured system of "production of human/musical capital" that found its spaces of artistic and professional accomplishment first in the religious sphere (churches, chapels, and congregations), then increasingly in the secular sphere, thanks to a growing demand for "musical services" coming from merchants, bankers, and government officials—interested in hiring house musicians, teachers of singing and musical instruments, or occasional performers—or from impresario who run theaters. A practice that grew rapidly from the mid-seventeenth century onward, finding its brightest moment in the eighteenth century. At the same time, as noted above, the increasing professionalization of the musician was expressed in a widespread corporate organization of monasteries and confraternities that, born with "mutualistic" functions, exercised an important "regulatory" role in the music market.

In the meantime, sacred music retained its role and spaces corresponding to its educational and, above all, liturgical function. The ecclesiastics, and among them the archbishops, became the city's greatest patrons. The religious institutions that produced and commissioned sacred music in Naples were innumerable: there were at least 500 churches and convents, and out of four hundred thousand inhabitants, at least ten percent were priests. Equally numerous were the religious festivities that celebrated, among other occasions, some 40 patron saints, for whom frequent religious festivals were organized. To St. Gennaro alone, the most important patron saint of Naples, three major celebratory events per year were dedicated.[38] Music was an indispensable ingredient on such occasions, and patrons began to turn, to an ever-increasing extent, to the four men's conservatories, which, in those very years, met an ever-increasing demand for "musical services," the quality of which we will explain more fully later, became "musical workshops".

Meanwhile, the market, already during the sixteenth century, had started to show new tastes and new musical genres: first the madrigal, an aristocratic production par excellence that saw its decline after 1621, then the villanella, a lighter and more popular genre of widespread consumption, and finally the opera.

The madrigal disappeared after 1621 and with it crumbled the sixteenth-century structure of a civil society centered on court life, the exercise of culture and chivalry as symbolic forms of exercising power and authority, and the ideal of urbanity and courtesy that the madrigal embodied was substituted.[39] In this same environment the villanella had been born, intended for a cultivated audience living in an urban context with the growing use of the Neapolitan language to openly show the intolerance toward the foreigners. There were many nobles who displayed anti-Spanish attitudes and were deprived of the right to take up arms and, perhaps for that reason, many young aristocrats took up the art of music. However, one cannot forget some great aristocratic families, such as the Spinelli, the Galatea or the Maddaloni, whose patronage supported the staging of so many musical performances.

Most famous was the Flemish banker Gaspare Roomer, who, besides being a great collector, was one of the greatest patrons in mid-seventeenth-century Naples. His most important exploit was his subsi-dizing of two musical conservatories out of the four active in the city.[40]

Between 1620 and 1624, connected to the decline of the madrigal, there was the phenomenon of the reduction of printed editions. These were years in which the entire Italian economy experienced an intense critical phase[41] and the publishing sector was affected everywhere.[42]

> The crisis of music publishing went hand in hand with the seventeenth-century economic recession also because of its technological obsolescence: the Italian techniques for producing printed musical characters [were] in the seventeenth century outdated, and with the rising prices of wood, paper and lead, the production costs of musical anthologies increased and [were] no longer competitive.[43]

In Naples, which suffered in that first part of the century from heavy viceregal fiscal pressure, the sector saw a drastic reduction in publishers and printers. Lorenzo Giustiniani states that the publishing sector lost as many as four hundred employees[44] to the point of disappearing almost completely after 1630.[45]

However, the indicator of publishing production was not always decisive to assess the state of the music market in Naples. It is well known that printers, typographers, and publishers made a living working for a varied group of clients who didn't hail only from the music sector. Francesca Seller argues that it was mainly religious orders and archiepiscopal curias that strongly conditioned patronage and publishing choices. Seventeenth-century printing, in fact, was "the subject of continuous and restrictive laws throughout the century, with a continuous rebound of competences between state and church, often in conflict with each other".[46] The prevailing activity of seventeenth-century printers was, therefore, not that of music, but that aimed at publishing religious, literary, philosophical, and legal works. However, although much material has been dispersed, recent studies have collected important printed repertories of vocal[47] and sacred music[48] and a particular attention of Neapolitan publishers to the madrigal, in contrast to the rest of Italy. These included Magnetta, Gargano, and Nucci, who printed madrigals, villanelles, and canzonettas written by composers active in Naples. Printed editions, throughout the seventeenth century, were associated with manuscript copies, which were more useful in reconstructing the context in which musical compositions were produced.

Music consumption turned increasingly to listening and less to performing. If this trend better defined the characters of a paying audience, expanding the demand to new social groups, it certainly generated a lowering of production quality. It changed the demand, which became broader and less elitist, and changed tastes, which were very different from the "reservist music" once demanded by the nobility. Music consumption sought and led to new genres, such as "concert music," with an important spillover effect on the industry. A more complex business organization capable of dealing with stage apparatus, choreography, and stage machinery became necessary. The cost of musical performances increased, requiring more voices, more instrumentalists, more dancers, more operators, and the audience, increasingly willing to pay a ticket, also increased. That was the beginning, in the eighteenth century, of a phase when the spectacle became a real undertaking, with an increase in the number of people working in this sector, an increased need for suitable spaces for a socially crosswise audience, and a growing demand for training and specialization courses. All this began to fuel an economic circuit that required capital investment, sometimes considerable, sometimes less.[49]

Although the musical genres in demand were evolving, as to the city theater scene, the power of the church and that of the religious orders were still prominent; the former controlled the sacred music circuit while the latter operated selectively in the colleges aimed at educating the offspring of the city's aristocracy.[50] One of the theatrical genres over which they exerted their influence was the *commedias de santos*, often staged in the convents and the oratory of St. Filippo Neri, interspersed with musical entertainments.[51]

By the mid-seventeenth century, Naples, like Venice, already had theaters and schools of music with which it met the growing demand for "musical services" and performances. The orientation toward a secular and mass music education, the multiplication of entertainment spaces and occasions, the number and variety of entertainment production workers, and their travels and trips abroad to "sell" musical and theatrical products that, without knowing it, were building a real *made in Naples*, were the components of a cultural fashion and a new way of *consumption*.

If Venice had the honor of embarking on the process of creating the Italian opera in 1637, it fell to Naples to bring it to completion in 1652. In those years, as to the musical styles, a synthesis between commedia dell'arte and melodrama was accomplished in Italy; on the economic-institutional level, a new audience was defined that contributed to the spread of mercenary companies in academic and princely theaters.[52]

After overcoming the economic crisis and the sociopolitical tensions of the Spanish period that characterized the second part of the century, and after the revolt led by Masaniello against the fiscal pressure imposed by the viceregal government, a policy of stability was implemented, with the magistrates as guarantor. The revolt, characterized exclusively by political, economic, and social specificities, after Masaniello's death, became an anti-feudal and anti-Spanish movement. It was for these reasons that one of the objectives of the cultural program of the Count of Oñate, upon his arrival in Naples in the phase of the political restoration, was to redefine the cracked relations between the baronage and the civil class.[53] The so-called "popularismo,"[54] the term with which Paolo Mattia Doria defined the protagonism of the civil population in Neapolitan public life instead of the aristocracy, is indicative of the function of opera in Naples, seen as an instrument of propaganda and therefore subject to the dictates of etiquette and ceremonial. From its beginnings, opera in Naples was conditioned by viceregal politics and its agenda, as if it were an emanation of palace ceremonial, where forms and functions obeyed more to a logic of sociopolitical mediation between the viceroys and the city than to the rules of musical and theatrical production.[55]

The theatrical events that mark, in this period, the history of the opera theater in Naples, already reveal some definitive traits, which continually recur until the end of the century: the configuration of different patterns of fruition, the dialectic between local and national identity (i.e., what happens in Naples is a function of what happens in other theatrical squares in Italy), and the dependence on the theatrical agenda of dynastic and political events through the will—and the formation, taste, intent—of the viceroy. Before 1650, musical theater in Naples was not so high in demand. At the viceroy's court, as in any Italian court, there was a tradition of performances with music interspersed with dancing and singing, much like the Florentine intermediums, the English pasques or the French ballet de cour.[56]

The initial sporadic appreciation of musical theater in Naples before 1650 was justified by some specific differences between Neapolitan and Venetian opera, although the production models of musical theater in the two cities had many points in common. In fact, the most striking difference is the size of the playbills: compared to the varied offers of Venetian theaters, which managed to run up to ten performances in a single season, the Neapolitan programming set a maximum of three, mostly performed by the same company. Probably such a limited playbill was conditioned by the practice, in force in Naples, of subjecting the librettos of the operas to be performed to judgment. The control of the performance supply, on the one hand, relates to market laws and public demand, on the other hand, reaffirms the role of influence of the viceregal court on the production and enjoyment of performance.[57]

In general, the range of entertainment occasions included a variety of instrumental, operatic, choreographic, or prose productions, especially after 1650. The perception at the time of such theatrical products often confused the various genres, without distinguishing, for example, between opera and prose comedies, which, perhaps because they were less conditioned by viceregal ceremonial, in addition to being performed in theaters, were particularly performed in private homes.[58]

The image consecrated by Benedetto Croce of Naples seen as a city of theaters and music has a well-founded historical consistency: during the seventeenth century, Naples became one of the main centers of production of works in music and a center of attraction for artists and intellectuals from all over Europe. Theater and music became the unfailing ingredients of the festivities—so locally important for a *festive* people— but at the same time, they became the symbol of the cosmopolitan projection of the city where the *grand tour* and the fascination with European models would land, involving in diverse ways and forms all social classes.

A dimension of spectacle is defined that characterizes the very daily life of Neapolitans. Every occasion was good for feasting and celebrating a religious or civil event. At least two were held every week, and since the patronage was purely viceroyal, the events could include viceroy rides, "possessions" of public offices by nobles or other titulars, festivities for events related to the royal family, processions for the feasts of patron saints or would-be patron saints, carnival celebrations, and many other occasions for celebrations of a different nature.

Every event was spectacularized and staged, in theatrical times and forms, in the most disparate city spaces which, with a big amount of creative energy and the involvement of many workers and artists, were transformed into incredible theatrical settings. Among the aristocrats there were some who loved to devote themselves to organizing the staging of comedies, often offering their own palaces, both the courtyards and the inner rooms (palazzo Celllamare, the residence of the idle academic Luigi Carafa di Stiglian, palazzo Sansevero, palazzo Cavaniglia, palazzo Bisignano, palazzo Carafa di Maddaloni, palazzo Gravina, ...).[59]

These were almost always very expensive events that could only be set up through subsidization guaranteed by the viceroy court. The financing of the spectacle took place in distinct ways, depending on the times and the will of individual viceroys, but always with propaganda purposes. The stage remained the most suitable and "democratic" place to flaunt royal magnificence.[60] The stage apparatuses were majestic, complex, and impressive, as evidenced by the iconography of that period, which was also fueled by a good market.[61]

The impetus given to entertainment in Naples by the viceroys is now well understood by scholars. They were the first great patrons of Neapolitan musical theater, and among those who dabbled in organizing performances were people of high cultural standing, such as the Count of Lemos, the Count of Monterey, the Count of Oñate who imposed Venetian-style musical opera in the city beginning in 1650, with the intention of creating a positive image of Spain after Masaniello's revolution; the Duke of Medinaceli—a case studied and rehabilitated only recently, and Gaspar de Haro Marquis of Carpio, great scholar, protector of Scarlatti, who managed to bring an international ambiance to Naples.

One of the arrangements sponsored by the latter, to celebrate the queen mother's name day in July 1685, was the setting up of a large arena on the sea rocks, opposite Mergellina. Domenico Confuorto describes the event:

> for not only was it full of all sorts of small and large boats; but the whole street of Chiaia, long and wide, all the way to Mergellina, was full of carriages, coaches and people on foot, who did not understand a millet, to such an extent that a plank was made in Mergoglino and a tarì was paid per head to get on it to see.[62]

The frequent and increasingly striking use of extraordinary stage apparatus, with attached machines to create what we would now call "special effects," characterized almost all spectacular events in Naples at that time, more or less impressive depending on the nature and importance of the event. What the sources hand down to us as "music," always provided in those stagings, were mostly musical accompaniments or simple marches that served more as background than as a performance to be listened to with great attention. Comedies set to music were then alternated with ballets, court dances, and several new dances began to take hold, such as the gagliarda, the moresca, the flashlight dance, the passo e mezzo, and many others.[63]

Each staging required direction, set design, choreography, a set of narrative plots combined with recitatives, music, dancing, masquerades, and, of course, the involvement of a huge number of artists (singers, actors, musicians, dancers, extras) in addition to the laborers necessary for the assembly and use of the stage machinery and all the sometimes very large scenic apparatus. All, of course, supported by very high costs that only the viceregal court was in a position to cover.

It is then necessary to question the taste of the Neapolitan public of the seventeenth century. What did they prefer? Which theatrical or musical genre was "mostly greeted and applauded"? The fact that opera was imposed from above and that it satisfied the court's needs for magnificence did not determine an obvious liking of the public which, depending on its own interests, musical competence, and social status, was still free to make judgments, sometimes amplified by the city press, but not necessarily true to the quality of the play.

Throughout the second half of the seventeenth century, city life was enlivened by a great cultural vivacity, and the historical reconstruction of the musical and theatrical scene often describes it to us in detail. There remained, however, the great social and economic problems of a great capital of the kingdom, about which the most attentive intellectual groups kept alive a constructive debate regarding the difficulties of the people and in so doing they became the promoters of a profound renewal of society. The Academy of the Investigati, in particular, from 1663 onward, tried to overcome the strict ecclesiastical conservatism, especially in the scientific and medical fields, but the Palace Academy of the Duke of Medinaceli, its convinced supporter, also dealt with scientific and cultural issues at the end of the century.[64]

The history of the Mezzogiorno and its ancient capital flowed between great contradictions, between strong social, political, and institutional contrasts, between great poverty and great pomp, between "misery" and "nobility." However, in the words of Croce, "the whole city of Naples became musical with the penultimate Spanish viceroy,"[65] and, in the new century, Naples would become a European capital of music, attracting foreign musicians, supporting music collecting and the spread of manuscripts copied in Naples The seventeenth century is also the century of foreign musicians in Naples, of music collecting and the spread of manuscripts copied in Napoli throughout Europe.

The irrepressible vibrancy of the Neapolitan musical and theatrical scene in the seventeenth century is full of banquets, carnivals, performances of various kinds, pyrotechnic displays, weddings, funerals, triumphs, entrances, processions, tournaments, jousts, *palii*, balls, *cuccagne*, and so on. These were all live entertainment occasions for which *machines* and *apparatuses* were set up with the involvement and the interweaving of a variety of skills: behind architects, painters, men of letters, poets, actors, and musicians, there were hundreds of workers and suppliers, an infinite number of workers with different professional profiles, who quantified, with their very presence and their remunerations, the economic value of the *festival* or any other form of entertainment. In analyzing the quantity, heterogeneity, and specialization of the craftsmen and suppliers involved and their swirling business turns, one cannot help but wonder, why, for so long, economics, economic history in particular, was not interested in such initiatives capable of mobilizing unparalleled crowds, talents, and economic resources.[66]

NOTES

1. A. Clementi, R. Del Prete, *Cultural Creativity and Symbolic Economy in Early Modern Naples: Music and Theatre as Cultural Industries*, in I. Van Damme, B. De Munck, A. Miles (eds.), *Cities and Creativity from Renaissanse to the Present*, Routledge, Taylor & Francis New York and London, 2017, pp. 107–126.
2. On the need to orient economic history toward the economic processes of art and culture, we have already spoken on several occasions. See, among others, the introductory paragraph to R. Del Prete, «che i suoni divengano visibili e che l'orecchio veda». Savinio e la musica, in T. Iermano, P. Sabbatino, Passione Savinio. Letteratura, Arte, Politica (1952–2012), Naples, Edizioni Scientifiche Italiane, 2013, pp. 121–148.
3. A. Amin, N. Thrift, *Cultural Economy and Cities*, "Progress in Human Geography", 31 (2), 2007, pp. 143–161; W. A. Friedman, G. Jones, *Creative Industries in History*, "Business History Review", 85, 2011, pp. 237–244.
4. See G. Muto, *Gestione politica e controllo sociale nella Napoli spagnola*, in C. De Seta, *Le città capitali*, Roma-Bari-Laterza, 1985, p. 73.
5. R. Del Prete, *La città del loisir. Il sistema produttivo dello spettacolo dal vivo a Napoli tra '800 e '900*, in A. Pesce, M. L. Stazio (eds.), *La canzone napoletana tra memoria e innovazione*, CNR Issm, Naples 2013, pp. 121–164, http://www.issm.cnr/pubblicazioni/ebook/canzone_napoletana.pdf.
6. On the subject of festivals and art markets in Italy see Guido Guerzoni, *Apollo e Vulcano. I mercati artistici in Italia (1400–1700)*, Marsilio, Venezia 2006.
7. C. Charle, *Les theâtre et leurs publics à Paris, Berlin et Vienne 1860–1914*, in C. Charle, D. Roche (eds.), *Capitales culturelles*, Paris, Publ. de la Sorbonne, 2002, pp. 403–420.
8. See F. Cotticelli, P. Maione, *Onesto divertimento ed allegria de' popoli. Materiali per una storia dello spettacolo a Napoli nel primo*

Settecento, Ricordi, Milano 1996; F. Mancini, *Feste ed apparati civili e religiosi in Napoli dal Viceregno alla Capitale*, ESI, Napoli 1968.

9. See again the extensive documentation in F. Mancini, *Feste ed apparati civili e religiosi*, cit.; Id., «*L'immaginario di regime. Apparati e scenografie alla corte del Viceré*, in *Civiltà del Seicento a Napoli* (catalogue of the 1984 Naples exhibition)», Electa, Naples 1984, II, pp. 27–35. The latter offers numerous other testimonies on the spectacular attitude of Neapolitan artistic production.

10. D. A. D'Alessandro, A. Ziino (eds.), *La musica a Napoli durante il Seicento*, Edizioni Torre d'Orfeo, Rome 1987; L. Bianconi, R. Bossa (eds.), *Musica e Cultura a Napoli dal XV al XIX sec.*, Olschki, Florence 1983, pp. 61–77.

11. On these issues see P. Besutti, *Note e monete. Strategie economiche di musicisti nella prima Età moderna*, pp. 167–204.

12. G. Russo, *Vita popolare napoletana dal 1860 a oggi*, in *Storia di Napoli*, vol. X ESI, Napoli, pp. 645–715, p. 697.

13. G. Galasso, *Breve premessa alla storia civile e sociale di Napoli*, in L. Bianconi, R. Bossa (eds.), *Musica e cultura a Napoli dal XV al XIX secolo*, Olschki editore, Florence 1983, pp. 13–27.

14. I. Zilli, «*El arbol de la cucana*»: *Ocio y tiempo libre en la Napoles del XVIII*, in L. Ribot, L. De Rosa (dir. por), *Trabajo y ocio en la Epoca Moderna*, Editorial Actas, Madrid 2001, pp. 267–294.

15. On musical practice in Naples in the seventeenth century, enlightening and rich in unpublished informations that shed new light on the musical and theatrical liveliness of seventeenth-century Naples, see the two monumental volumes published by the Centro di Musica Antica Pietà dei Turchini: F. Cotticelli, P. Maione (eds.), *Storia della musica e dello spettacolo a Napoli. Il Seicento*, Turchini edizioni, Naples 2019.

16. March 16, 1637 in Venice opened the Teatro 'San Cassian,' the first Italian theater to be paid for. It was an event of extraordinary importance that gave a new meaning to musical and theatrical production [E. Saracini, *Imprenditori del teatro e della musica*, in S. Cavaciocchi (ed.), *Il tempo libero. Economia e Società. Secc. XIII-XVIII*, Le Monnier, Florence 1995, pp. 751–763].

17. M. Columbro, P. Maione, *La Cappella musicale del Tesoro di San Gennaro di Napoli tra Sei e Settecento*, Turchini Edizioni, Napoli 2008.

18. G. A. R. Veneziano, «Napoli è tutto il mondo»: la cappella musicale del Pio Monte della Misericordia (1616–1749), in Camillo Faverzani (ed.), *Les capitales méditerrranénnes de la culture, Naples lieu de convergences: circulation langue set des arts en Meditérranéee*, Peter Lang, Bern 2013, pp. 29–40.

19. Naples became a geographically and culturally identified center of madrigal production, with a particularly vibrant musical life (A. Pompilio, A. Vassalli, *Il madrigale a Napoli nel Cinque-Seicento*, in D. A. D'Alessandro, A. Ziino (eds.), *La musica a Napoli durante il Seicento*, cit, pp. 9–16). See also the more recent work of G. Muto, *La Napoli spagnola*, cit. pp. 19–70, and, in the same impressive volume, the substantial contribution of D. A. D'Alessandro, *Mecenati e mecenatismo nella vita musicale napoletana del Seicento e condizione sociale del musicista. I casi di Giovanni Maria Trabaci e Francesco Provenzale*, pp. 71–604.

20. K. A. Larson, *Condizione sociale dei musicisti e dei loro committenti nella Napoli del Cinque e del Seicento*, in L. Bianconi, R. Bossa (eds.), *Musica e Cultura a Napoli dal XV al XIX sec.*, Olschki, Florence 1983, pp. 61–77.

21. A similar case to the Neapolitan one was that of the four Venetian conservatories intended exclusively for putte, that is, Venetian maidens, orphan or not (J. L. Baldauf-Berdes, *Women Musicians of Venice Musical Foundations, 1525–1855*, Oxford Press, 1993).

22. We limit ourselves, for now, to mention two milestones of musical historiography: G. Pannain, *Le origini della scuola musicale di Napoli*, Naples 1914 and F. Florimo, *La scuola musicale di Napoli e i suoi Conservatori*, Morano, Naples 1881–83, 4 vols. [anastatic ref. Forni, Bologna 1969].

23. There are already several studies on the subject: D. Fabris, *Strumenti di corde, musici e congregazioni a Napoli alla metà del Seicento*, «Note d'archivio per la storia musicale», n.s. I, 1983, pp. 63–110; Id., *Istituzioni assistenziali e congregazioni di musici a Napoli e nell'Italia meridionale durante il viceregno spagnolo*, in L. Bertoldi Lenoci (ed.), *Confraternite, Chiesa e società. Aspetti e problemi dell'associazionismo laicale europeo in età moderna e contemporanea*, Schena, Fasano (Br) 1994, pp. 779–800; M. Columbro, E. Intini, *Congregazioni e corporazioni di musici a Napoli tra Sei e Settecento*, «Rivista italiana di musicologia», XXXIII, 1998,

pp. 41–76; Ead, *Considerazioni sulla condizione sociale e lavorativa del musicista napoletano nel Sei e Settecento*, in M. Columbro, P. Maione (eds.), *Pietro Metastasio. Il testo e il contesto*, Altrastampa, Napoli 2000, pp. 17–27.

24. On trade corporations in Naples in the modern age there are insights and research of considerable interest: L. De Rosa, *Le corporazioni nel Sud della Penisola: problemi interpretativi*, «Studi storici Luigi Simeoni» XLI (1991), pp. 49–68; F. Assante, *Le corporazioni a Napoli in età moderna: forze produttive e rapporti di produzione*, ivi, pp. 69–83; Ead., *I profeti della previdenza: monti e conservatori nelle corporazioni napoletane in età moderna*, in A. Guenzi, P. Massa, A. Moioli (eds.), *Corporazioni e gruppi professionali nell'Italia moderna*, Franco Angeli, Milan 1999, pp. 601–612; L. Mascilli Migliorini, *Il sistema delle arti: corporazioni annonarie e di mestiere a Napoli nel Settecento*, A. Guida, Naples 1992; A. Mastrodonato, *La norma inefficace: conflitti e negoziazioni nelle Arti napoletane (secc. XVI–XVIII)*, «Mediterranea—ricerche storiche», Year X, April 2013, no. 27, pp. 65–92.

25. The chapters of the Congregazione delli Musici erected in Santa Brigida were transcribed by D. Fabris, *Istituzioni assistenziali*, cit. pp. 794–797.

26. D. Fabris, *Strumenti di corde*, cit. p. 83.

27. Ibid., pp. 93–100.

28. Ibid.

29. M. Columbro, E. Intini, *Congregazioni e corporazioni di musici*, cit. pp. 58–60.

30. Naples State Archives (A.S.N.), Fondo Cappellano Maggiore, *Cantori e musici*, Statuto, anno 1645, inv. 1188, inc. 58. The other Statutes of the Corporations of Musicians related to the seventeenth century, kept in the State Archives of Naples, Fondo Cappellano Maggiore, are: *Arte corde di liuto*, year 1653, inv. 1196, inc. 46; *Arte corde di liuto*, year 1684, inv. 1182, inc. 54; *Musici*, undated, inv. 1192, inc. 97; *Musici*, year 1699, inv. 1201, inc. 1; *Suonatori di trombetta*, year 1667, inv. 1201, inc. 31. This information, and the digital reproduction of two of those Statutes, comes to us from Prof. Giuseppe Rescigno, whom we thank infinitely for the generosity with which he agreed to share with us a part of the impressive work of transcription, to which he had been devoting himself for some time now, of all the Statutes

of the Artisan Guilds of Naples. A work that has since merged into an anthology entitled *Lo "Stato dell'Arte"*. *Le corporazioni nel Regno di Napoli dal XV al XVIII secolo*, X, coll. «Alle origini di Minerva trionfante», Ministry of Cultural Heritage and Activities, Rome 2016.

31. A.S.N., Fondo Cappellano Maggiore, Cantori e Musici, Statuto, anno 1645, inv. 1188, inc. 58.
32. Ibid.
33. Ibid.
34. Ibid.
35. U. Prota-Giurleo, *Francesco Provenzale*, «Archivisti d'Italia e Rassegna Internazionale degli Archivi», S. II, 25 (1958), p. 72.
36. We also learn from the statute that a bunch of guitar strings included 60 strings (these were in fact double strings) and a bunch of violin strings included thirty strings. The cost of a viola string was half a grain, while that of a sea trumpet string, one grain (D. Fabris, *Strumenti di corde*, cit. p. 88).
37. M. Columbro, E. Intini, *Considerazioni sulla condizione sociale e lavorativa del musicista*, cit., pp. 20–21.
38. D. Fabris, *La Capilla Real en las etiquetas de la corte virreinal de Nàpoles durante el siglio XVII*, in B. J. García García, J. J. Carreras (eds.), *La Capilla Real de los Austrias. Mùsica y ritual de corte en la Europa moderna*, Fundaciòn Carlos de Amberes, Madrid 2001, pp. 235–250.
39. L. Bianconi, *Storia della musica. Il Seicento*, EDI, Torino 1989, pp. 163–167.
40. D. Fabris, *Spettacoli e opera in musica alla courte di Napoli fino all'arrivo di Alessandro Scarlatti (1649–1683)*, in P. Di Maggio, P. Maione (eds.), *La scena del Re. Il Teatro di Corte del Palazzo Reale di Napoli*, Clean edizioni, Naples 2014, pp. 100–115; D. A. D'Alessandro, *Mecenati e mecenatismo nella vita musicale napoletana*, cit., pp. 71–603; on the typology of patronage nurtured by churches and convents on the four conservatories see chapters III and IV of this volume.
41. R. Romano, *Tra XVI e XVII secolo. Una crisi economica: 1619–1622*, «Rivista Storica Italiana», 3 (1962), pp. 480–531; G. Muto, *La crisi del Seicento*, in *Storia moderna*, Rome, Donzelli 1998, pp. 249–272.

42. For a closer look at the publishing industry in Naples in the seventeenth century, cf. S. Sbordone, *Editori e tipografi a Napoli nel '600*, Accademia Pontaniana, Napoli 1990; G. Lombardi, *L'attività carto-libraria a Napoli tra fine '600 e primo '700*, in A. M. Rao (ed.), *Editoria e cultura a Napoli nel XVIII secolo*, Liguori, Naples 1998; Id., *Tra le pagine di San Biagio. L'economia della stampa a Napoli in età moderna*, ESI, Naples 2000; F. Seller, *L'editoria musicale a Napoli*, in *Storia della musica e dello spettacolo a Napoli*, cit. tomo II, pp. 1815–1824.
43. G. Muto, *La Napoli spagnola*, in *Storia della musica e dello spettacolo a Napoli*, cit., pp. 19–70: p. 53.
44. L. Giustiniani, *Saggio storico-critico sulla tipografia nel Regno di Napoli*, Orsini, Naples 1793, pp. 161 passim.
45. L. Bianconi, *Storia della musica*, cit. p. 85.
46. F. Seller, *L'editoria musicale a Napoli*, cit. p. 1817.
47. Ibid, p. 1820; L. Bianconi, *Il Seicento*, pp. 75–82.
48. A. Caroccia, *Scelte editoriali al tempo di Calo Gesualdo: le fonti a stampa della biblioteca del Conservatorio «San Pietro a Majella» e dell'Archivio Musicale dei Gerolamini di Napoli*, in A. Caroccia, M. Columbro (eds.)., *Giornata Gesualdiana*, Atti della giornata di studio (Castello di Gesualdo, 7 dicembre 2015) Il Cimarosa, Avellino 2015, pp. 105–145.
49. Valuable on these observations is the summary offered by G, Muto, in *La Napoli spagnola*, cit.
50. B. Croce, *I teatri di Napoli*, cit. p. 138.
51. G. R. Ceriello, *Comedias de santos a Napoli nel '600*, «Bulletin Hispanique», XXII/2 (1920), pp. 77–100.
52. G. Staffieri, «*Versi, machine e canto*»: il teatro in musica del Seicento*, in A. Chegai et al. (eds.), *Musiche nella storia*, Carocci, Rome 2017, pp. 131–187; and in N. Badolato, *Amazzoni e sovrani, la festa e il teatro*, in S. Cappelletto (ed.), *Il contributo italiano alla storia del pensiero. Musica*, pp. 156–163.
53. Fundamental to fully understanding the political, social and cultural life of Naples in this historical period is the contribution of G. Galasso, *Napoli spagnola dopo Masaniello: politica, cultura, società*, Edizioni di Storia e Letteratura, Rome 2005 (1st edition Sansoni, Florence 1982).
54. M. Rivero Rodrìguez, *El mundo desordenado: el cambio de dinastìa en el reino de Nàapoles (1707)*, in Immaculada Arias de Saavedra

Alìas (ed.), *Vida cotidiana en la Espana de la Illustraciòn*, Universidad de Granada 2012, pp. 463–486.
55. L. Bianconi, T. Walker, *Dalla finta pazza alla veremonda: storie di Febiarmonici*, «Rivista Italiana di Musicologia», X (1975), pp. 379–454. More recent and rich in new research insights and information is the essay by J. M. Dominguez, *Napoli e l'opera italiana nel Seicento*, in F. Cotticelli, P. Maione (eds.), *Storia della musica e dello spettacolo*, cit. pp. 605–651.
56. J. M. Dominguez, *Napoli e l'opera italiana nel Seicento*, cit., pp. 605–651.
57. Ibid., p. 613. Compared to the ten Venetian dramas of the autumn season and the carnival season of 1681–1682, less than half of them were represented in Naples at the same time.
58. J. M. Dominguez, *L'opera durante il primo period napoletano di Alessandro Scarlatti*, in *Storia della musica e dello spettacolo*, cit, pp. 653–710.
59. G. Muto, *La Napoli spagnola*, cit.
60. P. Maione, *Le metamorfosi della scienza tra generi e imprenditoria nella seconda metà del Seicento a Napoli*, in A. Lattanzi, P. Maione (eds.), *Commedia dell'arte e spettacolo in musica tra Sei e Settecento*, Naples, Editoriale Scientifica, Napoli 2003, pp. 295–328. Maione refers to a document of fundamental importance for understanding the variable financial mechanism according to each viceroy's dispositions, published in F. Cotticelli, P. Maione, *Per una storia della vita teatrale napoletana nel primo Settecento: ricerche e documenti d'archivio*, «Studi pergolesiani. Pergolesi Studies», III (1999), pp. 31–115. Some preliminary inflections to this effect had already been set forth years earlier in his research on Giulia de Caro: P. Maione, *Giulia de Caro «seu Ciulla» da commediante a cantarina. Osservazioni sulla condizione degli «armonici» nella seconda metà del Seicento*, «Rivista italiana di musicologia», XXXII (1997), pp. 61–80, in which it is shown how "the generic wording of commedianti also includes the exercise of the operatic genre".
61. F. Mancini, *Feste ed apparati civili e religiosi in Napoli dal viceregno alla capitale*, Edizioni Scientifiche Italiane, Naples 1968 and *Capolavori in festa. Effimero barocco a Largo di Palazzo (1683–1759)*, Electa, Naples 1997.
62. D. Confuorto, *Giornali di Napoli da MDCLXXIX al MDCIC*, edited by N. Nicolini, L. Lubrano, Naples 1930, vol. I, p. 107.

63. J. Sasportes (ed.), *Storia della danza italiana dalle origini ai giorni nostri*, EDT, Turin 2011, p. 79. On seventeenth-century developments in Naples J. M. Domìn- guez, *Danza y baile en las celebraciones festivas de la corte virreinal de Nàpoles a finales del siglo XVII*, in M. P. Barrios Manzano, M. Serrano Gil (eds.), *Danzas ituales en los paìses iberoamericanos: maestra del patrimonio compartio: entre la tradiciòn y la historia. Estudios e informes*, Consejerìa de Educaciòn y Cultura. Junta de Extremadura, Madrid 2011, pp. 323–334.

64. M. Rak (vols. I–IV) and M. Conforti, C. Lombardi (eds.), *Lezioni dell'Accademia di Palazzo del Duca di Medinaceli. Napoli 1698–1701*, vol. V, Istituto Italiano per gli Studi Filosofici, Naples 2000–2005.

65. B. Croce, *I teatri di Napoli*, cit. p. 145.

66. We have been trying to ask this question since our first publication on the subject: R. Del Prete, *Un'azienda musicale a Napoli tra Cinquecento e Settecento: il Conservatorio della Pietà dei Turchini*, «'Storia Economica», 3 (1999), pp. 413–464.

CHAPTER 3

The Transformation of Orphanages in Conservatory of Music as a Production Place to Share Knowledge, Professional Development and Invest in Human Capital

1 FROM RENFERMEMENT TO MUSIC EDUCATION IN NAPLES AND VENICE

Starting from a historiographical reflection on the complex issue of assistance to abandoned children and reflecting on the continuity and extraordinary topicality of a timeless educational method, we will propose here one of the aspects that united, in the modern age, some particular Italian welfare institutions: the construction of a model of musical education that is still very relevant in some social contexts.

Let us first consider two issues: the prolongation of the welfare period—which turned, in many cases, into a period of more or less professional training and/or actual employment of labor—and the *gendered* approach, consolidated in the different welfare and educational models. Further reflection on a new and more recent educational/professional experience, conducted in contexts almost as difficult as those in which the first music schools were built, will demonstrate the effectiveness of an ancient method of social reintegration, now fully validated by pedagogical and sociological analyses, as well as by results. Every city had its welfare institutions aimed at the poor, the marginalized, the sick, and especially orphaned or abandoned children and adolescents, for whom a fundamental instrument of social control, was defined in Europe in the

© The Author(s), under exclusive license to Springer Nature Switzerland AG 2024
R. Del Prete, *The Neapolitan Creative Economy*, Palgrave Studies in Economic History, https://doi.org/10.1007/978-3-031-55903-7_3

modern age. This was the *renfermement*, a model of reception, education, and recovery to sociality that proposed reeducational strategies based on work, through the apprenticeship of a trade and the direct employment of the 'recluses' in work activities, The combination of the mercantilist principles then in vogue (escape from idleness, creation of new factories, training of new labor-force) with ethical-religious motivations defined two inescapable prerequisites for any charitable action that addressed a neglected, abandoned and only apparent "human capital" mind unable to work: *work-prayer* and *care-production*.

With work, the poor, especially the young, recovered, stimulating them to self-support, but they also found the necessary resources to accommodate them and rehabilitate them into productive citizens. With prayer, the masses were educated and alphabetized.

Over time, many of those children's homes, hospitals, orphanages, or conservatories activated early vocational education pathways, building a system of relationships with artisans and various craftsmen that guaranteed the youngsters a start in a job. With this in mind, placing young guests "in the workshop," where it was possible, certainly had a twofold meaning: on the one hand, initiating them into an *art* gave them a social *status* to spend in adulthood; on the other hand, it provided a replacement for an absent or failing family. The artisan and his family sometimes became the foster family of the young apprentices, and this practice of family fostering guaranteed them resources for maintenance, accommodation in a family environment, education to lawfulness, healthy coexistence behaviors, and training and initiation into an art to be reused in adulthood. Almost all "assisted" foundlings, between the ages of seven and thirteen, were trained in craft or manufacturing activities and, at the same time, received that much basic education which, most often, coincided with a manner catechism.

Music, especially singing, was everywhere a necessary and functional educational component for a more harmonious coexistence as well as for the fulfillment of liturgical obligations, but only in some institutes did it become a true professional orientation. The geography of the brephotrophs, transformed into the first music schools in the modern age, was therefore drawn from North to South of the Boot: first Venice, Naples, and Palermo, then Salerno, Aversa, Reggio Calabria, and Giovinazzo, to mention the realities already studied.

But the first real novelty came in the late sixteenth century with the two mirror-image cases of the four female conservatories in Venice and the four male conservatories in Naples. The case of Palermo, is less relevant at the moment, but it bears witness to another case of the transformation of an orfanotrophy into a music school.[1]

None of the welfare institutions, of which we speak, originated as a vocational training center for musicians, but such became their connotation, almost exclusively, during the seventeenth century. The reasons for this change were mainly economic in nature: the expenses for the maintenance, and education of the young inmates and their initiation into the acquisition of a trade were initially met with alms or bequests from benefactors. Soon it was realized that, precisely through music, the *children* themselves could help to increase income by providing "musical services" generally required for various liturgical services, for the accompaniment of Viaticum, processions, or funerals. A growing demand for music that, from the second half of the seventeenth century, began to turn increasingly toward secular uses (theaters, concerts, public and private festivals). The new artistic "consumption" also influenced the music chapels of the ecclesiastical tradition, which began to welcome singers and instrumentalists no longer trained in their sphere, but coming from the new "music schools."

In Naples, as in Venice, the vicissitudes of the music conservatories thus intertwined with those of a rising musical and theatrical market and, starting from the bottom, they contributed to structuring an educational system that laid the foundations for a European model of musical education, producing, in an increasingly structured way, a "human capital" that found its spaces of artistic and professional realization first in the religious, then, gradually, more and more in the secular sphere. The orientation toward music education, the growth in the number of entertainment producers, and the increasingly frequent engagement of youngsters in what came *to be* known as the *entertainment industry* were the components of a cultural fashion that, as noted above, exploded in the eighteenth century only to undergo new transformations in the following era.[2]

But, if the "professional" education reserved for young boys was always finalized to the practice of a profession, that reserved for girls became unproductive once their stay in the conservatory was over. The gender differences between the musical experience of Venice and Napoli determined the fates of many female musicians and influenced in no small measure the normalization of the system of music education that was put in place in the nineteenth century.

a. Case of Interest in "Gender" Care: The Puttees of the Four Venice Hospitals

In general, the welfare, educational, and formative approach intended for males and females in the Italian conservatories of the modern age was based on the confinement of both groups, but with different modes. First of all, the initial motivations for the help to maidens versus that to boys were different—the former risked to lose their honor, the latter could become dangerous to themselves and others—but even more different were the productive activities they were trained for and the formative principle behind it. For males, the initiation into a trade and the practice of work was part of a vocational training "project," which would be followed up in the practice of a profession upon leaving the conservatorship. On the contrary, the training reserved for girls, although considered to be of economic and productive value (as long as it was practiced within the "conservatory-workshop"), was not always used in the exercise of a job upon leaving the institution. As far as the employed maidens were concerned, their main function was to make a contribution to their own maintenance expenses during their stay in the conservatory and to accumulate the necessary dowry to contract marriage or to follow the religious path and become a nun. They ended all the experience gained through years of hard, often forced labor. Marriage, and the consequent delivery into the hands of the husband of one's "savings," nullified all the skills, abilities, and autonomy with which an orphan or a *perilous* maiden had "rebuilt" her social existence. In the policy of the women's conservatories, therefore, labor was simply a subsidiary path to that of pure livelihood for the maidens. Rather, the main program of their assistance was based on the respect for the moral function of guardianship and care around which the very meaning of the institution that received them revolved.

With this same essential motivation, *putte,* the Venetian waifs in need of help, were received in the four major Hospitals of Venice.[3]

The *Ospedale della Pietà*, founded by the Franciscan Friar Pietruccio in 1346, had the primary purpose of providing care for abandoned children. The *Hospital of the Incurables*, arose in 1522 to deal with a dangerous spread of syphilis, creating a place for the isolation and care of the contagious sick. The *Ospedaletto di S. Maria dei Derelitti*, originated to dispense relief to the poor, whose number was then enormously growing as a result of a persistent famine. The *Beggars' Hospital*, the oldest of all (it would date back to 1182), offered shelter to vagrants, the sick, the elderly, and the disabled for six centuries.

Their organization traced, though not strictly, that of the monastic institutions; but the management, entrusted to lay congregations and sustained by the massive support of benefactors, maintained wide autonomy, from both ecclesiastical and state authorities. At the head of each institute, there was a congregation, composed only of nobles at the *Ospedale della Pietà* and of an equal number of representatives from the aristocracy and the bourgeois in the other three hospitals; the number of governors ranged from twenty-four to fifty, including presidents and deputies in charge of supervisory or management activities in specific areas of the institute; the *deputies on the choir* supervised the organization of musical activity. The economies of the four hospitals were highly different because of the size of the host population; income was derived in part from the labor *of community daughters*, engaged in manufacturing acts, and, more substantially, from congruous bequests from benefactors.

As with other conservatories, the introduction of musical activity, which had always been a means of exalting the faith, responding first and foremost to a need for an image, increased the participation in religious services, procuring a greater number of supporters. Musical activity was carried out as early as the 1500s, but it was not until the following century that choirs were established with masters coming from the outside, the selection of *daughters,* and a well-chosen repertoire. The procedures followed by the governors with regard to the appointment of masters associates and the selection of *daughters* identified the insiders, dispensed from ordinary services, and the outsiders, such as *daughters at the expense of daughters in education.* Among these, they distinguished the *masters,* i.e., the elderly and experienced ones, who instructed the initiates in singing or playing. The size of the choir varied according to periods and hospitals: even more than a hundred daughters per choir in the seventeenth century, then reduced to about forty in the first half of the next century and again increasing significantly in the second half.

There were three classes of female students at The Beggars' Hospital: the first was the beginners' class, under the age of 16; the second was the rookies' class, who studied for 5 more years; the third was composed of the older women who, having completed their studies, were obliged to remain at the service of the choir—as performers or as teachers—for at least 10 more years. Only the most gifted entered the choir, in limited numbers and after passing a rehearsal audition: only eight of these girls were permanently admitted to the hospital. The most important role in the institution was that of the choirmaster, who had the obligation to compose the music, liturgical and otherwise, and to organize the performances. There are at least seventy names of musicians—many of them celebrated—who in the history of the hospitals were engaged in such positions. Alongside them, there were the masters associates, singing and instrumental, and *the choir master*, that is, the senior daughter who substituted for the highest authority during rehearsals or in brief periods of her absence. The *daughters of the choir* learned the basics of musical language from a singing master and often received music lessons from older girls who, under the mutual teaching system, helped the younger ones in their learning paths. Many could play as many as two or three instruments, and some of them were active as both singers and instrumentalists, but, once out of the Hospitals, they were obliged to abandon "public" musical performances. Those who embarked on "careers" as composers, instrumentalists, or singers, chose, in fact, to remain in the Conservatory all their life, and only in this way, some of them, were able to distinguish themselves by a long and great success.

The scribes were responsible for transcribing the music and copying the scores on behalf of the Hospital itself, which then distributed the teaching materials. After a period of apprenticeship, the best ones became active members of the choir; an *ensemble* of about forty singers and players who performed regularly in the Chapel of la Pietà. Within the ensemble, there were fourteen privileged daughters (including two *Choirmasters*) who had the exclusive right to act as guardians for *daughters in education* from noble and bourgeois families. The office of *Maestra* was the highest rank they could achieve and was limited to twenty of them at a time. The other eighteen teachers had various musical and administrative duties for which they were periodically confirmed or rotated.

The *putte* performed in the church on various liturgical occasions, and, hidden behind grates, they couldn't be seen by anybody. The sound of their instruments and their angelic voices were sought and appreciated by nobles and commoners, and even by numerous foreign visitors, but "the audience itself could not comment on or applaud those admirable performances: in order to show appreciation, listeners would just move their seats a little or clear their throats. And this was sufficient. The orphans knew they were the center of attention: those crunches, those coughs amounted to thunderous clapping." For more than a century, the Venetian *putte* were the pride and honor of the Serenissima and were cited by the great music connoisseurs in both Vienna and London, especially when, from 1703, they had the privilege of having the celebrated Antonio Vivaldi as teacher and author of the music they performed. He entered the Pietà as master of violin and fueled strong artistic competition among the various conservatories. Charles De Brosses, an educated French traveler, recounts that enthusiasts moved from one institute to another so as not to miss the '*academies*' (concerts) of the most gifted *puttees*, not to mention the convents where, among the most brilliant virtuosos, there were even nuns. Their lives generally flowed serenely, and in case of illness or fatigue, to regenerate themselves, they were sent with friends to the countryside where, also attending parties, they perhaps met their future husbands. A 'freedom' that gives us the measure of a cultured and uninhibited, as well as devout, city such as Venice was in the modern age.

Among the surnames coined *for* more famous *chorus daughters* are those of *Caterina della Viola, Lucrezia del Violon, Bernardina del Violin, Adriana della Tiorba, and Fortunata Cantora*. Once they attained notoriety, they were paid for their performances, but that money was often used to build the dowry to get married or enter a monastery, and whenever one of those talented orphans got married, she lost all her art and fame.

One of the most famous *putte* was Anna Maria (1695–1782), a choirmaster, singer, and instrumentalist of great renown for her time; an anonymous political satire was dedicated to her. Her talent emerged since the very beginning under Vivaldi's guidance and was one of five *daughters* who were given special permission to participate as concertmasters/instrumentalists in a dispute over Christian doctrine. She became the principal violinist of the choir and had a brilliant career that enabled her to rise to the highest institutional positions. In addition to the violin, Anna Maria could play the harpsichord, cello, viola d'amore, flute, mandolin, and theorbo, demonstrating a multifaceted and extraordinary musical ability that earned her the praise of high foreign personalities visiting Venice and international fame.

One of her most promising pupils was Chiara (known as Chiaretta and later as *Chiara del Violin*). Abandoned in 1718 when she was only two months old, she became a brilliant and virtuoso violinist, but spent her entire life in the Ospedale della Pietà. What remains of her is *The Diary of Clare*, preserved today by the Conservatorio 'B. Marcello' in Venice, a notebook of sheet music on which the young violinist practiced. Vivaldi himself composed "*for Ms. Chiara*" a demanding concert for violin and orchestra. When, much to the *putte*'s chagrin, Vivaldi went to Vienna and never returned to Venice, another highly-regarded teacher, Antonio Martinelli, composed beautiful viola concerts for Chiara (by then 40 years old). And Chiara became a virtuoso viola d'amore player as well. She was later herself a violin teacher at Pietà, and her virtuoso was known throughout Europe. She died in 1791, at the age of 73.[4]

On the music conservatories of Venice, the *storytelling* was certainly amplified by another book that was a considerable success: *Stabat Mater*, by Tiziano Scarpa, for Giulio Einaudi Editore. The book won the 2009 Strega Prize and was then brought to the stage with a play signed by Andrea Chiodi.

Research, meanwhile, waits to reveal new facts and stories. In the concluding chapter of his book, the only organic work of meticulous historical research on the four Hospitals of Venice, J. Baldauf-Berdes briefly dwells on the subject of the vast musical heritage of the hospitals, which still awaits to be investigated and repurposed: suffice it to recall the conspicuous funds of the Pietà housed in the Venetian Conservatory or the more than 200 envelopes of documents, preserved in the State Archives of Venice, until now only partially investigated.

b. A winning Educational Model: The System of the Ancient Conservatories of Naples

The extraordinary demographic increase that, in the mid-sixteenth century, had created in the city of Naples as well, social disproportions and serious conditions of misery,[5] had prompted the wealthy population, in the absence of a public welfare policy, to intervene against rampant poverty with a "system" of private assistance and charity.[6] Boarding schools, orphanages, hospitals, and other institutions were opened, generally entrusted to lay or religious congregations and arising, much more often, on the initiative of individual benefactors.

The history of the four Neapolitan conservatories is very similar to that of the Venetian Hospitals, but while in Venice they were "for girls" the four Neapolitan institutes were all "for young boys" and arose within half a century: the Santa Maria di Loreto in 1537, the Sant'Onofrio a Capuana in 1578, the Pietà dei Turchini in 1583 and the Poveri di Gesù Cristo in 1589. They were founded as brephotrophs, soon to take on more articulated social, welfare, and educative functions, with *music as* the center of their interests.[7]

These were institutions widely involved in the social, political, and cultural activities of communities, which we might describe as forerunners of many of the social services and professions fostered today by the provision of public funding. *Non-profit* organizations and initiatives expressed, in historically diverse forms, the need to build social and solidarity-based relationships, often complementary to or alternative to those on which market economies are based. The combination of civic and religious instances urged the wealthy to donate to the poor, fueling a centuries-old flow of goods. At the same time, promoters and administrators of charitable institutions performed fundamental mediation work, soliciting donations, raising funds, administering resources, and providing services for the less fortunate.[8]

For abandoned children, the European principle of *renfermement* proposed reeducational strategies based on work, a fundamental instrument of social control.[9] Combining the mercantilist principles then in vogue (escape from idleness, creation of new factories, training of new labor force) with ethical-religious motives, it defined two inescapable prerequisites for any charitable action that addressed neglected, abandoned, and only seemingly unfit-for-work "human capital": *work-prayer* and *assistance-production*. With work, the poor, especially the young, recovered, stimulating them to self-support, but they also found the necessary resources to accommodate them and rehabilitate them into productive citizens. From this point of view, placing the little guests of the conservatory "in the workshop" certainly had a twofold significance: on the one hand, by initiating them into a trade, they were given a social *status* to be spent in adulthood, and on the other hand, they were replacing an absent family, due to conditions of orphanhood or general neglect. The artisan and his family became the adopted family of the little apprentices welcomed into the workshop, which often coincided with the home of the artisan family.[10] The educational and symbolic value evoked by this practice of family fostering, which solved a number of problems (resources for the maintenance of the *son*, reception in a family environment, education in legality and healthy coexistence behaviors, training and initiation in an art to be reused in the adult phase, *fund raising* for the conservatory itself that made "cash" to guarantee assistance to a greater number of outcasts), was undoubtedly very high.

The craft or manufacturing activities to which the children of the four conservatories were initiated were different. At an early stage, the young boys, aged between 7 to 13, were almost exclusively prepared for crafts (*tinkerer, philaterer, beret maker*), and music was still used only as a catechetical tool and necessary complement to liturgical services.[11] The governors of the institutes entered into actual apprenticeship contracts with the artisans with whom the orphans were placed. The *instromento* [12] provided for a precise commitment on the part of the master craftsman: teach the son the trade,[13] offer him "full-board, clothing and treat him well for at least six continuous years," give him "a new suit of Naples cloth," and then deliver him to the governors, paying the conservatory 10 ducats for his service. Any delays in "deliveries" or payments would oblige the artisan to a penalty of another 6 ducats per month for the whole duration of the delay. This secured the master, but also the child's maintenance expenses, while an already productive workforce had joined the institute, thus contributing to its revenue.[14]

The demographic information, although fragmentary, effectively gives us an idea of the social, professional and geographical characterization of the children who entered the conservatories, identifying their routes in and out. Some of them were "collected" by the governors themselves, who periodically "visited" the city streets in search of orphaned or "misguided" children. Others, on the other hand, were reported by persons who took responsibility for them by guaranteeing the payment of their tuition. From the *Rolls* of the sons, we derive a long list of admissions that offers our investigation a set of interesting news: name, geographical origin, age, period of stay, "plegio" or consignee, mode of entry and exit, and, for the years after 1650, even the type of musical studies they were about to follow. Information that opens glimpses into the dynamics of Neapolitan poverty, suggests the typology of the artisans of the time, the social background of those who would become the students of the music conservatories, defining the protagonists of that particular and flourishing system of music demand and supply in Naples in the seventeenth and eighteenth centuries. The internal life of the conservatory was animated by numerous other "officials" in a hierarchical division of duties, which entrusted the father Rector with the "superintendence of both the House and the Church." His staff included the vice rector, the sacristan, the prefects, the teachers of grammar, music, and instruments, the sons, and the priests.

The overall movement of the children, all boys, who entered the conservatories was always very irregular, varying in relation to the exits of those who completed their *instromento*, the number of places in the *piazza franca* (i.e., without payment of tuition), but even more so in relation to the events that from time to time complicated their socio-economical conditions. There were at least three events that strained the city and had heavy repercussions on the four Conservatories as well: the Masaniello Revolution in 1647; the plague epidemic in 1656; and the 1688 earthquake.

The records of the four institutions never explicitly show any connection with those tremendous occasions. Yet contemporary chronicles often tell of the involvement of some of the children, mostly from the populace, with Masaniello's revolutionary uprisings. In general, in each of those periods, the number of admissions to the various institutes turned out to be lower than usual: at the Conservatorio di Sant'Onofrio, which had just recovered from the events of 1647, the outbreak of the plague nine years later reduced the number of sons to only 32; the same fate befell the other institutes. "At Lavinaio, at Porto, at Mercato, at Vicaria, at Porta Capuana, populous and filthy neighborhoods, people were dying like flies."[15]

Particularly noticeable, however, is the resumption of activities immediately after those events. All those institutes were full again almost immediately, and their books showed the various expenditures, sales or purchases of old and new buildings, payments of educational staff and music teachers, and tuition of the educated children.

At St. Onofrio's, in 1658, the list of "*provisionati*" shows quite a high number of monthly payments made by negotiable securities on the Bank of St. Eligius (Table 1).

At the Pietà dei Turchini, where the plague scourged more than two-thirds of the hospitalized patients (the Rector, Don Giuseppe Incarnato, the custodians, a hundred children, and several of the brethren of the Whites died); in July 1656, the pharmacist Pietro Paolo Fenice also died.[16] But even there, it took only a few years for the revival: "from 1662 to 1700, the Turchini gathered together the best of our seventeenth-century teachers and composers: the Salvatore, who is said to have been Alessandro Scarlatti's teacher, the Provenzale, a distinguished teacher and deservedly acclaimed musician, and others."[17]

Table 1 Provisionati at the conservatory of San'Onofrio in Capuana, Naples, 1658

Provisionati/Provised	Annual provision in ducats
Rettore	24
Maestro di Cappella	48
Maestro di Schola	18
Maestro di Violino	12
Cappellano e musico (cantor)	12
Lavannara (Washerwoman)	13
Barber	03

Source S. Di Giacomo, *Il Conservatorio di Sant'Onofrio in Capuana*, Naples, Remo Sandron Editore, 1924, p. 44

2   To the Origins of the Neapolitan School of Music

As the schools grew and the number of children increased, new staff and premises were needed: rooms, dormitories, storages for wood and food supplies; an infirmary, a place to make bread, one to be used for salting and bagging of meat, a stable for a couple of beasts of burden, and again a pharmacy.

At Pietà dei Turchini, the first four buildings attached to the Conservatorio were purchased by the governors between 1595 and 1634 at a total expense of 10,000 ducats, while the other houses owned by the institution were the fruit of inheritance or charity.

In the years 1627–1631 the Conservatory collected annual interest of ducats 1,524.98 on capital of ducats 14,382.94 and paid interests for 552.75 ducats annually on mortgages of 9,050.50 ducats. The other annuities generally came from capital invested in the purchase of shares in arrents. It was thanks to the bequests of personalities such as the Prince of Cellamare, the Marquis of Crispano, Councilor F. Rocco, Notary Agostino Fenizia, the Marquis of Arena or the Marquis of Collevisi (just to mention a few names) that the Conservatory was able to boast movable income, coming from public debt securities.[18] The Conservatories used, for their own payments and collections, the work of the public banks.[19] Investments in real estate were mostly dictated by the need to expand individual venues but, very often, real estate came from bequests and donations with the attached obligation to allocate part of the annuities to the celebration of masses in suffrage of the donors (enriched nobles and bourgeoisie).

In 1656 alone, the year of the plague, as many as seven bequests were received by the Pietà dei Turchini for a total capital of 12,920.70 ducats.[20] Among the donors appear the names of the ancient Neapolitan aristocracy, alongside congregations and benefactors belonging to the middle class. In those years the real estate of the Conservatorio della Pietà dei Turchini consisted of at least three apartments, two rooms, a *poteca* and "*un basso al vico di rimpetto dove erano le carceri di S. Giacomo*" (aka and a tiny ground floor apartment in front of the St. Giacomo jail):

- Home at Largo del Castello where there is the Corriero Maggiore
- Big house at Vico del Baglivo
- A fundaco of houses at Ponte de Tappia
- A large house behind S. Giorgio de' Genovesi
- A house in the streetof Fr. Francis (current St. Brigid Street)
- Casa Grande at Charity Chianche
- House in St. Nicolillo of Charity
- Various houses in Lettere, in vico dei Greci, in Chiaia, at Egiziaca in Forcella
- A farm house in Posillipo
- Two plots of land in Capri
- House with a schola bascio in S. Bartolomeo.

Revenues could vary considerably, even a few years apart, and the fluctuations were due to a threefold order of factors. They depended on the income from the gabelles, which were not, as it is well known, constant, due to the varying revenue from tributes; on the fact that in the years immediately following the plague there was, from the economic point of view, a general upheaval; and, finally, on the amount of the "entry" fees, that is, the sums that had to be paid by non-poor young people who intended to attend the conservatory to learn music. They were susceptible to variation depending on the number and payment possibilities of the "educating sons." The statutes set to one hundred the number of youngsters to be housed in the institute and at 12 ducats the enrollment fee. The total number of sons admitted to the Pietà dei Turchini in the years 1632–1676 was 322, that is, on average, just over 14 per year. Not at all negligible, therefore, was the incidence of the children's income and even less that of the fees received for representations and musical assistance services in which they took part, in the two decades following the plague. The cash movements recorded by the Treasurer in the thirty-year period 1660–1691 reveal the difficulties of those years, confirmed by the prevalence of expenditures over income, particularly between 1685 and 1691. The most significant deficit in that period was recorded in 1686, when expenditures exceeded revenues by as much as 2,593.19 ducats. It is contained in the following five years, around a few hundred ducats. The thirty years following the plague of 1656 were particularly difficult. In 1676 the Governors of the Pietà were forced to sell one of the houses inherited by the notary Fenizia to obtain 337 ducats from it, withholding an annual census of 2 ducats.[21]

Lacking records from 1665 to 1682, the extent of income and expenditures in that year is unknown, but the institution was probably forced to sell the property pressed by the needs of management. Only two instances of real estate alienation are recorded in the property accounts. The accounting records break down again from December 1687 until September 1689, that is, before and after the 1688 earthquake, which forced the conservatory, in the following years, to face huge expenses for the renovation of the building and the properties it owned. These more or less contingent management difficulties were common to all four Institutes.

With regard to the number of youngsters housed in the individual Conservatories, it fluctuated, on average, around 100, but in St. Mary of Loreto, which was more accustomed to diversifying the training and destination of its assisted, the total number of children could be far higher, as they did not all reside within the institute.

Contact with the artisan world continued, with some differences, even when music education and initiation into the "musical professions" of the sons. Musical activity has been carried out, since the sixteenth century, in support of devotional practices and pompous liturgical rites. Starting from the next century, and following the arrival of outside masters, the selection of the sons, and the choice of the repertoire, the real music school took over, with its threefold role: educational agency, center of professional training for musicians, and "music factory".

The turning point came in the mid-seventeenth century: it was then that music became the fundamental element of their educational-welfare structure by imposing itself as the *art* most in demand in the socio-religious market of the time. After initiating their reeducational mission by entrusting the children collected from the streets to the workshops, those institutes understood that that same music, used at first as an instrument of reeducation and salvation of the soul, could become the art to be practiced in places *other* than the artisan workshops. Thus, church institutions, squares, and, increasingly even private theaters began to be supplied with musicians and singers. The factors that concurred in the transformation of the four brefotrophs into music schools were essentially twofold: the need to find alternative sources of revenue to cover the operating and support expenses, and the need to meet the ever-increasing demand for "musical services" both religious and secular.

That was the moment when new productive sectors and new professional outlets were defined within a broader musical and theatre system which at the city level at first and then nationally, would expand its reach to foreign countries, stimulating, the demand for the services of the Neapolitan Musical School in the European circuit.[22] New professional figures sprung up, such as music masters, copyists, singers, and instrumentalists, as well as set designers, violin makers, tuners, and stage personnel, until glimpses of the "workshops armonics," where the more established chapel masters would surround themselves with particular and promising apprentices, as well as professionals, who could be counted on to form well established and perfectly close-knit "working groups."[23]

The welfare reality where the four conservatories operated, was a microeconomy of exchange: the system of economic inter-relationships with the society, starting with the analysis of the costs and returns of charity, authorize us to call the pious work a true business. In the exercise of charity, in fact, explicit economic reasons and more elusive, but no less decisive, motivations of social convenience, immediate individual interests and more complicated collective benefits converge.

The transformation of the four welfare institutions into places of production of knowledge and *know-how* and then into true "music factories" goes through the history of their institutional purposes, organization, and the prestigious collaborations from which those singular "factories" took advantage. Thus began a fervid web of cultural, aesthetic, social, and economic connections that would condition from a certain point onward the very rules of music composing. A new kind of industry, the theatrical-musical industry, was established, and its productivity played a role of great importance, especially from the mid-1700s when, with the birth of impresario theater, a new economic category was defined along-side the system of religious and secular, public or private patrons: the *paying audience*.

By the mid-seventeenth century in Italy, and in Naples in particular, artistic productivity discovered new *audiences*: no longer the *lord* and/or *monsignor*, but also an *audience* who, by paying an entrance fee to enjoy an occasion of entertainment and leisure, would offer new production opportunities to *composers*, increasingly influencing their creative vein, composing rules and results.

Audience *consensus* would later become decisive in reshaping the hierarchy of subjects in the Italian musical theater production chain.

3   The Educational Structure of Music Schools

The early seventeenth century marked a true artistic revolution in Italy: monodic singing with instrumental accompaniment prevailed over vocal polyphony and its complex and abstract forms. Everywhere in Italy's major cities, the musical word increasingly pandered to the tastes of a perhaps less courtly but increasingly broader public. In Naples, in 1607, Francesco Lombardi, master of the Viceregnal Chapel, sent to press his book of villanelles for several voices; other Neapolitan composers, such as Giovanni Maria Trabaci, Donato Antonio Spano and Giovan Domenico Mondella published other similar books, with madrigals and *madrigaletti*, while, the great Salvator Rosa, in the same period, gave to the press his Cantata officially opening the doors of the Parthenopean theaters to melodrama. The musical scene, however, was built within the four ancient Conservatories, then moved on to the Viceroy's Palace and, soon after, to the theaters of Naples, where, during a sumptuous seventeenth century, beside the Opera seria, the Opera buffa was established and, with them, the Naples School of Music.[24]

It was thus the seventeenth century, with its pomp, apparatus, and artistic revolution, that directed the change of the four Male Orphanages into Schools of Music. If the first practice of admission to the Conservatories had been suggested by a welfare-like management policy, the first half of the century saw a shift to a system of admissions established by rules of a didactic nature, more selective and suggested by a more articulated musical demand. Rules that were essentially the same in all four music conservatories,—although we were still quite far from a truly centrally organized system of public music education and each institution had always acted autonomously.

In fact, from the mid-seventeenth century onward, the purely welfare-like function of the four institutes, though without being totally abandoned, waned in favor of a more strictly educational and specialistic one: the boys admitted to the Conservatory were therefore selected on the basis of their aptitudes, separating those suited to the study of music (*educandi*) from those who proved to be more prone to learn an art or a trade.[25] It is difficult to say precisely in which year the individual conservatories decided to give priority to regular music teaching. For none of the four Institutes has come down to us a precise deliberative act, and the Statutes were updated only during the eighteenth century, but without making major changes to the seventeenth-century ones and including, almost as a matter of course, the rules inherent in the study and production of music. The documents from which it is possible to infer the gradual transformation into music schools are mainly accounting books. Thus, if at Santa Maria di Loreto, in the lists of paid personnel, there were at least three organists as early as 1586 and 1587, and, from 1630, the presence of secular music teachers; at the Pietà dei Turchini, regular music teaching appears from 1615; at the Poveri di Gesù Cristo, the first teachers appear in 1633; and at the Conservatorio di Sant'Onofrio a Capuana, the first expenditures for music date from 1653.

The largest orphanage among the four music conservatories was undoubtedly Santa Maria di Loreto. Between 1568 and 1590, more than one hundred children were received at the institute and were engaged in the manufacture of silk socks, felt caps, dyeing, and "cusitura." The orphans' welfare was particularly well cared for and effective. The institute maintained a fruitful network of contacts with the artisans in the area and was soon able to guarantee a very well-structured system of education and initiation into work, including musical work, which was also almost immediately aimed at the admission of students (*educandi*), aged between 8 and 12, capable of paying 12 ducats in *entrance* fees and an annual tuition of at least 25 ducats. The *educandi* children, with a contract stipulated before a notary, undertook to remain for a certain number of years in the Conservatory and to serve in the music activities that the institution would provide to the various patrons.[26]

Between 1586 and 1587, there are records of three organists regularly paid by the Conservatory, with a salary of 1 ducat per month: Stefano di Napoli, Giovan Cesare de Falco, and Giovan Bernardino de Filippis. In

1588, Francesco Roccia, the organist who taught singing, organ playing, and counterpoint to 5 children every day, was paid 2 ducats a month.

Since 1610, the books regularly present the so-called "Expenses of our Church" in which, for the most part, appear payments to music teachers, the purchase and tuning of instruments, and a few names of chapel masters. The first of them is Marco Viadano: from January 1621 to February 1622, he was compensated for one year's attendance with 21 ducats. In that same 1622 Lutio Oppici took service as first violin master and remained in office until 1628. In the same period, Bartolomeo Angelone was paid, as cornet master, 5 ducats per month. On December 4, 1633 we find a note regarding a *mastro de cappella* with a pay of 6 ducats a month; on January 29, 1634 there is mention of a *mastro de cornetta*, and in February of the same year of a *mastro de' violins*, with pay, each, of 5 ducats a month.

Between 1630 and 1640 secular musicians were called in to serve the church and processions: a Giovanni Gambardella, bass, and a soprano whose name is not given, were compensated with 1 ducat per the month each. Still, until 1644, there appear to be a number of organ masters, who no longer appear as such later on. The last will be Gio. Orsolini.

With the arrival of Francesco Provenzale—whose presence the sources detect first in 1651, then, with regularity, from 1661—the chapel master's compensation rose to 12 ducats per month, then fell clamorously to 6 or 7 ducats per month with his successors, Gaetano Veneziano, Nicola Acerbo, and Cataldo Amodei, in 1684 the first two, and in 1687 the third, respectively.[27]

These were the years when the orphanage changed into a music school: the first income from music performed outside the conservatory is recorded in 1644. In this year Marco Viadano (very probably a priest) still appears as the first chapel master, with a salary of 10 ducats a month, until 1651. He was succeeded by another priest, Antonio Murino, until 1657; and from 1657 to 1658 Don Pietro Coppola was the maestro of chapel, followed by Don Leonardo Fiata who occupied that position from 1658 to 1663. Each of the four chapel masters had a salary of 10 ducats a month and probably lived in the same Conservatory, of which Don Leonardo Fiata was also chaplain.

In the same years, here as in the other Conservatories, the induction of lay music teachers in place of priests would begin, and so, officially, on May 7, 1663, Francesco Provenzale, "the most distinguished musician of the time, the most illustrious theorist and practitioner," would take the place of Don Leonardo Fiata. Provenzale would remain at Santa Maria di Loreto until 1673 when he moved to the Pietà dei Turchini, where he remained until 1701.

Between 1678 and 1684 the first person to answer to the title of singing master was Giuseppe Cavallo, who received 120 ducats a year to teach singing to the Conservatory's children and to accompany liturgical services at the attached church. Cavallo appears to have served from 1672 to 1674 as second maestro (when he was also a colleague of the Provenzale) and from 1675 to 1684 as chapel master. After Provenzale moved to the Turchini, (in 1674) and following the death of Cavallo (on July 9, 1684), the two influential Maestri were replaced by two former sons of the Conservatory, Gaetano Veneziano and Nicola Acerbo, one as first maestro (maestro di cappella), the other as vice maestro (maestro pel cantare), with the pay of 6 ducats per month each.

A year later, as the number of pupils grew, Veneziano said he could "no longer attend to his sons because of his many occupations." Nicola Acerbo took his place and, as the first teacher, was required to give two hours of lessons a day with a monthly salary of 10 ducats.

The number of sons grew and the music school became better and better structured, but teaching at the conservatories, however prestigious was not very well paid. In 1686, the Governors of Loreto offered Don Giuseppe Scaramuzza a position as violin master, but he declined and the position went to Gian Carlo Cailò (or Chilò), for a monthly salary of 5 ducats. Meanwhile, just a year after his appointment, Maestro Nicola Acerbo also declared that he could no longer look after the musical education of so many sons. Don Cataldo Amodeo was called in his place, to give singing and music lessons in the mornings, but he too was forced to resign: his multiple musical occupations were difficult to reconcile with his teaching commitment.

At that point, the governors of St. Maria di Loreto, forced to replace Amodeo as well, opted to entrust the professorship to another distinguished lay musician, Alessandro Scarlatti. But even this appointment proved to be short-lived.

Scarlatti accepted the post of Chapel Master as of March 1, 1689, committing himself to give lessons "de canto e suono" in the morning, for a provision of 10 ducats per month. Nicola Acerbo was to collaborate with him as second Maestro while continuing to give his lessons in the evening, as he had been doing for some time now. Both of them, as chapel masters (first and second) maintained the obligation to produce music and compositions according to the conditions deliberated in the Conclusions of September 14, 1687. They, as chapel masters, were required to compose not only music for two choirs—and, each of them, every four months—a mass for four with instruments, and at the end of the year a mass for two choirs with instruments and every month a motet, but "whenever the occasion comes to make some composition of Prologue, intermezzo et ogni altra cosa recitativa they must be given the necessary paper. If the masters do not deliver one of these works it will be reheld on their provision d. 6 for each mass and d. 2 for each motroof."[28] But Alessandro Scarlatti, already a celebrated artist and acclaimed even far from Naples, was forced to ask for a thirty-day leave at the end of April (two months after his hiring) to go to Rome to attend to some of his affairs. However, the period of leave lengthened to over two and a half months, and as the summer progressed, his return was not expected soon. "Such delay evidently caused harm to the sons studying music because they had to skip practice, and also affected the interests of the Conservatory, as it no longer made those musics that used to be made." For these reasons, the Governors of the Conservatory decided to dismiss him and hire Don Pietro Bartilotti in his place. However, the choice was not liked by the sons, who protested saying that they had found themselves with two teachers (one declared first teacher and the other, Acerbo, second teacher, i.e., singing teacher) of practically equal status. A few years later, on April 2, 1695, Bartilotti resigned; Gaetano Veneziano, "known for one of the primarii maestri di cappella of that city," returned to serve the Conservatorio, with the position of the first maestro. His salary was set at 12 ducats per month, and the position included the obligation to give singing and music lessons every morning.

By the end of the seventeenth century, the Conservatory of Santa Maria di Loreto, the largest and most complex of the four, was an established music school. This is clearly confirmed by the resolution passed on August 23, 1699, by which it was stipulated that, from then on, the children would be admitted as *educandi (students)* and would have to pay not less than 30 ducats per year, with an early semester and the usual *entry* of 10 ducats.

At the Conservatorio della Pietà dei Turchini, De Lellis mentioned as early as 1626, masters of theorbo, cornet, and violin.[29] In fact, the books of Deliberations and Expenditures, record the appearance of the music lessons at the Turchini as early as 1615, under the name of Don Lelio d'Urso, singing master and organist at least until 1622, with a salary of 1 ducat, 2 tarì and 10 grana per month. From 1622 to 1626 the direction of music teaching was entrusted to a better-known chapel master, Don Giovanni Maria Sabino, with a salary of 10 ducats a month; he was followed by Francesco Lombardi and Giacinto Anzalone. What exactly these early masters taught is not hard to imagine: sacred music, certainly, to serve the liturgical services that were celebrated in the church attached to the Conservatory (Table 2). Throughout the seventeenth century, musical teachings in the four Conservatories were limited to simple songs and accompanying sounds for funerals, monkings, processions, viaticum brought to the dying, or for the sacred representations increasingly demanded by Churches, Monasteries, and Congregations. A more articulated, more eclectic, and deeper musical culture emerged only later:

> in the days of Sabino, Lambardi and Anzalone the children of the Pietà dei Turchini could not claim but that vocal, and scarcely instrumental, exercise, which helped them in the usual needs, humble and not difficult, to which their Governors destined them (the usual Sunday singing in the church attached to the Conservatory, the accompaniment of the viaticum, that of funerals, any performance of singing and music in the Conservatory itself and in the monasteries).[30]

Famous musicians who taught at the Pietà include Francesco Provenzale, who taught from 1673 to 1701 and died in 1704. His second teacher was, throughout his tenure, Don Gennaro Ursino. Among his pupils, we recall some who were already quite well known, who were at the Turchini between 1652 and 1676.

Domenicantonio Nola, composer of sacred music;
   Giovan Cesare Netti, from Putignano (Puglie), who entered in 1663 at the age of 8, had already been a pupil of Giovanni Salvatore, and after leaving the Conservatory in 1667, became supernumerary organist at the Royal Chapel.
   Don Gennaro Ursino, a Neapolitan who entered in 1663, at the age of 8, in 1686 succeeded Giovanni Salvatore as chapel master at the Poveri di Gesù Cristo with 6 ducats a month; in 1675 he was named second maestro at the Turchini, where he would later be first maestro from 1701 to 1705, when he would move on, again as chapel master to the Santa Casa dell'Annunziata.

Table 2 Masters in service at the Conservatorio della Pietà dei Turchini. Naples, 17th cent

Masters	Teaching	Service
Don Lelio d'Urso	1° Maestro di Cappella	1615–1622
Don Giovanni Maria Sabino	1° Maestro di Cappella	1622–1626
Francesco Lombardi	1° Maestro di Cappella	1626–1630
Giacinto Anzalone	1° Maestro di Cappella	1630–1657
Domenico Vetromile	1° Maestro di Cappella	1657–1662
Don Giovanni Salvatore	1° Maestro di Cappella	1662–1673
Francesco Provenzale	1° Maestro di Cappella	1673–1701
Don Gennaro Ursino	2° Maestro di cappella	1675–1700
Giuseppe Impiastro	Organista e Maestro	1626–1629
Don Gabriele Solfrizzi	Maestro di Pandòra	1675–1679
Toberio Coppola	Maestro di Violino	1630–1638
Gennaro Morone	Maestro di Violino	1638–1639
Giov. Francesco Melina	Maestro di Violino	1639–1640
Andrea Carmellino	Maestro di Violino	1640–1641
Francesco Anzalone	Maestro di Violino	1641–1657
Carlo de Vincentiis	Maestro di Violino	1657–1677
Nicola Vinciprova	Maestro di Violino	1677–1694
Chailaux Giov. Carlo	Maestro di Violino	1694–1722
Giov. Giacomo Anzalone	Maestro di Cornetta e Trombone	1626–1640
Geronimo de Nardo	Maestro di Cornetta e Trombone	1640–1647
Don Francesco Grieco	Maestro di Cornetta e Trombone	1648–1673
Pietro Guarino	Maestro di Cornetta e Trombone	1673–1675
Pietro Manto	Maestro di Cornetta e Trombone	1675–1701

Source S. Di Giacomo, Il Conservatorio della Pietà dei Turchini, Naples, Remo Sandron Editore, 1924, pp. 295–298

Tommaso Persico, also from Naples, entered the Pietà in 1665 at age 11. He sang as bass and in that capacity was later hired first at the Annunziata, in 1679, then at the Royal Chapel, in 1685.

Pietro Manto, Neapolitan, master of wind instruments from 1675 to 1701 at the Pietà, where he had been a pupil. From 1688 to 1701 he was a maestro at the Conservatorio di Sant'Onofrio, then, until 1705, he taught at the Poveri di Gesù Cristo. He sometimes played at the Cathedral. Di Giacomo calls him a "famous and sought-after" musician.

Finally, the Neapolitan violinist, *Bonaventura Veneziano*. He began his studies at the Pietà in 1666. From 1717 he began his career at the Royal Chapel, where he remained until his death in 1736.[31]

The Conservatory of the Poor of Jesus Christ already possessed music books and musical instruments in the years between 1630 and 1632. The list of *Libri de' Musica* included scores of masses, vespers, mottets and sonatas; books for four or eight voices; madrigals and paranze. And, after the books, the instruments are also listed: violins and violones, trombones, cornets, a cymbal, and a rebecchina for music (Table 3).[32]

April 1633 records the names of four *maestri de schola* entered for the first time in the account books: Francesco Rufolo, *magister musicae*, Marco Antonio D'Antonino, *ejus coadiutor*, Francesco Anzalone, *magister lyrae*, Jacopo Anzalone, *magister buccinae*.[33] In 1634, a son of the Conservatory, Diego Marcuccio, turns out as *mastricello* and teaches violin to his fellow students, rewarded with the monthly salary of

Table 3 Libri de' Musica, Conservatorio dei Poveri di Gesù Cristo, Naples, 1632

Partimenti de messe, vesperi, motteti et sonate	Libri due
Libri a otto, messe, vesperi, motteti et sonate	Paranze quattro
Libri a quattro voci, messe, vesperi, mottetti e frottole	Paranze cinque
Libri grandi di Morales a quattro voci, messe de defonti et feste	Libri due
Mottetti di Don Giovanni Maria Sabino, a due, tre e quattro voci	Paranze due
Madrigali a cinque di Pomponio Nenna	Paranze tre
Madrigali a cinque della scelta	Paranza una
Madrigali a quattro et cinque de Pomponio Dentice	Paranze due
Madrigali di Luca Marenzio a quattro	Paranza una
Madrigali di Rogiero Giovanelli a cinque	Paranza una
Uno libro grande dove se canta a quattro	
Sonate a quattro et cinque di Don Giov. Maria Sabino	
Due paranze de libri de madrigali del Prencepe de Venosa, coverti in pergamena	

Source S. Di Giacomo, *The Conservatory of the Poor of Jesus Christ*, Naples, Remo Sandron Editore, 1928, p. 77

Table 4 Masters in service at the conservatory of the poor of Jesus Christ, Naples 1660

Masters	Teaching	Provision in ducats
Carlo Acquaviva	Stringed instruments	3 per month
Giovanni Ferraro	Wind instruments	2 per month
Canon Ignazio Peliggi	Chapel Master	48 per year
Fr. Gian Lonardo De Blasio	Chapel Master	3 per month

Source S. Di Giacomo, *The Conservatory of the Poor of Jesus Christ*, Naples, Remo Sandron Editore, 1928, p. 83

one ducat, two tarì and 10 grana. Another son, Marcantonio d'Antonino, joins Rufolo as *maestro de cantare*.

The masters serving in 1660 were Carlo Acquaviva, Giovanni Ferraro, Canon Ignazio Peliggi, and Don Gian Leonardo De Blasio (Table 4).

Until 1699 the teaching staff of the Poor of Jesus Christ consisted of a chapel master, Gaetano Greco, and his helper, Matteo Giordano (formerly Ursino's deputy); a master of string instruments, Francesco Mirabella; and a master of wind instruments, Pietro Manto.[34]

There they continue, yes, to gather poor children from the street, but the new administrators take in even paying ones and thus effectively increase the income of the place. Discipline, as the number of the inmates increased, became more difficult to maintain among them, and so the illustrious visiting prelate found in the wardrobe - and perhaps he did not regret it - three iron rods, two iron bars and a pair of iron handcuffs, which evidently served to correct the frequent boiling of these youngsters, or their lack of assiduity in studying. For - this should also be noted - now the children are also taught music, among other things, and no longer in the primitive manner that trained them for very simple peripatetic needs, (that is, when they accompanied, singing and playing, the funeral transports or so also preceded the processions), but rather with a broader program, with more experienced and numerous teachers, with the intention, in short, of establishing in the Conservatory a true musical ephebe that could serve the daily and incessant philharmonic needs of Naples as well as the more worthy and more lucrative future of each of those youngsters. In what year precisely the Conservatory of the Poor of Jesus Christ began to change into a musical institute, we could not say[...].[35]

The external activity of the Conservatory during the seventeenth century was intense: in the year 1680 alone, the institution was engaged in more than 100 musical services, required by as many patrons distributed throughout the city of Naples and neighboring territories, which yielded the Institute, for that year alone and for music revenues alone, more than 700 ducats.[36]

At the Conservatorio di Sant'Onofrio in Capuana, the earliest useful date to which the Institute's musical activity can be traced is 1653, when the presence is recorded of the *mastro de schola* Don Giovanni Terracciano, who, for 15 ducats a year, "board, room, shoes, washerwoman and barber," was in charge of giving lessons only to the Conservatorio's children and no more than four or five other seculars; with him appears the Maestro di Cappella, Carlo Sica, with a salary of 4 ducats a month who, certainly, had been teaching there for some years because in the same year, he fell ill (he would later die in 1655) and was replaced by a son of the same conservatory, Pietro Guarino. The rector of the conservatory in those years was Don Aniello Russo, with a salary of 24 ducats a year. There were 11 paying sons: Pietro Leggiero, Salvatore Caserta, Francesco Riccardo, Honofrio Guadagno, Giovanni Passaro, Salvatore Vitto, Giambattista Vitto, Alessio Lembo, Felice Tofano, Salvatore Rubino, and Domenico de Colellis.[37]

The sons' musical performances took place, again, in the various churches of Naples, but also in Ischia, Nola, Amalfi, Avellino, Sessa Aurunca, Montecassino, and many other neighboring localities. Their participation was in great demand for performances of oratorios, intermezzi and sacred plays, especially in monasteries and convents; accompaniment of viaticum, funerals, and public festivals, and many of these services were repeated regularly from month to month or year to year, guaranteeing more or less constant income.

The Institute's income was then greatly increased by the gabelles for grain and flour, oil, soap, barrel and retail wine, silks of Calabria, manna, and the four salt warehouses. Thanks to these revenues, the conservatory was able to avail himself of new teachers again and again, chosen, as best as they could, from the city's increasingly dense and renewed musical corps, selecting from among the most worthy professionals. In 1653, for example, Carlo Riccio was hired as second chapel master. In 1658 Francesco Basso, an excellent player of wind instruments, was called, with a monthly salary of 2 ducats. He was hired as cornet master, but he was also asked to give lessons in trombone, oboe, flute, and bassoon (again for that pay); and this same workload, they will have, until 1742, all his successors.

Thus, while taking care of the final arrangement of the schools, the church chaplains (some of whom were already sons of the Conservatory), the rectors themselves (often mere pedagogized priests), and the Scolopian Fathers were called to conduct the Conservatory. We first find them at St. Onofrio in 1669, and from then on an intransigent system of severity was introduced, and the life of the Institute was more disciplined, more composed, and more fruitful, even at the cost of difficult decisions, as when the expulsion of the unruly and useless boys was proposed.

It was therefore no coincidence that the number of sons in 1670 increased to over a hundred in attendance, even considering that, starting in 1653, the government of that institute had resolved to admit there also paying students, who generally chose their schools on the basis of the fame and good reputation of their teachers. At Sant'Onofrio, between 1669 and 1690, chapel masters of the caliber of Abbot Francesco Rossi, canon of Bari, who staged at least four of his operas in Venetian theaters, taught; the no less well-known and esteemed Abbot Don Pietro Andrea Ziani; Caresana, also a Venetian, held in high esteem in Naples (more than 300 of his precious musical autographs were kept by the Padri Filippini in Naples); one of the most excellent wind masters, as Pietro Manto, a former son himself, distinguished himself for his bravura and thanks to his fame he taught cornet, oboe, and flute also in the Conservatories of the Pietà dei Turchini and the Poveri di Gesù Cristo.

In those years the Rector of Sant'Onofrio was *Don Angelo Durante*, uncle of the more famous Francesco, later Maestro di Cappella too, in substitution of Don Cristoforo Caresana, in 1690. Inexplicably, at that time, the number of *educandi* seems once again to have dwindled (a *scarparo* note from 1689 counts only 46). In the following decade the situation appears unchanged, to the point that in a supplication sent by the S. Onofrio's children to the Elect of the Most Faithful City of Naples, they declared that they were now reduced to great necessity, both because of the penury of the times and the scarcity of income, and for these reasons they asked for the charity of "four staia of oil," which the Elect, of course, granted them.

Having overcome the difficulties of daily life, the students of St. Onofrio continued to provide musical services throughout the second half of the seventeenth century. So, having defined their *mission*, as early as the mid-seventeenth century, the conservatories housed pupils and boarders.

The boarder entered at the age of 7 or 8 and paid an *entrance fee* and a separate annual fee depending on his status as "outsiders," "regnicoli," and Neapolitans. The figures were susceptible to further downward variations depending on economic possibilities, the child's talent, and accompanying recommendations. The pupil, on the other hand, was often of more advanced age, around 18–20 years, and already had harmonic competences; he paid only the tuition, was always accompanied by the *plegio* of artisans or shopkeepers, and pledged to *serve* the conservatory for the number of years agreed upon with the governors.[38]

The most deserving sons generally obtained the *post* of tenor, soprano, violinist, trumpeter, oboist, or chapel master, upgrading to the status of "non paying students" and in addition assuming the role of *mastricelli*, that is, assistant masters. Regularly conducted and supervised, their lessons were considered of great value for the education of their fellow students. Among the activities entrusted to the children, an important one was the copying of papers from music, which initiated and sustained the market of a still artisanal music publishing industry, fulfilling, first and foremost, a domestic demand.

The Conservatory, which based its livelihood on the charity from private individuals, demanded from its students "good manners" to be displayed in society, a kind of external presentability that would satisfy the benefactors' prejudices and expectations even before the needs of the benefactors. Once a week, a quarter of an hour was devoted to a lesson in good citizen and good Christian behavior; once a month, the Rules of the Conservatory were reread to the pupils "lest they be forgotten." The uniform provided to the sons had to be in perfect order at all times, though absolutely sober, especially on "musical outings." The sons of the four institutes were distinguished by the different colors of their uniforms: red and turquoise for the Poveri, white for the Loreto, and white and brown for the Sant'Onofrio. That of the sons of the Pietà dei Turchini, consisted of "sottana and zimarra torchina" without "silk shows or buttons" and was provided to the student upon entering the conservatory. In winter, the "cotta" was added to it, which was delivered to the checkroom upon return from the exits. The shoes, which were also all the same, could not be "French style" or with a "wooden heel," but had to adhere to the shape given to them by the master shoemaker, an employee of the Conservatory.

Devotion, good behavior, escape from idleness, modesty, silence, obedience, and commitment were thus the basic requirements for permanence in the conservatory. Religious duties involved service at daily Mass, observance of the office, and frequent confession. Extraordinary ones were scheduled three times a year—Christmas, Easter and before the patronal feast—but became indispensable in cases of insubordination, when confession was understood to be an irreplaceable remedy to reconciliation and good manners.

Over the children watched the father Rector assisted by the vice rector, the fathers *commissi*, the masters of grammar, instruments, and music.[39] They were divided into brigades, each assigned to a brigade leader and a chapel master. The rules to be observed were numerous and very strict and concerned the conduct to be kept in and out of the conservatory, in the church, during classes, and at the canteen. In particular, it was the rector's duty to teach the children good manners, engaging each of them, according to his ability, in the study of grammar, vocal, or instrumental music. From time to time the children received permission to return to visit their relatives. They would be accompanied home by a father *commisso* who was never supposed to leave the boy alone, but, once home, many decided never to return to the institution. The children were never supposed to go around the city alone, but always with their companions. In particular, on feast days and Carnival Thursdays, they could not go out except for "funeral" or "music" engagements. Overnight stays outside the Conservatory were rarely allowed by the governors, and permission to eat outside the Con servatory could only be granted by the *mensario* governor. The rector had to manage outings for "music" and could not send "paranze di figlioli"[40] to play music outside Naples, in places where it was necessary to stay overnight or in private homes. Nor could he allow the conservatory's sons to make music together with "stranger" musicians: only governors could authorize their employment on such special occasions. Conservatory teachers were also not allowed to give lessons to pupils from outside the House.

Each week the rector identified the children who were to serve in the church and set the time for grammar lessons, music lessons, and all other exercises of "devotion," study, or service to the Conservatory.

4   THE MUSIC MARKET BETWEEN PATRONAGE AND PRODUCTION

As noted above, the first professional jobs of the educated children were in musical services provided to private individuals, religious congregations, and folk festivals. For these the application could be for one or more soloists or a group of instrumentalists; private individuals could request "choirs of angels" on various occasions, but largely for funeral ceremonies; convents, congregations, or parishes made use of the participation of their children at masses, processions, or solemn liturgical ceremonies.

Through policies and trusts taken out at the city's public banks, religious congregations or private benefactors often guaranteed the payment of education fees for a child, or, in the best of cases, took on the role of "economic" supporter of one of the conservatories. A system, this one, that guaranteed the crediting of revenue policies for the life allowances of the orphans and later educandi, who often benefited from *grants* in favor of their education.[41] In order to create a kind of family bond for orphans, one of the most widespread practices was to give the donor's surname to the benefited child.

A commonplace of seventeenth-century religious musical culture did not allow women to be involved as singers in the church because they were traditionally considered to be devoid of worship.[42] This would be enough to explain why the four music conservatories were intended only for males.[43]

In the second half of the seventeenth century, an analysis of the conservatories' musical activities describes an essentially religious patronage: most of the services were absorbed by the churches or congregations of the urban area, monasteries or convents in the city, and its surroundings. Services for "funerals" requested directly by private individuals were also frequent: to redeem their sins, wealthy men and women "bound" part of their inheritance to the institution and to celebrate their passage to a better life under the conditions of forgiveness, they were accompanied by the "angels of music." The belief in spiritual investment pro remedio animae was strongly held at the time. Individuals' consciences were influenced by counter-reformist oratory that warned of the danger of eternal damnation for those who, at the time of passing away, did not care for their neighbors in need. Many testamentary dispositions thus favored the confluence of a large part of individuals' so—rooms into the coffers of welfare institutions conditioned by the spread of treatises on "well dying" and by the indications of many confraternities, which prepared their associates to a "good death".[44] The required musical services were for "music, paranzas, contracts, funeral and angels." Each contract detailed a description of the various times of the liturgical year when the musical service was required. It could consist of "simple or full paranzas," "choirs," "assistances to the chapel master," and entertainments (motets, symphonies, and others).

In view of real employment opportunities, there were several motivations for a young man to enter the institution 'voluntarily.' For a musician who did not belong to the madrigalist cenacle or to that of the court theaters, entering the conservatory meant not only training but also work and right away. The institute filtered, according to its own principles and their own needs, the children's various "professional" jobs, and for many of them, it was difficult to resist the enticements of artistic and musical offers that came from outside the conservatory.[45]

Also significant is the percentage of *eunuchs* among the pupils of the conservatories: the practice of castration at prepuberal age was widespread at that time, in order to make the most of the special vocal talents of children and to preserve their sweet, high-pitched timbre. Many families resorted to it, in spite of strict prohibitions, in order to encourage the inclusion of their children in church children's choirs, thus hoping for a future joining the ranks of the clergy.[46] The children were directed to an ecclesiastical career or to activities related to the life of the Church (thus music), in the hope of granting them social elevation, and a better and easier future.[47] It was not by accident, then, that many of the children came out of the conservatories to "become priests".[48]

Gradually, pupils later in age and studies began to be enticed by personal offers that would launch them into musical and theatrical careers of far greater magnitude. Nobles and the bourgeoisie, for example, hired musicians as house musicians, as teachers of singing and musical instruments, or as performers of music on special occasions, such as the Posillipo *merrymaking*, which, on summer evenings, fostered ostentatious display among the nobility, who competed to exhibit the most sumptuous fleets of boats on the water and, aboard, the richest liveries and uniforms for their sailors and musicians. Any occasion, religious, or civil, was good for organizing festivals with their respective ingredients (civil and religious apparatuses, floats, cuccagne, jousts, masquerades, etc.). Music, emphasizing the solemnity and merriment of these occasions, was im- posed as a spectacle, and the more astute viceroys used it in an increasingly refined and grandiose way to appeal to the people and receive their approval.

It is very difficult to reconstruct in detail the musical productivity of individual institutions. We know that masters and students were required to periodically produce a certain amount of musical compositions intended mainly for internal use, for teaching needs, but increasingly some of these compositions, sometimes performed in more complex stage settings, were intended for external audiences. At the Conservatory of Santa Maria di Loreto, from 1621 to 1658, the compensation of a chapel master remained at around 10 ducats per month. In 1661, Giovanni Ferraro was succeeded by Orazio Lucarelli with the provision of d. 7 per month, and only with the coming of Francesco Provenzale, in 1661, did the remuneration rise to d. 12 per month, to drop resoundingly to d. 6 or 7 per month with his successors, Gaetano Veneziano, Nicola Acerbo, and Cataldo Amodei, in 1684 the first two, and in 1687 the third, respectively. The economic value bestowed on those musical compositions can give an idea of the importance of that production, which tended to grow as we reached the eighteenth century. The difference in fees was due to the prestige and importance of the individual masters, or, more simply, to the financial situation of the conservatory, in relation especially to historical difficulties and related problems of survival. The teachings of the four music schools envisaged the presence of teachers of cornet, bassoon, trumpet, trombone, violin, singing, and composition.

The system of musical patronage mentioned above pushed the masters to some specific compositions suited to the most diverse performing occasions. The huge music manuscript holdings of the Historical Library of the Conservatorio di S. Pietro a Majella in Naples, preserve a fair number of autographs or manuscript copies of musical compositions intended for performance or operative representation "ne lo giardino de Lorito" or signed by some of the masters active in the four conservatories. That would be an archival fund that one could further tap onto to try to reconstruct the artistic productivity of the individual institutes. It is difficult to accurately compare the data collected to show the greater productivity of one institute over the other. The information gathered so far and the archival documentation already consulted have revealed all the heterogeneity of the available data, which, even though they contain very clear details regarding the socio-economic and cultural trends of the singular institutes, do not allow for more precise comparisons because of some chronological gaps in the documentation. For example, the productivity of the Pietà dei Turchini turns out to be more or less full-bodied during the eighteenth century because the documentation received is mainly that produced in that historical period; while for the Santa Maria di Loreto, the seventeenth-century support comes from a more heterogeneous and richer documentation.

Of great interest, for the conservatory of Santa Maria di Loreto, is the activity of musical theater, although it covers a very small percentage of the overall reconstructed patronage. It seems to be exclusively related to *sacred drama,* a particular area of musical practice in the Neapolitan conservatories that, in order to be on the borderline between the religious genre of oratorio and musical theater, requires a specific approach.[49] A constant in sacred dramas was thus the involvement of conservatory students: often in the composition of the music (a sort of final essay of the best), always in the staging and performance. From Fuidoro we learn that on November 6, 1664, some sons of Loreto participated in the performance of The martyrdom of *San Gennaro,* which was attended by the viceroy Cardinal d'Aragona.[50] And again, in 1672 the city chronicle reports the staging of *The Phoenix of Avila Teresa of Jesus,* by Don Giuseppe Castaldo with music by Provenzale. The event took place inside the same conservatory, once again in the presence of the Viceroy, who, in the words of Croce, "understood it with particular gusto and at 6 o'clock at night, was escorted home with songs and sounds by the captains of the octinas and the students of the conservatory."[51]

One more opera by Castaldo with music by Provenzale, *The life os Saint Rose,* was staged on October 28, 1679, at S. Maria di Loreto and then repeated twice at the Royal Palace, as *La Fenice d'Avila Teresa di Gesù.* The number of these performances would grow by leaps and bounds in the eighteenth-century period of the conservatory's life, with the relations between it and the theaters:

- Nov. 6, 1664, The martyrdom of San Gennaro "was performed at Palazzo…by the sons of the Conservatory of S. Maria di Loreto, before Mr. Cardinal d'Aragona, and he had them brought to the Palace in three carriages, where there was a concourse of Dames, Nobles and Titled." The libretto was by D. Gennaro Paolella, the music by Provenzale.
- April 13, 1663, the poet G. Paolella and the rector of the conservatory, D. Geronimo Barzellino, signed a contract with the scenographer Gian Battista Magno (the Modanino), to paint all the scenes of

the opera with an agreed compensation of 115 ducats, a certainly not small sum when compared to the monthly fees of the conservatory's teachers.

- 1653, the Somasque Father Gio. Francesco del Gesù had the same sons perform in three acts with Prologue, "lo Sponsalizio del B. Girolamo Emiliani Fundatore della Cong.ne de' Somaschi con l'Orfanella, a musical drama composed by Fr. Gio. Franco di Gesù, Priest at Scole Pie, dedicated to the eminent S.r Diego Bernardo Sofia, President of S.R.C. and Protector of the Holy House of Loreto in Naples" (the verso of the manuscript's title page reads, "The work was set to music by the late *D. Andrea Murino* Mastro di Cappella of the same Holy House of Loreto in Naples in the year 1653".[52]

In particular, some of them excelled in the performance of musically sacred operettas. It seems that the sons of St. Onofrio were indeed very good and very well-liked in this type of performance. One of these occasions has remained particularly famous: in 1671 they staged an operetta in honor of the banker Gaspare Roemer, who was very well known in the city for being a righteous man and great benefactor. The operetta[53] had been written by the Rector of the Conservatory, Don Tomaso Valuta. The libretto was printed in a rudimentary typographic form, probably at the expense of Roemer himself. The drama had as many as 18 characters, and the soliloquies of the protagonist *Nardo* (the type of the plebeian Neapolitan, foolish and cowardly) were alternated with frequent scenes of comedy, which the children enjoyed playing. Thus, the younger ones were given the role of the little angels singing lauds, the older ones were reserved for the more difficult parts of the old men and old women, and the eunuchs preferred to play the role of the busty damsels. The drama had, in this case, only one chorus, that of the Angels. All other parts were acted. Two other sacred operas came out in those same years from the Conservatory of Sant'Onofrio: one entitled *San Giugliano*, staged in Giugliano (in the province of Naples) in 1688 and the other entitled *La gara amorosa tra il cielo, la terra e il mare*, by Dr. Nicola Orilia, music by Rev. Don Angelo Durante, Naples, for Benzi, 1696. For the performance in Giugliano, the registers note the recruitment of two "outside" comedians selected from those best known in the city; expenses for the journey of the sons and transportation of the scenery; expenses for music

paper (1 tarì); for "ink and arena," 1 tarì; for transportation of a harpsichord, for transportation of the rector, for compensation to Gioacchino
Rago and Pietro Rezza (those two comedians), reciters, about ten ducats.
Net ducats 35 came into the Conservatory, no small sum at that time: the
libretto of S. Giuliano, written by the Reverend Don Carlo Capuano, cost
8 ducats; the music was composed by such Don Nicola Pallottino, and he
was compensated for it with 6 ducats.

The older sons were actively involved in this kind of pleasant and profitable labors and one or two of them played the role of the *zanni*, acting
in vernacular, those foolish or cunning servants who were a fixture of
every play and were especially appreciated by the public. The younger sons
were still destined to represent turbs or choirs of angels at public festivals, sacred performances, mortuary accompaniments, and processions to
honor the saints. St. Onofrio's *angels* were in great demand, and in 1689
they were also invited to the Conservatories of the Pietà dei Turchini and
St. Mary of Loreto.

5   ENTREPRENEURIAL THEATER TURNS ARTISTIC CAPITAL INTO WEALTH

Among cultural activities, music appears, therefore, as a dominant component of both the practice of the so-called "living arts" and the individual
and collective imagination that underlies the production and consumption
of all artistic forms. It's essential and emblematic nature and its properties as a *public good* have strong implications from an economic point of
view and allow its characteristics and manifestations to be used as representative phenomena of the more general relationship between economy,
society, and artistic expression. It is necessary to take into account these
phenomena and all their possible connections with markets and economic
policy.

Within the urban fabric, different performance venues tend to distinguish themselves topologically. In seventeenth-century Naples, public
halls for performances were concentrated in a clearly identifiable area of
the city, the so-called "theater district," confined to the area adjoining
Largo di Castello (Castel Nuovo) and located above and below today's
Via Medina, in the area around the Tribunals and finally close to the
port.[54] The Conservatorio della Pietà dei Turchini, for example, located
in the northern part of the city, was surrounded by the main theaters
of the time: the "room" of S. Giorgio dei Genovesi, known as "alla

commedia vecchia," destroyed in 1620; the Teatro dei Fiorentini,[55] active in the so-called "entertainment district" since 1618, known as alla "commedia nuova," which saw continuous metamorphoses on the threshold of the new century, its seventeenth-century structure having become dilapidated; the theater in the street known as alla Duchesca, which revived with the arrival of the Scolopi at the Conservatorio di Sant' Onofrio[56]; the Teatro di S. Bartolomeo[57] adjoining the Conservatorio della Pietà dei Turchini, active until 1737, when it yielded the baton to the Teatro di San Carlo.[58] Both in the seventeenth-century rooms and in the new theater spaces, the chain of comic operas, which were generally performed in numbers of four per season, alternated with acting-only performances, but prose theater and the so-called speech actors also made use of sound, often requiring the collaboration of small orchestras.[59] The viceregal city of theaters, produced, in the seventeenth century, a separation of the levels of enjoyment of theatricality: as opposed to the public halls, there was a phenomenon of privatization of the spectacle assimilated within the noble palaces. The various theatrical halls, frequented mainly by the petty bourgeoisie and the populace, would later constitute a circuit on the fringes of the official theater, in which a variety of theatrical and musical representations went to enrich the usual seasonal calendar. Three types of spaces were possible for representations: the courtyard, the garden, and the hall.[60] The small "Ciardiniello," outside Porta Capuana, was one of the outdoor spaces, already in existence in 1657 and active until 1740. Then there was "lo ciardino de lo Rito," adjacent to the Conservatorio di Santa Maria di Loreto, where various sacred dramas were performed, alongside private houses, monasteries, and convents.

The theatrical space, with the rise of impresario theater, took on an architectural structure that became itself a stage: the structure of the halls, traditionally rectangular in shape with an arrangement of the audience on the long sides gradually assumed a horseshoe shape, where the hierarchical arrangement of the audience became increasingly explicit and "staged" the *kermesse* between classes. The occasions for entertainment, as noted above, were numerous and punctuated the solar and social calendar by offering musical and theatrical *performances* of all kinds. The theatrical and harmonic skills, like an inheritance, were handed down from one generation to the next, in families that also "expanded" on horizontal lines into kinship and collateral relationships. Areas of employment ranged from teaching to composition to musical performance, and employment opportunities, even in multiple forms, were certainly not lacking, even if the salaries were never particularly high. Certainly, teaching guaranteed, more than any other employment, a certain stability and continuity of remuneration. With the consolidation of the category of musicians and their corporate spirit, conservatory teachers were preferably chosen among alumni, but the scene of Neapolitan music teaching, as mentioned above, was enriched by 'private' teachers, who gave lessons in their own homes or at their workshops, in which teaching became an 'apprenticeship,' guaranteeing a form of training and/or professional refinement. Soon, however, the supply of musicians hailing from these training places exceeded local demand, forcing them to seek work elsewhere. Theater impresarios, for their part, were increasingly interested in the singing and instrumental performances of those young students, but the theater environment was notorious for its unruliness, absence of guarantees, and "looseness of customs." Year after year, musicians completing their studies at the conservatories came to terms on the one hand with an increasingly rigidly articulated teaching structure and on the other hand with the increasingly attractive organization of the performing arts world for which they worked. Starting from the end of the seventeenth century, when the laws of the market, of supply and demand, began to rule Italian theatrical life and production, the professional energies of the musician and the opera performer were mainly channeled toward obtaining success, the economic one in particular.

The theatrical industry fed an extremely articulated "creative" labor market, nurturing an extremely important supply chain and requiring first and foremost skilled labor: from composers, librettists, actors and singers, orchestral players, dancers, music professors, as well as theatrical scenographers and architects, to suppliers of textiles and costumes, scenic materials, carpentry, and construction, and finally to the publishing market. The latter, initiated by the manual work of copyists within the Conservatories, passed through a more artisanal evolution of the printer's trade to reach a more "industrial" setting with the publisher. In Naples, the trade in theatrical texts, opera librettos, sheet music of cantatas, and then canzonettas was very lively from the middle of the seventeenth century. The seventeenth century was thus for Naples the springboard for a very lively cultural and creative market that would find its maximum realization in the following century. The explosion of such cultural vivacity can only be understood by recalling the transformations experienced by the city in the Renaissance and especially the Baroque age when Naples became a collector of human resources and a generator of artistic skills in a complex relationship between a new and growing regulatory system of political order and market dynamics. In Naples as in Venice, the theatre industry found its roots and, thanks to the *patronage* and financial support of the Spanish viceroys, "popular" and "impresarial" theaters were able to channel the professional energies of musicists toward achieving "market" success, despite the fact that the only outlets for "stable" and guaranteed work remained the church and the conservatories. The world of entertainment exerted a special fascination on young Neapolitan artists, forcing them, in the absence of particular guarantees to acquire a kind of managerial skill and entrepreneurial *savoir-faire* to safeguard their interests and procure engagements.

Having overcome the youthful fervor, the more mature musicians, who felt all the precariousness of their "artistic" work, aimed for the so-called permanent position: a stable job as chapel master, preferably in an ecclesiastical institution or a teaching position in one of the four music conservatories. Such jobs would have guaranteed continuity of employment, residency, a certain authority, and even additional benefits and rewards by virtue of possible seniority, but they were almost always jobs with relatively low wages compared to the income a musician could have made in the theater. In 1689, Alessandro Scarlatti earned 120 ducats in one year as maestro of the conservatory of S. Maria di Loreto while, three years earlier, operatic engagements, concentrated in just a few months, had earned him as much as 300 ducats.[61]

The theater, which had begun as an effective response to a social need for "spectacularity," only later turned into an incubator of opera in music, presenting itself, at a time of stagnation in the Italian and Neapolitan economies in particular, as a profitable form of investment for its promoters and producers. We could even consider the construction of theaters and the start-up of operatic enterprises as one of the few forms of investment in a society anchored to land rents, which, in the nineteenth century even took the form of civil entertainment, certainly ephemeral, but prestigious and institutional.[62]

The system of the theatrical enterprise stimulated the energies of a diffuse impresario class, with both a popular and aristocratic or bourgeois origin, which found in it a centrally recognized container of lucrative activities, in which the market balance is far more cogent and the enterprise does not resist unless it is able to increase the number of its users, going towards the tastes of a socially heterogeneous fruition. The impresario theaters were competitive in the market, and this made the influence of popular taste strong on their cultural offers, which were increasingly oriented toward the comic and choreographic genres.

What used to be an occasion of "platonic debate" for an elite of intellectuals (nobles, aristocrats, academics...) now became *a spectacular event*, with all that it entailed on the level of the productive management of the event (think, for example, of the stage machinery that inevitably lead to the emergence of an artisanal industry of carpenters, dyers, blacksmiths, costume designers, tailors, and more) and even on the public relations level (to use more contemporary terms) if we consider that the presence of the *claque* (at the San Cassian in Venice entirely run by the gondoliers) or the pursuit of *sponsorship* are almost contemporary to the spectacularization of melodrama.[63]

There is no doubt that the most conspicuous effect caused by the operation of a paid theater was the rise of the impresario of the opera house, a phenomenon completely ignored for a long time by musical historiographers, because of that misunderstanding of aesthetic thinking that led to the exaltation of the finished product-especially if it was a masterpiece—rather than shedding light on the circumstances and the political and socio-economic conditions that fostered the gestation and birth of the theatrical product. And if sometimes they have been forced to show some interest in it, they have limited their analysis to the fringes of the phenomenon, finding it quite weird that Antonio Vivaldi (1678–1741) in Venice, Georg Friederich Händel (1685–1759) in London or Marc'Antonio Cesti (1623–1669) in Vienna had *also* been impresarios— and in certain moments of their careers, *only* impresarios—maybe spurred by the desire to make the most of their investment on their own operatic productions in order to maximize the profits.[64] The creative city is, in short, the result of power dynamics, market dynamics, but above all of a system of training and circulation of artistic knowledge produced by the city's attractiveness, by an underlying system of education originally oriented to perform another function, that is the care of the poor, and by the gradual affirmation of a cultural institution, which grows to the extent that it is able to pander to widespread cultural consumption, overcoming the elitist and "political" characterization that the absolutist eighteenth century will try to impose on the theater as an institution of power. However, it is not credible that the refinement of propaganda directorship was enough to ensure, for centuries on end, such an enduring consensus. The political perspective would offer too narrow an interpretation, which does not take into account the economic spin-offs and social implications of the many cultural and spectacular initiatives recorded over the centuries. Perhaps we should begin to think that the enthusiasm with which different classes shared certain events and the consensus derived from that broad participation, could also derive from another form of participation, which was more closely related to the benefits that flowed from it.

In financial and employment terms, that 'system' of live performance, supporting a growing demand, provided "services" and produced "ephemeral artifacts" that, if different from the "durable" goods, normally studied, were nonetheless traceable to managerial mechanisms, accounting procedures, intersectoral transfers of technical and technological knowledge, worker mobility or the development of *organization capabilities*, factors for which an exclusive industrial relevance was often assumed. On the contrary, operators in that system are required (and the situation today is not so different) to have exceptional design, management, administrative, and implementation capabilities. Forced to move in cramped spaces and in very short time frames, workers, accountants, machinery, tools, animals, and suppliers, were able to solve in the space of a few hours, if not minutes, problems of enormous complexity: permits and passes for out-of-town workers and artists, lodgings, contracting per diems with taverns, supplies, daily reporting, controls, payments and cash flow, needs for raw materials, tools and semi-finished goods, finding substitutes and helpers, routes for the passage of bulkier machinery, management of day and evening shifts, public order and safety in the workplace, a host of tasks to be performed under pressing working conditions that were never actually guaranteed. In short, "such achievements did not rest on pindaric flights of fancy at all. The culture of the ephemeral rested on a solid, earthy, industrious culture of doing, because, under normal conditions, not a single nail was wasted."[65]

Notes

1. Of the Orphanage of the Good Shepherd, which arose in the Sicilian capital in 1617, also known as the *Casa degli Spersi*, because it was dedicated to the care "de li spersi mascoli," we know little: its foundation was at the behest of Viceroy Count De Castro, in the fourteenth-century Church of the Santissima Annunziata; its social purpose was the salvation of abandoned children and adolescents, mostly devoted to petty crimes, who were

guaranteed a dignified life and the learning of a trade. "That House produced valiant players, not masters skilled in composing operas and conducting orchestras: however, they were required from outside." From the end of the seventeenth century, music teaching took on an increasingly important role, and, over the next century, the future prestigious vocation of the Conservatory, namely the professional training of musicians, took shape. From the mid-eighteenth-century music became exclusive teaching, and in the nineteenth century, under the direction of Baron Pietro Pisani, a theater was added in what is recognized as a small jewel of fourteenth-century architecture, while teaching activities were intensified with the use of new instruments and the study of new manuscript and printed music (www.conservatoriobellini.it).

2. We have often spoken of these topics. See among others: R. Del Prete, *Musical Education and Job Market: The Employment of Children and Young People in the Neapolitan Music Industry with Particular Reference to the Period 1650–1806*, in G. Arrighi, V. Emeljanov (eds.), *Entertaining Children. The Participation of Youth in the Entertainment Industry*, Palgrave Macmillan, New York, 2014, pp. 15–32.

3. J. L. Baldauf-Berdes, *Women Musicians of Venice*. Cit.

4. Fabio Biondi wanted to pay tribute to her, recording with his orchestra Europa Galante nine concerts of the repertoire that had made her famous and made the Pieta Institute great. Biondi, moreover, produced a short fictional work, attached to the CD, directed by Lucrezia Le Moli and scripted by Amedeo Guarnieri, whose protagonist is Chiara: as the young violinist, who recounts the years of her successes, and as the mature teacher, who takes stock of her life.

5. C. Petraccone, *Napoli moderna e contemporanea*, Guida Editore, Naples 1981.

6. We refer for brevity to one of the most recent works on poverty in Italy in which several regional cases offer a variety of bibliographic references: V. Zamagni (ed.), *Povertà e innovazioni istituzionali in Italia dal Medioevo a oggi*, Il Mulino, Bologna 2000.

7. In addition to the unparalleled studies by Salvatore Di Giacomo, *Il Conservatorio di Sant'Onofrio a Capuana e quello di S. M. della Pietà dei Turchini*, Sandron, Palermo 1924 and *Il Conservatorio dei Poveri di Gesù Cristo e quello di S. M. di Loreto*, Sandron, Palermo

1928, see the works we have published over the years, for which see the list in the bibliography.

8. Cf. B. Farolfi, V. Melandri (eds.), *Fund raising in Italia. Storia e prospettive*, Il Mulino, Bologna 2008; on the use of bequeathing legacies to conservatories see R. Del Prete, *Legati pii, patronati e maritaggi,* cit.

9. In Naples the requirement was reiterated in Prammatica I, *De Vagabundis seu erronibus*, May 31, 1586, in L. Giustiniani, *Nuova collezione delle prammatiche del Regno di Napoli*, t. XV, Naples 1808, p. 16.

10. On the models of the artisan family, its breadth, and the transmission of the trade from father to son, see G. Da Molin, A. Carbone, *Gli artigiani nel Mezzogiorno d'Italia nel XVIII secolo: modelli differenti delle famiglie, del matrimonio e del controllo degli assetti produttivi*, in S. Cavaciocchi (ed.), *La famiglia nell'economia europea dei secoli XIII-XVIII*, Fondazione Internazionale di Storia Economica "F. Datini," Prato 2009, pp. 305–324.

11. Chanting was the basis of the conservatories' educational project, and the use of pueri cantores in liturgies boasted a millennia-old tradition.

12. This was the name given to the contract that sealed the child's entry into the conservatory and regulated the relationship with the craftsman who accepted him at his workshop. Instructions were drafted with the help of a notary public trusted by the institution.

13. A.S.M.L., Sezione Alunni e Convittori IV. 1. 1., *Notamento degli orfani*, 1586–1594.

14. This practice was implemented in all four institutes, but it was much more frequent and systematic in the Conservatorio di S. Maria di Loreto, the oldest one located in the suburb of Loreto, which being near the Port, stood out as one of the city's most flourishing artisan and commercial suburbs (R. Del Prete, *La trasformazione di un istituto benefico-assistenziale*, cit.).

15. S. Di Giacomo, *Il Conservatorio di Sant'Onofrio in Capuana*, Remo Sandron Editore, Naples 1924, p. 29.

16. It was decided not to replace it, but to reopen the apothecary shop anyway to prevent the "robbe aromentarie" from rotting (about 62 ducats were thus recovered from their sale).

17. S. Di Giacomo, *Il Conservatorio della Pietà dei Turchini*, Remo Sandron Editore, Naples 1924, p. 192.

18. R. Del Prete, *Un'azienda musicale a Napoli*, cit, pp. 420–421.
19. The eight Neapolitan public banks (Banco della Pietà, Banco dei Poveri, Banco della SS.ma Annunziata, Banco di S. Maria del Popolo, Banco dello Spirito Santo, Banco di S. Eligio, Banco di S. Giacomo e Vittoria, Banco del SS.mo Salvatore), progenitors of the Banco di Napoli, were founded (except one) in the mid-1600s on the initiative of moral entities (hospitals, orphanages, confraternities, monti di pietà) and soon replaced the discredited merchants' banks. They favored the acceptance of deposits, and their functions were: accepting deposits of sums that they undertook to keep and return at the customer's request, without paying any interest; issuing receipts to depositors, who could endorse them to others, transferring their credit to the bank; paying sums to third parties on the customer's written order; paying third parties by means of giro accounts (E. Tortora, *Raccolta di documenti storici e delle leggi e regole concernenti il Banco di Napoli*, Napoli, Giannini, 1882; R. Filangieri, *I banchi di Napoli dalle origini alla costituzione del Banco delle Due Sicilie, 1539–1808*, Napoli 1940; E. De Simone, *Storia della Banca. Dalle origini ai nostri giorni*, Arte Tipografica, Napoli 1985, pp. 106–113; L. De Rosa, *Il Mezzogiorno spagnolo tra crescita e decadenza*, Milan, Mondadori, 1987; P. Avallone, *Stato e banchi pubblici a Napoli a metà del 700. Il Banco dei Poveri: una svolta*, Naples 1995).
20. R. Del Prete, *Un'azienda musicale a Napoli*, op. cit, p. 421.
21. Ibid.
22. See M. F. Robinson, *Naples and Neapolitan Opera*, Clarendon Press, Oxford 1972.
23. F. Cotticelli, P. Maione, *Le carte degli antichi banchi e il panorama musicale e teatrale della Napoli di primo Settecento 1732–33*, «Studi pergolesiani», 5 (2006), pp. 21–54, with accompanying cd-rom (*Spoglio delle polizze bancarie di interesse teatrale e musicale reperite nei giornali di cassa dell'Archivio del Banco di Napoli per gli anni 1732–1734*).
24. S. Di Giacomo, *Il Conservatorio dei Poveri di Gesù Cristo*, Remo Sandron Editore, Naples 1928, pp. 74–75.
25. Over time, admission methods varied in relation to the demands that came from outside and the internal needs of the institution itself.

26. R. Del Prete, *La trasformazione di un istituto benefico-assistenziale*, op. cit.
27. Ibid, pp. 678–679.
28. (R. Del Prete, *La trasformazione di un istituto benefico-assistenziale*, cit., pp. 678–680).
29. S. Di Giacomo, Il Conservatorio della Pietà dei Turchini, Remo Sandron Edi- tore, Naples 1924, p. 180.
30. Ibid., pp. 203–205.
31. S. Di Giacomo, *Il Conservatorio della Pietà dei Turchini*, cit., pp. 222–223.
32. The inventory of the musical material owned by the Conserva- tory included in addition to books, musical instruments (3 soprano violins; 3 tenor violins; 2 trombones; 3 old cornets; 1 harpsichord; 2 violones; 1 violin of the *quondam* Don Antonio Gabriele; 1 rebecchina for music). (S. Di Giacomo, *Il Conservatorio dei Poveri di Gesù Cristo*, cit., pp. 77–78).
33. Ibid., pp. 67–68.
34. Ibid., pp. 77–78.
35. Ibid., pp. 78–79.
36. Ibid., pp. 88–95.
37. S. Di Giacomo, *Il Conservatorio di Sant'Onofrio a Capuana*, cit. pp. 22–23.
38. The *pleggeria* consisted of a guarantee offered mostly by artisans or shopkeepers to the pupils and sometimes to the boarders, which generally amounted to 50 ducats. The sum was paid for precau- tionary purposes, and the guarantor assumed the responsibility to answer in the first person in the event that the pupil left the conservatory without completing his "istrumento" (by which he undertook to "produce" for the institution for a certain number of years) or caused damage to the house or persons (R. Del Prete, *Un'azienda musicale a Napoli*, cit., pp. 435–436).
39. The distinction between instrument masters and music masters can be attributed to the opinion of the Chapel Master as a music master.
40. A *"paranza"* comprised a certain number of sons (between 12 and 20 sons) to be sent to congregations or in procession, to accom- pany with songs and sounds the celebration of a particular religious or popular ceremony (R. Del Prete, *Un'azienda musicale a Napoli*, cit., pp. 440–441).

41. The piazze were a kind of scholarships that enabled the financing of studies, professional careers, religious vocations, and entrepreneurial activities. They consisted of an annuity established on land and real estate assets that served to accumulate girls' dowries or boarding school annuities.

42. On the consideration of women in music and musical religiosity in the seventeenth century, see G. Stefani, *Musica barocca. Poetica e Ideologia*, Bompiani, Milano 1974.

43. The presence of maidens is sporadic and in some cases yet to be confirmed such as the presence of a girls' singing school within the conservatory of S. Maria di Loreto (F. Florimo, *La scuola musicale di Napoli*, cit. II, p. 54, discusses this). However, we know of the later existence of a women's music school: R. Cafiero, *Istruzione musicale a Napoli tra decennio francese e resaturazione borbonica: il "collegio musicale delle donzelle" (1806–1832)*, in R. Cafiero, M. Marino (eds.), *Francesco Florimo e l'Ottocento musicale*, cit., pp. 753–825.

44. A. Tenenti, *Il senso della morte e l'amore della vita nel Rinascimento*, Einaudi, Torino 1977, pp. 62–111; R. Del Prete, *Legati pii, patronati e maritaggi*, cit., pp. 7–17.

45. Recall that, by contract, students could be employed for "music services" but only with the consent and mediation of the institution to which they belonged, and that a large part of the income went, by contract, to replenish the conservatory's common treasury.

46. P. Barbier, *Gli evirati cantori*, Rizzoli, Milan 1991.

47. G. Galasso, C. Russo, *Per la storia sociale e religiosa del Mezzogiorno d'Italia*, Guida Editore, Naples 1982, pp. 258–260.

48. In the decade 1652–1662, out of 85 Turchini sons, 18 went out to become "monks," 4 took up service as chapel masters, among them, one kept his commitment to serve the institute on the occasion of Corpus Christi, playing the trombone and another went out as a eunuch, that is, as a singer (R. Del Prete, *Un'azienda musicale a Napoli*, cit., p. 438).

49. The genre has not yet been thoroughly studied. Reports around it define it to us as an operatic genre of religious subject matter, in vogue between the seventeenth and eighteenth centuries in Naples, in which elements from the lives of the saints and buffoonish elements are blended. Benedetto Croce proposes the derivation of the "dramma sacro" from the commedias de santos, thus claiming

that Spanish influence on seventeenth-century religious music (B. Croce, *I Teatri di Napoli*, cit. pp. 154–155).

50. National Library of Naples (I-Nn), I. Fuidoro, *Giornali di Napoli dal 1660 al 1680*, ms. C.B.14, f. 78.

51. B. Croce, *I teatri di Napoli*, cit.

52. R. Del Prete, *La trasformazione di un istituto benefico-assistenziale*, cit. p. 683.

53. S. Onofrio, Drama by D. Tomaso Valua—O il ritorno d'Onofrio in padria—Dedicato all'Ill.mo e nob.mo signore Gasparo Roemer. In Napoli, for Roncagliolo, 1671.

54. P. L. Ciapparelli, *I luoghi dei teatri e dell'effimero. Scenografia e scenotecnica*, in F. Cotticelli, P. Maione, *Storia della musica e dello spettacolo a Napoli*, vol. II, *Il Settecento*, tomo I, Turchini Edizioni, Napoli 2009, pp. 223–329; p. 225.

55. There are several papers on the history of the Theater. We highlight among the most recent ones: F. Cotticelli, P. Maione, *"Onesto divertimento, ed allegria de' popoli"* cit., pp. 95–136; P. L. Ciapparelli, *I luoghi dei teatri e dell'effimero*, cit., pp. 226–230.

56. S. Di Giacomo, *Il Conservatorio di Sant'Onofrio a Capuana*, op. cit., pp. 60–62.

57. F. Cotticelli, P. Maione, *Per una storia della vita teatrale napoletana nel primo Settecento* cit., pp. 48–61; A. Cappellieri, *Il Teatro di San Bartolomeo da Scarlatti a Pergolesi*, ivi, 4 (2000), pp. 131–156.

58. The seventeenth-century rooms were joined by two other new theatrical spaces between 1723 and 1724, both in areas other than those identified as venues for the city's spectacular: the Teatro della Pace, at the alley of Lava and the Teatro Nuovo above Montecalvario. [P.L. Ciapparelli, *Due secoli di teatri in Campania (1694–1896). Teorie, progetti e realizzazioni*, Electa, Naples 1999, pp. 14–15; S. Tortora, La nascita di un modello per l'architettura dei teatri partenopei: il Teatro Nuovo a Montecalvario, in B. Gravagnuolo, F. Adriani (ed.), *Domenico Antonio Vaccaro sintesi delle arti*, Guida, Naples 2005, pp. 251–264].

59. B. Croce, *I teatri di Napoli*, cit. pp. 385–386.

60. P. L. Ciapparelli, *I luoghi del teatro a Napoli nel Seicento.*, *Le Sale "private"*, in D.A. D'Alessandro, A. Ziino (eds.), *La musica a Napoli durante il Seicento*, Rome, Torre d'Orfeo 1987, pp. 379–412. An extensive overview of spaces and places for musical

activities is also in R. Di Benedetto, P. Maione, F. Seller, *Napoli Itinerari Armonici*, Electa, Naples 1998.

61. F. Degrada, *L'opera napoletana*, in G. Barblan, A. Basso (ed.), *Storia dell'opera*, I, Utet, Turin 1977, pp. 237, 275, 332.

62. R. Del Prete, *L'avventura imprenditoriale della musica nell'Ottocento: i luoghi, i protagonisti, il sistema di produzione e di fruizione, l'editoria*, in E. Careri, E. Donisi (ed.), *Prima e dopo Cavour: la musica tra stato sabaudo e Italia unita (1848–1870)*, CLIOPRESS, Naples 2015, pp. 17–66.

63. E. Saracino, *Imprenditori del Teatro e della Musica*, in S. Cavaciocchi (ed.), *Il Tempo libero. Economia e Società*, Le Monnier, Florence 1995, pp. 751–759.

64. Ibid.

65. G. Guerzoni, *Apollo e Vulcano. I mercati artistici in Italia (1400–1700)*, op. cit, pp. 211–229: p. 218.

CHAPTER 4

The Experience of the Conservatorio della Pietà dei Turchini (1584–1807)

1 THE FOUNDATION OF THE CONSERVATORIO DELLA PIETÀ DEI TURCHINI AND ITS PATRIMONIAL STRUCTURE

The reconstruction of the functioning mechanisms of the Conservatorio della Pietà dei Turchini, taken as a model for Neapolitan music education institutions,[1] allows, through the examination of its financing and expenditure flows, to analyze various problems. Among these is the question of whether there is continuity or rupture with the more traditional welfare structure. In reality, the music conservatory fully fits into it, both in its patrimonial configuration and in its intervention policy. It was born as a foundling hospital based on an educational program aimed at education and learning a trade[2] manages "the patrimony of the poor"[3] like many other contemporary charitable institutions, but what is most surprising in its functioning is the setting of a singular educational agency, which, while referring to welfare models common to the practice of *renfermement*, aims at the maintenance of poor and abandoned children through a music school with a continuous exchange of tasks and functions. Music, in fact, did not respond to a simple need for image but, in addition to being a means of exalting faith, the institution, and the city, increased the participation in religious functions, procuring a greater number of supporters and introducing, on the market, musicians and musical productions of various kinds, both sacred and profane.

© The Author(s), under exclusive license to Springer Nature Switzerland AG 2024
R. Del Prete, *The Neapolitan Creative Economy*, Palgrave Studies in Economic History, https://doi.org/10.1007/978-3-031-55903-7_4

The policy of renfermement, during the seventeenth and eighteenth centuries, suggested vague intentions of re-education of young people, recovered through the practice of work. The work-prayer and assistance-production binomials, in fact, supported the mercantilist principles then in vogue—escape from idleness, creation of new factories, formation of new workforce—and, more often, motivations of an ethical-religious nature.[4] Work, understood in a mystical sense, thus became the discriminating factor of the new charitable institutions and became an element of conscious detachment from the old models of private charity. The financial situation of the four institutes sometimes reveals strong differences due to the consistency of the guest population: the proceeds came partly from the work of the «figlioli»[5] engaged in manufacturing activities first and in "musical services" subsequently, and more significantly, from substantial bequests of benefactors.

The first statute of our Conservatory dates back to 1583 and was approved by Philip II in 1584.[6] The request for the approval of the Archbishop of Naples and especially the protection of Philip II and the Viceroy was probably aimed at obtaining favors, tax privileges, and possible financial contributions. The government of the institution was entrusted to six governors appointed every year, on August 15. The six (three nobles, two lawyers, and a merchant) had to be appointed in the following way: two by the ottina,[7] or district, of Rua Catalana, two from the confreres of the Oratory of the Most Holy Piety, and two from any other street in the city. Their task was to administer for 13 months and, in turn, perform the role of Mensario, who was responsible for overseeing the general accounting of the institution, held by a "Secretary-Rational." They enjoyed wide autonomy in the management of the institute, decided on investments, hired staff, authorized expenses, and made any other decision concerning the life of the Conservatory, without the participation of the Royal Delegate, who had only jurisdictional functions. No compensation was provided for carrying out these tasks, sometimes very demanding, since the administration of a pious place was considered an act of charity, from which one could not escape. The government met twice a week, on Sundays and Thursdays.

To analyze the role of the Conservatory in the society of the time, we will consider the moment of the formation of the institution's "capital" and that of their subsequent distribution, trying to identify the economic and social motivations that guided the actions of the administrators and to

reconstruct the difficult balance between individual and collective interests in the exercise of charity. The musical "productivity" plays a role of
great importance, especially from the mid-seventeenth century, when the
Conservatory gradually and without precise statutory indications—transformed from a simple orphanage into a music school, thus entering an
economic circuit in which professions intertwined with trades, art became
commodified, and production became increasingly specific and sought
after.

The initial capital of the Conservatory was essentially constituted by
the self-taxation of the confreres of the Oratory of the Bianchi, by alms
given by wealthy citizens in search of easy indulgences, by the proceeds of
the alms boxes located in the churches, and by donations or inheritances.

From the patrimonial writings[8] that have come down to us from 1594
to the early 1700s, albeit discontinuously, we can see a modest increase
in the assets of the Conservatory, due to bequests and donations and,
perhaps, to the greater income from begging and the fame that the
Conservatory was acquiring from the point of view of producing musical
activities.

The institution used, for its payments and collections, the work of
public banks.[9] Investments in real estate were mostly dictated by the
need to expand the headquarters of the Conservatory, but very often
the properties came from legacies and donations on which the obligation
to allocate part of the income to the celebration of masses in suffrage
of the donors (nobles and enriched bourgeoisie) weighed. In fact, the
first four buildings annexed to the Conservatory were purchased by the
governors between 1595 and 1634 with a total expenditure of 10,000
ducats,[10] while the other houses owned by the institution were the result
of inheritance or charity.

In the years 1627–1631, the Conservatory collected annual interest
of 1,524.98 ducats on a capital of two. 14,382.94 and paid interest of
552.75 ducats per year on mortgages of 9,050.50 ducats.[11] The other
came from capital invested in the purchase of shares of leases.[12] And
thanks to the bequests of personalities such as the Prince of Cellamare,
the Marquis of Crispano, the Counselor F. Rocco, the Notary Agostino
Fenitia, the Marquis of Arena, or the Marquis of Collevisi (just to mention
a few names), the Conservatory could boast of income from movable
assets, coming from public debt securities. In 1656 alone, the year of
the plague, the Conservatory received as many as seven bequests for a
total capital of two. 12,920.70. Among the donors are the names of the

ancient Neapolitan aristocracy, alongside congregations and benefactors belonging to the middle class.[13]

The income varied significantly even within a few years, and the fluctuations were due to a triple set of factors. They depended on the income from leases, which were not, as is well known, constant, due to the varying collection of taxes[14]; from the fact that in the years immediately following the plague, there was, from an economic point of view, a general upheaval[15]; and, finally, from the amount of «entratura», that is, the sums that non-poor young people who intended to attend the conservatory to learn music had to pay. These were subject to variations depending on the number and payment possibilities of the «educandi» children.[16] The Statute set the number of young people to be hosted in the institute at one hundred and the registration fee at 12 ducats. The "sons" admitted to the Conservatory in the years 1652–1676 were a total of 322, on average, that is, just over 14 per year.[17] The economic impact of the «entratura» fees of the "sons" was not negligible, and even less so the compensation received for performances and musical assistance services in which the Conservatory students took part in the twenty years following the plague. The city, which was decimated by the plague, only slowly began to make up for the losses suffered. The cash movements recorded by the Treasurer in the thirty-year period 1660–1691 reveal the difficulties of those years, confirmed by the prevalence of expenses over income, particularly between 1685 and 1691. The most significant deficit in that period is recorded in 1686, when expenses exceeded income by as much as 2,593.19 ducats. It was contained, in the following five-year period, at around a few hundred ducats (Table 1).

The thirty years following the 1656 plague were particularly difficult. In 1676, the Conservatory was forced to sell one of the houses inherited from Notary A. Fenitia for 337 ducats, retaining an annual census of 2 ducats. The registers from 1665 to 1682 are missing, so the extent of that year's revenues and expenditures is unknown, but the institution was probably forced to sell the property due to management needs. In the asset accounting, only two cases of real estate alienation are recorded. The accounting registers are interrupted again from December 1687 to September 1689, i.e., before and after the 1688 earthquake, which forced the Conservatory, in the following years, to face significant expenses for the renovation of the building and its properties.[18] The second real estate sale by the institution dates back to 1690: the Governors alienated to

Table 1 Conservatorio della Pietà dei Turchini Income and expenses in 1660–1664 and 1683–1691

Period		Income	Expenses
September 1660–August	1661	6889.69	6736.44
September 1661–August	1662	7594.74	7166.27
August 1662–September	1663	5557.12	6428.50
August 1663–September	1664	6347.33	5939.81
August 1683–September	1684	5427.06	4066.76
August 1684–September	1685	4621.71	1754.82
August 1685–September	1686	4635.04	7228.23
August 1686–September	1687	4430.39	4894.70
September 1687–December	1687	1276.38	1651.91
September 1689–December	1689	1535.05	1672.39
January 1690–December	1690	4117.03	4616.36
January 1691–August	1691	3491.16	3547.34

Note Among the revenues and expenditures are the cash funds of the previous year's budget
Source A.P.T., Treasurer's Revenue and Expenditure Journals, years 1661–1691

Gennaro Paduano a "small house with several rooms" located in the S. Giacomo quarters at the price of 195 ducats. Of these, only 35 were paid at the signing of the contract, with the buyer, who had no other "ready" money, committing to pay the remaining 160 after one year, with an interest of 6%.[19]

The Conservatory's assets included, however, not only a fair number of real estate properties,[20] but also numerous "items" of leases and taxes or fiscal duties, annual revenues, some exemptions, and various legacies.

The asset and income situation of the Conservatory was quite different a century later. Revenues and expenses had doubled and, in some cases, even tripled, indicating that the institution had grown and established itself. The surplus of revenues over expenses was constant, although it varied from year to year, as can be seen from Table 2.

The increase in revenues was particularly significant starting from 1774. The reasons for this substantial growth will be discussed shortly. What is noteworthy is that, with the increase in revenues, the Conservatory's assets also increased.

The first indicator of this growth was the increase in real estate properties, which can be inferred from a document signed in 1751 by engineer Pascale De Simone, listing and describing "all the houses." In reality, he

Table 2 Conservatory of Pietà dei Turchini. Expenses and income in the years 1761–1779, in ducats

Year	Expenses	Income
1761	9,159.16	11,306.87
1762	8,076.30	9,130.32
1763	6,744.31	7,832.74
1764	7,358.72	8,792.50
1765	7,420.29	9,066.89
1766	7,566.76	9,237.89
1767	6,986.60	7,385.88
1768	6,432.57	7,165.86
1769	6,503.26	8,436.76
1771	7,761.24	9,065.88
1772	7,585.91	8,677.70
1774	8,175.10	15,781.33
1775	7,657.70	10,165.16
1776	8,445.11	11,982.29
1777	7,747.16	11,251.17
1778	8,216.11	10,226.91
1779	8,412.37	10,723.53

Source A.P.T. Introito and Esito di Mensario (Monthly Budgets) 1761–1779; Annual Budgets 1761–1779

only reports 15 buildings compared to the 35 identified by our investigation. It is difficult to understand this different description by the engineer, perhaps referring only to a certain type of property, among those that the Conservatory had acquired over time through bequests and donations. The assets had thus been enriched by a substantial group of houses and shops that were gradually rented out, and the only two recorded house sales were those of 1676 and 1690.[21] Between 1771 and 1775, from the alienation of other assets, the Conservatory received about 10,000 ducats, part of which was spent in 1771 (two. 707.83) for the "reconstruction" of the Casa al Baglivo and partly used, two years later, in purchases of annual revenues (two. 4,340).[22] The accounting documents related to rents and leases report the annual income collected by the Conservatory for the rent of some houses. In particular, there are rents for the building at S. Tommaso d'Aquino from May 4, 1719, to May 4, 1755,[23] a building described as consisting of a shop "mezzanine with convenience and cellar below, and inside which there is a small door from which you access three rooms one above the other, and has formal water".[24] From 1719 to 1721 it was rented for two. 50 per year, remained vacant for three years, and in 1723 it was rented again for two. 45 per year until 1747. From '47 to '49 it was not rented due to the "construction," that is, the works that were being carried out[25]; from 1749 to '50 the first and second apartment of the aforementioned "rebuilt" house were rented to D. Nicola Ingenito for 58 ducats. From 1750 to '51 the amount of rent rose to two. 100 and the following year it dropped to two. 98, but rose again to two. 125 just one year later and continued to grow in the following years (two. 134 in 1755 and two. 136 in 1756). There were, therefore, three years, from 1747 to 1749, during which the houses located in St. Thomas Aquinas did not provide any income because of the work that was carried out there. But, to provide no income must have been other houses as well, if the complex of rents marked a setback precisely in those years. From the data collected it does not seem, however, that there was stability in the income from the properties, as we find other involution in 1757, and again in 1759.[26]

And yet it is clear that the total income derived from rents was not without consistency, as is evident from Table 3.

It is worth noting that the Conservatory's real estate assets were generally located in the urban area of Naples, particularly near the Conservatory itself, confirming that many of the donors lived in the same "northern" part of the city where the House of the "Turchini" "sons" was established.

Even more than real estate, the Conservatory's assets were expanded by the income from Leaseholds, that is, the shares of public debt that it gradually came into possession of. The growth of these shares took on considerable dimensions already in the first half of the eighteenth century, but reached a significant level in the second half of the century. This is confirmed by the fairly continuous series that can be seen, starting from 1751, in the Conservatory's accounts.[27] Many of these shares came to

Table 3 Conservatorio della Pietà dei Turchini. Real estate income in the years 1746–1750 and 1755–1780, in ducats

Years	Rents	Years	Rents
1746	1,396.98	1755	1,990
1747	1,386.66	1757	1,331
1748	1,115.30	1758	1,694
1749	1,138.60	1759	1,348
1750	1,481.10	1762	1,412
		1780	1,644

Source A.P.T. Accounting, Rents, leases, and censuses, 26–29

him from bequests and legacies, but others were certainly purchased by him, considering the security of the investment and, above all, at least for a part of them, the convenient remuneration that, in general, they guaranteed (Table 4).

The shares owned weighed on several leases which, due to the fact that they referred to taxes that affected general-use food commodities, ended up being highly appreciated and sought after in the capital market. And, in fact, it does not seem that they, except for some, suffered particular damage after the first conversion of the income produced by the Repurchase Board in 1751. It turns out that quite a few of them further improved their revenue. This was the case for the Precipui del Sale of the 4 warehouse,[28] the flour tax, the silks of Bisignano, the Customs of Puglia, etc. The extension of the reduction of the capitalization rate from 7 to 5 and 4%,[29] however, ended up affecting their capital value, so much so that, in the three-year period 1758–1760, the Leases yielded just 2,155.13 ducats compared to the 5,767.34 ducats of the three-year period 1753–1755.[30] Until 1769, investments in leases were predominant; subsequently, especially after the second conversion of public income, with the reduction of the interest rate of capitalization from 4 to 3.50%, investments in houses, shops, and workshops located in urban areas increased.

2   Legacies, Patronages, and Marriages

The religious associative phenomenon became increasingly evident, and the number of confraternities multiplied due to the impulse of the Catholic Reformation, which modified their structure according to the new religious orientations with charitable functions.[31] Inflation, the continuous reshuffling of fortunes, the growing increase of the population, and the constant disbanding of mercenary armies had produced masses of poor and vagabonds who, especially in cities, inspired fear and repugnance. Miserable and vagabonds were now judged harshly, as parasites and antisocial beings, guilty only because they were "marginalized." In fact, vagrancy often turned into banditry and, as such, worried both the ruling classes and the common people. An undeniable social malaise was, therefore, at the origin of the "segregation" of the poor and querulous miserable. The Catholic world responded with the creation of countless charitable and welfare institutions that, through the exercise of charity, favored the "redemption" of benefactors. Their functions relied

Table 4   Conservatory of Pietà dei Turchini. Annual income from lease installments collected in the years 1753–1755, in ducats

Arrendamenti	1753	1754	1755
Tabacco	215.18	184.44	184.44
Regi Censali	21.60	40.41	12.48
Regia Dogana di Puglia	526.60	555.20	458.30
Sale de' 4 fondaci	30.42	30.42	28.08
Franchigia del Sale de' 4 fondaci	54.57	64.00	0.00
Precipui del grano a rotolo del Pesce	10.00	14.50	10.00
Gabella della farina	26.25	0.00	60.19
Gabella delle I grana 5 a tomolo di farina	29.45	41.39	65.08
Gabella delle II grana 5 a tomolo di farina	35.35	11.46	4.78
Gabella delle II grana 3 a tomolo di farina	60.26	79.55	48.00
Sale di Puglia	31.18	21.16	11.16
Docato a Botte	48.64	41.61	39.83
Farina Vecchia	82.80	68.80	86.40
Seconde grana 3 a tomolo di farina	10.84	0.00	5.42
Regia Dogana di Napoli	58.63	58.63	58.59
Franchigia della Regia Dogana	50.49	50.59	50.59
Sete e Zafferano	1.40	2.10	1.68
Ferro	59.23	47.81	49.22
Oglio	11.72	8.80	3.04
Sale d'Apruzzo	0.08	0.08	2.09
Prime grana 5 a tomolo di farina	14.91	12.39	8.18
Seconde grana 5 a tomolo di farina	0.84	0.42	0.89
Prime grana 5 a Libra di Seta	13.09	15.47	15.47
Sale d'Otranto	5.09	4.40	7.69
Peso del Regno	8.00	71.32	12.00
Regia Zecca	8.50	8.50	12.85
Fiscali di S. Severino	24.00	48.00	0.00
Carte da gioco	22.92	15.28	19.11
Sete di Calabria	73.65	73.65	73.69
Sete di Bisignano	179.21	200.82	243.52
Mezzo grano a rotolo	24.75	13.50	27.00
Vino a minute	41.34	41.34	42.93
Tratte	32.09	32.09	32.08
Oglio e Sapone	13.77	13.67	15.20
Carlini 5 a botte di vino	0.32	0.00	0.00
Oro ed Argento	0.23	3.58	11.08
Conto di Tufo	56.78	34.00	0.00
Regia Dogana di Puglia e Tufo	15.58	8.37	40.00
Gab. Farina sotto riparuo dei Banchi	18.00	18.00	0.00
Totale	1946.93	1951.41	1869

Source A.P.T., Journals of Income and Outcome of the Monthly Treasurer (Monthly Budgets) 1753–1755

exclusively on humanitarianism and the charitable spirit of individuals, and therefore they were largely supported by legacies and testamentary provisions, which required the governors of the various entities to have managerial skills that, in some cases, were the origin of very profitable investments and speculations.[32]

In modern times, numerous institutions with welfare or moralization purposes operated in Naples. Religious congregations, conservatories for girls, for women separated from their husbands and for widows, city hospitals, orphanages, monti di pietà, provided for the protection of the common people, and their welfare work was supported not only by Christian charity but also by economic reasons and strong motivations for social stability.[33] Although the viceregal government did not consider assistance a state task or the responsibility of the Health Office, charitable institutions enjoyed some privileges that, although not institutionalized, guaranteed alms, exemptions, exemptions from fiscal taxes, and jurisdictional privileges.[34] The mutualistic and economic functions of such institutions are indicative of an urban reality characterized by great social heterogeneity. The Neapolitan confraternities themselves had a diversified social structure. Some were made up only of nobles, others of representatives of more modest social classes. All had specific devotional and welfare functions: alms, dowries, food and lodging, clothing, medical care, education, interest-free pawn loans, essential services to support the "common people" whose standard of living was precarious and insecure.[35] The four Neapolitan music conservatories, for example, managed to build a planned and solid structure that led them to high levels of efficiency and effective usefulness for the community. The relationships between welfare institutions and music are already known. They historically determined the operatic production of a geographically and culturally identified musical center, Naples, where mass music education was established in a complex network of relationships that involved conservatories, musicians, "educating children," patrons, and public banks in the practice of a set of musical activities, first in the city of Naples and then—with different modalities—also in Venice, in relation to the Counter-Reformation devotional apparatus and the cultural and ritual manifestations of popular religion.[36] The various congregations were accustomed to accompany particular liturgical festivities of the year with music and songs, and to gain the protection of a Saint, they resorted to generous monetary offerings that contributed to making the celebrations more unique and surprising, supporting large expenses for vestments, wax, "machines of artifice" and especially music. Like many other welfare institutions, which spread from the second half of the fifteenth century, the four Neapolitan music conservatories were "custodians" of Christian charity. Their assets were largely made up of real estate, leasehold accounts, or other public securities, which yielded their fruits, to which were added the sums from alms collected in the church collection boxes. The four charitable institutions developed on common models, providing assistance to orphaned or poor young people in the city and developing an original form of apprenticeship, but not unusual for the society of the time, that of initiation into the art or study of music, which soon proved to be full of prospects. The welfare activities of the four music conservatories must be placed within the broader charitable work carried out by Neapolitan welfare institutions in the modern era, which aimed to exercise Christian charity toward both the living and the dead, in the forms of mutual aid, the granting of marital dowries, assistance to the sick, burial of deceased beggars, often in their own cemeteries, suffrages for the deceased, and charity to the poor.[37] The Conservatory of Pietà dei Turchini, in particular, was founded as a non-profit organization and was maintained thanks to the contributions paid by its founders (the Confratelli of the Oratory of the Bianchi), donations from congregations and private individuals, collections in the attached Church, bequests, and testamentary legacies from wealthy people. It provided its charitable work to the "misguided" children of the city, introducing them to musical apprenticeship and, from the very beginning, used the proceeds from the musical performances of its «figlioli» (sons/children), whose services were in high demand by Churches, Confraternities, or private benefactors. The choirs of white voices or the "paranze of children" thus became an indispensable component in the celebration of Mass, whether solemn or ritual, in processions, and in the commemoration of the deceased. With musical services, theatrical performances, and the evolution of a music school, "the conservatories'" expenses increased enormously and were no longer limited to providing food and lodging for the children collected from the streets, but had to be used for the purchase of musical instruments, the payment of increasingly diverse and numerous professional figures, and the organization of religious and popular festivals. Moreover, the management of bequests and testamentary legacies involved administrators in the purchase of annual incomes, shares of rentals and taxes, in the collection of rents or censuses, requiring them to perform economic and financial functions of no small responsibility.[38] The charitable institutions most responsible for managing money were the Monti di Pietà,[39] which were characterized as both a religious assistance and economic phenomenon. In Naples, they arose in the sixteenth century, affiliated with various city Holy Houses that were driven by events to open a public treasury. Citizens, in fact, due to the difficult economic conditions in which the city found itself and concerned by the decisions of the viceregal government in matters of economic and monetary policy,[40] to avoid keeping their money at home, began to "deposit" it with these institutions. The Monti di Pietà thus found themselves managing a capital that they employed in their institutional activity of helping the poor, by granting small loans on pawn, which prevented them from falling into the clutches of usury. As "banks of the poor",[41] although they charged modest interest on loans, they made good profits, which they used to cover management expenses, support pawn lending activity, and other charitable works. The "purchase of annual incomes," for example, was a safe investment to make a capital grow without excessive worries.[42] The Neapolitan welfare reality, in the seventeenth-eighteenth centuries, therefore, appears, despite the absence of precise political measures, as an articulated system of economic and social interrelations.

The pro anima legacies—The use of legacies, as mentioned, was quite common: numerous were those in cash, almost non-existent those in kind. The Turchini appear to be fully in line with the customs of the time, since the pro anima legacies of the seventeenth century were generally constituted by sums of money.[43] The relationship thus established between the donors, mostly from the ranks of the aristocracy, and the clergy, only served to increase, due to mutual interests, the ties between the two classes. The legal formula of the legacy, as it appears in the Conservatory's records, was that of the testamentary legacy. In particular, pious legacies were patrimonial provisions dictated for religious reasons of worship or charity. They were generally accepted by the diocesan Ordinary through donation or testament in favor of ecclesiastical entities or an entity to be established, as in the case of pious places. These pious bequests, as they were also called, also contained all the dispositive acts in favor of the heir with the imposition of a modus that bound him to disburse sums or carry out activities for religious or worship purposes. In particular, the legacies we are talking about could also be defined as pro anima, when they established that acts of worship were to be performed for the benefit of one's own soul. The acquisition of the legacy took place ipso jure without the need for acceptance, which, however, the governors of the Conservatory expressed equally as confirmation of the acquisition or as a willingness not to renounce.[44] At the time, the belief in spiritual investment *pro remedio animae* was still widespread. The work carried out by the Church through preaching could not but influence the consciences of individuals. Among the recurring arguments in Counter-Reformation oratory, in fact, we find warnings about the danger of eternal damnation for those who, at the time of passing, did not care for the needy neighbor. Moreover, among the elements that heavily and for a long time influenced the choice of testamentary provisions, favoring the confluence of most of the individual's assets into the coffers of welfare institutions, we must include a certain success of some treatises on "dying well"[45] and the multiplication of confraternities, which aimed at preparing their associates for a "good death." These entities generally invested their money in purchases of public debt securities, so that, as it has been rightly noted, the forms of organized charity, which remained virtually unchanged until the nineteenth century, "on the one hand responded to traditional and centuries-old concerns for particular human cases, on the other, as institutions fully integrated into social reality, [they were] a particularly sensitive sounding board for the transformations of economic life and society in Southern Italy".[46] Following a principle of Tridentine observance, the practice of accepting legacies with the obligation of masses in suffrage of the testator began in the early years of the conservatory's life. The registration of the "masses" was kept by the Sacristan (Book of Masses) and the accounting is rich in precious details for the reconstruction of one of the "hinge" aspects in the relationship between the Conservatory and society. In 1595, Lonardo Genoino bequeathed to the Conservatory an annual income of 40 ducats with the "weight" of one mass per day in perpetuum, to be celebrated in the Church of Pietà dei Turchini. The same Genoino was granted the Chapel of the Rosary, the second on the right of the nave when entering the Church.[47] The Chapel then passed to Genoino's heirs: first to his nephew, Giacinto Romano di Francesco, then to Francesco, Giuseppe, and Nicola di Fiore, and from them to their nephew Casimiro Galzerano di Fiore.[48] In 1623, Francesco Lombardo, a musician in service at the Royal Chapel, left 2,750 ducats to the Turchini, which obliged the governors of the Conservatory to celebrate twenty-five masses per month in perpetuum, thirteen of which were to be celebrated at the privileged altar of the Church of Pietà dei Turchini. A large part of the sum received, 800 ducats, was spent on the "service" of the Church, so that the Conservatory was left with 1,950 ducats, which yielded 78 ducats per year at 4%, as was provided for by the acceptance of the legacy in the acts of the archbishop's Curia.[49] The case of Gaspare Roomer, although exceptional, is nevertheless symptomatic. A Flemish merchant, firmly established in the commercial and financial reality of the Kingdom, he bequeathed and left for charitable purposes a sum of about 30,000 ducats.[50] Gaspare Roomer was one of the major financiers of the century who managed to profit from the financial needs of the State. In the early 1640s, in fact, Roomer and his business partner Giovanni Vandeneyden—governor of the Conservatory of Pietà dei Turchini in the four-year period 1652–1656—accumulated large capitals thanks to maritime and commercial traffic and loans to the Government. They thus managed to gain possession of large public revenues, such as the tax on flour in the City of Naples.[51] It seems that Roomer himself lent his help to the Conservatory of Pietà dei Turchini before and after the plague of 1656. He is, however, among the benefactors who contributed to the construction of the new church in 1633, alongside other illustrious figures such as Tommaso D'Aquino, Matteo Pironti, Cornelio Spinola, and the Prince of Cellamare.[52] In 1638, Gaspare Roomer and Giovanni Vandeneyden donated to the Conservatory a capital of 4,445 ducats, which yielded an annual income of 266.70 ducats on the silks of Bisignano. The governors paid 2,000 ducats for the Banco di S. Eligio (October 1, 1638) with the money received from Luise della Banda, on condition that they were paid, during her lifetime, 180 ducats annually.[53] Moreover, in the same four-year period in which his business partner served as governor, Giovan Francesco Melina—who left the Conservatory as heir to all his assets—and Andrea Mastellone, Roomer's biographer, also held the same role.[54] In 1657, Giovanni Vandeneyden again came to the aid of the institute, lending it 313.14 ducats. Among the donors were also the Marquis of Crispano, who, in 1688, left 1,500 ducats for a daily mass in perpetuum in "his" Chapel of the SS. Crucifix. The governors undertook to pay the chaplains designated by the heirs for the celebration of the masses with the "usual alms" and employed the sum received in the lease of the salt of the four warehouses.[55]

The testamentary provisions of the benefactors had various forms of use for the bequests. In addition to the celebration of suffrage masses, the income could be used for church expenses, construction and reconstruction works, and often also for carrying out other types of charitable activities. It should not be forgotten that it was precisely thanks to the respect of the clauses provided by some donations that the governors managed to embellish and decorate the Conservatory and establish a series of chapels inside the Church of Santa Maria della Pietà, as they were obliged to use the money in this way. There are also cases where the religious themselves, at the time of their profession, as Rector, Vice-Rector, or Sacristan, donated substantial (perhaps the most substantial) legacies to the Conservatory. One example is that of the Judge of the Vicariate and President Giovan Battista Rocco, consisting of 278.35 annual ducats on the lease of the Jus Prohibendi of Tobacco, for a capital of 4,639.27 ducats. Giovan Battista Rocco, son of the Royal Counselor Francesco, also the holder of a substantial inheritance left for charity and which we will discuss later, in his last will, drawn up on April 17, 1684, in Cosenza by notary Giuseppe Mazziotti, left his wife Anna Pironti as usufructuary heir of a capital of as much as 9,000 ducats, in addition to other "bodies." Upon the death of Mrs. Pironti, the 9,000 ducats would have gone to charity, half to the Church of Sanità of the Dominicans and the other half to the Church of the Conservatory of the Turchini, with the "burden" of masses for both churches. Upon the death of Giovan Battista Rocco, the 9,000 ducats were deposited at the Banco dell'Annunziata, which returned them to his wife in 1687, and the noblewoman used them in tobacco lease installments. Upon the death of Anna Pironti, on May 9, 1696, the Conservatory came into possession of half of the capital income of that installment.[56] In the middle of the seventeenth century, the Kingdom went through a terrible economic and financial crisis, from which the Fathers[57] of the Turchini could not escape.[58] On March 16, 1652, the governors were forced to resort to the Tridentine commission of cardinals to obtain a reduction of the masses that the Church was obliged to celebrate by virtue of six legacies. Since the income of those six legacies "had deteriorated," the governors "requested a reduction in the burden of the masses, taking into account not only the amount of the usual alms but also the annulled fruits corresponding to the respective capitals".[59] Archbishop Ascanio Filomarino, on April 27, 1652, authorized the reduction of the masses, indicating the amount of alms, in relation to the customs of the city, and the number of masses according to the capital income.[60] In the same year, the governors again appealed to the Congregation of Cardinals to request a further reduction of masses. This time it was about 33 pious legacies. On November 16, 1652, the Congregation replied that it had already authorized the reduction, and on October 9, 1654, the amount for each mass was set at 2 carlini. A third reduction was requested on September 1, 1657. The Congregation entrusted everything to the prudence of the archbishop, who delegated the general vicar Paolo Garbinati protonotary. On November 15, 1663, the reduction was authorized, still setting the "alms" for each mass at 2 carlini. The devaluation of income had, inevitably, also affected the governors of the Pietà dei Turchini.[61] The heritage grows over the years and is enriched by further bequests that benefactors linked to the Conservatory for various purposes: the most recurring were the celebrations of masses for the rest of their own soul or that of their deceased relatives, but these were also accompanied by suggestions on how to use the inherited capital, sometimes in public annuities, sometimes in purchases of annual income or renovations of properties owned by the Conservatory, or, again, in works of ornamentation and expansion of the Chapels of the small Church of St. Maria della Pietà dei Turchini. In 1751, the state of income from various leasehold, fiscal, or other collections by the Conservatory recorded a total of 42,420.88 ducats of capital, compared to the 45,802.36 ducats of 1736.[62] In 1759, the priest Giuseppe Aveta, rector of the Conservatory, in his last will, drawn up by notary Gaspare Del Giudice, left the Conservatory 52.50 annual ducats, for a capital of 1,050 ducats at 5%. The sum was paid by brothers Gennaro, Nicola, and Ignazio Spanò, through two "instruments" drawn up by the same notary on February 27, 1752, and June 17, 1756.[63] The inheritance also included 20 annual ducats for a capital of 410 ducats, owed to Aveta by Andrea Aniello Cozzolino of Resina. The sums reached the Conservatory in 1762. The governors invested 500 ducats in the Gabella of old flour, starting from February 4, 1763.[64] Another 500 ducats were invested with the Monastery of St. Maria della Libera of the Order of Preachers of the Land of Quercia.[65] Of the initial capital, 50 ducats remained, which, with the "mandate of liberation" of the royal Counselor Mancini at the appointed actuary Gaetano Racioppi, were paid to the Conservatory on March 15, 1768, and immediately used for the renovation expenses of the houses that the Conservatory owned between the two streets of Ponte di Tappia and Baglino.[66] The examples reported show the continuity of bequests to the Conservatory and therefore, the formation of the institution's heritage over the years, as evidenced by the asset registrations. The decline in movable assets was, however, offset by the endowment of real estate, especially urban-type, inherited from other benefactors. Unfortunately, this type of asset is not quantifiable because their description, of a structural and architectural nature, does not report their monetary value. The only reference is given by the income from rents or emphyteutic censuses of those houses, titles of income extremely variable because determined by the trend of prices and the conditions in which the properties were.

The income from patronages—The institution of testamentary legacies found further application in the juspatronage of the chapels. Within the Church of Pietà dei Turchini, eleven chapels were erected[67] wanted by faithful nobles or wealthy people, confirming the importance and spread of the institution of the juspatronage of altars and chapels in the Neapolitan diocese. Although not large in size, the Church of St. Maria della Pietà dei Turchini managed to accommodate along its aisles those privileged altars, desired by benefactors who provided for both their "construction" and their "maintenance," through bequests that arranged for the celebration of masses at specific altars and with specific chaplains. The accounting of these chapels was essentially separate from that of the Conservatory. The most imposing chapel, in terms of size, ornaments, and accounting, was that of St. Anna,[68] erected by the will of the Royal Counselor Francesco Rocco, for which the founder left precise instructions, providing for an accounting strictly separate from that of the Conservatory. The concession to build a chapel dedicated to St. Anna was given to Rocco in 1667 and recommended that the works should not cause damage to the ceilings and warehouses below the church, on the side of the street of St. Bartolomeo.[69] The construction of the Chapel cost a total of more than 2,200 ducats.

Counselor Rocco, a representative of the wealthy Neapolitan aristocratic circles, assumed a role of great importance in the economic life of the Conservatory. From an investigation opened on him by the Viceroy Don Pietro d'Aragona in April 1666, it appears that, probably, the extraordinary amount of his assets was the result of illicit enrichment connected to the performance of his official duties.[70] Ten years before Rocco made his will, his assets, in particular all the funds deposited in his name at the Neapolitan banks, had been confiscated. However, the assets he left to his family and the bequest to the Chapel of St. Anna suggest that he was a man of great resources.[71] In his closed will dated September 30, 1675, he arranged for his body to be buried in his own Chapel and, after leaving his son Giovan Battista as the universal heir to all his assets and his daughters, wife, and daughter-in-law Anna Pironti as usufructuary heirs, he left a legacy of 20,000 ducats with an annual income of 800 ducats to the Chapel of St. Anna. The bequest was divided as follows: 12,000 ducats invested in the lease of the Salts of the four warehouses and 8,000

ducats in the purchase of annual income with the Bank of the Annunciation. The income of 800 ducats, according to the modus provided by
the legacy, was to be used to pay ten chaplains called to celebrate masses
for the rest of his soul, all his ancestors, his children, his two wives, his
sisters, and Pietro Corignano, who had left him heir to his "property." It
is impressive the meticulousness with which he indicates the amounts to
be spent on the payments of the chaplains and the expenses for the festivities "hat were to be held every year". From the income of the 20,000
ducats, the Chapel of St. Anna was to pay 70 ducats annually to the
Conservatory to be used as follows: 20 ducats for the litanies that the
children sang every week in the chapel; 30 ducats to pray to God for his
soul and to have all the children communicate on one day of the week;
another 10 ducats to be spent on the "recreation" of the children on the
feast day of St. Anna, as he had done every year of his life; and another
10 ducats to be divided among the children (1 carlino each) so that they
could buy whatever they liked most on November 2nd. Finally, 12 ducats
were intended for the Conservatory's Accountant for the keeping of a
separate "income and expenditure" book for the Chapel of St. Anna. In
total, the expenses of the legacy amounted to 743.27 ducats, distributed
as follows: 540 ducats to the ten chaplains at 4.50 ducats each per month;
121.27 ducats for the expenses of the three festivities; 70 ducats for the
children of the Conservatory and 12 ducats for the accountant.[72] Since
the income amounted to 800 ducats, there remained 56.73 ducats that
should have been deposited in the Bank[73] so that once accumulated they
could be used "for a large silver Cross proportionate for said Chapel".
This was followed by a myriad of other provisions with a detailed list of
all his assets (movable, immovable, furnishings, etc.), investment conditions, organizational indications, and more.[74] The heritage book provides
the exact location of the chapels along the aisles of the church, the date of
foundation, and recalls the various concessions in patronage, sometimes
also referring to the musical and religious performances of the Conservatory's "sons" (for example, the execution of two musical choirs on the day
of the patron saint or other). The Chapel of the Holy Guardian Angel,
owned by the Company of the Oratory of the Whites, was donated to the
Conservatory in July 1641.[75] During the plague of 1656, many brothers
of the Company were buried in the chapel, but following the provision
of the "Deputies of Health" to "close" all infected burials, the governors allowed the brothers of the Oratory to build another chapel at their
expense. The Chapel of the Holy Guardian Angel was then sold in June

1653[76] to the Couriers of the Office of the Chief Courier at the price of 400 ducats paid through the Bank of the SS. Annunciation. In 1778, the patronage of this chapel belonged to Gerardo Martinetti, who annually paid 12 ducats to the Church to keep a perpetual lamp lit there.[77] The other chapels, on the other hand, were all granted at the price of 200 ducats, to which the bequests of any annual income were then "bound" with the obligation to have masses celebrated. The right of patronage thus took on a meaning, albeit not exclusively, economic, insofar as this institution allowed, with the foundation of benefits and chaplaincies at the family altar, to exempt some assets from taxes and, at the same time, to establish a secure income base for some members of the family itself. It is no coincidence that the appointment of the beneficiary or chaplain was very often the cause of sharp contrasts within the family group, especially when, after the death of the founder and through various hereditary successions, the number of those entitled to patronage multiplied, making it extremely difficult to agree on the choice of the candidate. Cases of disputes between aspiring chaplains and beneficiaries of lay and family patronage can be found, for example, for the chapel of the Most Holy Crucifix, granted to the Marquis of Crispano. He was a member of the Confraternity of the Cross, which explains why, evidently, his right of patronage was on the Chapel of the Most Holy Crucifix.[78] This chapel had been granted in 1615 for 200 ducats to Giuliano Belenda, a creditor of the Royal Customs[79] and governor of the Conservatory of Pietà. On commission from Belenda himself, the painter Belisario Corinzio had executed a painting depicting the Annunciation.[80] In 1688, the notary Luca Montefusco of Naples drew up the instrument of concession of the Chapel to the Marquis of Crispano, upon payment of 200 ducats.[81]

The institution of Marriage Funds—The post-Tridentine congregations became interpreters of new forms of welfare, welcoming the poor to catechize them, defining and legitimizing charity, linking it to the meaning and value that the Counter-Reformation attributed to good deeds.[82] Among the various forms of assistance, there was one, suggested precisely by some testamentary provisions of some of the main benefactors of the institution: the task of dispensing dowries for "marriages" to poor but respectable young women. This activity expressed a common concern for almost all confraternities of the time.[83] For some social classes bearing the expenses of a marriage was almost impossible, and charitable aid became the only possibility to make matrimonial unions.[84] The phenomenon of marriage funds is of great importance for the study of the social and professional structure of the poorer population.[85] The institution of marriage funds was very common among confraternities or pious places starting from the seventeenth century.[86] Many are mentioned by Summonte,[87] such as the confraternity of St. Andrew of the Shoemakers, which assigned four marriages of 60 ducats, the conservatory of St. Mary of the Virgins of the Silk Art, which distributed six marriages of 50 ducats, the congregation of the Whites of St. Mary Succurremiseris, the Oratory of the Whites of the Holy Spirit, in addition to the various Funds established by nobles, whose marriages envisaged "a large dowry".[88] In Naples, the practice of charity under the guise of marriages was quite widespread both in lay and religious congregations and in the corporations of arts and crafts, each of which provided a dowry for at least four girls per year.[89] As with the Monti di Pietà, for other welfare institutions, the activity related to marriages was an ancillary activity, but not negligible: the deposit of funds to be dispensed as marital dowries allowed the use of capital for their own needs until the girl was chosen and then married.

As already observed, the activity of welfare institutions was particularly directed toward abandoned children,[90] the disabled, and women. Social investment in child assistance was taken for granted: both ethically and economically, they would constitute the new productive force of society; and if the sick had to be helped to prevent epidemics and contagions, women were to be controlled because of the high birth rate, In particular, the attention of welfare institutions for women increased to the point that they established ad-hoc boarding schools and retreats but, above all, they supplied marital dowries, provided that the recipient girls had preserved their honor.[91] The Monti di Maritaggi thus indirectly exercised a form of birth control and especially of those destined to balance the number of abandoned infants. Since the Renaissance, daughters had represented a growing problem for families who would have had to marry and endow them, but it is also true that families were a growing problem for daughters, who had to endure a strategy in which they always played the role of pawns and never of protagonists. With the rise of Protestantism, the social landscape underwent a change. Marriage was revalued, and all women were invited to establish "productive" or rather "reproductive" marital bonds.[92] Through different paths, but with identical results, both the Council of Trent and Protestant ethics affirmed that sexuality was permissible only within marriage and only if subordinate to the purpose of procreation. Lust became the sin par excellence, more important even than the sins of pride and greed, condemned with greater severity by medieval morality. Therefore, it seems that at the root of the benefactor's interest in poor girls was also the control of female fertility, recalled by the indispensable condition for the granting of marriage dowries, namely the state of virginity of the girls. It was not, therefore, an individual problem, but a group one, aimed at identifying the rules for its own continuity by incorporating fertility into a general control system. The status of wife was determined not so much by consent to the partner, but by her willingness to become a mother. Marriage, therefore, as a social investment. The dowry constituted a capital whose productive investment ensured, beyond a return on the money deposited, the "production" of a social nucleus, the family, morally and economically controlled, and the continuation of the species and the workforce through the children of the married woman. The concept that 'family' and 'society' are practically extensions of one another or that a progressive society not based on the family unit is inconceivable has always been widespread. The concern to create welfare funds to support poor girls, all in all, fell within a complexity of attitudes and political actions that had to face a global problem: economically, women constituted the most exploited group, but also the psychologically inferior one. In the Conservatory of Pietà dei Turchini, the activity of marriages was carried out, so to speak, indirectly by the governors, except for one case, the one mentioned in the testamentary legacy of Francesco Rocco, who established a real Fund of Marriages at the Chapel of St. Anna. The other donors who left funds for marriages indicated more or less precisely the names of the girls destined to receive the marital dowry and asked the governors of Pietà dei Turchini to manage their inheritance, trusting in their experience in the investment sector. The three main testamentary legacies, established in favor of the Conservatory, were those of Francesco Rocco, Teodoro Alianelli, and Giovan Francesco Melina. All three disposed of a part of their inheritance in favor of "marriages." The documentary material relating to this particular welfare activity, while proving sufficient for the interpretation of the phenomenon and the description of the practice of assigning dowries, is chronologically incomplete. Currently, three volumes and about 200 files are preserved in the Conservatory's archive, covering a period of time from the last decades of the seventeenth century to the beginning of the nineteenth. The "albarani"[93] drawn up by the governors of the Conservatory, the certificates of the *complateari* or captains of the ottina to which the future bride belonged, the marriage process signed by the parish priest, the certificate of the conclusion of the marriage chapters, another notarial act in which the future husband declares that he has received the dowry and undertakes to return it in case of the wife's death without legitimate and natural children, and some payment policies are preserved. The documentation is not complete for each practice, but the variety of papers gives a good idea of the bureaucratic practice that preceded the assignment of the marriage. Sometimes there are also baptismal certificates and certificates from the confessor, which the girls presented as further confirmation of their poverty and honesty.

The Melina inheritance—Among the donors of the Conservatory, the first to leave funds to be assigned to marriages was the physician Giovan Francesco Melina, one of the members of the Oratory of the Bianchi. Originally from Carife, in the Principality Ultra, he lived in Naples and frequented the aristocratic and most prominent circles of the city. In his will, opened and published on March 22, 1654, by the notary Giovan Lonardo Campanile of Naples, he indicated the Venerable Church and Conservatory of St. Maria della Pietà dei Turchini as his universal and particular heir. He also ordered that his inheritance be "governed" by the governors of the Conservatory and the prior of the Oratory of the Bianchi then existing within the same Conservatory.[94] The will is very clear regarding the management of the capital left as inheritance[95]: the Conservatory could take from its assets "for its own use and benefit, by reason of its labors", only what would remain from the capital of 4,100 ducats assigned for the celebration of five perpetual masses every week. Melina also established that the income derived from his inheritance should be made into a "cumulus" to be deposited at a public Bank of the city in an account in the name of the governors and the prior so that the legacies, marriages, and other burdens that would have to be paid could be satisfied. The accounting of Melina's inheritance had to be kept in a separate Book of income and expenditure, in order to avoid confusion between its income and that of the Holy House.[96]

Melina arranged marriages for the daughters in capillis,[97] descendants of his sisters or other relatives.[98] To each of these young girls, Melina left "for one time only" 100 ducats for the marriage. The sum had to be "promised" to the groom in the marriage articles: it had to be converted into the purchase of annual income or stable assets in the territory of the Land of Carife,[99] with the consent of the governors and the prior. In case of dissolution of the marriage, without legitimate and natural children "ex corpore," the girl could dispose of only 50 ducats. The other 50 ducats had to go to the future heir of the testator. Melina also left to the daughters who would be born from the young girls identified in the will, "both of the male line and the female line", up to the fifth generation, 60 ducats for the marriage of each of them. Also in this case, if the marriage were dissolved, the sum would be divided in half between the married girls and his future heir. Since the lineages became complicated, it was decided to keep a "tree" from which one could more easily, trace the descendants entitled to the marriage. The validity of this *albarano* was attested by the mayor, the elected officials, and the abbot pro tempore of the Land of Carife. Melina also ordered that every year, in perpetuum, five other daughters of the Land of Carife should be married, this time orphans, poor but always in capillis. To each of them, 30 ducats had to be given. In the absence of girls with the above-mentioned requirements, five other girls could be chosen who, although not orphans, had to be in conditions of extreme poverty.[100] He left instead to Felice (Felicia) Varratumolo, his niece in capillis, who then lived in her uncle's house, 1,200 ducats for her marriage. The sum consisted of 400 ducats in cash and another 800 invested in annual income at 8% with the convent of the Fathers of the Third Order of St. Francis, of St. Catherine Virgin and Martyr, located beyond the Porta di Chiaja.[101] The benefactor doctor left two more marriages, each of 30 ducats, to the two daughters of Marco Riccio (Orsola and Silvia) and another 100 ducats to Cassandra Sporlino, the youngest daughter in the service of his house, as a subsidy for her dowry. It is not possible to define the sum destined by Melina for marriages, since we do not know the exact number of girls entitled to the marital dowry during the five generations indicated. Certainly, however, the doctor left a truly substantial sum in inheritance to the conservatory. Just take a look, even a summary one, at the Book of income and expenses of his account to get an idea of how articulated and complex the management of the inheritance was.

The Rocco Marriage Fund—Of great importance, as mentioned, was the inheritance that the royal councilor Francesco Rocco left to the conservatory. A printed copy of his will is preserved, which highlights not only the size of his estate but also the precise distribution of his assets, even in view of future investments. The funds to be allocated to the marriages left by Rocco in 1675 were part of the inheritance of 20,000 ducats left to the Chapel of St. Anna. Among the various testamentary provisions, some of which have already been analyzed, there was one relating to the establishment of a marriage fund. The governors of the

Conservatory, as well as the administrators of the Chapel of St. Anna[102] would have to bestow, every year, starting from 1676, ten marriages, of 50 ducats each, to ten "maiden girls, poor, honorable" and named Anna, coming from the district and the ottina of Pietà, or, if there were none, from neighboring districts. The question of origin was very delicate. In 1711, the problem arose of defining the alternative district of origin of some girls.[103] On July 26 of that year, the governors expressed conflicting opinions on the origin of the girls. Rocco's testamentary provisions indicated, as the area of origin, all the streets surrounding the Church of Pietà dei Turchini, as long as they were the "closest." Some governors argued that all the girls residing in the district and in the ottina of Pietà dei Turchini should be eligible for the dowry and that those coming from the Strada della Pietà should be excluded, because although living near the Church and therefore in the same district, belonged to the ottina of St. Joseph and not to that of Pietà, which was, in reality, the ottina of Rua Catalana. Since the city of Naples was divided into 29 ottine, it seemed that Councilor Rocco had not made a substantial distinction between the terms ottina and district, but had wanted to indicate the area closest to the Conservatory as the origin of the poor girls, limiting his charity to that part of the people of the city of Naples who most frequented the Church of Pietà and took advantage of the activities of the Conservatory. The governors, therefore, decided that the origin of the girls eligible to the "Rocco" marriages should include only certain areas of the city. The specification of the places of origin was essential for the correct dispensation of the ten "Rocco" marriages. The marital dowry was highly sought after and there were no shortage of attempts at fraud against the Conservatory. In 1754, a potential eligible girl, Anna Nicoletta Moccia, in order to receive the 60 ducats of the marriage, declared that she lived in Diego Scala's house, where she had moved, since she did not come from either the district or the ottina of Pietà. In reality, the expedient proved futile and the issue lasted about four years, during which that marriage was never assigned to Moccia nor transferred to another girl.[104] The ten marriages were to be assigned on the day of St. Anna (July 26) in the homonymous Chapel, where the young girls to be drawn would have to attend, confess and communicate, take indulgences from the Church and then apply them in suffrage for the soul of their benefactor and his family members. At that point, the ten marriages would be "drawn." The documentation also preserves some petitions submitted by the governors for admission to the marriage draw of the Chapel of

St. Anna. The names of the girls drawn from the lottery are all recorded in the "Rolls of the daughters." The number of applicants for marriage was always very high and fluctuated around 300 units.[105] The drawing, as mentioned, took place according to certain conditions and procedures: all the poor but honorable girls living in the Rua Catalana district or nearby were included in the lottery. The origin, for the most part, is recorded from the Rua Catalana district, but there are also titles from other districts such as the Porta del Caputo and the S. Spirito di Palazzo. The admission of the proposed girls to the lottery took place with the consent of the six governors who constituted the board, and two or three of them presented reports on the qualifications possessed by the admitted girls. Ten names were then drawn. If the girl was found suitable, she was sent the *albarano* valid for two years,[106] but the dowry was not paid before the marriage chapters were stipulated and before the applicant's conditions were ascertained. The provisions in this regard were very strict: the girl had to be visited by one of the governors to establish that until the day of the marriage contract she had lived a virginal and honored life. There could be delays in the payment of dowries, as can be inferred from a "memorandum," unfortunately without a date, submitted to delegate Iannucci to request the payment of a marriage from the chapel of St. Anna.[107] Once the sum was received, the groom and a guarantor had to commit to returning it in case of dissolution of the marriage due to the death of the bride without legitimate and natural children. In the event of the bride's death, however, it was difficult to recover the dowry amount. It could happen, in fact, that the husband, having spent the sum received for the dowry and all he possessed due to his wife's illness, unable to return the dowry, appealed to the governors' mercy. Requests for the allocation of the dowry were addressed directly to the governors by the girls' relatives or by the captains of the districts from which they originated. There are no detailed indications that allow us to accurately reconstruct the mechanism of the "lotteries." The girls were generally between 13 and 30 years old, with very rare exceptions. For example, in 1811, Anna Orsola Di Fiore was 41 years old when she married Massimo Raffaele, who was 27 years old.[108] However, it seems that there were no predetermined age limits to access the marriages. There are cases of renunciation of the dowry, such as that of Anna Rosa Sorrentino who, in 1735, decided to renounce the dowry to become a «bizzoca».[109] The renunciation of marriages could occur in favor of others, for the choice of becoming a nun, «pinzochera» or «bizzoca», or due to the death of the interested party. In case of renunciation of the marriage, the ten marital dowries allocated for that given year could become eight or nine or even less. The marriages not assigned in one year were paid the following year. For example, in the lottery of July 26, 1774, fourteen marriages were drawn, that is, "ten as usual" and other "four returned in previous years".[110]

Other marriages—As can be seen from the first patrimonial writings and from the declaration of income made in 1751, the great benefactors were, in general, religious people. United by a true "corporatist" spirit, those who could, such as sacristan Teodoro Alianelli or priest D. Giuseppe Aveta, of whom we have already spoken, did not hesitate to make donations to the Conservatory. The Rev. Teodoro Alianelli, in his last will and testament closed on August 21, 1737 by notary Lonardo Marinelli of Naples, left all his stable assets, credits, bodies, income, and any other property in the land of Missanelli, his birthplace, to his brother Cosmo Alianelli. All his movable assets, gold, silver, cash, reasons, censuses, bodies, and income he possessed in the city of Naples, he left instead to the Church of Pietà dei Turchini, with a series of weights and legacies. Having died on June 11, 1745, on July 3, the Conservatory came into possession of a capital of 11,600 ducats with an annual income equal to 486.50 ducats. Of this large inheritance, the Conservatory spent "as a subsidy for the expenses of restructuring some houses" 7,600 ducats.[111] Reverend Alianelli was the last donor of funds intended for marriages. As a sacristan, he received an annual salary of 30 ducats[112] and was part of the Holy House family in every respect. The marriages he assigned were tied to the daughters of his brother Cosmo Alianelli. The dowries could be used either for their marriages or for their possible monasticism. This testamentary provision was added in the form of a nuncupative codicil[113] to the will. In the instrument relating to the chapters stipulated for the marriage between Giacomo Carisoni and Stella Alianelli, dated 1752 and 1754, the dowry in question amounts to 350 and 171 ducats left, precisely, in codicil by the Sacristan.

In the order of payment, it is then specified that the aforementioned sum was not subject to the conditions provided for by the will, but only to the condition contained in the nuncupative codicils drawn up on June 6, 1745 by Alianelli himself, according to which the cash found after his death should have gone to the benefit of his brother Cosmo Alianelli who, in turn, would have divided the sum equally among his daughters.[114] We do not have enough data to be able to define the exact number of marriages assigned each year. In general, we believe we can confirm the figures arranged by the legatees, since the five marriages per year destined by Melina and the ten established by Rocco were dispensed more or less regularly. However, we cannot ignore some elements that could have influenced those figures and the methods of application. The relative devaluation over time of the capital and income intended for marriages could have played a role of imbalance in the management of the "mountains" of marriages, especially for the last years of the seventeenth century and those of the following century. However, the available documents do not reveal problems of this kind. As already mentioned, the sporadic variations in the number of marriages dispensed are due more to the renunciation of marital dowries for personal reasons of the girl chosen than to economic contingencies. From a balance of marriages satisfied from 1711 to 1727, a total expenditure of about 8,500 ducats dispensed for 170 marriages is obtained.[115] From the discussion of the Marriage Funds established at the Conservatory of Pietà dei Turchini, it is evident that their allocation was mostly limited to daughters related to the legatees or coming from a well-defined geographical and social context: that of the Land of Carife for the Monte Melina, and that of the ottina of Pietà for the legacy of Francesco Rocco. M. G. Rienzo, referring to the distinction of Naples into four zones, adopted by Petraccone, notes that the area of origin of the largest number of girls eligible for the draw was the southern one, followed by the northern zone—where the Conservatory was located—, the peripheral strip, and finally, the Spanish quarters.[116]

The city's physiognomy proposed by Petraccone showed a strong discrepancy between a wealthy aristocracy and bourgeoisie, on one hand, and the small bourgeoisie, "also ragged and miserable",[117] and the very poor popular classes, on the other. This situation indicates a fundamental weakness of the productive structures that had remained stagnant compared to demographic development. The similarities found in the methods of granting marriages among other congregations and the Conservatory of Turchini are so many and such that we can once again argue the importance of the four musical conservatories in the history of assistance in Naples. Government policy supported a complex, decentralized charity system, which could be traced back to a plurality of reference centers such as lay and religious congregations or arts and crafts corporations. The forms of assistance of the four musical institutes have been neglected so far, perhaps because the history of the conservatories has been wrongly considered the prerogative of more specific historical competences, such as musicological ones. However, the reality that has unfolded before our eyes is quite different. The complex activity of those singular charitable entities presents all the essential characteristics of the main lay and religious congregations operating in the city, but unlike them, thanks to music, they open up to national and international cultural exchanges, becoming the spokesperson for an important musical and theatrical culture, that of the Neapolitan School.

3   A COMPLEX ADMINISTRATION

Before dwelling on another source of income, it seems appropriate to try to clarify the type of administration that presided over the management of the Conservatory. Since its foundation, the Conservatory of Pietà dei Turchini has been configured as a "company" with complex management, in which an essential administrative organization is opposed to a variety of assistance and training tasks. The examination of its functioning shows a generalized "good governance" of its administrators. The division of competences among the six governors is also consistent and respects, over time, the statutory rules. The figures of the Mensario, the Rationale-Secretary, the Father Rector, the Vice-Rector, and the Sacristan remain fixed, each of whom was entrusted with the accounting of a specific sector.

The division of competences among the various administrators was quite simple. The figure of the Mensario guaranteed a certain unity of direction on the administrative level, but did not always resolve the fragmentation of accounting management. The principle of the division of competences had given rise, in fact, in the Conservatory, to a multiplication of separate accounts, causing confusion in the numerous payment practices[118] which resulted in a series of delays in the settlement of mandates.

If for the entire seventeenth century the accounting had been kept by the Treasurer, who was one of the governors[119] and ratified the monthly accounts of the Mensario, in the eighteenth century, this seems to have been replaced by the Razionale-Secretary, a paid employee who appears to have belonged to the religious Order present in the Institute. The figure of the Razionale assumed greater importance during the eighteenth century and the fact that the "direct"[120] management of the institute was entrusted to him, the Rector, the Vice-Rector, and the Sacristan, who were also employees, suggests a stronger "religious" presence and a more active participation of the clergy members of the Conservatory in the financial management of the institution and not only in the educational one.

It cannot be stated with certainty to which order the religious of the Conservatory belonged since the consulted documentation refers only to the Congregation of the Bianchi, while the information drawn from historical literature reports the presence of Somaschi and Jesuits.[121] The only certain presence is that of the Confreres of the Oratory of the Bianchi,[122] but even clearer is the rivalry in the management of the institution between the secular government linked to the Sacred Royal Council,[123] through the royal delegate,[124] and the "patronage" exercised by the Company of the Oratory.[125] Most of the "internal" roles within the institution were, in fact, held by the Confreres, while the collection service of income, not directly coming from the public treasury—including real estate assets and older movable income (censuses, capital, legacies)—was entrusted to receivers or external collectors of the Conservatory, on whose speculative maneuvers it is not easy to express considerations.

The externalization of the collection service suggests a kind of concern for the management of a complex heritage, such as real estate, for which, however, the government of the Conservatory retained the prerogative to proceed with rentals. The entrusting to third parties of the collection service of censuses and rents stemmed from the fact that neither the governors nor the religious of the Conservatory were in a position to deal with them directly. The former because they were all external to the Conservatory and often, especially if very old, managed it directly from their own homes[126] the latter, because they were all "internal" and probably too busy with the management of the House and not very experienced in financial matters to also deal with real estate assets and movable income. But, more often, the concession of collection services was linked to the Conservatory's need for cash, difficulties in collecting income, or particular periods of crisis. The collectors thus contributed to the recovery of the "piggioni".[127] In taking on the contract for the collection service, they were required to sign, in the presence of the Conservatory's notary, an "instrument" of proxy that often reported the "State of the piggioni of the Houses of the Royal Conservatory," from which also resulted in the dislocation of individual properties, the rent share, and the names of the tenants, many of whom belonged to the same musicians who gravitated around the schools or the musical chapels of the city.[128]

This concerns certain revenues. But the Conservatory also provided resources. The institution presented itself, in fact, as a sort of multi-demand company aimed at various sectors of the unproductive urban market, and can be considered an important resource distribution center of the capital.[129]

The operating costs of the company, obviously, expanded in relation to the number of "sons," especially during the eighteenth century, when the dynamics of expenditure fueled a process of bureaucratization, common, moreover, to all other welfare institutions of the time, judging by the employment of half of their income in salaries, fees, wages, masses, Church and Sacristy, lawsuits and expenses of all kinds. In particular, the costs of the actual welfare activity (food, infirmary, clothing) and those of management (interest on passive capital, expenses for worship, salaries, maintenance of real estate assets, furnishings and musical instruments, collection costs, and all various and possible other expenses) were, for example, in our Conservatory, in the three-year period 1753–1755, substantially equivalent, except for the year 1754 in which management expenses exceeded those for assistance by as much as 1,252.53 ducats[130]; a phenomenon that intensified in the years 1761 and 1762, when a significant increase in administration and maintenance expenses was recorded. However, from 1763, when the first signs of the subsistence crisis of 1764 began to appear, these expenses decreased, while those for the purchase of supplies and food increased, also in relation to the increase in the level of food prices that hit everywhere in Europe in the last forty years of the century, as a result of the growth in demand, caused by the significant demographic increase. In particular, from 1762 to 1767, each year the Conservatory spent, on average, for the supply of food goods, 1,300 ducats, compared to about 800 ducats per year spent between 1753 and 1761. In the year of the famine, the gap between assistance expenses and those of house management amounted to about 2000 ducats, maintaining this difference until 1766. From that moment on, management expenses were even lower compared to the costs of actual assistance, which is very surprising, considering that in those years the number of "sons" present in the Conservatory constantly fluctuated around 80–100 units, as can be deduced from the periodic "shoe orders" in which the same quantities of shoes were commissioned, while the musical activities of the Institute multiplied, and with them, the staff who exercised them. In those same years, the set of officers serving the institution appeared, in fact, quite numerous, as can be seen from the payments to the masters and other "provisioned" of the House, including the collectors and contractors with whom, in that same period, the Conservatory stipulated contracts for the granting of related services.

The trend of management expenses and those for assistance in the period under examination shows, however, a sort of stability in the figures (Table 5). The fact that management expenses decreased in some years could be an indicator of better-guided administration, but we believe that the variations in those figures are also and above all linked to the delays with which payments were made for all those activities—which with an anachronistic term we could define as "tertiary"—such as teaching or occasional service provision of various kinds. A merchant supplier of food or fabrics and other materials would hardly have anticipated his goods without a short-term payment. The teachers and all the administrative staff, on the other hand, being largely "internal" to the Conservatory (at least as far as the religious are concerned) or—as in the case of some music teachers—providing their service in several places, were more willing to wait for payments. On the other hand, in the second half of the eighteenth century, the cost of living had increased, but the Conservatory did not change the salary levels of its employees, except in sporadic cases.

Table 5 Conservatory of Pietà dei Turchini Welfare and management expenses in the years 1761–1769, in ducats	*Year*	*Assistance expenses*	*Management expenses*
	1761	3,578.65	5,521.28
	1762	3,745.32	4,346.79
	1763	3,399.08	3,332.39
	1764	4,558.13	2,714.03
	1765	4,697.42	2,779.17
	1766	4,527.27	2,904.83
	1767	3,833.21	3,300.85
	1768	3,671.75	2,648.65
	1769	3,394.30	2,969.26

Note Assistance expenses include those for food, nursing, clothing; in management expenses, passive capital, expenses for worship, salaries, expenses for the maintenance of buildings, furnishings and musical instruments, collection costs and all various and possible other expenses are included

Sources Journals of Income and Expenditure of the Monthly Treasurer (Monthly Budgets) 1761–1769 and Journals of Income and Expenditure of the Rector (Books of the Rector), 1761–1769

4   REVENUES FROM EDUCATIONAL
AND MUSICAL ACTIVITIES

The connection between the activity of the Turchini Conservatory and the economic situation seems to emerge also from the number of poor and abandoned children hosted in the institute. Unfortunately, demographic information related to the members of the Institute's family is rather fragmentary and refers only to certain years. Some elements to reconstruct the social, professional, and geographical characterization of the first "sons" and to identify the paths through which they came into contact with the new welfare reality are provided by the Rolls of the "sons," the Students, and the Boarders, which, although covering a fairly wide time span, from 1652 to 1809, present two large gaps: the first, related to the first seventy years of the Institute's life, and the second, ranging from 1676 to 1745. These registers, together with other lists found in loose and not always dated folders, constitute the few remains still preserved that refers to the movement of a part of the Conservatory's occupants during the second half of the seventeenth century and throughout the eighteenth century. The information found in the Rolls, not always in complete form (name, geographical origin, age, period of stay, "plegio" or recommender, mode of entry and exit, and sometimes also the type of musical studies)[131] opens up insights into the dynamics of Neapolitan poverty, suggests the typology of craftsmen of the time, and defines the protagonists of that particular and flourishing system of musical supply and demand in Naples in the eighteenth century.

The overall movement of males[132] entering the Conservatory between 1652 and 1676, it has been said, was 322 units, but the number per year was always very irregular, ranging from 12 admissions in 1657 (a year in which many localities were still suffering from the plague), 42 in 1664, and 19 in 1674. Later, there were still 7 admissions in 1795 and 14 in 1808. In 1687[133] the «Nota del Pane» informs us of the presence of at least 91 "sons".[134] The number of young people hosted in the Conservatory, between 1765 and 1794, oscillated, on average, around 130 units (including children, students, and boarders).[135] In the same years, the total number of students admitted was 32 boys for whom the "plegi"[136] paid a deposit of 50 ducats for a total of 1,600 ducats, to which were added 384 ducats in total registration fees for a total income of 1,984 ducats. From 1791 to 1801, there was a total presence of 133 boarders. In 1793 alone, the annual fees paid by 36 boarders amounted to an annual income of about 1,300 ducats. The figure is approximate because in some cases it appears to have been reduced by order of the governors. When lists of "sons" are missing, accounting documents allow, from some administrative "incomes" related to clothing and musical activities, to hypothesize plausible but not precise estimates, since such fees, paid *tertiatim* or *semestratim*, were never separated from other accounts. The figures we have reached are those indicated in the "Instruments of Admission"[137] and which therefore made the idea more or less reliable of the income for the annual fees of the "sons" as established at the time of registration. The bureaucratic procedure for admission to the conservatory was quite rigorous and required precise documentation: the *instrumento*, drawn up between the parties by the Conservatory's notary, was accompanied by the baptismal certificate, the declaration of the "pledge," the certificate of good conduct, the family status, and the certificate of deposit of the entrance fee, that is, the registration fee.

If we limit ourselves to considering the final entry and exit dates, we observe a great variability in the period of stay. The stay in the Conservatory was hardly uninterrupted, and the obligation of permanence established in the admission instrument was not always respected. Both the student and the boarder were committed to "serving" the House for a period of time ranging from 5 to 12 years. The duration depended a lot on the age of the child at the time of admission, the type of musical studies he would undertake (violin, singing, choral direction, or other), his economic possibilities, and the payment methods.

So far, we have spoken indifferently of students or boarders, but in reality, there was a significant difference between the two categories. The Boarder entered at the age of seven or eight and paid an annual fee that for the entire eighteenth century amounted to 60 ducats for "foreigners," 40 ducats for "subjects" and 30 ducats for Neapolitans, in addition to the "entrance fee" of 12 ducats. In fact, these figures were subject to downward variations depending on the economic possibilities, the "talent" of the "son" and the presentations or "recommendations" that accompanied him. The Student, on the other hand, was almost always older, around 18–20 years old; he was already able to play or sing and paid only his "entrance fee," also equal to 12 ducats, in addition to always being accompanied by a "*plegio.*" Those who guaranteed for the student, and sometimes for the boarder, were mostly artisans or merchants, not always from Naples and not always from the same area of the Conservatory. The student committed himself to serve the Holy House in music, assistance, and funerals for the number of years agreed with the Governors, also in this case between 5 and 12 years of stay. Furthermore, in the admission *instrumento*, the young musician's commitment to "correspond and pay" everything he had earned outside the Conservatory for the remaining time of his instrument was reaffirmed in case he left before the established deadline. The commitment to serve the Conservatory for a certain number of years obliged the student to "produce" for the institution for the entire period, even if he decided not to be part of the Conservatory community anymore. The institute did not provide for external students: both students and boarders were guests of the musical college. The Pietà dei Turchini Conservatory, like the other three Neapolitan conservatories, provided hospitality to poor "children" and at the same time to paying "children," the latter being the vast majority.

Unlike the S. Maria di Loreto conservatory, the Turchini one has proved to be less oriented toward a manufacturing training of its beneficiaries.[138] In the Conservatory of Loreto, as in that of S. Onofrio in Capuana, a large number of "children" were dedicated to the art of silk and learned that of «*trenettaro, filatoraro, and berrettaio*». In the first period of the Conservatory's life, the "children" were, in fact, almost exclusively prepared for trades. The governors of the institute stipulated real contracts with the master craftsmen with whom the orphans were placed. The instrument provided, on the part of the master craftsman, first of all to teach the "child" the trade, then to offer him "food, clothing, and to treat him well for at least six continuous years," at the end of which he should have given him a new suit of Neapolitan cloth and then handed him over to the governors, paying the Conservatory 10 ducats for the service that the orphan had offered him all those years. In the event that the terms of delivery and payment were not respected, a penalty was provided that obliged the craftsman to pay another 6 ducats per month for the entire time of the delay. In this way, the Conservatory not only secured the master but also all the expenses related to the established period, while a productive workforce already entered the Institute, thus contributing to increasing its income.[139] It should be remembered that the Conservatory of S. Maria di Loreto was close to the Port and in the midst of one of the most flourishing artisan and commercial villages of Naples,[140] while the Pietà dei Turchini, located in the northern part of the city, was surrounded by the main theaters of the time (the "room" of S. Giorgio dei Genovesi destroyed in 1620, the Theater of S. Bartolomeo adjacent to the Conservatory and that of the Fiorentini first, the S. Carlo and the Teatro Nuovo later).[141] Therefore, the "productive" stimuli to which its guests were subjected were more artistic than artisanal. It is no coincidence that the Pietà dei Turchini survived the other conservatories and constituted, on a national level, the ancient reference of the Neapolitan musical school before the foundation of the Conservatory of S. Pietro a Majella.

The epidemic of 1764 and the years of crisis that followed placed a heavy mortgage on the ancient city hospital institutions and on the development of public and private charity. These elements of uncertainty seemed not to touch the Conservatory, which in the meantime had modified the welfare system into a proper educational-musical one, introducing original and implicitly selective productivity factors into the management of the institute: the governors were forced to implement sometimes severe selections on the would-be "studying sons." Over the years, the organizational and educational structure of the Conservatory consolidated, and the presence of renowned masters meant that admissions were examined with specific tests of instrument or composition. There were also recurring decisions to ban entry to those who had previously fled from that or other conservatories,[142] or for repeated, and unobserved, recalls to those who had disobeyed the rules of the House.

The statistics of the entrances and exits of the "little children" in the Conservatory provide an even more fragmented panorama and indicate the motivations that led them to enter the institute: for a musician who did not belong to the circle of madrigalists or to that of the court theaters, entering the Conservatory meant not only training, but work and immediately. The temporary character that the "sons" attributed to their stay in the Conservatory is often felt. Escape remained a widespread aspiration, especially among the youngest. But the longing for freedom was often frustrated by precarious physical conditions that required staying in the hospice or returning home. In about a third of cases (30%), the interruption of the stay in the Conservatory depended on the child's illness, for another share (15%) on bad conduct or poor performance, and for another 15% on the decision to "become a priest"; for the remaining part for having exhausted the *instrumento.*

As it is well known, quite a good number of few families in order to guarantee a better and more comfortable placement of their children, but also to rise socially through them, pushed their children, if not to the ecclesiastical career, at least toward activities connected with the life of the Church. They sometimes even resorted to prepubescent castration, despite the severe prohibitions, to promote their inclusion in the white voice choirs of the churches, in the hope of future aggregation to the ranks of the clergy.[143] We mentioned earlier a 15% of "sons" who left to "become a priest." From 1652 to 1662, out of 85 "sons" of the Pietà Conservatory, 18 left to become "monks," 4 to take service as a chapel master, one at San Gennaro, another at Viesti, with Monsignor Mastellone,[144] a third committed to serve the institute on the occasion of Corpus Domini, playing the trombone, and the fourth left as a eunuch, therefore, as a singer. Of one student, it is known that, dismissed on May 10, 1666, he "went to the painting workshop of Vaccaro"[145] to learn a completely different art, but of the other 53 guests in those 10 years, it is not known what occupation they undertook after leaving the school.[146] Certainly, some decided to remain in the Conservatory as music teachers.

Beyond the proclaimed purpose of hosting all the misguided children of the city, in the eighteenth century, when it had already established itself as an excellent School of Music, the Conservatory attracted almost exclusively young musicians from the Neapolitan hinterland, except for a small percentage of "regnicoli" in the broad sense and groups of foreigners coming from Rome, Pisa, Florence, Milan, Genoa, or even from abroad: Lyon, Paris, Malta, Moscow, Bavaria, and Portugal.[147] The small number of non-Campanians listed is made up of episodic presences, people who came to Naples from other port cities (Livorno, Genoa) or were stationed there as soldiers of the Bourbon troops. Immigration from Genoa was significant, thanks to the commercial relations between the two cities[148] but there were also students coming from Flanders, Sicily, Calabria, and Apulia. In practice, compared to the immigration movements toward the capital, the new charitable institution seemed to carry out an indirect action, aimed at forming, since the mid-1600s, an abundant musical workforce: singers, virtuosos, music teachers, chapel masters, who in the 1700s would achieve European fame. The admission of external students—boarders who accessed the institute for the specific purpose of acquiring a musical education—was encouraged by the fact that their registration fees guaranteed a basis for the more proper welfare functions of the institute. The educational activity was mainly aimed at already urbanized elements and, if at least in the early days it revealed a rather random recruitment, which was expressed in the absence of well-defined "musical" purposes and through multiple channels, in a second moment, identifiable with the first half of the 1700s, the activity of the Conservatory changed, taking on the characteristics of a regular educational-training system, aimed at a specific professional category. The procedures that formalized entry into the Conservatory were essentially based on three types of decisions, corresponding to as many personal and administrative references. There was, first of all, an informal system of "recommendation" that spread from the Court to the father rector and to the governors of the Conservatory themselves. And it was through this path that, throughout the eighteenth century, a good part of the "educating children" entered the Conservatory. The Rolls of the "sons" and the admission instruments indicate precisely in the governors of the pious work the main link with the outside. In these years there were "sons" admitted thanks to the intervention of various nobles, from the Prince of Caramanico to the Marquis of Cariati, while others were accompanied by the presentation of the king and others still by that of the rector or vice rector who "guaranteed" for the good faith of the child to be received.[149]

Accepting "children" already experienced in music meant having immediately the so-called "workforce," indispensable for being able to carry out remunerative work. The musical performances of those "children" dressed in turquoise gradually intensified, creating a customary relationship between conservatories and eighteenth-century theaters. The Conservatory officially became a School of Music, probably from the early years of the 1700s, even if, already in the mid-seventeenth century, it produced a copious musical workforce mostly engaged for religious purposes. The massification was evident in the number of students, as mentioned, and in the type of instruction, efficient but brief, entrusted to just five teachers in all (one for singing, another for the harpsichord, another for counterpoint, one for string instruments and one for wind instruments).

The "sons" began to ensure income for the Conservatory already in the first years of boarding, when they were employed as beggars on the streets of the city, but they increased it considerably when they began to practice musical activity, for the exercise of which, on the suggestion of the teachers, they were selected by the governors among those exempted from ordinary services (dispenser, wardrobe, sacristan, porter, nurse, and prefect) and those defined as "educating children," employed in music services, assistance and funerals, crews, angels, etc. The first "professional, employments" of the "studying sons" were in services external to the institute, for example in a "paranza",[150] which provided for a certain number of "children," established at the discretion of the rector, to be sent to a congregation on the occasion of some ceremony. It could also include 25 "sons" to whom another 2 or 4 "angels"[151] were added. The cost of a "simple paranza" of "sons" varied from 5 to 8 carlini in the first half of the 1700s. It involved an average of twelve "sons," but the number varied depending on the commission. More complex were the "full paranze," which involved about twenty-five "sons": the twelve from the simple paranza plus four, six, or twelve "angels," the Cross, and another six "sons for the bats of the Pallico." Its cost reached about 25 carlini. A Choir, on the other hand, consisted of an organist, four voices, four violins, a cello, an oboe, or a trumpet.

The most deserving "sons" generally obtained the "position" of first or second tenor, soprano, violinist, trumpeter, oboist, or maestro di Cappella, that is, they moved to the condition of "non paying pupils," that is, without payment of any fee and also taking on the role of «mastricelli», that is, assistant masters. Regularly carried out and controlled, their lessons were considered very "profitable for the instruction of the sons".[152] Among these, we remember Don Serafino Miglietta, whose fee was reduced from 50 ducats per year to 18 ducats as a one-time payment, with the obligation to be a master of letters. Another case is Don Michele Riccio, appointed prefect and cellist at 35 ducats instead of 50 ducats. In 1794, Antonio Campi stipulated his *instrmento* for 5 years: he played the violin and was the character master of the "sons."

In the seventeenth century, the School aimed to train mainly singers and, in the following century, instrumentalists, mostly violinists. In particular, between 1745 and 1762, it has been calculated that, out of ninety "sons," thirty studied to become singers (11 sopranos, 10 contraltos, 6 tenors, 3 basses), eight to become Maestri di Cappella, thirty studied Violin, three Cello, two Double Bass, eight Oboe, six Trumpet, and one Bassoon.

Among the "sons" who studied as Maestro di Cappella, we remember in 1752 the musician Giacomo Tritto[153] who, from 1785, held the role of second master alongside Nicola Sala[154] first master. The latter was "retired," that is, relieved of his position in 1799, and replaced by Tritto, who held the position of first master until 1800 with a salary of 5 ducats per month (Nicola Sala took 8 per month).

When a student showed particular musical talent, the Conservatory tried to extend his stay in the institute. This was the case with Giovanni Calderano, who entered in 1789 to stay for 5 years, but since he proved to be "good" and sang well as a "buffo",[155] he was "maintained." On

January 12, 1798, however, he was hired by the Band of the Hunters of the Prince of the Forest and thus obtained his release. The case of Domenico Lamarra, on the other hand, confirms the Conservatory's attention to maintaining an internal musical system in which each role, vocal or instrumental, was covered and ready to be employed. Lamarra had entered the Conservatory on July 2, 1793, stipulating a 10-year *instromento*, but, due to the "scarcity" of contraltos, he moved to "non paying student". He sang and played the cello, the instrument chosen at the time of registration.

But the Conservatory also welcomed students from other welfare institutions; in fact, in 1793, four students arrived at the Turchini from the Albergo dei Poveri and were admitted to the Conservatory as violin players (2 of them) and clarinet players (the other 2), all with the commitment to pay two. 20 per year each. The four students came to perfect their skills after attending the Music School established at the Albergo dei Poveri, probably also following the principles of *renfermement*.[156]

The study of music had indeed become a possibility for the social recovery of the inmates, who could be included in musical bands, thus taking on professional or artisanal characteristics. The fact that some of these inmates then needed to study at the Conservatory confirms, on the one hand, their artistic talent; on the other hand, it underlines the official value of the "degree" obtained in that school. Moreover, the commitment to pay the fee by the institution of origin suggests, in addition to the continuity of the assistance offered even outside the reclusorio, a sort of profit that came from the musical activity of its inmates, just as it happened for the "children placed in a workshop" by the Conservatory of S. Maria di Loreto.

From 1791 to 1806, out of 193 boarders, 19 embarked on a musical profession, some in the Band of the Terra di Lavoro regiment, some at the Teatro Nuovo, some in the Conservatory as a Chapel Master or instrumentalist. Of the others, all musicians, we do not know for certain what activity they carried out after leaving the Conservatory. A small number enlisted as soldiers or sailors, later finding a place in the regiment's band, others, as mentioned, took the path of the priesthood, but often without abandoning music, still others were involved in the revolutionary movement of 1799 and were therefore arrested as state criminals. The last years of the eighteenth century were, after all, quite turbulent, and the Jacobin revolts involved many young Neapolitans. Among these was the famous musician Gaspare Spontini,[157] also a student of the Conservatory. As a "foreigner," he should have paid 60 ducats a year for his fee; instead, he was exempted from payment with the obligation to copy papers, but two years later, in 1795, he fled the Conservatory for "some crimes".[158] It is not known if, among the students of the Conservatory, who the registers label as incorrigible or state criminals and expelled from the institute, there were other musicians who embarked on their profession after the turmoil of the 90s. It is certain that the growing musical reputation of the Conservatory brought privileges and remunerations to the "sons," lightening the burden of the physical work they would have had to undergo and increasing their earnings. It is worth noting that the "sons," within the Conservatory, could also carry out another activity, also of some importance: the "copying of music papers."

Copyists were, in general, those who could not pay the full fee and offered a service to the House.[159] The financial accounts, in the chapters related to Music expenses, include, alongside the expenses for repairs, tuning, or purchasing musical instruments, mostly wind or string instruments, those for sheet music and compensation (when it was not an obligation) for the young person in charge of the "copying." Is it possible to think of a "handwritten," "manufacturing" publishing activity within the Conservatory? As far as we know, none of the publishers, printers, and music booksellers documented in Naples from 1575 to 1700 dedicated themselves exclusively to music. For all of them, it was only one branch, never the majority among their many activities, just as it happened throughout Italy, with the exception of Venice. In this period, very few music books were printed in the city of Naples, and all of them were characterized by some exceptional prerogative compared to the norm of music publishing itself. Neapolitan publishing was too submissive to censorship, which weighed on the entire cultural life of the city and which, in fact, was exercised between the sixteenth and seventeenth centuries by two authorities: the viceregal government and the archbishop's curia. The printers of the time, such as Carlino, Vitale, Stigliola, Pace, Marescalchi.[160] However, the Neapolitan musical publishing tradition is still to be studied, and therefore many hypotheses are still possible. To think of the copying activity of the "young people" as a productive activity, replacing an indispensable service for an already organized and specialized school system, is therefore legitimate. Especially since the masters and the young teachers were required to produce a certain type of musical works, which certainly required at least one copy for the institution and another for the eventual performance. In that case, it was then necessary to distribute the individual parts to the respective musicians. Therefore, the activity of the copyists within the Conservatory was certainly aimed, in the first place, at the production of an "internal" service that subsequently required an "external" destination. But what did the musical activity that the "sons" were commissioned to carry out externally, both in churches and in theaters and private homes, represent in terms of income?

An answer comes from Table 6, where the income from the Conservatory's musical activities is compared, albeit limited to some years in the mid-eighteenth century, with that derived from employment in real estate, as well as in leases.

It is evident that the volume of income from leases and real estate exceeded that of a musical nature several times, a sign of the patrimonial consistency achieved by the Conservatory.

The prevalence of patrimonial income is even more significant in the second half of the eighteenth century, as shown in Table 7, when musical income fluctuated, compared to the total of other income, between the tenth and the fourteenth-fifteenth part.

Additions from the previous year's active cash fund have not been considered. Percentages are based on total income.

It should be noted, however, that in the expansion of other income, income from real estate took on considerable importance, as a result of the significant increase in population, especially the Neapolitan population.[161] Housing rents had indeed grown rapidly and continued to increase. An example is provided by a rental contract stipulated by the Conservatory itself. In 1776, it rented out the bakery inside its building,

Table 6 Conservatory of Pietà dei Turchini revenues in the years 1753–1755, in ducats

Year	Music	%	Lease	%	Other	%	Total	%
1753	1,629.07	19.5	1,946.93	23.3	4,265.89	51.1	8,347.92	100
1754	1,795.83	18.7	1,951.41	20.4	5,399.20	56.3	9,587.14	100
1755	1,474.21	18.2	1,869.00	23.1	3,716.67	46.0	8,083.59	100

Notes Music: revenues for Music and Contract Assistance; Music and Assistance outside Contracts; Funerals and Angels as from the Rector's income item. Rent: all Revenues for Rentals effectively collected. Other: collection of the Censor of censuses, rents, legacies, and children's income
Sources A.P.T. Journals of Income and Expenditure of the Monthly Treasurer (Monthly Budgets) 1753–1755; Journals of Income and Expenditure of the Rector (Rector's Books) 1753–1755

Table 7 Conservatory of Pietà dei Turchini. Revenues in the years 1774–1779, in ducats

Year	Music	Other
1774	967.76	14,813.57
1775	999.82	9,165.34
1776	1112.52	10,869.77
1777	948.40	10,302.77
1778	918.42	9308.49
1779	1060.45	9663.08

Notes Music: income from music services, funerals, and assistance; income from angels and funerals; income from music contracts; Other: income from leases; income from rents, fixed incomes, and annuities
Sources Monthly Income and Expense Journals and Rector's Journals (Monthly Budgets, Rector's Books), years 1774–1779

which consisted of an "upper room, a small side room, the courtyard atrium, the basement, and all other amenities" to D. Francesco della Selva for 80 ducats per year: the agreement also included, in addition to the payment of rent, the obligation on the part of the landlord to provide the necessary bread to the Conservatory every morning[162] and, therefore, given the number of people living there, a considerable overall figure.

5   Types of Income from Musical Activity

Although quantitatively inferior to the total of other types of income, those derived from musical activity constituted the result of a very wide range of musical services offered. The attempt to ascertain the importance assumed by each of these services, and also the evolution of their demand, can represent a contribution to the reconstruction of the socio-economic framework of seventeenth-eighteenth century Naples, capital of a Viceroyalty until 1734, and from that year, capital of a Kingdom, the largest in Italy at the time, and where, in addition to the Bourbon court and the government of the entire country, foreign embassies resided and the majority of national and international trade was concentrated. It has been said that musical performances were made up of "music, paranze, contracts, funerals, and angels." Limiting ourselves to the eighteenth century, and benefiting from the discovery of a particular volume, the so-called "contracts" book, relating to the years 1752–1755, we can ascertain the nature of the patronage that was linked to the Conservatory. In this way, it can be determined that the musical services provided by the "sons" to private individuals, religious congregations, and popular festivals varied according to the occasion and the type of musical ensemble. For example, for popular festivals, the demand could be for one or more soloists or a group of instrumentalists. Private individuals, on the other hand, could request "choirs of angels" on various occasions, but mostly for funeral ceremonies. Convents, congregations, or parishes made use of the participation of the "children" in masses, processions, or solemn liturgical ceremonies.

In the analysis of musical activities and their related patronage, contracts stipulated for "music and assistance" describe a patronage represented essentially by churches, monasteries, and congregations of the Neapolitan diocese.[163] It seems, in fact, that most of the musical activities carried out during the considered period were related to religious functions. Out of a total of 34 services, about 50% were absorbed by churches, mostly in the city; 13 services referred to religious congregations, also predominantly urban; the remaining services concerned monasteries and convents in the city and its surroundings. The musical activity requested by devout laypeople was episodic and negligible.

In each contract, the description of the moments of the liturgical year in which the musical service was required is always very detailed.[164] This consisted of simple or full "paranze," "choirs," "assistance to the Maestro di Cappella," entertainments (motets, symphonies, and others). The most requested service was the "paranza." Not all contracts contained the established compensation, but when the annual compensation is reported, it is possible to calculate with some approximation the annual income of the Conservatory for this type of service. Sometimes, however, the document reports the cost of each service without defining the total number, but leaving its execution to the will of the Governors of the commissioning places.

This type of contract was stipulated only between the representatives of the two contracting parties; it did not require witnesses or notarial registration. The possible interruption of the commitment made by the Conservatory or the commissioning Church or Congregation could occur at any time, provided it was notified at least one month in advance.

One of the recurring clauses concerned the observance of the obligations of the "sons" dictated by the Rules of the Conservatory: if one of the musical services coincided, for example, with the Saturday dedicated to confession and general communion, or with the week of spiritual exercises, it had to be moved to times when the "studying sons" were free from any other canonical commitment. However, their presence must have been in high demand if, in the contract of the Church of St. Maria dell'Anima, the service was set early "to give room to the "children" to serve other Churches".[165]

Payments were made tertiatim or semestratim, that is, every four or six months and often on different dates from each other, so it is complex to trace the annual income. If in the contract with the Congregation of the Third Order of St. Francis of Assisi in St. Mary La Nuova, to the ten ducats that were paid annually in December, a candle was added for the rector on the day of purification, in the one with the Church of St. Mary of Grace in Toledo, the payment was subject to a "scaling" of as much as twenty annual ducats due to a period of economic difficulties suffered by the aforementioned Church. It was also frequent that the contractor owed nothing for music services because the Conservatory was already in possession of a legacy intended for masses, paranze, or litanies.

A final example can clarify another payment practice, that of "tickets." In a contract agreed upon in 1747 with the Parochial Church of St. Liborio, the Conservatory committed to sending its "children" for "full paranze", according to the requests of the parish priest of the Church. The latter, every time he wanted to request such a service, would have had to forward the request to the Conservatory through a "ticket" that would have been kept by the rector to exhibit it, once the service was done, to the Monte dei poveri vergognosi[166] on which the deputies and the parish priest of the Church would have issued a payment order "at the rate of eight carlini each".[167]

We have already mentioned the imprecision of the dates related to the duration of individual contracts. Although the analyzed Book reports the dates of the three-year period 1752–1755, many contracts appear to be open since 1737; for some of them, the date of suspension and reopening is reported, but this is not enough to give a clear picture of the continuity of commitments and therefore of income. Based on an approximate and purely indicative calculation, of the shares established in the contracts in that three-year period, music services seem to have yielded about 700 ducats per year. However, this figure is not confirmed by the accounting documents, from which it appears that in 1753 the Income for music contracts amounted to 505.2 ducats, in 1754 to 612.7 ducats, and in 1755 to 587.6 ducats.[168] The difference found is probably due to delays in the collection of contracts or their reduction over time. In the following years, from 1761 to the early years of the nineteenth century, income from music services marked a significant increase as shown in Table 8.

Table 8 Conservatorio della Pietà dei Turchini Revenue for musical services in the years 1761–1790 and 1804, in ducats

Year	Music-Parances	Funerals and angels	Total
1761	1382.46	82.85	1465.31
1762	4926.17	81.43	5007.60
1763[a]	693.03	69.08	794.51
1764[a]	734.68	62.79	927.34
1765	876.36	60.61	936.97
1766	912.44	63.81	976.25
1767	897.82	45.21	943.03
1768	828.29	60.83	889.12
1769	855.75	36.56	892.31
1770	911.64	42.03	953.67
1771	895.79	67.70	963.49
1772	1045.05	35.94	1080.99
1773	995.97	64.56	1060.53
1774	943.65	24.11	967.76
1775	914.45	85.37	999.82
1776	1022.49	90.03	1112.52
1777	886.78	61.62	948.40
1778	888.42	30.00	918.42
1779	968.50	91.95	1060.45
1780	796.77	48.80	845.57
1781	928.28	46.80	975.08
1782	1132.10	48.60	1180.70
1783	1069.35	24.40	1093.75
1784	1147.25	33.90	1181.15
1785	1046.05	13.00	1059.05
1786	1045.72	1.20	1046.92
1787	617.70	0.60	618.30
1788	1109.78	–	1109.78
1789	827.28	–	827.28
1790	815.10	–	815.10
1804	1062.72	–	1062.72

[a]Revenues for these two years also include those for the staging of Intermezzi and Musical opera
Note Items shown are those recorded in the Dean's revenue batch, which is responsible for this type of music service
Sources Journals of Introit and Outcome of the Rector in the years 1761–1804 (Rector's Books)

The revenues for Music show an apparently constant trend over the years, recording some very high peaks, such as that of 1784, with an income of duc. 1,181.15, and some very low ones, such as that of 1787 with two. 618.30. Exceptional is the income of 1762, amounting to two. 5,007.60, a staggering figure compared to the others recorded in the table, difficult to explain except by thinking of the increase in theatrical activity. It should also be noted that the revenues of the period 1765–1770, that is, the one immediately following the crisis of 1764, do not undergo significant variations, while the five-year period 1782–1786 shows an increase in revenues for the main productive activity of the Conservatory. Generally maintained below one thousand ducats, they exceeded that level in the years from 1782 to 1786, to collapse to around 600 ducats the following year and rise to over 1,100 ducats in 1788. The progressive disappearance of income for "funerals and angels" could indicate a change in religious customs and habits, but also a greater professionalism of the musicians provided by the Music School. Surprising is the collapse of revenues for "music and paranze" that occurred in 1763 at only 693.03 ducats after an inexplicable peak of 4,926.17 ducats in 1762, a golden year for the musical performances of the "turchini" children. In reality, the productive activity of the institution multiplied in a series of interventions in theaters, private homes, royal halls, which provided certain revenues not recorded in the budget books, probably because the competence of the rector was limited to the control of "religious" musical services. However, the revenues recorded in 1763 and 1764, relating to theatrical performances, if on the one hand surprise, as the only budget items considered, relating to less "religious" musical services, on the other hand confirm a productive activity of the Conservatory of a higher artistic level that, evidently, will have to be confirmed by other sources.[169]

The performances took place during the Carnival season (January–February–March, up to the time of Lent excluded). In 1763 there were four, and they gave a total income, as mentioned, of two. 32.4. The places, times, and costs of the individual performances are significant (Table 9).

The 1764 Carnival season yielded much more: the same works with the same intermezzo had 10 reruns, bringing in revenue equal to 129.87 ducats.

Table 9 Conservatorio della Pietà dei Turchini, revenues from performances during the Carnival of 1763

Year 1763	Performance	Location	Revenues
January 30	Intermezzo	Monastery of S. Severino	6.0
February 3	Intermezzo and Opera	Monastery of the Maddalena Nuns	7.4
February 9	II Intermezzo (replica)	Monastery of the Maddalena Nuns	4.0
February 15	Opera and Intermezzo	House of Mr. Duke Coscia	15.0

Source Journal of Income and Outcome of the Rector in the year 1763 (Rector's Book 1763, January–February)

For that season as well, the highest compensation for the theatrical performances of the Conservatory's "sons" came from a private individual. In 1763, Baldassarre Coscia, Duke of Paduli, paid 15 ducats for the opera and intermezzo, compared to the 7.4 ducats paid for the same performance by the Monastery of the Nuns of Maddalena; in 1764, the same duke commissioned three theatrical performances which he paid for, through a bank policy of March 19, 1764, with 50 ducats. The amount also included the expense note recorded later in the outcome and comprising the rental of costumes for the scenes, payment to the hairdresser, and other expenses for the staging. In the same year, the Duke of Monteleone, for an opera in music performed in his residence, paid 14.4 ducats (Table 10).

The intermezzo seems to have been entrusted to the "little ones," that is, less experienced and responsible for a less demanding theatrical part. The intermezzo, in fact, was born as a divertissement between one act and another of the represented opera, a sort of modern "commercial break" that interrupted the serious "monotony" of the serious Opera.[170] It is not clear whether the work of "S. Gaetano," already represented in 1763, was an opera in music or in prose. It certainly recalls the sacred drama, a Neapolitan version of the comedios dos santos imported to Naples by the Spaniards.[171] The information concerning it defines it as an operatic genre of religious argument, popular between the seventeenth and eighteenth centuries in Naples, in which elements taken from the lives of the saints and buffoonish elements are combined. It seems to constitute, albeit to a very limited extent within the overall scope of patronage, a particular sector of the Neapolitan conservatories' musical practice, which,

Table 10   Conservatory of Pietà dei Turchini. Revenues from performances during the 1764 Carnival

Year 1764	Performance location	Revenues
Opera in Music	Monastery of S. Severino	7.00
//	Monastery of S. Teresa	6.00
//	Monastery of S. Apostoli	7.00
//	House of the Duke of Monteleone	14.40
Opera in Prose of the "little ones"	Monastery of Monteoliveto	9.00
Opera in Music	Monastery of Pietrasanta	7.00
Opera of S. Gaetano	Monastery of Miss Nuns of S.	8.00
Opera of S. Gaetano (2nd time) with	Chiara	
Intermezzo of the "little ones"	Monastery of Miss Nuns of S.	9.47
	Chiara	
3 Works: 2 in Music and 1 of S. Gaetano	House of Duke Coscia	50.00
II Opera of the "little ones" in Prose	Monastery of S. Severino	12.00

Source Journal of Income and Outcome of the Rector in the year 1764 (Rector's Book 1764)

being at the border between the religious genre of the oratorio and musical theater, requires specialist study. A characteristic of sacred dramas was the involvement of the Conservatory students: often in the composition of music (a sort of final exam for the best), but always in the staging and execution.[172]

The number of these musical representations grew considerably in the eighteenth century and constituted one of the artistic expressions with which the city's patron saint or other examples of moral and religious life were honored.[173] These theatrical representations, in addition to constituting one of the productive activities of the Conservatory, mainly advertised the sponsoring institution in the best possible way. We remember some of them. On March 4, 1786, the Prince of Belmonte, Pignatelli, president of the Deputation of shows and theaters, paid a policy of 10.04 ducats for the participation of 16 "little ones" in the opera in music Alceste, represented in the domestic theater of Caserta in the presence of the royal family on the evening of January 12, 1786.[174] Another policy of as much as 50 ducats dates back to February 1, 1787 as compensation for "two months of illumination" on the occasion of the "Real Passeggio di Chiaia" in which the "children" of Pietà had played, alternating with those of S. Onofrio and S. Maria di Loreto.[175] Furthermore, in November 1789, 23 "sons" provided assistance to the choirs of the drama Rinaldo, performed for eleven nights at the Teatro San Carlo. The compensation amounted to 25 grana for each son and for each night. In March of the same season, another 24 students from Pietà returned to San Carlo, again with a compensation of 25 grana each, for the choirs of Catone in Utica.[176]

6 Expenses for Musical Activities

Musical services were not without expenses, however. Among the extraordinary expenses were the rental of candlesticks, damasks, festoons, and other apparatus necessary for the decoration of the church on the occasion of feasts, and often, but not always, for the scenic material necessary for the musical performances staged on special occasions, generally in February, at the end of the theater season. The expense notes for the staging of the works in music and prose performed during the Carnival season of 1763 and 1764 included expenses for stage materials (plants, «Sevo» candles, «Sevo teanelle», wire, nails, tin «micciarelli», chairs, flowers, plates, and then ribbons, pins, cotton, needles, powder, etc.), the "transport and return" of clothes, shoes, clothing accessories, the rental of guns for extras, who were in turn paid, as well as the wages for the working days of carpenters, hairdressers, painters, porters, and so on. For the staging of the Carnival season of 1763, the Conservatory spent 55.06 ducats to obtain an income of only 32.40 ducats; the following year, it totaled an expense of 176.62 for an income of 129.87 ducats. Although exceeding the revenues, the expenses for the staging did not create significant deficits in the budget of musical activities, especially considering that the expense notes reported a number of performances higher than that indicated in the revenue items. This suggests that some performances were carried out without any compensation for the purpose of making known, and therefore "publicizing," the operatic activities of the Conservatory.

The ordinary or daily expenses, consisting of wax, oil, laundry, and adjustments to clothing and shoes, as well as those for food, had a significant impact on the Institute's budgets. The salaries paid to some "provisioned" employees also constituted recurring items of expenditure. In particular, the payments made by the rector concerned a "laundress," a "sweeper," a "tailor," a "barber," a "solapianello," a "harpsichordist," a watchmaker, a "coppersmith," a gatekeeper, and a "trombonist." The last three received their salary every six months (in June and December), all the others, except the watchmaker, were paid monthly. In the period 1761–1790, the expenses for the provisioned employees made by the rector amounted, on average, to two. 130 per year. Table 11 summarizes some salary levels of the staff serving the Conservatory in those years.

The barber's payment is recorded sporadically. The salary indicated is the one paid monthly in the year 1790. Other times, the barber receives the salary directly from the rational-secretary.

The violinist is recorded in the years 1772–1790, under the name Gagliano. His role, as well as that of the trombonist, is not very clear. They are certainly not masters, but while in the case of the harpsichordist, there may be a connection with the religious service of daily assistance to the celebration of Mass, and in the case of the trombonist, a reference to the hours of silence or study during the day, the presence of the violinist is not easily justifiable. He was probably used to accompany the children in their music studies as well as for tuning the instruments.

The clockmaker is also not always present. The payment indicated is the one made in February 1761 to complete a year.

In 1804, the rector paid, in addition to the already listed salaried employees, a cook and an assistant cook, respectively with two. 1.5 and two. 1.3 per month. The "monthly payment" of the tailor had risen to two. 1.5, while that of the porter remained unchanged, however, assisted by an underporter with 1 ducat per month. There is still a record of the

Table 11
Conservatory of Pietà dei Turchini. Monthly salaries in the years 1761–1790, in ducats

Provisioned	Salaries
Laundress	5.00
Chimney sweep	1.00
Tailor	0.90
Window cleaner	0.50
Harpsichordist	0.25
Barber	1.30
Doorman	0.25
Branch worker	0.375
Trombonist	0.216
Violinist	0.625
Clockmaker	0.166

Note The variations that salaries underwent over the years were not of great significance

Sources Rector's Income and Expenditure Journals in the years 1761–1790 (Rector's Books 1761–1790)

monthly payment of two nurses at two. 0.20 per month each and, a new figure among the provisioned, the "keeper of the papers," who received a monthly salary of two. 0.30. The papers were probably those of music that the expenses for "Musical instruments" calculate as papers to be copied, for which a copyist was employed, paid on a "piecework" basis, that is, based on the number of papers copied and the type of music (instrumental parts, masses, motets, Te deum, madrigals, etc.). In 1755, the copy of 19 sheets of music paper of different writings was paid to Matteo Alteriis, copyist, with two. 3.77 (13 grains per sheet). In August 1764, the music papers used for the copy of the "new Mass for the Virginity of St. Irene" cost two. 12. In the same year, five concert books entitled "of St. Martin," by the violin master, with the necessary papers and the copy of the parts, "for the use of the Conservatory sons" cost two. 2.95. In April 1770, the "copying" and the papers for 168 sheets of music were entrusted to the son Aversano "with the understanding" of Salzani and master Tarantini, who would have had to copy a Miserere, Responsorij, Improperi^ Passio, Holy Land Lessons, Magnificat, Credi, and Motets. The whole cost 84 ducats.[177]

The expenses under the title of "Musical instruments" included, in addition to the purchase of reeds for oboe or other wind instruments (these being the most recurring expenses), bows for violins and cellos, or the instruments themselves, the repair and tuning of instruments owned by the Conservatory or its masters. It is not possible to trace back to the first purchases of musical instruments, and we do not know when and which instruments the Conservatory was equipped with. Certainly, the Church had a harpsichord or an organ, the only musical instrument allowed to be used during religious functions.[178] The alternative was a cappella music, that is, without musical accompaniment. On the other hand, the figure of the harpsichordist is present from the origins of the Institute, so to exercise his functions, he almost certainly had to have the instrument inside the Conservatory or the Church (Table 12).

Among the salaries paid by the monthly budget, those for the rector, vice rector, sacristan, an under-sacristan, an actuary, the notary, the royal engineer, the rational-secretary, a litigation attorney, a surgeon, a confessor, two physicians for the "children," and all the teaching staff, musical and non-musical, of the School. It is evident that the professional level of these employees was higher than that of the manual labor staff paid by the rector, confirming a hierarchy of roles within the Institute based on a criterion of social superiority of these "professionals."

Table 12   Conservatory of Pietà dei Turchini. Annual salaries of administrative and teaching staff in 1752, in ducats

Personnel serving the institution in 1752	Salaries
Notary Giovanni Tufarelli	10.0
Royal Engineer D. Biase De Lellis	6.0
Actuary appointed by the Delegation of Cons. Salvatore Arnese	8.0
Litigation attorney D. Giov. De Franciscis	24.0
Physician (children's doctor) R.do D. Valentino Mazzoni	12.0
Physician (children's doctor) D. Giov. Batt.a Balbi	12.0
Surgeon D. Francesco Riccio	9.0
Accountant and Secretary R.do D. A. Mammana	96.0
Rector Don Giuseppe Aveta	30.0
ViceRector R.do D. Teodoro Tirinato	24.0
Sacristan Franco Ferrara	18.0
Assistant Sacristan D. Giuseppe Perciante	14.4
Confessor Don Nicola Russo	30.0
Confessor D. Diodato D'Andria	30.0
Confessor Don G. Aveta	30.0
Schoolmaster Rev. D. Nicolò Grotti	21.6
I Chapel Master Lorenzo Fago	96.0
II Chapel Master Gio. Gualberto Brunetti	60.0
Violin Master Orazio Gravina	48.0
Retired Violin Master Nicola Natale	24.0
Oboe, flute, and transverse Master Ferdianndo Lisio	30.0
Trumpet and hunting horn Master Gennaro Piano	30.0

Notes Some of the masters paid by the Conservatory have been identified: L. Fago (Naples, 1704–1793), organist and composer, was chapel master from 1731 at the Treasury of San Gennaro, where he succeeded his father; from 1737 to 1793 he taught at the Conservatory and in 1744 succeeded L. Leo as the first master; Giovan Gualberto Brunetti (Pistoia, 1706–Pisa, 1787) studied first in Pistoia, then at the Pietà dei Turchini (1728) with the intention of cultivating the violin, but was forced to become a singer. Later he became chapel master of the Duke of Monte Nero, in Sicily, then he was in Genoa as a teacher at the oratory of the Filippini fathers, and from 1744 he was chapel master at the Turchini for ten years (DEUMM, cit., vol. I, p. 734); Gennaro Piano could be identified with Germano Piano [Piana, Piani] (Naples, 1709–1781), one of the brothers of an entire family of Neapolitan musicians, but originally from Bologna. All the brothers seem to have studied at the Pietà dei Turchini; Germano is the only hunting horn player. He played in the orchestras of the Teatro S. Bartolomeo, S. Carlo, as well as the Royal Chapel. He taught at the Pietà dei Turchini for forty-four years (DEUMM, cit., vol. V, p. 702). No useful information is available for the identification of the other masters listed

Sources Monthly Income and Expense Journals in the year 1752 (Monthly Budgets 1752)

Comparing the salary levels of the Conservatory staff with other salaries of the time, the salaries paid by the Pietà dei Turchini appear very low.[179] Probably many of the services were occasional and not continuous, but the modesty of the salaries was compensated by gratifications of another kind that often guaranteed not negligible integrations of the basic salary. Doctors and surgeons, for example, were used to receiving gifts "in kind" (poultry or veal meat); music teachers often taught in several conservatories and each of their performances on the occasion of festivals or ceremonies was paid with fees established from time to time. The administrative staff coincided for a long time with the religious staff and enjoyed, in addition to the salary, board and lodging in the Conservatory. The benefit of living in the same Conservatory or in its properties was invaluable and often reserved also for external masters. The continuous integration of funds for litigation expenses constituted a significant source of additional income for the lawyers employed for the management of matters related to the conservatory's assets. The rationale and the first maestro di cappella received the highest remunerations, given the importance of their functions, one in the administrative sector, the other in the formative-productive sector. Not to mention the annual salary received by the cook, sporadically paid by the Mensario, who, in 1752, collected as much as 138 ducats for his one-year provision, almost to underline the importance of the person who was responsible for the first form of "survival" within the community: food. It is worth noting the presence of two doctors for the "children" and three confessors. Among the latter, there was often the one who also held the role of rector, for which he received another salary. Other payments, more occasional because they were linked to supplies and various services—such as the "puzzaro" who provided water to the Conservatory and one who provided it to all the "formals" of the houses he owned—offer a broad and complex picture of the outgoing notes. Lawyers, notaries, collectors, but also shopkeepers, small artisans, domestic workers, and above all musicians, all figures "at the service of the house," remunerated more or less through modalities dictated by archaic "patronage" schemes, rather than by a more current relationship of commission and performance, draw a dense web that, branching out from the Conservatory, connected to the local settlement system.[180] A system in which, at the beginning of the eighteenth century, in Naples, as in other European cities, the long process of settlement of aristocratic families was consolidated, opposed by a very weak productive structure, constrained by the rigid rules of the artisanal corporate system or dispersed in the immense circuit of retail distribution and small shops: a productive apparatus made up of a host of craftsmen, freelancers, and laborers. However, if the image of eighteenth-century Naples is that suggested by Luigi De Rosa, that is, of a city of consumption that felt "the stagnant atmosphere of an overcrowded city with scarce resources and initiatives",[181] it is also true that it was precisely from that elite of property owners and nobles who crowded the capital that a musical patronage was born, linked to questionable and often superstitious religious principles, but which, however, had outlined a new physiognomy of work. By inserting musicians into the city's professional groups, partly giving up the ancient and noble superiority of musical practice to the lower classes, the "sterile class" of Naples, strongly influenced by the post-Tridentine climate, generated a sort of commodification of music and musicians. Neapolitan nobles hired musicians as "house musicians," singing and musical instrument teachers, or as performers of music on special occasions. This practice was carried out from 1500 to 1800 with more or less similar modalities, which then modified nineteenth-century musical consumption and production, contributing to the cultural definition of the "salon." Thus, the high levels of production of the Conservatory, the Neapolitan musical industry, met the demand for musical services that the "aristocratic" city market posed to it. The staff at the service of the Conservatory grew especially during the eighteenth century when the accounting sector, but even more so, that of those responsible for the discipline and education of the "children" absorbed a large part of the new "provisioned" staff.

In the payments, the items related to music teachers, in addition to those of the more generic "schoolmaster," appear with increasing frequency. Among the violin, trumpet, horn, wind, and cappella teachers, we find the names of Antonio Pagliarulo, Gennaro Piano, Francesco Papa, and the more resounding ones, Leonardo Leo, Nicola Sala, Giacomo Tritto.[182] Their salaries confirm the "musical" hierarchy, already identified, in which we find the Maestro di cappella in the first place with a salary equal to duc. 96, followed by the Violin Master with two. 36, the wind master with two. 14.05.[183]

In addition to these, there are retired teachers who continue to receive a salary as a pension. In 1752, Nicola Natale, a retired violin teacher, was paid 24 ducats annually, equal to half the amount received by the current violin teacher.

While, therefore, the expenses borne by the rector were mainly related to the ordinary management of the house, those of the rational-secretary, or rather the mensario, were mostly expenses for construction, procurement, wages for personnel—we could define it as "contractual," to distinguish it from the "fixed" staff paid by the rector-, and, again, expenses for the celebration of masses including what was needed for the function (wine, oil, wax, funeral apparatus, clerics, jus sagrestiae etc.). The cost of a mass, over the two centuries, was 2 carlini, but the total number of celebrations charged to the Conservatory, which in the seventeenth century exceeded 2,000 annual masses, varied considerably due to the three "reductions" that the governors were forced to ask the Congregation of Cardinals between 1652 and 1657, due to the "deterioration" of some legacies' income. In fact, they had become inadequate for the "weights" of masses they were accompanied by, due to the decrease in the interest rate on some leases. During the eighteenth century, the so-called "worship" expenses underwent other significant changes, recording decreases in difficult years for public income, such as 1753 and 1754, and in the years between 1765 and 1768, to stabilize, immediately after, at around 1000 ducats per year for mass expenses alone. The number of masses celebrated in a year was almost halved compared to the previous century. Worship expenses were distributed between expenses for the celebration of suffrage masses and those for the "church and sacristy," sometimes also related to renovation or embellishment works of the Church, in addition to the necessary ritual for the celebration of religious services (Tables 13 and 14).

A separate discussion is needed for the construction expenses, which refer to the maintenance of the church and the adjoining oratory or to the good preservation and increase of the stable assets. From the accounts examined, the "repairs," both to the building and to the furnishings of the Conservatory, were quite frequent. The expenditure for construction works and repairs in the years 1754, 1761, and 1762 was significant, amounting to two. 2,531.28, two. 2,539.03, and two. 1,115.18. These are very high figures, which are far removed from those recorded in the other years shown in Table 15.

Among the most recurring items, we find roof and pavement repairs due to continuous rainwater infiltrations, but above all carpentry work for doors, cabinets, stalls, and other furniture. The intervention of the blacksmith for the repair of locks, gates, and external fixtures was equally frequent. More sporadic are the items related to masonry work for the

Table 13
Conservatory of Pietà dei Turchini. Expenses for the "provisionati" under the responsibility of the Mensario in the years 1753–1779, in ducats

Year	Expenses for provisional
1753	684.82
1754	721.93
1755	586.10
1761	901.33
1762	861.98
1763	873.76
1764	881.84
1765	810.68
1766	854.62
1767	775.82
1768	80,622
1769	863.60
1771	847.10
1772	1,009.40
1774	910.85
1775	813.90
1776	856.98
1777	608.30
1778	870.06
1779	840.09

Notes For the missing years, no documents have been received
Sources Journals of Income and Expenditure of the Monthly in the years 1753–1779 (Monthly Budgets 1753–1779)

construction of houses or expansions, such as the one, for example, related to the construction of a room for the Eunuchs, so that their dormitory would be far from that of the "half-children." Expressing a judgment on the administration of the Conservatory is certainly not easy, partly due to gaps in the archival documentation and partly due to the scarcity of specific studies that can provide a background for the interpretation of the data, even in relation to the varying purchasing power of money from the end of the sixteenth century to the entire eighteenth century. The period was marked, on the other hand, by moments of important transformations in the social, political, and religious fields (affirmation of the Counter-Reformation, pressing Spanish fiscalism, creation of an autonomous kingdom in 1734, Concordat of 1741, earthquake and plague that decimated the Neapolitan population). However, overall, the management of the Conservatory appears incisive, apparently correct, and mostly oriented toward necessary expenses rather than superfluous ones.

Table 14
Conservatory of the
Pietà dei Turchini.
"Worship expenses" in
the years 1753–1779, in
ducats

Year	Masses	Church and sacristy
1753	869.18	387.85
1754	960.18	174.77
1755	1,876.38	263.24
1761	1,084.28	240.52
1762	1,088.18	324.25
1763	1,067.23	241.80
1764	1,008.55	208.62
1765	788.07	181.11
1766	950.79	249.17
1767	987.60	207.43
1768	961.58	202.54
1769	1,183.58	200.44
1771	1,121.12	208.87
1772	1,042.31	172.92
1774	1,072.53	218.35
1775	1,041.87	305.04
1776	1,198.26	344.48
1777	2,013.15	465.12
1778	1,091.17	208.16
1779	1,187.77	238.29

Sources A.P.T., Giornali di Introito ed Esito del Mensario negli anni 1753–1779 (Monthly Budgets 1753–1779)

The Conservatory of Pietà dei Turchini, at the end of the eighteenth century, sought to reorganize its internal life and its relationships with the outside world on better-defined models, specifying the boundaries of its possible users and the tools to contain the risks associated with the decline of its fame. The intentions corresponded to the results: the transfer to the Royal College of San Sebastiano, the Supplication to the King for the safeguarding of musical education in Naples, and its transformation from an orphanage into a School of Music.

In the meantime, in 1751, Charles III of Bourbon established the largest Hospice in southern Italy, intended for males and females, adults and children, which was the Royal Albergo dei Poveri.[184] The first evidence of its music school, created mainly to provide instrumentalists for the numerous military bands, dates back to 1792. The teaching of wind instruments was privileged, but string instruments, spinet, and harpsichord were also taught, and even a dance school was established, whose dancers were often employed in the choreographies of the San Carlo

Table 15
Conservatorio della
Pietà dei Turchini.
"Construction expenses
and repairs" in the years
1753–1779, in ducats

Year	Construction expenses and repairs
1753	866.37
1754	2,531.28
1755	909.61
1761	2,539.03
1762	1,115.18
1763	370.75
1764	5,822
1765	117.47
1766	156.87
1767	91.59
1768	94.60
1769	54.15
1771	227.49
1772	435.46
1774	325.17
1775	144.42
1776	312.09
1777	156.56
1778	505.39
1779	411.64

Sources Introito and Esito Journals of the Mensario in the years 1753–1779 (Monthly Budgets, 1753–1779)

Theater. Here too, music constituted an important source of income, as well as for other charitable institutions of the Kingdom, almost all male: in Salerno, the Provincial Orphanage,[185] in Aversa, the Hospice of San Lorenzo,[186] in Reggio Calabria, the Royal Provincial Orphanage and, in Giovinazzo, the Royal Apulian Hospice.[187] Between 1815 and 1816, some decrees established the expansion of the staff of the infantry regiment bands. The teaching of music thus became functional to another phenomenon that also characterized certain male institutions: the militarization of childhood, also considered a valid instrument of social control.[188]

Meanwhile, in 1804, Marcello Perrino had drawn up the "Plan for a General Institute of Music for the Kingdom of Naples," and, alongside the establishment of a single college for men, had also planned a "facility for Women [...]. These, educated with the strictest discipline, could learn to play the harpsichord, to sing, and even counterpoint." The Plan was taken up and implemented in 1806 by Joseph Bonaparte who, by prohibiting the admission of eunuchs to the Conservatory of Music, established the Female College of the Holy Spirit, providing teachings in singing, harpsichord, harp, dance, and acting.[189]

From a system of musical education, in fact managed by private individuals, strongly influenced first by the Church and then by entrepreneurial theaters, increasingly massified and gradually regulated in a system of public musical education, we thus arrived, during the French period, at the establishment of the Royal Colleges of Music, later State Conservatories of Music.

7   Life as Conservatory Students: The Sons of Pietà dei Turchini in the Second Half of the Eighteenth Century Between Study Paths and Professional Opportunities

The studies focused on the issues of musical education in Naples and committed to evaluating the evolution of the professional training of musicians, although having provided general interpretative lines, now well established, have not yet completely dissolved the shadowy areas that remain on the functioning of the four Neapolitan musical institutes, on their primitive welfare models, and especially on the crucial phase of transition from private charity to public music school.[190]

The material history of the four conservatories[191] is closely linked to that of assistance and charity institutions and, as we have suggested in the past,[192] especially in relation to their legal nature and social functions, it can reveal the complexity of a story that played a significant part in the genesis and formation of the modern welfare state. The existence of the only Italian case of transformation of the four Neapolitan conservatories, from charity institutions for poor and abandoned children to professional training institutes for musicians, is therefore of considerable interest. This transformation was based on a process governed by economic principles and was crucial for the advent of a music market often managed, in turn, by "families of musicians."

Among cultural activities, music appears as a dominant component both in the practice of the so-called "living arts" and in the individual and collective imagination that underlies the production and consumption of every artistic form. The essential and emblematic nature of music and its properties as a public good have strong implications from an economic standpoint and allow its characteristics and manifestations to be used as representative phenomena of the more general relationship between economy, society, and artistic expression. Therefore, such phenomena and their possible connections with markets and economic policy should not be overlooked. The welfare reality in which the Conservatory is embedded presents itself as a microeconomy of exchange. It was enough to analyze its system of economic interrelations with society, starting from the analysis of the costs and returns of charity, to represent the pious work as a company. In the exercise of charity, in fact, explicit economic reasons converge with more elusive, but no less decisive, motivations of social convenience, immediate individual interests, and more complicated collective advantages. A new type of industry, the music industry, emerges, and its productivity plays a significant role, especially from the mid-seventeenth century when the conservatory gradually transforms—without precise statutory indications—from an orphanage into a music school.

The history of the ancient Neapolitan music schools necessarily passes through the history of institutional purposes, organization, administration, and prestigious collaborations from which those singular "workshops" benefited. To the news concerning the masters, often famous musicians, it seemed appropriate to add information about the living conditions of the "sons," the timing and characteristics of the musical offer, extraordinary events and performances, the income and expenses incurred by theatrical representations, and the variety of instrumental teachings imparted. All this information can be deduced from documentation that is essentially of an accounting nature, often fragmented and indirect, but extremely varied and full of surprises.[193]

If the Conservatories owed their life throughout the seventeenth century to an educational program aimed at instruction and learning a trade, according to the principles of *renfermement*,[194] the orientation toward musical education, the multiplication of theaters and theatrical opportunities, the growth in the number of workers in the production of shows, and the increasing frequency of their travels outside the kingdom to sell texts and the image of what was beginning to be called the *Neapolitan school*, were the components of a cultural trend in significant growth during the first decades of the eighteenth century.

During the previous century, musical "occasions" of an essentially religious nature had intensified, and the "music services" of the children had responded to an ever-growing demand.[195] With the consolidation of its educational structure, the Conservatory was soon able to produce "specialized labor" (singers, instrumentalists, composers, chapel masters) now mainly demanded by Neapolitan theaters.

The Statute of the Conservatorio della Pietà dei Turchini established that, on the first Sunday of each month, the deputies would communicate to the Governors how many and which children in need of help should be admitted to the Conservatory.[196] On the same day, the teachers to whom the children would be entrusted were summoned—to "govern, punish, and teach them"—by selecting those who showed aptitude for the study of letters and therefore music (studying sons) and those who, on the other hand, appeared more suitable for learning a trade or craft or simply for the ordinary services of the House (*steward, wardrobe keeper, sacristan, etc.*).[197]

The educational orientation adopted by the school in the eighteenth century seemed to be mainly aimed at training instrumentalists, mostly violinists.[198] There were also students of wind instruments, especially toward the end of the century, when the personnel of the line regiments' bands began to increase.[199] From 1791 to 1806, out of 193 boarders, 19 undoubtedly embarked on a musical profession, some in the Band of the Terra di Lavoro Regiment, some at the Teatro Nuovo, and some remaining in the same Conservatory.

There is never any reference to a maximum number of sons to be accommodated, and the admission procedures varied over time in relation to external requests and the internal needs of the institution itself (for example, there is occasionally a need for "musicians" with bass voices or horn players, etc.).[200]

The information found, not always in complete form—name, geographical origin, age, period of stay, "plegio"[201] or recommender, mode of entry and exit, and sometimes even the type of musical studies, sheds light on the dynamics of Neapolitan poverty, suggests the typology of artisans of the time, and defines the protagonists of that particular and flourishing system of musical supply and demand in Naples in the eighteenth century. Among the guarantors of the students, we find not only numerous city artisans but also some "music artisans" such as Gaetano Albano, trombone master, who guaranteed for student Gaetano Costa admitted to the study of "winds, strings, or singing"; or Nicola Mancini, organ master, who guaranteed for Ferdinando Murganza and Giuseppe Domenicucci. There is also the case of Filippo Corelli, son of the Conservatory's trumpet master, Onofrio Corelli, who was examined and admitted in 1781.[202]

The registers of the four Neapolitan conservatories increasingly fill up with sons from the middle and lower classes: more and more immigrants with musical ambitions enroll, many of whom reach prestigious positions.[203] The "Rolls of the sons," lists of boarders and loose documents related to admission instruments, insubordination practices, permits, or even the legal documentation necessary for registration in the Conservatory, such as birth certificates, residence, baptismal faiths, certificates of good conduct, inform us about the presence of a significant number of students. Demographic information, related to the number of sons admitted to the institute, is however rather fragmentary and concerns only a few years. The absence of clear guidelines on who could have access to the Conservatory is evident in the definition of the channels through which admission to the institute was realized. The procedures that formalized entry into the Conservatory, for the entire second half of the eighteenth century, were essentially based on an informal system of "recommendation," which branched out from the Court to the rector, and even to the governors themselves. Throughout the second half of the eighteenth century, in particular, admission and permanence in the Conservatory were subject to the payment possibilities of the child, who only in special cases could benefit from the condition of "non paying student", that is, exempted from the payment of the tuition fee.[204]

Students and boarders were both guests of the college and, upon admission, committed to "serving" the Conservatory for the entire duration of their stay (sometimes even beyond), guaranteeing the institution a musical and economic "production" of vital importance. The former entered at the age of 18 or 20 and already had a musical education, while the latter entered at the age of about eight and followed a more regular course of study, when they managed to complete it by "resisting" for the period provided by the admission instrument, which varied between 5 and 12 years. The length of stay depended a lot on the sons' age at the time of admission, the type of musical studies they would undertake (violin, singing, choral direction, or other), their financial possibilities, and payment methods.[205] It was rare for the stay in the Conservatory to be uninterrupted, and the obligation to stay established in the admission act was not always respected. Escape, however, remained a widespread aspiration, especially among the youngest. The intolerance of the Rules was strong also because the "closure" in the Conservatory had not been a free choice for most of the boarders.

In case of a child's escape from the institute, teachers and governors should have looked for him and then punished him, forbidding him, for a certain period, to leave the Conservatory, and implementing any expedient suitable for the recovery of his good conduct.[206] The severity with which the fugitives or those sons who rebelled against the order and the rigid and inescapable respect of the rules were punished is striking, but in most cases, the social background of those boys was not the highest, and their "education" obeyed more to the laws of the street than to the ethical-religious ones of the family and the Church. Moreover, the conservatory, as a "public" structure supported by private charity, demanded from its guests "good manners" to be exhibited in society, a sort of external presentability that satisfied the prejudices and expectations of the benefactors, before even the needs of the "beneficiaries." In fact, once a week, a quarter of an hour was dedicated to the lesson of "duties of a good citizen with those of a good Christian." Furthermore, once a month, the Rules of the Conservatory were read to the children, "so that they would not be forgotten".[207] The uniform provided to the children had to always be in perfect order, even in its absolute simplicity, especially during the "musical outings." It consisted of a "torchina skirt and robe" without "silk displays or buttons" and was provided by the house at the time of entry into the conservatory. In winter, the "cotta" was added, which was returned to the wardrobe upon returning from outings. The shoes, all identical, could not be "French style" or with a "wooden heel," but had to conform to the "style" given to them by the master shoemaker, one of the "provisioned" of the house.[208]

Devotion, good behavior, avoidance of idleness, modesty, silence, obedience, and commitment were the basic requirements for staying in the conservatory, as highlighted in the Statutes. Religious duties, applicable to all, involved serving daily Mass, observing the office, and frequent confession. Extraordinary confessions were scheduled three times a year—Christmas, Easter, and before the patronal feast—but became indispensable in cases of insubordination, as mentioned above, when confession was understood as punishment and an irreplaceable remedy for reconciliation and good education.

The sons had the duty to serve the Oratory of the Bianchi, which was located inside the Conservatory, assisting for free in the celebration of masses, processions, and other necessary tasks for the confreres. They

were supervised by the rector, assisted by the vice rector, the commissioned fathers, the grammar teachers, the instrument teachers, and the
music teachers. They were divided into brigades, each entrusted to a
brigade leader and a chapel master. The rules to be respected were
numerous and very strict, concerning the conduct to be maintained
inside and outside the conservatory, in the church, during lessons, and
at meals. In particular, it was the rector's task to teach the children
good manners, engaging each of them, according to their abilities, in the
study of grammar, vocal or instrumental music.[209] From time to time,
the sons were allowed to visit their relatives. They were accompanied
by a commissioned father who should never have left the child alone,
but many decided not to return to the institute. The sons should never
have gone around the city alone, but always with their companions. In
particular, on holidays and on Carnival Thursdays, they could not go out
except for "funeral" or "musical" commitments. Overnight stays outside
the Conservatory were rarely allowed by the governors, and permission
to eat outside the Conservatory could only be granted by the monthly
governor. The rector had to manage the outings for "musicals" and could
not send "paranzas of sons"[210] to make music outside Naples, in places
where it was necessary to spend the night or in private homes. He could
not even allow the conservatory children to make music together with
"foreign" musicians: only the governors could authorize their employment on such special occasions. Furthermore, it was not allowed for the
Conservatory teachers to give lessons to students outside the House.

Every week, the rector identified the sons who had to serve in
the Church, established the schedule of grammar, music, and all other
"devotion," study, or service exercises at the Conservatory.

In a meeting of the governors on July 23, 1785, the criteria for
assigning sick children to the infirmary were established. Until then, the
duration of the "hospitalization" varied between ten and twenty days
assigned by the doctor from the first day of illness. Subsequently, the
prohibition of prescribing a long period of illness was followed by the
obligation to indicate, every two or three days, the state of the child's
illness. If, after a medical examination, the period was prolonged, there
followed the prohibition of administering coffee, sorbets, milk, and other
things to the sick, except in cases of actual need: milk in extreme cases,
sorbet in high fevers, etc. Day by day, the names of the sick sons had
to be recorded, especially those who did not eat so that the cook could
subtract them from the count of "mouths." The doctor also had the task

of recording all the medicines not included in the pharmacist's note, distinguishing them carefully and annotating them next to the son's name.[211]

A son admitted to the Conservatory could not receive the robe unless he had first stipulated the *instromento*, which had to specify the length of stay, and unless he had paid 12 ducats for the "entrance fee." In addition to the robe, he was also given a bed complete with mattress and blanket. Those who were poor and unable to pay the "entrance fee" would give up the bed or blanket, which they sometimes brought with them. The children were housed in dormitories divided into the dormitory of the little ones (25 beds), the dormitory of the eunuchs[212] (13 beds), the dormitory of the middle ones (21 beds), and the dormitory of the big ones (31 beds).[213]

Their day began at dawn, at the sound of the bell of one of the prefects. The prefect or committed father of each dormitory intoned the *Psalm Laudate Pueri Dominum* and, while the sons put on their dresses, they recited the *Miserere mei Deus*. After washing and preparing, they went in pairs to the oratory and, taking their places, devoted 15 minutes to "mental prayer," another 15 minutes to prayers and litanies, and finally participated in the daily mass. After fulfilling their devotional duties, each took their books and went to the school of letters. Here too, the lesson began with a prayer, the oration *Veni Creator Spiritus*. The "school exercises" lasted two hours, marked by the teacher's hourglass.[214] At the end, the prefects waited for their sons at the door to lead each of them to their own singing or playing classroom, where the music teachers would assign them the part to study first individually and then "to make the concert of all the musicians, both of voice and instruments." The music lesson was followed by the recitation of the third part of the rosary and immediately after the meal, during which someone would read a spiritual lesson or a *Life of the Saints*. Lunch was followed by half an hour of recreation and immediately after the silence was sounded, the interruption of which was punished as a "serious crime." In the afternoon, they attended the school of letters and the music lesson held by the chapel master, often replaced by the mastricelli,[215] then another hour of sacred history and "civic education" and finally the litanies recited in church. The day ended with another moment of freedom before dinner and immediately after with the withdrawal to the dormitories.[216]

The internal life of the Conservatory was animated by numerous other "officials" in accordance with a hierarchical division of tasks, which entrusted the father rector with the "supervision of both the House and the Church." He was responsible for the vice rector, the sacristan, the prefects, the teachers of grammar, music, instruments, the children, the priests, and the master "shoemaker." Periodically, the rector gave an account of the progress of the House and the Church first to the *mensario*[217] and then to the governors "in session." The rector's functions were very important, as he acted as an intermediary between the sons and the entire *staff* of the governors.

The control exercised over the teachers obliged the rector to keep a register in which he recorded their lessons in order to calculate their absences every month. At the end of the month, he presented it to the governors before paying the "monthly fees." In the second part of the eighteenth century, the general impression, regarding salaries and wages, is that there was a situation of stability that, although contrasting with the contemporary increase in prices, was common to those of other city institutions.[218]

The eighteenth century passed for the Pietà dei Turchini without any particular moments of crisis. Even the severe famine of 1764 was faced by the institute's governors with great balance, and the rhythm of musical performances seemed to intensify, as, on the other hand, happened in the entire city, where the proliferation of satires and theatrical performances constituted a sort of popular reaction to hunger and misery. Some problems in the life of the institute were determined by the climate of tensions, arising from the Concordat with Rome of 1741, which also had repercussions in the Conservatory, where accusations of mismanagement and harassment by the religious against the lay governors of the institution became increasingly consistent. In 1762, Counselor Borgia, then delegate of the Conservatory, tried to introduce a new system of election of the governors, but the prior and the brethren of the Congregation of the Whites[219] protested, invoking their rights. In 1768, new rules were drawn up, which established that the election of the governors belonged to the same brethren, without royal consent. The decision sealed the autonomy of the institute and, from that moment on, the history of the Conservatory of Pietà was entrusted, almost exclusively, to the "good" administration of the governors and the Prior of the Congregation of the Whites. Meanwhile, the decline in the value of music influenced the tastes

of the public, which forced composers to modify their style to accommodate the vocal artifices of the "castrati" and theaters drew more heavily
on the conservatories to form their choirs. And, if on the one hand, the
singing performances of the sons were paid for by the theater impresarios,
on the other hand, the frequency with which the Conservatory students
took part in those performances contributed to sowing disorder and lack
of respect for disciplinary rules to the point that, in 1759, the governors were forced to turn to the king. They complained about the laxity
of discipline and good manners that the sons found in the theaters, to
the detriment of the good name and interests of the pious place. Partic-
ipating in the operas staged at the Teatro di San Carlo, for example,
prevented them from respecting one of the most firm rules of the institute, that of not going out at night. Moreover, the preparation for the
choirs organized by the theater impresario prejudiced the availability for
daily exercise marked by the hours of lessons and prayer. In particular,
the sons neglected the evening lessons held by the "mastricelli," "the
most profitable ones." Not to mention the bad friendships struck up in
theatrical environments: singers and dancers, card and dice players, who
led the young conservatory students to the "relaxation of morals".[220]

The Conservatory was even forced to dismiss four highly skilled children, who contributed to its income, due to their lifestyle, which had
become too indecent to be accepted by the local pious morality. The
governors were particularly concerned when they recalled the contracts
for music and paranzas[221] that the institute had with various churches
in the city, where the sons' performances were generally required in the
early hours of the morning. It became impossible to send the sons who
had retired at dawn after singing in theaters, and the institution, to maintain the commitments made with those churches, would have had to hire
external musicians for the occasion. In short, under these conditions, the
interests of the Conservatory were at great risk from the participation
of its students in theatrical works, and the profit from them was not so
significant if, for the service of 27 participations of 54 children for the
Carnival opera of 1758, it had been paid ("after a long suffered dispute")
by the impresario of the San Carlo Theater with only 125 ducats.[222]

For these reasons, the governors of Pietà begged the king to forbid
the impresario of the San Carlo Theater from contacting the children
of the Conservatory. The response to that plea established that for the
performance of November 4, 1759, the children of the Pietà dei Turchini

Conservatory would take part in the choirs, but after that, the impresario would have to contact singers external to the institute.

However, the measure was disregarded, and on January 14, 1763, the governors of Pietà still begged the king to preserve the order and discipline of the music school by avoiding the performances of its students in theaters.[223] But even this intervention by the governors fell on deaf ears. Meanwhile, Neapolitan music was losing its tones, and a few years later, the plan for a *Theatrical Academy for the Profit of Young Conservatorists* was presented to the king, which advanced reform proposals aimed at refocusing the students' attention on beautiful, ancient, and traditional music, as well as requalifying the taste and technique of the students. In that same year, 1770, Charles Burney expressed his doubts about the level of solo singers trained by the conservatories, reporting extensively on the unsatisfactory quality of the *standards* of execution of the students.[224]

The supply of musicians trained in the conservatories had exceeded, since the early years of the 1700s, the local demand. More and more of them had to look for work outside Naples. Gathered in small groups of emigrants, either residing in European cities or circulating between one capital and another, they worked to impose the idea of a "musical" Naples on the attention of the international public.[225]

There are no obvious possible explanations for the undeniable decline. Its symptoms, however, were clear: the number of students who became famous decreased considerably, and criticism of the Conservatories grew. To these internal difficulties were added more serious ones during the 1780s and the first decades of the following century. The scarcity of cash had meanwhile begun to afflict the kingdom due to the flight of capital abroad, due to the favorable exchange rate and the trade balance deficit. Finally, the poor harvests of the years 1792–1795 led the city administration and the state to resort more frequently to interest-free loans from public banks, always granted for the regular supply of annona, compromising their liquidity, already affected by numerous loans to the nobility.[226] The Conservatory, without drastically changing its economic and managerial policies (the budgets seem not to suffer from significant fluctuations in income or expenses), had a desperate need for cash and tried to meet this need by granting the contract for the collection of some of its movable and immovable income.[227]

Nevertheless, during the 1980s, payments for the musical services of the sons increased, but above all, payments for participation in performances in the city's theaters increased.[228] Villeneuve, in the eighteenth century, well described the social and economic advantages for the conservatories of the frequent performances of the students in various parts of the city and elsewhere.[229] These practices were particularly appreciated by the student musicians, as they enlivened their monotonous life as conservatory students and highlighted all their talent and the technique acquired in their studies. They also served the more advanced sons to gain independence and authority. In fact, both the musicians and the administration, despite its protests, benefited from a system that offered great advantages as long as the income from musical activity was sufficient to guarantee the conservatories their autonomy from higher authorities (for example, the Court) whose demands began to push the artistic resources of the institutes beyond their limits.

Since 1791, the Conservatory's balance sheet acquired new revenues and, with them, a more clearly "public" appearance. 1791 was also the year in which the royal delegate Saverio Mattei was given the task of intervening in the management of the Conservatory to improve its conditions both in terms of teaching and economics. Thus began what we might call the "commissioning" phase of the institution[230] in which an attempt was made to establish a new «ordo studiorum» that required sons to engage with plain chant, with the cantatas of Leo, Durante, and Scarlatti, as well as with the best treatises on theory.[231] Therefore, the commissioning entrusted to Mattei resulted in the resumption of teaching of strict contrapuntal forms and the so-called ancient style. Teachings that had never been lacking in the Neapolitan Conservatories, which, however, had always kept up with new trends, favoring the affirmation of the modern style. On the other hand, the four institutes had always been characterized by more pragmatic than doctrinal teaching inclinations and, above all, had had the need, since the beginning of the musical school, to accommodate the tastes and demands that the clientele, indispensable support for their activities, asked of them.

The "musical outings" of the conservatory students continued: their performances, although Neapolitan music began to feel the crisis, were still in high demand. In November 1798, four music professors (two clarinetists, one bassoonist, and one hunting horn player) received the order from the vice-director to accompany four groups of sons to Catanzaro to perform music.[232]

We are now at the end of the eighteenth century, and among the documentation relating to those years, we find the "list of students" of January 1, 1798: there were 65 in total. Among these, in July 1799, there were 17 who left the institute for various reasons: of these, 13 were arrested because they were "state criminals." On the eve of the events of 1799, as can be seen from the situation of the Conservatory's income, the ties with the financial administration of the State had partly consolidated, despite the plurality of sources directly or indirectly attributable to the public sector. We are at the dawn of a new economic structure of charitable institutions, as well as music schools, characterized by a progressive loss of autonomy and dependence on the weak and often insolvent public funding. This process, also detectable in other European realities under Bourbon rule, does not mean that the state assumed responsibility for the assistance of the poor, but rather that it contributed to the management of those institutions, without severing ties with the previous arrangements of private charity. Moreover, the practice of charity among private individuals, in addition to being less exercised than in the past, was burdened by constraints and motivations scarcely attributable to the charitable attitudes of the old aristocratic *élites*. But the fall of the conservatories' economy is mainly linked to the artistic decline felt in the last years of the eighteenth century in Naples: all prices rose and the conservatory administrations found themselves forced to "save" on expenses. It began with the drastic reduction in the number of students. However, it was necessary to safeguard the efficiency of the school and therefore a downsizing of the institutions was carried out, in an attempt to stabilize the financial situation. But the contractions of income from musical performances, together with the scarcity of cash, led to a progressive closure of the four conservatories, which, amid the indifference of the successive sovereigns, saw the "virtual" survival of only one conservatory, that of Pietà dei Turchini.

Those were difficult years that saw the entry of French troops into Naples and the Conservatory, like everyone in the city, was forced to face ever greater difficulties, especially in the exchange of its bank policies, on which the agio, always increasing, weighed.

The cash movements recorded by the Conservatory of Pietà's accountant in the years 1797–1800, show a financial situation decidedly different from previous years. In 1797, the expenses for the "provisioned" amounted, in total, to 893 ducats and provided for the remuneration of an already expanded number of employees: tenant, accountant, rector, vice rector, sacristan, a retired sacristan, an assistant sacristan, a master of ceremonies, three confessors, two chapel masters (Nicola Sala and Giacomo Tritto were still there), two extraordinary chapel masters (don Giovanni Salina and Baldassarre La Barbiera), two violin masters, one cello master, one oboe master, one trumpet master, a surgeon, a doctor, an extraordinary surgeon, an engineer, a master of acts, his assistant, a notary, two "puzzari," the archivist don Giuseppe Sigismondi (with an annual provision of d. 24) and a clarinet master.[233]

Furthermore, from the expenses for shoes, the number of children present in the Conservatory can be deduced. In 1798, 94 pairs of shoes were ordered, while the following year the purchase was 51 pairs.[234] The titles of the Conservatory's annual income between 1797 and 1800 underwent a significant decline that also affected expenses.[235] The last years of the Conservatory's life passed between institutional changes, unfortunately recorded very sporadically, and a review of the state of income. That of 1802 informs us that for the years 1799–1801 the "subscribed income reasoned on the fruit of 1798" was missing. The revenues in that year were d. 8,583.34 against a total of expenses equal to d. 8,704.08. In 1802 it was declared that in the span of those three years, d. 3,695.08 had not been collected, and the overall "arrears" amounted to d. 3,893.90, for which the Conservatory asked the Court for a loan of 1,000 ducats.[236] As if that were not enough, on July 26, 1805, there was a strong earthquake in Naples, and the governors of Pietà, to repair the damage caused by the earthquake, were forced to ask for another thousand ducats in loans, to be repaid in four years with an interest of 8%. The damage had mainly affected the vault of the Church, but also some rooms of the Conservatory.[237]

During the eighteenth century, the logic of private charity transformed, the abrupt accelerations, induced from the outside, in the economic and social fabric made the structure of private charity inadequate. The State intervened, increasingly thinning the consistency of private welfare intervention. Moreover, there was a kind of cultural revolution that changed, among others, the traditional attitudes toward poverty, reducing the resources of charitable institutions. To this was added a greater demand, in the music market, for virtuoso singers, in the face of the abundant supply of instrumentalists produced by the Conservatories, which contributed to the wavering fortunes of the four institutes.

The decree of merger of the three remaining conservatories (the first to close was that of the Poor of Jesus Christ) was signed by the King on November 26, 1806. The transfer of S. Maria di Loreto to Pietà dei Turchini took place at the beginning of the new year. On June 30, 1807, the new institution became, by royal decree, the College of Music[238] and only a year later followed the transfer by the economic director Marcello Perrino to the Monastery of the Ladies of S. Sebastiano, where it seemed to find a definitive arrangement. From that moment, and for at least another fifteen years, the Royal College seemed to be supported by two administrations: that of the new public school and the surviving one of Pietà dei Turchini.[239]

The Royal College of S. Sebastiano thus marked a first step toward the "nationalization" of the Music Conservatory, sealed by the definitive transfer to the Monastery of the Celestine Fathers of S. Pietro a Majella, still today the pride and glory of the Neapolitan music school. The good thing was that all the students gathered at the Turchini and then settled in the Royal College of Music remained in a college for musicians only. The French decade was decisive for the long-awaited "reform" of the state music conservatory and for the establishment of a female music college, probably due to the ban imposed by Joseph Bonaparte on November 27, 1806, to admit other eunuchs to the Music Conservatory.[240]

Thus ended the story of a monumental institution that arose from nothing. Its long life saw the birth of music, musicians, theatrical opera, and marked the social, cultural, and economic development of a city from which a long and complex series of threads have branched out, linking Neapolitan music to distant cities (Tables 16, 17, 18, 19, 20, and 21).

Table 16 Students admitted to the Pietà dei Turchini Conservatory between 1765 and 1794

Figliolo/child	Study classes	Year of admission	Years of stay	Age	Pledge	Origin
AQUILAR Carlo Leopoldo Ranieri	Oboe	1781	8	17	Gaspare Aquilar, padre	Bologna
BENAVENTO Antonio Francesco Geltrudo	—	1796	—	—	—	—
BIANCONCINI Giuseppe	Oboe e violino	1792	8	—	Pascale De Sio, negoziante di canape e funi	Livorno
BUCCELLA Andrea	Fiati, corde o canto	1779	8	—	Felice Pedone Maestro sartore	—
CAPRIOLO Raffaele Gennaro	Fiati, corde o canto	1779	10	15	Francesco Braj Maestro sartore	Napoli
COLSON Natale	Fiati, corde o canto	1767	12	21	Tommaso Piccolo Maestro perucchiero	—
COMPARETTI Gaetano	Fiati, corde o canto	1779	10	—	Luigi Zaurenghi Maestro indoratore	—
CONTI Giuseppe Giovanni Romualdo	Fagotto	1794	7	15	Vincenzo Conti	Napoli
CORELLI Filippo	Fiati, corde o canto	1781	10	14	Onofrio Corelli Prof. di tromba	Napoli
CORNET Alessandro	Fiati, corde o canto	1776	8	—	Nicola Gramigna, calzolaio	—
COSTA Gaetano	Fiati, corde o canto	1779	10	16	Gaetano Albano Maestro trombonaro	—
DEL VECCHIO Michele	Fiati, corde o canto	1779	8	—	D. Luigi Gonzales, orologiaio	Napoli
DI LEONARDI Thomas Francisus	—	1769	—	—	Pasquale Audico	Palermo

(continued)

Table 16 (continued)

Figliolo/child	Study classes	Year of admission	Years of stay	Age	Pledge	Origin
DI LORENZO Alessandro Francesco Saverio	Musico	1765	10	12	Domenico Di Lorenzo Maestro scarparo	Napoli
DOMENICUCCI Giuseppe	Fiati, corde o canto	1792	8	–	Nicola Mancini Maestro organaro	–
FINOCCHIO Alessandro Stefano	Fiati, corde o canto	1782	12	13	Ranieri Bartalini Pr. Caramanica	Pisa
FORCIGNANO Giuseppe Maria Quintino	Tenore	1769	10	20	Gennaro Pompilio, negoziante	Gallipoli
GARGANO Joseph Maria Raphael	–	1794	–	10	–	–
GUIDA Gaetano	Canto	1779	10	–	Giovanni Sportello Maestro frangiaro	–
LAUDANNA Michelangelo Costanzo	Fiati, corde o canto	1768	8	20	Bartolomeo Renzi Maestro sartore	Frasso (BN?)
LIBERATO Michele Carlo alias Bologna	Fiati, corde o canto	1779	12	–	Gaetano Zuccaio Maestro vetraro e Biase Bologna, patrigno	–
LICIO Arcangelo	Musico	1766	6	18	Ferdinando Licio Prof. Di oboe	Napoli
LISIO Giuseppe Maria Salvatore	Oboe	1779	10	13	Giuseppe Parlati officiale Banco di S. Giacomo	Napoli
MARGARITA Ferdinandus Francis	tromba	1781	10	–	Nicola Mancino Maestro organaro	Sovivo

Figliolo/child	Study classes	Year of admission	Years of stay	Age	Pledge	Origin
MARZANO Eliseo	Fiati, corde o canto	1781	–	16	Antonio Manfredi Maetrso Calzolaio	Castel di Sangro
MORRONE Gaetano Luigi Crispino	Violino	1791	10	12	Antonio Sapio Capo Mastro Fabricatore	Napoli
MURGANZA Ferdinando	Fiati, corde o canto	1781	10	–	Nicola Mancini Maestro organaro	–
PIAZZA Pascale	Musico	1766	5	20	Pascale Mennillo Maestro Carrozziero	–
PITTALUCA Giuseppe Tommaso Francesco	Fiati, corde o canto	1781	12	21	Emanuele Conversano negoziante di porcellane e vini stranieri	Napoli
RAIMONDI don Filippo, sacerdote	Canto da tenore	1791	3	–	D. Raffaele Raimondi, padre, notaro	Bitonto
RONGHI Augustinus Maria, sacerdote	–	1791	–	19	Agostino Connio, negoziante in Compagnia di Vallin e Wolsinglon	Genova
SANSONE Santi	Fiati, corde o canto	1768	5	23	Saverio D'Amico Maestro cordaro	–
SCOLART Giovanni Domenico	Fiati, corde o canto	1791	12	13	Vincenzo Muccardi Maestro falegname	Napoli
SERUGHI Giuseppe	Musico	1766	8	18	Giovanni Cristiani Maestro sartore	Tropea

(continued)

Table 16 (continued)

Figliolo/child	Study classes	Year of admission	Years of stay	Age	Pledge	Origin
TILLE Giuseppe	Fiati, corde o canto	1779	10	15	Domenico Monelli Maestro. sartore	Parigi
VEREREI Pietro Luca Benedetto	Musico	1766	10	15	Carmine Milone	Napoli

Note The dash indicates that the data is not known
Source A.P.T., Section Students and Boarders

Table 17 Children admitted to the Conservatory of Pietà dei Turchini between 1745 and 1762

Year of admission	Name	Years of stay	Qualification in musical studies
1758	ACCRESCA Agostino	10	Soprano
1752	AMICONE Antonio	8	Maestro di cappella
1755	ANTONINO Sabbato	10	Fagotto
1761	ARSIDI Pietro	8	Oboe
1758	ATTENA Giovanni	10	Violino
1761	AUGENTI Damiano	10	Soprano
1759	AULETTA Ferdinando	10	Tenore
1754	BELLI don Sabbato	10	Contralto
1761	BLASCO Giovanni	10	Non stabilito
1760	BLASCO Pietro	10	Violino
1760	BRUNO Giovanni	10	Soprano
1758	CALDAROLA Niccolò	10	Tenore
1759	CALENZA Luigi	10	Tromba
1758	CARPUTI Giuseppe	10	Violino
1761	CARRATURA Giovanni Antonio	8	Violino
1758	CASTELLANO Giuseppe	10	Maestro di cappella
1761	CAUOLO Pasquale	7	Contralto
1758	COLLURA Giuseppe	10	Tromba
1761	COMITAS Gregorio	10	Violino
1753	COPPOLA Niccolò	10	Soprano
1757	COSCUI Uomobuono	10	Contralto
1756	CUCCI Carlo	10	Violino
1754	CURCI Antonio	10	Tromba
1759	CURCI Leonardo	10	Soprano
1755	D'ANTONIO Niccolò	10	Contralto
1761	D'ELIA Giovanni	9	Violino
1758	D'ORZI Tommaso	10	Oboe
1761	DAVID Antonio	8	Maestro di cappella
1758	DE DOMENICO Emanuele	10	Oboe
1761	DI FALCO Giuseppe	8	Violino
1757	DI ZANNI Giovanni	10	Violoncello

(continued)

Table 17   (continued)

Year of admission	Name	Years of stay	Qualification in musical studies
1759	ELFER Niccolò	10	Violino
1762	EXTRAFALLACE Gaetano	6	Oboe
1762	FAVALE Francesco	6	Basso
1761	FERRETTI Cesare	5	Maestro cappella
1757	FIERI Giuseppe	10	Violino
1752	FINI Saverio	10	Contralto
1759	GABRIELLI Antonio	8	Tenore
1762	GALLO Andrea	10	Tromba
1758	GALLO Giovan Battista	10	Oboe
1760	GALLO Vincenzo	8	Tenore
1761	GHIALRDI Angelo	10	Violino
1754	GRAVINA Gaetano	10	Violino
1757	GRISOLIA Emanuele	10	Violino
1759	GROSSO Giovanni	10	Violoncello
1753	IGNESTI Michele	8	Violino
1757	INCOCCIA Lorenzo	10	Contralto
1755	IOVERAS Francesco	10	Violino
1761	LANGELLOTTI Niccolò	10	Soprano
1759	LANGLE' Onorato	8	Violino
1753	LENZI Francesco	10	Maestro di cappella
1757	LEOCI Francesco	10	Violino
1759	LONGO Giuseppe	8	Basso
1755	LONZI Marco	10	Contralto
1752	MAENZANO Giovanni	8	Contrabbasso
1751	MAIO Antonio	10	Soprano
1755	MASIELLO don Niccolò	10	Basso
1759	MASULLO Ignazio	10	Soprano
1754	MOROSETTI Gaetano	10	Violoncello
1758	NARDILLO Costantino	10	Tromba
1760	NATALE Tommaso	10	Violino
1761	PALLERINI Carlo	8	Oboe

(continued)

Table 17 (continued)

Year of admission	Name	Years of stay	Qualification in musical studies
1757	PARAVICINO Agostino	10	Oboe
1758	PARISI Gaetano	10	Violino
1762	PELLINI Giacomo	10	Contrabbasso
1754	PETRUCCI Francesco	8	Maestro di cappella
1759	PIETRICONE Flaminio	10	Violino
1759	PINTO Andrea	10	Violino
1758	POLIDEI Angelo	10	Tenore
1755	POLITO Aniello	10	Violino
1758	POLLONI Gaetano	10	Violino
1759	PRATO Nunziante	10	Violino
1759	QUINTAVALLE Tommaso	10	Contralto
1753	RANA Gennaro	10	Oboe
1762	RICCA Tommaso	10	Soprano
1757	ROMANO don Angelo	10	Violino
1757	ROMANO Francesco	10	Tenore
1759	RONDANINI Benedetto	10	Violino
1761	ROSSETTI Antonio	12	Violino
1754	RUIZ Filippo	10	Violino
1760	SALA Domenico	10	Violino
1761	SALZANO Niccolò	8	Maestro di cappella
1759	SCOTTI Giuseppe	10	Violino
1755	SENECA Pasquale	10	Contralto
1759	SPAGNOLO Filippo	10	Tromba
1760	TARNASSI Gaetano	4	Soprano
1745	TORNESE Gioacchino	8	Contralto
1762	TREMOLITI Michelangelo	10	Non stabilito
1752	TRITTO Giacomo	8	Maestro di cappella
1758	ZAMBROTTI Francesco	10	Soprano

Notes The period of stay at the institute varies between seven and ten years, and we believe that this variation is related to the child's age at the time of admission. Of course, we have no certainty that the period of stay reported in the table was actually respected, for the reasons already expressed earlier

Source A.P.T., Section Students and Boarders

Table 18   Students of the Conservatorio della Pietà dei Turchini in the years 1781 and 1791–1806

Figliolo/child	Year of admission	Anno di Licenza	Note
AGIANESE	1781	–	Entra il 22 giugno: suona il violino male
ALTIERI Raffaele e Michele	1806	–	Fratelli
ALTOBELLO Donato	1798	–	Uscì nel Governo Repubblicano come Reo di Stato, fu preso con le armi alla mano
ALTRUI	1781	–	Entra il 22 giugno: suona il violino mediocremente
ANGELOTTI Nicola	1803	–	Suona il contrabbasso e canta da tenore Per essere arrivato alla piazza di II tenore passa agli alunni
AUXILIA Francesco	1795	1799	Palermitano. Riammesso nel 1803 come alunno
AVETA Raffaele	1793	–	Napoletano
AZZELLINI Nicola	1795	1796	Uscito con licenza, fu riammesso nel 1798 a piazza franca
BARDARO' Vincenzo	1793	1798	Regnicolo. Per non poter pagare il Delegato lo situa nel Conservatorio di S. Onofrio; rientra alla Pietà dei Turchini a piazza franca, per 5 anni, come I violoncello
BARESE Raffaele	1794	1796	Espulso
BARTILOMO Pietro	1805	1806	Di Gravina. Licenziato
BASILE Giovanni	1800	1801	Tornato al suo Paese no è più rientrato
BELLOT Giovanni	1806	–	–
BENOVEI Raffaele	1794	1797	–
BERLENTIS Giovanni	1795	1796	Uscito con licenza
BERLENTIS Stefano	1795	1796	Uscito con licenza
BETRONICI Giovan Battista	1797	1799	Uscito per non poter pagare
BILLEMA Luigi	1793	–	Napoletano

(continued)

Table 18 (continued)

Figliolo/child	Year of admission	Anno di Licenza	Note
BIRAZZO Luigi	1803	–	–
BOCCARDI Filippo	1805	–	–
BOLOGNA	1781	–	Inetto e birbo. Espulso con fede dei maestri
BOSSI	1781	–	Entra il 22 giugno: appena solfeggia
BRANCACCIO Gaetano	1804	1806	Si è fatto soldato
BUONAMICI Ettore	1805	1806	Uscito per non aver voluto pagare
BUONNICI Antonio	1794	1795	Uscito con licenza
CALABRESE Francesco	1802	–	Passato agli alunni per non poter pagare con obbligo però di servire per 6 anni forzosi nel suono del Corno da caccia invece del violino e di copiare un foglio di carta di musica al giorno
CALDERANO Giovanni	1789	–	Entrò per 5 anni, ma dal momento che si rivelò «buono» e che Cantava bene «da buffo2, fu mantenuto»
CAPALDO Modestino	1796	–	Nel 1800 passa agli Alunni
CAPOLINO Gennaro	1798	1799	Licenziato
CAPRANICA Giovan Lorenzo	1792	1796	Basso. Esonerato dal pagamento con l'obbligo di copiare carte
CARACCIOLO Vincenzo	1802	1805	Ritiratosi per motivi di salute
CARAMELLI Giuseppe	1805	1805	Rimpatriato a Roma
CARLINI Lorenzo e Luigi	1806	–	Fratelli
CARLUCCI Nicola	1793	1793	Regnicolo. Uscito e rimpatriato per sue serie e gravi indisposizioni
CASSANO Luigi	1804	1805	Rimpatriato a Lecce
CASTELLANO Michele	1796	–	Essendo partito dal Conservatorio, non è più tornato
CASTIGNACE Giuseppe	1799	1802	Uscito per non poter pagare

(continued)

Table 18 (continued)

Figliolo/child	Year of admission	Anno di Licenza	Note
CAVALLERI don Bartolomeo	1806	1806	Licenziato
CECCARINI Carlo	1804	–	–
CERVELLI Francesco Paolo	1793	1796	Regnicolo.Essendo asceso al Sacerdozio si ritirò nel suo Paese
CHERUBINO Francesco Paolo	1794	1796	Regnicolo. (fratello di Salvatore) Esce per non poter pagare
CHERUBINO Salvatore	1794	1796	Regnicolo (fratello di Franceso P.) Esce per non poter pagare
CHIOCCA Giuseppe	1796	1799	Suona il corno da caccia. Per la sua abilità passa agli alunni Arrestato come Reo di Stato
CIORMONE Pasquale	1798	1801	Licenziato
CIPOLLA Giacomo	1806	–	Convittore per 6 anni: tre anni col pagamento di d. 45 e tre anni franco in qualità di alunno, come da istrumento
CIRALLO Gaetano	1794	1795	Siciliano
COLAVITO Rocco	1796	1797	Licenziato
COLONNA don Gabriele	1803	1805	Suddiacono. Gli fu abbassata la retta per aver l' incarico di insegnare a leggere e a scrivere ai figlioli Uscito per sua grave malattia è passato a miglior vita
COSTANZO Salvatore	1795	1796	Espulso
COZZI Gennaro	1793	1799	Napoletano. Passato a piazza franca perché I oboe, viene espulso per essere mancato alle musiche di S. Maria delle Grazie
CRISTIANO Federico	1796	1799	Licenziato per problemi di salute
D'ALIA don Michele	1801	–	Fuggito
D'ANDRIZZA Giuseppe	1803	–	–
D'ASPURA Giacomo	1804	1806	Sortito dal Conservatorio. Si è situato nella Marina
DACOSTA Custodio	1797	1798	–
DE CARO Nicola	1794	1795	Si ritirò nel suo Paese perché «inutile»
DE DOMINICIS don Antonio	1801	1802	Partito con suo padre

(continued)

Table 18   (continued)

Figliolo/child	Year of admission	Anno di Licenza	Note
DE GREGORJ Domenico	1805	1805	Uscito per non aver voluto pagare
DEL PRETE Carlo	1805	–	Problemi di pagamenti
DEL VECCHIO	1781	–	Maestro di Cappella: se non profitta in 4 mesi espellerlo
DELLA BARRA Luigi Giuliano	1792	1793	Esonerato dal pagamento per essere I violino
DEMETRIO Francesco	1805	1805	Suona il violino. Ricevuto per alunno, è stato mandato via prima di mettere la veste
DEONCHIA Donato	1794	1800	Esonerato dal pagamento con obbligo di copiare carte (30 fogli al mese). Contrabbasso
DI FRANCESCO Saverio	1793	1795	Regnicolo, espulso
DI GIORGIO Carlo	1794	1796	Espulso
DI GREGORIO Domenico	1791	1794	Regnicolo.Grazie all'intervento del Mattei, paga d. 40 anziché d. 60
DI RAIMONDO Pietro	1800	1806	Espulso per non aver rispettato la regola di non uscir solo poi riammesso e licenziato
DOGLIO Giuseppe	1803	–	–
DONINI Francesco	1795	1797	Licenziato per non aver voluto più pagare; è entrato nella Banda del Reggimento di Terra di Lavoro
FANIZZI Pasquale	1804	–	–
FATICATI Antonio	1793	1796	Napoletano. Suona il clarinetto Proveniente dall'Albergo dei Poveri. Espulso dal Conservatorio
FATTORINI Alderano	1802	1802	Si è licenziato per non volersi applicare alla musica
FERRANTE Antonio	1800	1802	Tornato a casa perché ammalato Entra nel Seminario di Nola per farsi sacerdote
FIANO (ZIANO) Luigi	1803	–	Gli fu abbassata la retta
FISCARELLI	–	–	Entra il 22 giugno: appena solfeggia
FONTANA Agostino	1795	1799	Ischitano. Riammesso nel 1801 come alunno
FORMIGLI Giovanni	18 04	–	Licenziato per non voler pagare

(continued)

Table 18   (continued)

Figliolo/child	Year of admission	Anno di Licenza	Note
FRANCHINI Giuseppe	1806	–	–
FRODI Vincenzo	1794	–	Regnicolo. Per le sue abilità passa a piazza franca nel 1800
GALLO Camillo	1794	–	Napoletano. Si è applicato alle scienze ed uscito dal Conservatorio
GALLO Vincenzo	1796	–	Passato agli Alunni nel 1798 dopo una fede di d. 24, pagata dal padre Ignazio presso il Banco dei Poveri
GAMBERALE Giovanni	1804	1804	Milanese, è fuggito dal Conservatorio
GARGANO Nicola	1798	–	Espulso per non aver pagato
GARGANO Vincenzo	1803	–	Uscito per non poter pagare
GARGIULO Raffaele	1797	–	Uscito, si è fatto soldato di cavalleria
(GAZZARINI)Francesco	1800	–	Ritirato dal padre poiché è stato licenziato il fratello maggiore
(GAZZARINI) Roberto	1800	1801	Espulso perché incorreggibile
GENTILE Federico	1804	1806	Gli fu abbassata la retta per profitto. Fu ritirato a Firenze dai genitori
GENTILE Filippo	1806	–	Palermitano. Ammalatosi è tornato a casa ed è esonerato dal pagamento per tutta la durata della sua malattia
GERMANO Francesco	1792	1793	Rimpatriato
GIANCOLA	1781	–	Eunuco, soprano, tenore, non profitta per volontà. Espulso
GIANNATTASIO Basilio	1793	1793	Espulso
GIANNI Pasquale	1806	–	–
GIARROCCHI Giuseppe Antonio	1794	–	Gli vengono restituiti 25 d. anticipati per il semestre perché ha rinunciato all'ammissione in Conservatorio
GODINO Gaetano	1797	1798	Ricevuto perché utile al Conservatorio. Espulso perché ladro; reintegrato per essere stato discolpato Arrestato in Conservatorio, nel 1799, come Reo di Stato

(continued)

Table 18 (continued)

Figliolo/child	Year of admission	Anno di Licenza	Note
IACONO Paolo	1794	1797	Regnicolo. Fuggito dal Conservatorio
LA MARRA Domenico	1793	–	Napoletano. Contralto. Passato a piazza franca come I contralto Arrestato con armi alla mano nella resa di Castellammare come reo di stato
LA MARRA Pietro	1805	1806	Rimpatriato
LAFAJA Carlo	1804	–	Gli fu abbassata la retta
LARICCHIA Giacomo	1796	1797	Licenziato con la restituzione del semestre anticipato
LASTRINO Carlo	1805	1806	–
LEGGI Vittorio Raffaele	1795	1801	Licenziato per mancanze gravi
LEONGITO Marco	1793	1794	Regnicolo. Sortito dal Conservatorio
LIBERATORE Teofilo	1802	1802	Uscito
LONGONE Francesco Antonio		1796	Uscito con licenza del Vicerettore Carlo Fiorillo
LONGONI Francescantonio	1797	1796	Uscito con licenza
LUCIANO Tobia	1805	–	Passato agli alunni
MAGLIONE Pasquale	1797	1801	Espulso perché indisciplinato
MAGRINA Giuseppe	1793	1793	Napoletano. Si è licenziato
MANCINO	1781	–	Cattivo soprano, viene affidato al mastricello Cornetti con una dilazione di quattro mesi
MANFREDI Venanzio	1793	1793	Regnicolo. Espulso perché incorreggibile
MANFROCI Nicola	1805	–	Gli fu abbassata la retta
MANNI Nicola	1805	–	Nel 1806 gli fu abbassata la retta
MARCHELLI Domenico	1800	–	Genovese. Passa agli alunni
MARCHESE Ignazio	1793	1796	Napoletano. Fuggì dal Conservatorio per farsi soldato
MARESCALCHI Ercole Michele	1802	1805	Uscito per non aver voluto pagare
MARINI Luigi Giovanni	1793	1794	Estero. Uscito per non poter pagare
MAROTTA Raffaele	1795	1796	E' stato cacciato via
MARTINO Pietro	1804	1805	Licenziato
MAURINO Antonio	1793	1793	Napoletano. Si è licenziato per alcuni giusti motivi
MAURINO Ferdinando	1793	1794	Napoletano. Uscito

(continued)

Table 18　(continued)

Figliolo/child	Year of admission	Anno di Licenza	Note
MAURINO Pasquale	1793	1793	Napoletano. Si è licenziato
MAZZARDI Giuseppe	1797	–	Uscito per non poter pagare
MEGLIO Donato Antonio	1801	–	Nel 1802 passa alla piazza di II tenore e poi a tenore dei Reali Ordini
MERLI primo	1781	–	Entra il 22 giugno: suona il violino da principiante
MERLI secondo	1781	–	Entra il 22 giugno: tenore, principiante
MIGLIETTA don Serafino	1796	–	Nel gennaio del 1798 percepisce d. 18 come alunno; Obbligato a far da Maestro di Lettere
MODUGNO Raffaele	1798	1798	Uscito per non poter pagare
MONTI don Filippo	1793	1795	–
MONTUORI don Baldassarre	1802	–	Passato agli alunni nel 1806
MORRONE Desiderio	1793	1798	Estero. Rimpatriato con licenza
MORRONE Michele	1804	1806	Espulso per gravi delitti
MUSTO Gabriele	1795	1801	Entra con l'obbligo di servire per 12 anni; espulso perché incorreggibile
NANI Angelo	1804	–	Maldese, è trapassato
NANULA Raffaele	1803	–	Gli fu abbassata la retta
NARDULLI Vito Antonio	1793	–	Napoletano. Se ne è uscito per esser matto
NERI Pietro Francesco Paolo Benedetto	1792	1796	Uscito per non poter pagare
NICASTRO	1781	–	Basso. Perentorio: se non profitta in quattro mesi espellerlo
ORLAN Ferdinando	1795	–	Uscito con licenza
ORLANDO Antonio	1802	–	Ritrovandosi abile nel servire viene esonerato dal pagamento dopo il primo semestre; nel 1806 passa agli alunni
PADUINO Domenico	1803	1803	Uscito per non poter pagare
PALMA Gaetano	1804	1805	Rimpatriato a Lecce
PANCALLO	1781	–	Entra il 22 giugno: tenore, principiante e di cattiva voce
PANIGADA Antonio	1794	1795	Napoletano. Si è fatto soldato
PAOLINO Giovanni	1806	–	–
PASANESE Pasquale	1806	–	–

(continued)

Table 18 (continued)

Figliolo/child	Year of admission	Anno di Licenza	Note
PAUSI don Saverio	1804	1806	–
PELLETTIERI Renato	1793	1795	Espulso
PEROCINO Vito Antonio	1797	1798	Partito dal Conservatorio non è più tornato
PERRINO Domenico Angelo	1793	1793	Napoletano. Sortito dal Conservatorio
PERSICO Giovanni Maria	1794	–	Nel 1801 passa agli Alunni
PETRAROLO Luigi	1802	1804	Licenziato per non aver pagato
PEZZONI don Raffaele	1804	1805	Uscito per non aver ricevuto licenza dal Vescovo di Aversa
PIACENZA don Domenico	1804	1806	–
PIESCHI Michele, seu Carlo	1793	1793	Napoletano. Si è licenziato per alcuni giusti motivi
PIGNATARI Spiridione	1805	–	–
POFFA Francescantonio	1795	1801	Estero. Passato a piazza franca perché in Concorso il 12 marzo 1797; ha occupato per sei anni la IV piazza di Maestro di cappella
POPOLIZIO Vincenzo e Michele	1806	–	–
QUARZOLI Luigi	1796	–	Suona l'oboe e per la mancanza di tale strumento paga meno Fuggito sulle navi inglesi
RAI Giovanni Pietro	1793	1794	Estero
RECUPIDO ANTONIO	1798	1798	Si ritirò al suo Paese per servire da Officiale Militare
RECUPIDO Giuseppe	1794	1797	Essendo I tenore gli viene abbassata la retta Si è licenziato per «istrumentarsi» nel Teatro Nuovo
RECUPITO Pascale	1796	1799	Uscito per non poter pagare
RICCI don Michele	1800	–	Abbassata la retta e abbonato l'attrasso perché serve da Prefetto e da I violoncello
RISOLO Giuseppe	1796	1796	· –
RODRIGUEZ Pasquale	1794	1802	Napoletano. Passato a piazza franca per 8 anni forzosi per il bisogno del luogo di corni da caccia

(continued)

Table 18   (continued)

Figliolo/child	Year of admission	Anno di Licenza	Note
ROMAGNOLI Giovanni	1797	1798	–
ROMANI Stefano	1794	1799	Per le sue abilità gli fu abbassata la retta. Rimpatriato a Pisa
RONDANINI Diodato	1793	1794	Napoletano; studia violino.Proveniente dall'Albergo dei Poveri Passa a miglior vita
RONDANINI Gaetano	1793	1796	Napoletano, studia violino. Proveniente dall'Albergo dei Poveri Fuggì per entrare nella Banda di Caltanissetta
ROTOLO	1781	–	Entra il 22 giugno: principiante di solfeggio
RUBINO Salvatore	1801	–	Obbligo di servire per 10 anni
RUGGIERO Giuseppe	1794	1797	Napoletano. Fuggito dal Conservatorio con la veste
SAFIO Santo	1793	1796	Regnicolo. Abile a servire. Fuggì Si fece soldato in Capua, nel Reggimento del Re
SALOMONI Raffaele	1803	1805	Ha preso l'abito religioso
SALVAGGIUOLO Giuseppe Oronzio	1798	1799	Tornato al suo Paese, non se hanno più notizie
SAMMARTINO don Donato	1800	1803	Prescelto come Prefetto, licenziato
SAPIENZA Pietro	1802	1806	Moscovita. Gli fu abbassata la retta per aver profittato nella musica
SARACINO Antonio	1804	1806	Leccese. Uscito per non aver pagato
SARAGONI Angelo	1795	1799	Fuggito dal Conservatorio
SARONE Giovan Battista	1806	1806	Ritirato in Bavaria
SCALIGINE Angelo Maria	1800	–	Passato agli Alunni
SCOTTO Francesco	1794	1797	Genovese. Rimpatriato con licenza
SECANTE Antonio	1796	–	Passato subito agli alunni
SIGISMONDI Domenico	1792	1797	Estero, esce per rimpatriarsi a Roma
SORIANI Vincenzo	1806	–	Clerico

(continued)

Table 18   (continued)

Figliolo/child	Year of admission	Anno di Licenza	Note
SPALLETTA Raffaele	1795	1800	Gli viene abbonato l'attrasso
SPONTINI Gaspare	1793	1795	Estero. Esonerato dal pagamento con obbligo di copiare carte Fuggì dal Conservatorio per alcuni delitti
STICHELER Antonio	1805	1806	–
SUSINNO Michele	1797	1798	Espulso perché incorreggibile
TAFURO Gennaro	1804	–	Essendo morto il padre si è ritirato dal Conservatorio
TAGLIAFERRI Gaetano	1793	1794	Napoletano. Suona il clarinetto. Proveniente dall'Albergo dei Poveri Fuggì dal Conservatorio
TARANTINO Gaetano	1798	1799	Si appartò dal Conservatorio come Reo di Stato, fu preso con la resa di Castellammare
TELLA (ZELLA?) Pietro	1797	1798	Licenziato per non aver voluto pagare
TERDONE Giuseppe	1799	–	Licenziato
TESTA Vincenzo	1806	–	-
TINTO Francesco	1803	1804	Passato da alunno a convittore. Uscito per non voler più pagare
TORDE Felice	1801	–	Gli fu abbassata da retta perché serviva da prefetto Per essere un buon maestro di cappella passa agli alunni
TROTTA Placido Cesario	1794	–	Regnicolo. Fuggì dopo aver rubato alcuni argenti della Chiesa
URGESE don Rocco	1794	1796	Regnicolo. Suddiacono. Uscito con licenza
VALVASSANI Giacomo	1804	–	Nel 1806 gli fu abbassata la retta
VEGORIO Francesco	1794	–	Napoletano. Licenziato e riammesso più volte per mancati pagamenti
VICECONTE Giuseppe Vincenzo	1794	1802	Napoletano. Licenziato per alcuni delitti

(continued)

Table 18   (continued)

Figliolo/child	Year of admission	Anno di Licenza	Note
VICECONTE Pietro	1802	–	–
VINACCI Giuseppe	1796	–	Suona il violoncello. Licenziato per non poter pagare, riammesso a piazza franca
VITULA Giuseppe	1795	1799	Passato a miglior vita

Note The dash indicates that the data is unknown
Source A.P.T., Section Students and Boarders

Table 19   Boarders transferred from the Santa Maria di Loreto Conservatory to the Pietà dei Turchini Conservatory

Convittori/Boarders	Data del trasferimento/Transfer date
BONACCHI Gennaro	1 marzo 1803
BOSSA Raffele	5 giugno 1805
CARRIERI Carlo	22 novembre 1802
COCCIA Raffaele	14 luglio 1804
(CORELLI) Ferdinando	31 ottobre 1804
CRIVELLI Domenico	5 luglio 1804
ERCULANO Filippo	12 marzo 1804
FESTA Ottavio e Giovanni	16 giugno 1804
FURNO Raffaele	1 marzo 1805
LOVERI Pietro Paolo	6 novembre 1804
NASCI Giovan Giuseppe	8 luglio 1801
PARISI Francesco	10 maggio 1802
PERRUCCI Aniello	22 novembre 1802
PETRUCCI Francesco e Gennaro	2 marzo 1806
PETRUCCI Gabriele	2 luglio 1806
RINALDI Raffaele	21 luglio 1804
SACCARDI Antonio	s.d.
VALENTE Pasquale	18 novembre 1806

Source A.P.T., Section Students and Boarders

Table 20 List of students and boarders transferred to the Conservatory of Pietà dei Turchini (no date)

AIELLO Raffaele	FONTANA Agostino
ALTIERI Michele	FRANCHINI Giuseppe
AMALFITANO Gaetano	FURNO Pascale 2°
ANDRIZZA Giuseppe	FURNO Raffaele 1°
AUGELLETTI Nicola	GENTILE Filippo
BARIONUOVO Francesco	GIANNI Pascale
BELLOTTI Giovanni	GIGLI Carlo
BILLEMI Luigi	GIOSUE' Andrea
BIRAGO Luigi	GRISI Domenico
BOCCARDI Filippo	LABRACHE Luigi
BOFFA Raffaele	LOVERI Pietro Paolo
BONACCHI Gennaro	LUCIANO Tobia
BONITI Giuseppe	MANFROCE Nicola
BRANDI Raffaele	MARCHETTI Domenico
CALABRESE Francesco	MARINO Nicola
CAPUANO Francesco	MASCIANGIOLO Raffaele
CARLINI Lorenzo 1°	MEGLIO Antonio
CARLINI Luigi 2°	MILOFICE Michele
CARRIERI Carlo	MONTEFUSCO Felice
CECCARINI Carlo	MONTUORO Baldassarre
CELESIA Gaetano	NANOLA Raffaela
CERRETELLI Antonio	NESCI Domenico 1°
CIAFRONE Francesco	NESCI Giovanni 3°
CIAFRONE Raimondo	NESCI Raffaele 2°
CIMAROSA Domenico	NONELLI Ferdinando
CIPOLLA Giacomo	PAOLINO Giacomo
COCCIA Raffaele	PARISI Francesco 2°
COLUCCI Gaetano	PARISI Saverio 2°
CRIVELLI Domenico	PECORARO -
CRIVELLI Giovanni 2°	PERRUCCI Antonello
DARIA Raffaele	PESCE Raffaele
DE LORENZI Giovanni	PESSETTI Giuseppe
DE MAIO Michele	PETRUCCI Francesco 2°
DEL PRETE Carlo	PETRUCCI Gabriello 2°
DELABONA Federico	PETRUCCI Gennaro 3°
DELASTAJA Carlo	PIACENZA don Domenico
DOGLIA Giuseppe	PIGNATARO Spiridione
DOMANDA Domenico	PIRAS Antonio
ERCOLANO Filippo	POPOLIZIO Michele 1°
FABIANI Gennaro 2°	POPOLIZIO Vincenzo
FABIANI Raffaele 1°	PORPORA Francesco
FENIZZI Pascale	RINALDI Raffaele
FERRERO Raffaello	RUBERTI Camillo
FESTA Giovanni 3°	RUBINO Salvatore

(continued)

Table 20   (continued)

FESTA Ottavio 2°	SANTUCCI Andrea
FESTA Vincenzo	SANZONE Giovanni
FIANO Luigi	SCALIGENA Angelo
FILIBERTI Nicola	SELVAGGIO Filippo
SORIANO Vincenzo	VALLE Antonio 1°
TARQUINIO Moisè	VALLE Tommaso 2°
TINELLI Angelo	VALVASSORE Giacomo
TURNER Giuseppe	VICECONTE Pietro
VALENTE Giuseppe	VILLANI Francesco
VALENTE Pascale	VITOLO Gennaro

Source A.P.T., Section Students and Boarders

Table 21   List of female boarders present at the Conservatory of Pietà dei Turchini in 1809

Convittrici/Boarders	Note
AVELLONE Luisa	–
BASILE Gaetana	–
BATTESTA Maria Raffaela	–
CELESIA Sig.ra Luisa	–
CELESIA Sig.ra Nicoletta	–
CESARANO Michelina	Ammessa a piazza franca
CONSO Errichetta	–
DE BLASIIS Costanza	–
DI MARTINO Luisa	–
ERCOLANO Marianna	–
GUIDETTI Teresian	–
INTERLANDI Diana	–
INTERLANDI Giuseppe	–
LASTRUCCI Sig.ra Marianna	–
MAITRE Adelaide	Uscita il 27 agosto per tornare a Parigi
MARCORELLI Gabriella	-
MARCIRELLI Gaetana	-
ROSSO Ottavia	-
TOSSELLI Francesca	-
VATTORTI Sig.ra Giuseppa	Ammessa a piazza franca

Note As mentioned, it seemed to us that for the first fifteen years of the nineteenth century, the Royal College was based on two administrations: that of the new public school, which also provided for the establishment of a female college, and the surviving one of Pietà dei Turchini. This is perhaps why this list of female boarders was also included among the lists of boarders of Pietà. The subject was nevertheless studied by R. Cafiero, *Musical education in Naples*, cit.
Source A.P.T., Section Students and Boarders

NOTES

1. The entire archival heritage relating to the ancient Neapolitan conservatories is kept in the Archive of the Conservatory of St. Peter in Majella in Naples. Our research was conducted between 1984 and 1996. In those years, for the first time the Archival Superintendency for Campania, after the studies of Salvatore Di Giacomo, began a phase of reorganization of that very important historical archive that we partly shared. The only Conservatory to have received complete cataloging and filing up to that point was that of the Turchini.

2. The Conservatory of Pietà did not welcome orphaned children (those were already taken care of, since 1537, by the Conservatory of Loreto), but all those children, aged 7–15, who, despite having a father, lived abandoned on the streets of the city, poorly guided and in extreme poverty. On the subject of abandoned childhood, see G. Da Molin, *Nati e abbandonati. Aspetti demografici e sociali dell'infanzia*, Cacucci Editore, Bari 1993.

3. Marriage Funds were also established at the Conservatory of Pietà dei Turchini, and the governors were tasked with dispensing dowries for "marriages" to poor but respectable girls.

4. J. P. Gutton, *La societé et le pauvres. L'exemple de la généralité de Lion*, Paris, 1970, p. 324.; B. Geremek, Il pauperismo nell'età preindustriale (XIV–XVIII secolo), in *Storia d'Italia*, Torino 1973, vol. V, pp. 669–698; Idem, *Renfermement des pauvres en Italie (XIV–XVII siécle). Remarques préliminaires*, in *Melanges en l'honneur de Femand Braudel*, Toulose 1973, vol. I, pp. 205–217.

5. This is what the young people hosted in the institute were called.

6. In 1573 the Confraternity of the Whites under the title of St. Mary of the Incoronatella founded an oratory. Ten years later, the same Confraternity drew up the statute of the conservatory and moved from the Incoronatella to Pietà dei Turchini. A reference to the Company of the Whites is in E. Pontieri, *Sulle origini della Compagnia dei Bianchi della Giustizia a in Napoli e sui suoi statuti in 1525*, «Campania sacra», 3 (1972).

7. At the end of the sixteenth century, and even more so towards the middle of the eighteenth century, Naples was divided into five squares or seats: Capuana, Nido, Montagna, Porto, and Portanova, each of which belonged to a group of nobles who

took their respective names. The representatives of each group met in their respective seat or assembly to discuss, deliberate, and form the various delegations that would preside over the branches of city administration and to choose the elected officials (one per square, except for Nido, which had two, but with only one voting right). Alongside the five noble squares, there was the people's assembly, distributed in 29 octaves, administrative districts that also extended to some villages and hamlets outside the city walls.

8. The sources on which we have relied to attempt a reconstruction of the management of the Conservatory of Pietà dei Turchini are essentially the income and outcome journals kept by the Treasurer, the Rector, and the Mensario.

9. On Neapolitan public banks, see note 19 in Chapter 3.

10. The figures are expressed in ducats and grana.

11. Historical Archive of the Banco di Napoli (from now on A.S.B.N.), *Banco dello Spirito Santo*, g. matr. 19—share of 40 ducats., May 24, 1599; ibidem, g. matr. 88—share of 64 ducats. And 84 grana, June 2, 1614. Archive of the Conservatory of Pietà dei Turchini (from now on A.P.T.), Main Book, matr. 2 (1627–1631), ff. 1–2. 190.

12. The arrendamenti were taxes on consumption. They originated from duties established in the Kingdom of Naples both on the import and export of goods, and on domestic consumption. The arrendamenti system spread in the South during the Spanish domination and consisted of the following: the government or individual cities of the Kingdom entrusted via a contract (in Spanish arrendar = to contract) private contractors with the collection of duties pertaining to them; those, in exchange for an annual rent, took charge of collecting them on their own account, deriving a further profit margin. The financial life of the country revolved around the arrendamenti for at least five centuries, and their existence, organization, and functioning involved every other aspect of social life, influencing trade, industry, agriculture, and directly penetrating the lives of individuals by conditioning their investments and industriousness. On this subject, see L. De Rosa, *Studi sugli Arrendamenti del Regno di Napoli. Aspetti della distribuzione della ricchezza mobile nel Mezzogiorno continentale (1649–1806)*, L'Arte tipografica, Napoli 1958.

13. A.P.T., Main Book of the Patrimony, II, 2. 27 (Platea 1751), *passim*.
14. L. De Rosa, *Studi sugli arrendamenti del Regno di Napoli*, cit, *passim*.
15. For the economic-financial crisis that affected the Neapolitan ecclesiastical institutions in the 1640s and 1650s, see C. Russo, *I monasteri femminili di clausura a Napoli nel secolo XVII*, Naples 1970; A. Lepre, *Rendite di monasterie nel Napoletano e crisi economica del '600*, «Quaderni storici», 15, pp. 844–865; E. De Renzi, *Sull'alimentazione del popolo minuto di Napoli*, Naples 1863.
16. The tuition fees and registration taxes of the children were recorded in a rather confused manner. The related items, recorded in the budgets, do not always give the total number of children admitted. For some years, the «entratura» taxes can be found in the Rolls of Students and Boarders.
17. A.P.T., Accounting III, 1, 2.
18. For the verification of building expenses, see A.P.T., Treasurer's Journal of 1690.
19. A.P.T., Platea, II.2.27, ff. 252v–253r.
20. A part of the real estate assets ensured the Conservatory annual income for censuses, equal, in 1751, to two. 843.55 ducats (A.P.T., Platea, II.2.27, ff. 56v–69v).
21. A.P.T., Platea II.2.27, ff. 252v–253r.
22. A.P.T., Accounting Section, rents, leases and censuses, 26 bis.
23. May 4th, was the deadline for leases, while the collection of rents took place in three annual installments. See E. De Simone, *Houses and Shops in Naples in the Seventeenth and Eighteenth Centuries*, "International Review of the History of the Bank", 12 (1976).
24. A.P.T., Description of buildings 1751, f. 20.
25. Elsewhere we may find the note of expenses corresponding to the maintenance and renovation works of the houses; A.P.T., Accounting 31 "Notes of works carried out for the Conservatory and related expenses," 1748.
26. A few years later some of these houses guaranteed the Conservatory the following annuities: between May 4, 1779, and May 4, 1780, the Casa accosto il Real Conservatorio yielded two. 151, that at the Gate of St. Bartholomew two. 322, that at the Baglivo

two. 144 and so on, for a total of 1644 ducats. The same properties, some twenty years earlier, in 1761–1762, had yielded 1,412
ducats. Cf. A.P.T., Accounting Section, rents, rents and censi,
26a.
27. A.P.T., Budgets, years 1751–1795.
28. L. De Rosa, *Studi sugli arrendamenti*, cit., pp. 27–28.
29. Ibid., p. 42 and following.
30. Ibid.
31. G. Alberigo, *Contributi alla storia delle confraternite dei disciplinati e della spiritualità laicale nei secoli XV e XVI*, in *Il
Movimento dei Disciplinati nel settimo centenario del suo inizio*,
Perugia 1960, pp. 156–252; B. Pullan, *Povertà, carità e nuove
forme di assistenza nell'Europa moderna*, in D. Zardin (ed.), *La
città dei poveri*, Milan, 1996; B. Geremek, *La pietà e la forca*,
Bari-Naples 1991; S. Cavallo, *Charity and Power in Early Modern
Italy*, Cambridge 1995.
32. R. Salvemini, *La difficile combinazione tra assistenza e credito in
età moderna*, «Rassegna Storica Salernitana» 29 (1998), pp. 29–
67.
33. C. Russo, *La storiografia socio-religiosa e i suoi problemi*, in C.
Russo (ed.), *Società, Chiesa e vita religiosa nell'Ancien Régime*,
Napoli 1976, p. CVIII. On the phenomenon of Italian confraternities see C. Black, *Le confraternite italiane del Cinquecento*,
Torino 1992; *Napoli sacra del XVI secolo. Repertorio delle
fabbriche religiose napoletane nella Cronaca del Gesuita Giovan
Francesco Araldo*, edited by F. Divenuto, Napoli 1990; G.
Muto, *Forme e contenuti economici dell'assistenza nel Mezzogiorno
moderno: il caso di Napoli*, pp. 237–258; A. Musi, *Pauperismo
e pensiero giuridico a Napoli nella prima metà del secolo XVII*,
in G. Politi, M. Rosa, F. Della Peruta (eds.), *Timore e carità.
I poveri nell'Italia moderna*, Cremona 1982, pp. 259–274; R.
Salvemini, *L'asistencia en la ciudad de Nàpoles en loss s. XVI–
XVII*, in *Ciudad y Mundo urbano en la Epoca Moderna*, Madrid
1997, pp. 271–299; A. Musi, *Medici e istituzioni a Napoli in età
moderna*, in P. Frascani (ed.), *Sanità e Società*, vol. V, Bologna
1990, pp. 19–66; G. Boccadamo, *L'antico ospedale di San Nicola
a Molo*, «Campania Sacra», 19 (2) (1988), pp. 311–340; the
volume *Chiesa, Assistenza e Società nel Mezzogiorno*, edited by
C. Russo, Lecce 1994; G. D'Addosio, *Origine e vicende storiche*

e progressi della Real Casa dell'Annunziata di Napoli, Napoli 1883; R. De Maio, *Società e vita religiosa a Napoli nell'Età moderna*, Napoli 1971, pp. 137–138; Idem, *L'Ospedale dell'Annunziata il «migliore e più segnalato di tutta Italia»*, in *Riforma e miti nella Chiesa del '500*, 2nd ed., Napoli 1992, pp. 241–249.

34. B. Capasso, *Catalogo ragionato dei libri o registri esistenti nella sezione antica o prima serie dell'archivio Municipale di Napoli*, vol. I, Napoli 1879, p. 112; L. De Rosa, *Studi sugli arrendamenti*, cit.; V. D'Arienzo, *L'arrendamento del sale dei Quattro Fondaci*, Salerno 1996, pp. 184–185.

35. B. Pullan, S. J. Wolf, *Plebi urbane e plebe rurali: da poveri a proletari*, in *Storia d'Italia, Annali*, vol. I, Torino, Einaudi p. 1021.

36. D. Carpitella, *Musica e tradizione orale*, Palermo 1973; Idem, *Folklore e analisi differenziale di cultura*, Roma 1976; R. Pozzi, *Vita musicale e committenza nei Conservatori napoletani nel Seicento. Il S. Onofrio e i Poveri di Gesù Cristo*, in A. Pompilio, D. Restani, L. Bianconi, F. A. Gallo (eds.), *Proceedings of the XIV Congress of the International Musicological Society, Trasmissione e ricezione delle forme di cultura musicale, III*, Turin 1990, pp. 915–924.

37. E. Vecchione, E. Genovesie, *Le istituzioni di beneficenza nella città di Napoli*, Naples 1908, p. 561.

38. R. Del Prete, *Un'azienda musicale a Napoli*, cit.

39. G. Garrani, *Il carattere bancario e l'evoluzione strutturale dei primigeni monti di pietà*, Milan 1957, pp. 144–161, 225–258; H. Holzappel, *Le origini del Monte di Pietà (1462–1515)*, Rocca San Casciano 1905; M. Maragi, *Cenni sulla natura e sullo svolgimento storico dei Monti di Pietà*, in *Historical Archives of Credit Companies*, vol. I, Rome 1956, pp. 291–314; G. Barbieri, Origini ed evoluzione dei Monti di Pietà in Italia, in *Economia e Credito*, Palermo 1961; S. Majarelli, U. Nicolini, *Il Monte dei Poveri di Perugia. Le origini (1462–1474)*, Perugia 1962; M. Monaco, *La questione dei Monti di Pietà al V Concilio Laterano*, «Studi Salernitani» 7 (January–June 1971), pp. 109 et seq.; P. Avallone, R. Salvemini, *Dall'assistenza al credito. L'esperienza dei Monti di Pietà e delle Case Sante nel Regno di Napoli tra XVI e XVIII secolo*, in *Nuova Rivista Storica*, Year LXXXIII, Fasc. I, Rome

1999, pp. 21–54; A. Placanica, *Moneta, prestiti, usure nel Mezzogiorno moderno*, Naples 1982; E. De Simone, *Il Monte di Pietà di Cusano. Origini e funzioni (1797–1811)*, in *Annali della Facoltà di Economia di Benevento*, Naples 1996, pp. 61–97; Idem, *Il Banco della Pietà di Napoli, 1734–1806*, Naples 1987.

40. A. Silvestri, *Sui banchieri pubblici napoletani nella prima metà del '500. Notizie e documenti*, in *Bollettino dell'Archivio Storico del Banco di Napoli*, vol. II, 1951; Idem, *Sui banchieri pubblici napoletani dall'avvento di Filippo II al trono della costituzione del monopolio. Notizie e documenti*, in *Bollettino dell'Archivio Storico del Banco di Napoli*, vol. IV, 1952; P. Avallone, *I banchi pubblici napoletani tra XVII e XVIII secolo: strategie e gestione*, «Sintesi», 1 (1999); AA.VV, *Banchi pubblici, banchi privati e monti di pietà nell'Europa preindustriale*, vol. II, Genoa 1991; G. M. Galanti, *Della descrizione geografica e politica delle due Sicilie*, Naples 1780 [new edition edited by F. Assante and D. Demarco, Naples 1969].

41. We have appreciated as very effective the expression proposed in the study day "The "poor" goes to the bank. The Monti di Pietà in the ancient Italian states (Fifteenth–eighteenth centuries)", Naples, February 12, 2000, Banco di Napoli—Sezione Pegni (edited by the Institute of Historical Research for the South, CNR, Naples).

42. A. Placanica, *Il patrimonio ecclesiastico calabrese nell'età moderna*, Chiaravalle 1972, p. 44.

43. R. Giura Longo, *I beni ecclesiastici nella storia economica di Matera*, Matera 1961, p. 61.

44. Often, governors would wait for authorization from the Archbishop's Curia before accepting.

45. A. Tenenti, *Il senso della morte e l'amore della vita nel Rinascimento*, cit., pp. 62–111.

46. A. Musi, *Pauperismo e pensiero giuridico a Napoli*, cit.

47. Archive of the Pietà dei Turchini (from now on, A.P.T.), Patrimony, II, 1, 17, f. 55; see also Libro Maggiore matr. 25, f. 196.

48. A.P.T., Libro Maggiore matr. 25, f. 239.

49. A.P.T., Patrimony, II, 1, 17, f. 191.

50. G. Ceci, *Un mercante mecenate nel secolo XVII, Gaspare Roomer*, «Napoli Nobilissima», XVI (1970), pp. 160–164.

51. L. De Rosa, *Il Mezzogiorno spagnolo tra crescita e decadenza*, Milan 1987, p. 61.
52. A.P.T., Libro Maggiore, 1633, matr. 4, f. 122.
53. A.P.T., Patrimonio II, 1, 178, f. 28.
54. On this subject, see S. Di Giacomo, *Il Conservatorio di Sant'Onofrio*, cit., pp. 206–207.
55. A.P.T., Patrimonio, I, 2, 16, f. 84 and Platea, II, 2, 27. One of the privileges granted to Neapolitan charitable institutions was the delivery of 6 *tomola* per year of alms salt.
56. A.P.T., Platea, II, 2, 27, f. 199r.
57. It is not yet known with certainty when the Conservatory associated a religious leadership with the secular government, at least in the "educational" activity of the institute. However, the presence of religious people in the Conservatory is undisputed. According to Di Giacomo, from 1607 to 1608, the Somascan Fathers took part in the government of the Conservatory (S. Di Giacomo in *Il Conservatorio di Sant'Onofrio*, cit., p. 181).
58. For the economic and financial situation of the Kingdom of Naples in those years, see the studies by L. De Rosa, and in particular, *Il Mezzogiorno spagnolo*, cit.
59. The interest rate on leases was decreasing, thus making the income from bequests inadequate for expenses (A.P.T., Platea, II, 2, 27, ff. 186v–187r).
60. A.P.T., Platea, II, 2, 27.
61. Again, on the consequences of the devaluation of income on the revenues of monasteries, see C. Russo, *I monasteri femminili di clausura a Napoli nel secolo XVII*, cit., pp. 40–42.
62. A.P.T., Libro del Patrimonio, II.2.17 and II.2.27.
63. The copies of the two instruments and the will are contained in A.P.T., IV vol. of the Cautele, f. 49. The chapels were dedicated to St. Anne, St. Guardian Angel, St. Charles Borromeo, St. Joseph, SS. Crucifix, SS. Rosary, St. Liberator, St. Nicholas, St. Mary of Grace, St. Anthony of Padua, and SS. Annunciation.
64. A.P.T., Cautele, vol. IV, f. 132.
65. A.P.T., Cautele, vol. I, ff. 144 and 159.
66. A.P.T., Platea II, 2, 2, 7, ff. 178r–179r.

67. The chapels were dedicated to St. Anne, St. Guardian Angel, St. Charles Borromeo, St. Joseph, SS. Crucifix, SS. Rosary, St. Liberator, St. Nicholas, St. Mary of Grace, St. Anthony of Padua, and SS. Annunciation.↑

68. The chapel is located to the right of the main altar of the Church of Pietà dei Turchini, where Nicola Vaccaro painted episodes related to the Rocco spouses, who had assumed the patronage of the chapel after considering themselves beneficiaries of the miraculous interventions of St. Anne.

69. A.S.B.N., Banco dell'Annunziata, g. matr. 409—50 ducats share, May 21, 1667.

70. The administrative diligence of Viceroy Don Pietro d'Aragona was aimed at identifying and containing the illicit enrichment that, by old tradition, characterized the world of business in closer relation to public offices. Among the extraordinary procedures, carried out energetically, especially with the aim of raising funds for the treasury, there was the investigation conducted quickly and surely against Counselor F. Rocco (see *Storia di Napoli*, vol. III, Naples 1976, p. 405).

71. A.P.T., Sezione Patrimonio, Printed Will of Counselor Rocco, Naples, September 30, 1675.

72. Ibid., *passim*.

73. Evidently, the Bank also managed the furniture account.

74. Printed Will of the Royal Counselor F. Rocco, cit.

75. A.P.T., Libro Maggiore (1633–1651), f. 18.

76. A.P.T., Platea, II.2.27, f.18.

77. A.S.B.N. Banco di San Giacomo, g. matr. 2110—entry of 12 ducats, August 21, 1778.

78. Diego Soria, Marquis of Crispano, pro-regent of the Vicariate in 1663. See G. Galasso, *Napoli spagnola dopo Masaniello*, Naples 1972, *ad indicem*, and S. D'Aloe, in *Storia dell'Augustissima Compagnia della Santa Croce*, Naples 1882, *passim*.

79. A.S.B.N., Banco dello Spirito Santo, g. matr. 109—entry of 75 ducats, February 25, 1616.

80. Ibid., g. matr. 104—entry of 30 ducats on March 16, 1616.

81. A.P.T., Libro Maggiore, Matr. 25, f. 238.

82. See in this regard J. P. Gutton, *La società e i poveri*, cit.; and in particular B. Geremek, *Il pauperismo nell'età preindustriale*, cit.

83. B. Pullan, S. J. Wolf, *Plebi urbane e plebi rurali: da poveri a proletari*, cit., p. 1022.

84. E. Vecchione, E. Genovese, *Le istituzioni di beneficenza nella città di Napoli*, cit., p. 571.

85. J. P. Gutton, *La société et les pauvres en Europe*, Paris 1974, p. 52; M. C. Galan-Vivas and J. Bonmariage, *Signification démographique de la nuptialité*, «Recherches économique de Louvrain», 4 (1969); A. Golini, *Omogamia secondo il luogo di origine in Italia*, in *Proceedings of the XXI Meeting of the Italian Statistical Society*, Rome 1961; P. H. Karmel, *The Relations Between Male and Female Nuptiality in a Stable Population*, "Population Studies", I (1948), p. 4.

86. F. Schiattarella, *Maritaggi di cuccagna*, Naples 1969; S. Cavallo, *Assistenza femminile e tutela dell'onore nella Torino del XVIII secolo*, in *Annali della Fondazione L. Einaudi*, vol. 14, Turin 1980, pp. 127–156.

87. G. A. Summonte, *Historia della città e regno di Napoli*, vol. I, Naples 1675, pp. 282–287.

88. Ibid., p. 287.

89. G. Muto, *Forme e contenuti economici dell'assistenza nel Mezzogiorno*, cit., pp. 237–258.

90. G. Da Molin (ed.), *Trovatelli e Balie in Italia, secc. XVI–XIX*, Bari 1994; C. D'Ario, *Gli esposti a Napoli nel XVIII secolo*, in *Chiesa, Assistenza e Società nel Mezzogiorno moderno*, cit., pp. 515–567; J. Boswell, *L'abbandono dei bambini in Europa occidentale*, Milan 1991; V. Hunecke, *I trovatelli di Milano*, Bologna 1989; AA.VV., *Enfance abandonné et société en Europe, XIX–XX siécle*, in *Collection de l'école Francaise de Rome*, 140, Rome 1991.

91. E. Cordella, *Sulla storia della beneficenza nei domini continentali del Regno*, «Annali civili del Regno di Napoli», CXXII (1857), pp. 113–126. On the relationship between property systems and dowry funds, C. Conte also insists, *Gli stabilimenti di beneficenza di Napoli*, Naples 1884, pp. 8–10. For a general analysis of the phenomenon, see G. Delille, *Un esempio di assistenza privata: i monti di maritaggio nel Regno di Napoli*, in *Pauperismo e assistenza negli antichi stati italiani*, cit. pp. 275–295.

92. M. L. King, *Le donne nel Rinascimento*, Editori Laterza, Rome-Bari 1991, p. 158; E. Novi Chavarria, *Sacro, pubblico e privato. Donne nei secoli XV–XVIII*, Napoli 2009.

93. The sources examined suggest that the albarano is a document drawn up between the parties: in this case, the governors and the young women or the spouses and their relatives. Unlike the instrumento, the albarano did not require the signature of a notary.

94. The role of the prior is described in the statute of the Conservatory and reappears in some regulations subsequent to the institute. In reality, the impression is that his power to intervene in the organizational life of the Turchini was essentially formal and disappeared over the years and with the transformation of the welfare policy into the productive activity of the Conservatory.

95. In the Turchini Archive, there are several references to the Melina will. A copy of the will, which we will refer to, is in the 1751 plate, location II. 2. 12 (ex II. 2. 27) in which we find a summary of the effects of the Melina inheritance modalities. Another copy of the Melina will is preserved in volume A of Cautele ed Istrumenti at pages 103 and following.

96. "The main book of the writing of the inheritance of the late Giovan Francesco Melina, administered by the Governors of the Royal Conservatory of Pietà dei Turchini and Prior of the Oratory of the Bianchi, erected within the royal Conservatory, which is worth from the first of January 1763 to all [...] 1763—1808", is located in A.P.T., the Patrimony at II. 2. 37. The Book opens with a Pandetta and on the lower sheet is stamped the word "Melina."

97. The *figliole in capillis*, that is, with long hair, were those of marriageable age.

98. The testator indicated the names of the figliole with precision.

99. The documentation of the "Melina" marriages attests to the conversion into purchases of real estate of the sum received by the groom or the bride's family. (Instruments of sale and caution of the Melina legacy marriages 1760, 1764, 1779, 1789, in A.P.T., Assistance and Charity V-5.)

100. Their identification by the mayor, the elected officials, and the abbot of Carife took place, according to the testator's provisions, on August 15, and, in case there were not enough marriageable girls, poor widows could be admitted, starting from thirty years old and below, under the same conditions as the virgin maidens. Also for this type of marriage, the rule of dividing the sum in half

between the bussolata and her potential heir remained valid in case of dissolution of the marriage.

101. The act of this employment was drawn up by the Notary Giovan Francesco Antonio Giangrande of Naples. In the event that the Convent of St. Catherine had repurchased the annual incomes sold for the capital of 8,700 ducats, the future groom would have had to convert the sum into another purchase.

102. The accounting of this Chapel was separate from that of the Conservatory, even though it was managed by the same governors. The accounting documentation is extensive and detailed, requiring a long and detailed study that we preferred to postpone.

103. The declarations of the governors on this matter are still preserved, as well as the "minutes" of a meeting held at the home of the regent Carlo Antonio De Rosa, Marquis of Villarosa, on the morning of August 4, where governors Francesco D'Agostino, Nicola D'Aulisco, Giacomo Piscopo, Giuseppe Criscuolo, and Francesco Guarracino were present; the sixth governor Alfonso Garofano was absent.

104. A.P.T., Assistance and Charity, vol. s.n., «Rollo delle figliole», years 1754–1758.

105. In 1730, the ten girls who were drawn were chosen from 279 names. Between 1730 and 1739, the number of applicants ranged between 279 (1730) and 350 (1733) (Rollo delle figliole, in A.P.T., Assistance and Charity, vol. s.n.).

106. If after the draw the marriage was not contracted within two years, the albarano lost its validity [A.P.T., Assistance and Charity, n. 1 (1711–1727) «Libri d'assegnazione di maritaggi», July 26, 1718].

107. The request was "pushed" by counselor Ciavalti, since the girl Anna Maria Carolina Fiore, already married to Raffaele Trombetta, was the daughter of one of his "lackeys" (A.P.T., Assistance and Charity V-7).

108. A.P.T., Assistance and Charity V-14.

109. A.P.T., Assistance and Charity, vol. s. n., «Rollo delle figliole che si estraggono dalla Bussola dei maritaggi (...) di S. Anna», July 26, 1735.

110. A.P.T., Assistance and Charity.

111. A.P.T., Platea, II, 2, 27, ff. 169v.–177r.

112. A.P.T., Monthly Balances, Salary Account.

113. The term codicil refers to the last will provisions that refer to a previous will to partially modify or integrate its content. The term nuncupative, on the other hand, derived from the Latin nuncupare (to name), was defined in intermediate law as the will made orally in front of a witness, which then had to be put in writing (Legal Dictionary, edited by Federico Del Giudice, Edizioni Simone, Naples 1992 and Encyclopedia of Law, Rizzoli).

114. The nuncupative codicils attached to the Alianelli will were drawn up by the notary Lonardo Marinelli. The Alianelli marriages also have the Fedi for 'assignment', dated 1751 and 1754.

115. A.P.T., Assistance Section, Charity and Worship, Marriages, years 1711–1727.

116. M. G. Rienzo, *Nobili e attività caritative a Napoli nell'età moderna. L'esempio dell'Oratorio del SS. Crocifisso dei Cavalieri in San Paolo Maggiore*, in G. Galasso, C. Russo (eds.), *Per la storia sociale e religiosa del Mezzogiorno d'Italia*, Naples 1982, p. 270.

117. Galasso defines it as such in *Intervista sulla storia di Napoli*, Bari 1978, p. 72.

118. There is reason to believe that payment mandates were settled in the vast majority in bank policies but, sometimes, also in cash, thus creating, for administrators, the problem of finding metallic currency not always offered by the market at a convenient premium.

119. This is how it is indicated in the frontispieces of the Treasurer's Books.

120. Not that the management of the Governors was indirect, but compared to their administrative functions, more linked to operations and economic investments, that of the Religious Fathers was more executive and above all in close contact with the "family" of the Conservatory.

121. C. D'Engenio, *Napoli Sacra*, I ed. by Ottavio Beltrano, Naples 1624, p. 487 and C. De Lellis, *I sunti di Carlo d'Angiò*, Caserta 1893 in S. Di Giacomo, *Il Conservatorio di Sant'Onofrio a Capuana e quello di Santa Maria della Pietà dei Turchini*, cit, p. 180. Both the Somaschi and the Jesuits belong to the order of the Regular Clerics, congregations that arose after the Council of Trent, therefore from the sixteenth century onwards, to educate young people. On the subject, see G. B. Del Tufo, *Historia della religione de' Padri Clerici Regolari*, Rome 1609 and R. De Maio,

4 THE EXPERIENCE OF THE CONSERVATORIO DELLA PIETÀ ... 205

Società e vita religiosa a Napoli nell'età moderna, 1656–1799, Naples 1971.

122. A.P.T., Platea II, 2, 27.
123. The Sacred Royal Council was one of the three governing bodies of the State that Naples hosted, in addition to being the seat of the Viceroy and his court. The other two were the Collateral Council and the Chamber of the Summaria, two of the highest magistracies of the kingdom. The administrative function was accompanied by the judicial one, held by the imposing Vicarìa tribunal. See M. Schifa, *Il Regno di Napoli al tempo di Carlo Borbone*, Milan-Rome-Naples 1923, I, pp. 26–27, 29, 36–40.
124. The royal delegate was appointed by the viceroy and was chosen from among the magistrates of the main courts.
125. In fact, in 1720 the White Confreres asked and obtained from Emperor Charles VI a further royal assent to the new statutory rules that confirmed their validity and, in particular, reaffirmed that the election of the governors of the Conservatory should take place through the confreres. In 1751, the rational Don Andrea Mammana, drafted, at the opening of the new Platea, a memory of the Conservatory and his words reflect the bitterness of those who are forced to acknowledge not too flourishing living conditions due to the "lay misgovernment." In 1756, the elective principle received another royal assent, but six years later, Counselor Borgia, then Delegate of the Conservatory, tried to introduce a new system of election of governors that excluded the White Confreres. The reform, initially approved by the king, was contested by the Whites because it was "harmful to their rights." Thus, they obtained, on May 31, 1768, the king's confirmation of the new rules, according to which the governors could be elected among the confreres themselves and without royal approval (A.P.T., Platea II, 2, 27, Memory of the Conservatory).
126. This could be one of the reasons why the Conservatory's documentation, despite its abundance, appears to have gaps. Probably the Governors took with them, outside the Conservatory, documents that were then lost or simply remained in their homes or offices.
127. For example, the five-year period 1745–1750 saw Francesco and Biase Crisaiolo as collectors, who, out of a total of 6,518.64 ducats for rents, collected 265.51 ducats as collection rights

(A.P.T., Accounting, Rents, leases and censuses, 26 bis, *Nota dell'esazione delle pigioni del Conservatorio*, 1745–1750).

128. Among the musicians identified, we recall Tommaso Persico, Gaetano Veneziano, Nicola Serino, and others.

129. In 1660, the total wages for the staff at the Conservatory amounted to two. 353.45 (A.P.T., Libro Maggiore 11, 2, 20), expenses for food, infirmary, and other extraordinary expenses amounted to two. 1,220.10, those for the Church and Sacristy amounted to two. 133.88, while the expenses for the shoes and stockings of the children were equal to two. 148.8. These last expenses rose to two. 282 in 1661; they decreased the following year to two. 194.75 and amounted in 1663 to 243.05 ducats (A.P.T., Libro Magg. 11, 2, 20, Expenses for Shoes and Stockings for the children in the years 1660–1663).

130. Conservatory of Pietà dei Turchini. Welfare and management expenses in the years 1753–1755, in ducats.

Years	Welfare expenses	Management expenses
1753	3,316.45	3,133.07
1754	3,947.86	5,200.39
1755	3,747.18	3,209.58

Source Giornali d'introito ed esito del Mensario (Monthly Budgets) 1753–1755.

131. The documentation cataloged in the "Students and Boarders" Section has been fully consulted.

132. Female students never appear among the children of the Conservatory. The only female presences in the Rolls are those of 20 non paying boarders, one-time only, but only at the beginning of the nineteenth century and in the documentation relating to the dispensation of marriages.

133. It should be remembered that from 1673 to 1701, Francesco Provenzale, one of the greatest composers of the seventeenth century, taught at the Conservatory of Pietà dei Turchini.

134. A.P.T., Accounting, III, 1, 2.

135. The distinction between the three categories, sons-students-boarders, is in this case linked to the heading of the lists found. The term son is, however, the one that identifies the boy hosted in the Conservatory, whether a student or boarder. The difference

between the last two is instead more marked and will be explained later.

136. Plegio was the one who guaranteed the good conduct and good will of the boy by signing a policy of 50 ducats for precautionary purposes and was personally responsible in case the student ran away from the conservatory or caused damage to the institution or people.

137. The Istromento di Ammissione was a kind of contract that was drawn up in the presence of the Conservatory's Notary, one or two of the Governors, the "son" to be admitted, his guardian or more often his "Plegio." It established the duration of the stay in the Conservatory, the fee and payment methods, the registration fee (the so-called entrance fee of 12 ducats), and the type of studies the son was about to undertake. Those that have come down to us refer to the registration of older students, often already possessing musical knowledge and skills, but the admission instrument was drawn up in any case, even when the son was admitted to be trained in a trade.

138. Both F. Florimo and S. Di Giacomo, the only two authors of an "integral" history of the four Neapolitan conservatories (the second being decidedly more faithful in historical and archival reconstruction), overlook the manufacturing activities of the "Turchini sons" while dwelling on those of the sons of Loreto and S. Onofrio a Capuana. See F. Florimo, *La scuola musicale di Napoli e i suoi Conservatori*, cit., and S. Di Giacomo, *Il Conservatorio di S. Onofrio e quello di S. Maria della Pietà dei Turchini*, cit., and Id., *Il Conservatorio dei Poveri di Gesù Cristo e quello di S. Maria di Loreto*, cit.

139. In a register of the Archive of the Conservatory of S. Maria di Loreto (A.S.M.L.) which reports the *Notamento* of orphans between 1586 and 1594, "it notes all the orphans who are received, raised daily in this blessed House of S. M. di Loreto" and, together with the names of the orphans, the trade they were about to learn, the name of the master and the location of his residence or his workshop.

140. In fact, there are frequent contracts made with local master craftsmen for the training and employment of the sons in the manufacturing sector (spinners, hat makers, glove makers, etc.)

(see A.S.M.L., *Notamento degli orfani*, archival source already cited).

141. "Within the urban fabric, the different places of entertainment tend to be topologically distinguished; in particular, the public halls are concentrated in some clearly identifiable areas of the city. Numerous theatrical halls are located near the Largo del Castello, which, frequented mainly by the lower middle class and the people, constituted a circuit on the margins of the official theater. In the viceregal city, in fact, the levels of enjoyment of theatricality are separated: in opposition to the public halls, there is a phenomenon of privatization of the show, which is absorbed within the noble palaces. There are three possible spaces for performances: the courtyard, the garden, and the hall" (P. L. Ciapparelli, *I luoghi del teatro a Napoli*, cit., pp. 379–412; B. Croce, *I teatri di Napoli*, cit.).

142. Archive of the Conservatory of S. Onofrio a Capuana (A.S.O.), IV.2.107. The governors of the conservatory of S. Onofrio in a representation to the king asked that the other conservatories be ordered not to accept children who had run away from another institute or who had not fulfilled the obligations provided for in the contract.

143. G. Galasso, C. Russo, *Per la storia sociale e religiosa del Mezzogiorno d'Italia*, cit. pp. 258–260.

144. The sources do not help us in identifying the priest, probably also a Chapel Master in Viesti.

145. The painter Nicola Vaccaro was buried precisely in the Pietà dei Turchini and his friendship with the musician Alessandro Scarlatti was well known (B. De Dominici, *Vita de' pittori, scultori e architetti napoletani*, 3 vols., Francesco and Cristoforo Ricciardi, Naples 1742, III, p. 154).

146. A.P.T., section Pupils and Boarders.

147. L. De Rosa reports the news of the arrival of a group of young Portuguese in Naples in 1760 who came to study music. See L. De Rosa, *Navi, merci, nazionalità, itinerari in un porto dell'età industriale. Il porto di Napoli nel 1760*, in *Saggi e Ricerche sul Settecento*, Naples 1968.

148. C. Petraccone, *Napoli dal '500 all'800*, cit, p. 114 and R. Romano, *Napoli dal Viceregno al Regno*, Turin, Einaudi 1976.

149. A.P.T., Correspondence Section.

150. The term *"paranza"* generally refers to a typical fishing boat equipped with a single triangular sail called a Latin sail. In the Conservatory, however, it identifies a group of sons called to accompany the "exit" of the statue of this or that saint, the Madonna or the Corpus Domini. The connection with the nautical etymology of the word could be the reference to the boat's mast and the triangular sail. Venturing a more extensive hypothesis, the term *paranza* could also recall the tradition of processions at sea.

151. The angels were probably the roles assumed by the youngest sons. It is evident the respect for a scenic liturgy dictated by the use of the time.

152. A.P.T., Printed Rules of 1769, p. IX.

153. Giacomo Tritto (Altamura, Bari, 1733–Naples, 1824) was first a student at the Conservatory, then a junior teacher (1759), and later an extraordinary teacher (1785). In 1787, he became the Director of the Teatro di San Carlo, and from 1799 to 1807, he taught counterpoint and composition at the Pietà dei Turchini. Along with Paisiello and Fenaroli, he assumed the direction from 1806 until 1813. He was the Master of the Royal Chapel and the Royal Chamber. Among his students were Bellini, Spontini, Raimondi, and Mercadante. He wrote a large number of theatrical works, comic dramas, intermezzi, comedies for music, including the famous *Le nozze contrastate* (1754), *La scuffiara* (1784), *La donna sensibile o sia Gli Amanti riuniti* (1798). He also composed serious and semi-serious works, cantatas, sacred music, and didactic works (DEUMM, Utet, Turin 1988, *The biographies*, vol. VII, p. 97).

154. Nicola Sala (Tocco Caudio, Benevento, 1713–Naples, 1801) was a theorist, composer, and teacher. A student at the Conservatory since 1732, he had teachers such as Fago and Leo; he became first a junior teacher and then a full-time teacher from 1785 until his death. Among his students were Tritto, Farinelli, Fioravanti, and Spontini. He wrote theatrical works such as Vologeso, oratorios, and didactic works (DEUMM, cit., vol. VI, p. 539).

155. That is, he was suitable for the interpretation of comic operas, probably as a bass.

156. G. Moricola, *L'Albergo dei Poveri*, cit., p. 122.

157. Gaspare Spontini (Maiolati, Ancona, 1774–1851) was an Italian composer and conductor, naturalized French. He entered the Conservatory in 1793 and studied with N. Sala and G. Tritto. He escaped in 1795 and, at the invitation of impresario Sismondi, went to Rome, where he was commissioned to compose a farce that made him famous. In 1803, he left for Paris, where he debuted at the Opera-Comique with success and began to adopt French texts. His restlessness continued even in his maturity: in 1840, he was tried for lese-majesty and sentenced to nine months in prison. Among his works, we remember *La Vestale* with a text by Victor-Joseph Etienne de Jouy (DEUMM, cit., vol. VII, pp. 411–414).

158. A.P.T., Students and Boarders Section.

159. On June 7, 1794, Donato Deonchia enrolled for eight years at the Conservatory but, "being poor, having learned the double bass and with the obligation to copy 30 sheets of music paper per month", in November 1797, he moved to the stayus of non paying student (A.P.T., Students and Boarders, IV).

160. A. Pompilio, *Editoria musicale a Napoli e in Italia nel Cinque-Seicento*, in *Musica e Cultura a Napoli dal XV al XIX secolo*, cit, pp. 79–139. For more on Neapolitan publishing, see L. De Matteo, *Tra "arte" e industria. L'editoria napoletana nella seconda metà del Settecento*, in *Storia Economica*, year I, phase. I, Edizioni Scientifiche Italiane, Naples 1998, pp. 7–26.

161. P. Villani, *Note sullo sviluppo economico e sociale del Regno di Napoli nel Settecento*, «Rassegna economica», 1 (1972), p. 34; G. Pardi, *Napoli attraverso i secoli*, Naples 1924.

162. A.P.T., 1.2,11, 1779.

163. The Pietà dei Turchini serves, in those three years, the following places, churches, monasteries, convents, and congregations: College of St. Joseph in Chiaja, Congregation of St. Thomas Aquinas, Congregation of the Rosariello of the Palace, Congregation of the Holy Spirit of the Palace, Congregation of the Most Holy Rosary of Monte di Dio, Congregation of Carmine erected in the Monastery of Concordia, Congregation of the Third Order of St. Francis of Assisi in St. Mary of the New, Monastery of St. Mary Apparete, Monastery of St. Antoniello outside Porta Medina, Church of St. Mary of Poliero, Church of St. Mary of Help, Church of St. Bridget, Church of St. Mary of Grace in

Toledo, Church of St. Mary of the Soul, Church of St. Francis of Paola, Church of St. John the Greater, Square or Street of the Lancers of St. John the Greater, Square or Street of St. Peter Martyr, Square or Street of the New Banks at Mezzo Cannone, Church of St. Clare, Church of St. James of the Italians, Church of St. Joseph, Church of St. Mary of all good, Church of St. Liborio, Parish Church of the Incoronatella on Pietatella, Church of St. Mary of the Angels at Pizzo Falcone, Parish Church of St. Joseph, Congregation of the Most Holy Rosary of St. Lucia at Sea, Congregation of the Most Holy Sacrament in St. Dominic Major, Church of St. Charles of the Mortelle, Monastery of St. Mary of Consolation, Church of St. Mary Star of the Sea, College of St. Aspreno of the Crucifer Fathers outside Porta St. Gennaro, Parish of St. Mary of the Rotonda.

164. One of the most detailed contracts seemed to be the one signed with the Church of St. Charles at Mortelle. The commitment undertaken by the Conservatory of Pietà dei Turchini consisted of sending, on the second Sundays of each month and on the Sundays of Lent, at twenty-one o'clock, an "appropriate" number of "musical sons," i.e., singers, and other sons with instruments to "sing" Vespers or to perform a "musical entertainment" with Motets, Litanies, and Symphonies during the Sacred Function. And again, every Friday in the month of March (except on Good Friday), only in the morning, the sons would have to sing Mass or the Hymn or provide "entertainment"; on Holy Thursday and Holy Saturday, another Choir of sons would sing Mass. Moreover, on Holy Thursday, the same sons would have to accompany the Most Holy Sacrament to the Sepulcher. The contract also provided for another Choir of sons on the four days of the Circular Forty Hours, which begin on November 1st, for a sung Mass in the morning and to sing, in the "after lunch" the Vespers, the Motet, the Hymn Pange Lingua, and the Litanies. The list of performances by those sons continues with the music to be performed on the day of St. Charles, and on other days of the year for which it is always specified which songs were reserved for the morning and which for the "after lunch."

165. A.P.T., Book of Contracts, f. 37.

166. One of the public banks that operated in Naples, between the sixteenth and eighteenth centuries, was the Monte e Banco dei

Poveri, which had very particular origins thanks to the action of a typical sector of the Neapolitan bourgeoisie: the Bar (L. De Rosa, *Il Mezzogiorno spagnolo tra crescita e decadenza*, cit., pp. 110–121).

167. A.P.T., Libro degli Appalti, f. 59.

168. A.P.T., Annual Budgets, 1753–1755.

169. It will be necessary to examine the numerous bank policies settled in favor of the Conservatory by other entities (in this case theaters) or by private individuals.

170. The intermezzo is at the origin of the comic opera, and its artistic quality and content will become increasingly important in the evolution of melodrama. It could be musical (singing, instrumental, or dancing) or in prose, as in the case of the one performed by sons of the Turchini at the Monastery of Monte-oliveto. In the tradition of the intermezzo, some elements of the eighteenth-century comic style are already fully defined, from the fast comic syllabication to the humorous use of the instrumental. Some, like G. Lazarevich (*The Neapolitan Intermezzo and its Influence on the Symphonic Idiom*, "The Musical Quarterly", 1971), argue that the intermezzo would even have influenced the definition of the eighteenth-century symphonic style. On the whole issue of the intermezzo, see I. Mamczarz, *Les Intermedes comiques italiens au XVIIIe Siècle en France et en Italie*, Paris 1972.

171. Benedetto Croce indeed proposes the derivation of the "sacred drama" from the comedios dos santos, thus claiming that Spanish influence on the theater and religious music of the seventeenth century. "The sacred dramas, having abandoned the naive form of the sacred representation, and recently that of classical tragedy, had become an imitation of the famous comedios dos santos of Spanish literature. Strange dramatic expositions, divided into three days, of the life of the saint, in which angels and demons and allegorical figures, such as Profane Love, Purity, Lust, and city characters, such as the saint's parents, and the saint's lovers, and the servants, and the usual Spanish graciosos, changed into the usual Neapolitans. Various temptations, various victories, some miracles, a final triumph were the fabric of it" (B. Croce, *I Teatri di Napoli*, cit., p. 82).

172. Some performances of sacred dramas by the children of the Neapolitan conservatories are reported in the newspapers of the time. From Fuidoro, in fact, we learn about the participation of the children of S. Maria di Loreto on November 6, 1664, in the performance of *"The Martyrdom of St. Gennaro,"* which was attended by the Viceroy Cardinal D'Aragona (I. Fuidoro, ms. X.B. 14, f. 78 National Library of Naples). Again in 1672, the city chronicle reports the musical performance of *"The Phoenix of Avila Teresa of Jesus,"* by Don Giuseppe Castaldo with music by Provenzale, in the same Conservatory of S. Maria di Loreto, once again in the presence of the Viceroy, who, to quote B. Croce, "listened to it with particular taste and at 6 o'clock in the evening, was accompanied home with songs and sounds, by the captains of the ottine and the students of the Conservatory" (B. Croce, *I teatri di Napoli*, cit., p. 84). Another work by Castaldo with music by Provenzale, *"The Life of Saint Rosa,"* was performed on October 28, 1679, at S. Maria di Loreto and then repeated twice at the Royal Palace (Fuidoro, ms. X.B. 19, f. 66).

173. In particular, the Carnival Season of 1764, almost in response to the great crisis of that year which manifested itself precisely in the month of February, was an extraordinarily rich season of shows. The exceptional nature of that situation is extensively and accurately described by L. Barletta, *Il Carnevale del 1764 a Napoli Protesta e integrazione in uno spazio urbano*. Società Editrice Napoletana, Naples 1981.

174. A.P.T., Journal of Income and Expenditure, in the years 1787–1790.

175. Ibid.

176. Ibid.

177. Journals of Income and Expenditure of the Rector for the years 1761–1790, Expenses for Musical Instruments.

178. The post-Tridentine church, in addition to redefining the "musical forms" suitable for religious functions, censoring those called "profane," considered the use of other musical instruments in the Church sacrilegious.

179. The Razionale of the Banco della Pietà of Naples earned a good 600 ducats per year, to which an extra 120 ducats were added (E. De Simone, *Il Banco della Pietà di Napoli, 1734–1806*, cit., p. 1045). Galiani calculated that a married man without children

could not live on less than 8 ducats per month, or 96 ducats per year.

180. For a comparison of salaries with those of some figures in the executive ranks of the most important jurisdictions of the time, see G. Aliberti, *Economia e Società da Carlo III ai Napoleonidi*, p. 377. See also G. A. Lauria, *Napoli alla fine del XVIII sec*, Naples 1877.

181. L. De Rosa, *Navi, merci, nazionalità, itinerari in un porto dell'età industriale*, cit., p. 370.

182. The identification of these musicians has not always been possible. Of L. Leo (Brindisi, 1694–Naples, 1744), it is known that he was admitted to the Conservatory in 1709 to study cello, harpsichord, counterpoint, and singing. His debut as a composer took place in 1712 with the sacred drama *L'infedeltà abbattuta*. He was an organist at the Royal Chapel, where he became Maestro di Cappella. He also taught at the Conservatory of S. Onofrio (1725). His theatrical production was very extensive, and he supervised many of the productions of his works in Venice, Rome, Bologna, Turin, and Milan. Of N. Sala and G. Tritto, it has already been mentioned in notes 80 and 81.

183. The salaries considered are those for the years 1738 for string and wind instrument teachers, 1741–1799 for Maestri di Cappella. In general, the annual salary was agreed upon for the entire period covered by the Master's service, and during the eighteenth century, it does not seem subject to significant variations.

184. T. Chirico, *Music in the Royal Albergo dei Poveri of Naples and in the Dependent Institutes (1817–1861)*, in R. Cafiero, M. Marino (eds.), *Francesco Florimo and the Musical Nineteenth century*, Reggio Calabria, Jason editrice 1999, pp. 827–860.

185. L. Aversano, *La scuola di musica dell'Orfanotrofio Provinciale di Salerno nel XIX secolo*, in A. Carlini (ed.), *Accademie Società Filarmoniche in Italia. Studie e ricerche*, Treno, Società Filarmonica Trento 2004, pp. 9–56.

186. The Ospizio di San Lorenzo opened on October 20, 1818, in Aversa, for the Provinces of Terra di Lavoro and Molise. Music schools were introduced later, but they did not have much success, and it was decided to transform it into an artistic-mechanical institute, dedicated to the training of future workers

(E. Donisi, *Le scuole musicali dell'Orfanotrofio di S. Lorenzo di Aversa*, City of Aversa, Department of Culture, 2012).

187. T. Chirico, *La scuola di musica del Real Orfanotrofio provinciale di Reggio Calabria e le istituzioni musicali napoletane*, «Nuova Rivista Musicale Italiana», 3 (July/September 1988), ERIRAI, pp. 462–491.

188. G. Da Molin, A. Carbone, *Un mondo al maschile: il Real Ospizio di Giovinazzo nell'Ottocento*, in G. Da Molin (ed.), *Senza famiglia. Modelli demografici e sociali dell'infanzia abbandonata e dell'assistenza in Italia (secc. XV–XX)*, Cacucci, Bari 2000, pp. 407–440.

189. R. Cafiero, *Istruzione musicale a Napoli*, cit., pp. 753–825.

190. The present work constitutes a further contribution to the history of the four Neapolitan institutes, which the author has already dealt with.

191. The Neapolitan "musical" conservatories, perfectly integrated into the European perspective of renfermement, were born as assistance institutions for poor and abandoned children with the aim of reintegrating them into society through the learning of an art or a trade. The Conservatory of Pietà dei Turchini was one of the four institutes, all established in Naples between the sixteenth and seventeenth centuries, into which the other three conservatories (St. Maria di Loreto, St. Onofrio a Capuana, and the Poor of Jesus Christ) merged, through a series of events.

192. R. Del Prete, *Un'azienda musicale a Napoli*, cit.

193. All of this has been, as mentioned, the subject of previous publications; in this context, only additions to what has already been discussed elsewhere will be provided, without any claim to exhaust the topic which, given the consistency of its sources, is still largely to be developed.

194. B. Geremek, *Renfermement des pauvres en Italie (XIV–XVII siécle)*, cit. pp. 205–217.

195. The musical performances required of the children were made up of "music, paranze, contracts, funerals, and angels." The demand varied depending on the situation: for popular festivals, generally one or more soloists or an ensemble were requested, while private individuals often asked for "choirs of angels" on various occasions, but mostly for funeral ceremonies. Convents, congregations, or parishes made use of the participation of the "children" in masses,

processions, or solemn liturgical ceremonies. The income derived from the musical activity of the children thus constituted a very wide range of musical services offered (R. Del Prete, *Un'azienda musicale a Napoli*, cit.

196. This practice of "shelter," suggested by a management policy still of an assistential type throughout the 1600s, will gradually be abandoned and replaced, during the 1700s, by a system of admissions established by rules of a "didactic" nature, more selective and suggested by a "musical" demand formulated not only by religious clients, but by private individuals, nobles, and the Viceroy himself.

197. The Platea of the Conservatory, from 1751, reports all the rules established in the Statute of 1583 and the subsequent integrations or modifications (Archive of the Conservatory of Pietà dei Turchini, from now on A.P.T., Platea, II.2.27). On the different uses of the children, see R. Del Prete, Un'azienda musicale a Napoli, cit.

198. Between 1745 and 1762, out of 90 children, 30 studied singing (11 as soprano, 10 as alto, 6 as tenor, and 3 as bass), 8 as chapel masters, 30 studied violin, 3 cello, 2 double bass, 8 oboe, 6 trumpet, and 1 bassoon (A.P.T., Section Students and Convicts).

199. In reality, band teachings prevailed in the music school of the Albergo dei Poveri, from which some children also came to the Turchini (R. Del Prete, *Un'azienda musicale a Napoli*, cit, p. 442). On the Albergo dei Poveri, see G. Moricola, *L'industria della carità*, cit., and T. Chirico, *Le scuole musicali del Real Albergo dei Poveri di Napoli*, cit., pp. 827–859.

200. Some elements to reconstruct the social, professional, geographical characterization of the first sons and to identify the paths through which they come into contact with the new assistential reality are provided by the Appendix attached to this work.

201. The "pleggeria" consisted of a guarantee offered mostly by craftsmen or merchants to students and sometimes to boarders, generally amounting to 50 ducats. The sum was paid as a precautionary measure, and the guarantor assumed responsibility for responding personally in case the student fled the Conservatory without completing their «istrumento» (with which they had committed to "produce" for the institution for a certain number of years) or caused damage to the House or people.

202. See Table 16.
203. Unfortunately, the data in the appendix cannot be exhaustive of the entire "scholastic platea" of the Conservatory of Pietà dei Turchini, but combined with the data of Guido Oliviero, Aggiunte a La scuola musicale di Napoli di F. Florimo: i contratti dei figlioli della Pietà dei Turchini nei prootocolli notarili (1667–1713), in *Francesco Florimo e l'Ottocento musicale*, cit., pp. 717–752, and the older ones of S. Di Giacomo, The Conservatory of Sant'Onofrio a Capuana and that of S. Maria della Pietà dei Turchini, Remo Sandron, Palermo 1924, can provide further biographical information on the musicians of the time.
204. See Table 18.
205. The stay of the sons in the Conservatory varied, for the years 1745–1762, between six and ten years. As it is still the case today, the years of study planned for the violin class were at least ten, as well as for the cello and other instruments. The ten years of stay represent a constant in the period 1755–59, while in the following years, 1759–1762, the duration of the stay tended to vary between five and ten years.
206. In the documentation, there is still a file concerning insubordination practices and the subsequent imprisonment of some sons in the San Felice al Cavone Prison. The file refers to the episode of December 1781, when the Royal Counselor, delegate of the Conservatory, ordered the rector Don Matteo Lambiase to include the eunuchs in the services of the House, who until then had been exempt from any domestic activity within the community of the Turchini. It was then that the rector, following that order, published the list of all the students destined to "perform duties," including the eunuchs Antico and Rosselli, appointed as stewards. One of the previous stewards, Giovanni Pagano, out of spite, stole the keys to the pantry. The eunuch Rosselli reported it to the rector who scolded the guilty student. At the time of the bread distribution, in the dining hall, by the two new stewards, no son wanted to verify it. The rector called the "seditious" ones, but they ran away and stayed out of the Conservatory for two days. Upon their return, they justified themselves by saying they had "gone to make music in Castellamare for a nun's ceremony." The fact was reported to Counselor Vincenzo Borragine, royal delegate. The following document is the report of the official of the

Sacred Royal Council, Michele Spadette, who, having personally gone to the Cavone of S. Eframo Nuovo (in the House of Don Filippo Stromino) to arrest the six sons who had taken refuge there, found as many as 13 who "made music" and opposed the imprisonment of the six reported sons. They were all arrested on January 15, 1782, but by order of the delegate, those not included "in the list" were immediately released. [In the list were Paolo della Corte, Giovan Battista Perano, Antonio Antico, Andrea Verde, Luigi Platone, and Tomaso Negri (A.P.T., Sez. Students and Boarders, IV.3.20)]. It was Michele Spadette who asked the royal counselor to remove the turquoise robe from the six imprisoned sons, "which was not suitable to keep because it was of no decorum for the royal conservatory." But the prisoners did not even obey the order to return the robes.

207. A.P.T., Printed Rules of 1769, pp. VII–VIII.

208. Ibidem.

209. The distinction between instrument teachers and music teachers can be attributed to the consideration of the Chapel Master as a music teacher. About instrumental musicians in Naples in this period, see A. Del Donna, *Instrumental Music in Late Eighteenth-Century Naples: Politics, Patronage and Artistic Culture*, Cambridge University Press 2020.

210. A "paranza" included a certain number of sons (between 12 and 20 sons) to be sent to congregations or in procession, to accompany with songs and sounds the celebration of a particular religious or popular ceremony (R. Del Prete, A Musical Company in Naples Between the Five and Six Hundred, cit.,pp. 440–441).

211. A.P.T., I, 4–20 (1785).

212. In some documents, the eunuchs are housed in the infirmary, probably because they are more delicate and in need of care (A.P.T., II.3.42). There is no mention of any castration practices carried out in the same institute.

213. A.P.T., Platea, II.2.27 (1751).

214. The Rules insist a lot on the conduct to be observed during lessons and on the order in which to keep one's school material, sometimes specifying even the smallest details.

215. In fact, teachers were not always able to personally guide the students, therefore, often older or more skilled students took their place, carrying out a large part of the lessons.

216. A.P.T., Printed Rules, 1769.
217. One of the governors, in turn, performed the role of the monthly officer, who took care of "all the necessary things for that month, kept the money and spent when necessary with the consent of the other governors" (A.P.T., Statute of 1583 and Platea of 1751).
218. The rigidity of wages is common, in that period, to various categories of Neapolitan workers (Cfr. E. De Simone, *Case e botteghe a Napoli nei secoli XVII e XVIII*, Genéve, Droz 1977 and the data of R. Romano, *Prezzi, salari e servizi a Napoli nei secoli XVII e XVIII*, Milano, 1965). Between 1741 and 1799, for example, a chapel master of the Pietà received an annual salary of 96 ducats. In general, the annual amount was agreed upon for the entire period covered by the master's service record. On the remuneration of the Conservatory staff see Table 13.
219. In 1573, the Confraternity of the Whites under the title of St. Mary of the Incoronatella founded an oratory. Ten years later, the same Confraternity drew up the statute of the Conservatory of the Pietà dei Turchini and moved from the Church of the Incoronatella to that of the Pietà dei Turchini.
220. State Archive of Naples, from now on ASN, Theater Bundles 1759–1760. The supplication is also reported by S. Di Giacomo, *Il Conservatorio di Sant'Onofrio*, cit. p. 241.↑
221. R. Del Prete, A musical company in Naples between the sixteenth and seventeenth centuries, cit., pp. 446–449.
222. ASN, Theater Bundles 1759–1760.
223. A.P.T., Correspondences, Supplications and Memorials, January 14, 1763.
224. Charles Burney, *The Present State of Music in Italy*, Becket, London 1771 (Italian translation. *Viaggio musicale in Italia*, edited by Enrico Fubini, EdT/Musica, Turin 1979, p. 294).
225. Katherin Preston, *Opera on the Road. Traveling Opera troupes in the United States, 1825–60*, University of Illinois Press, Urbana and Chicago 1993.
226. Luigi De Rosa, *Il Mezzogiorno spagnolo tra crescita e decadenza*, Mondadori, Milan 1987.
227. A.P.T., I, 2, 12.
228. In August 1781, Carlo Parise, probably an impresario, paid the Conservatory d. 55. Of that sum, 40 ducats were for "gratification" to the Conservatory and 15 ducats were divided among the

sons who had sung at the Teatro dei Fiorentini for 13 evenings in the opera titled Il Matrimonio Inaspettato. In September 1781, Vincenzo Montalto, probably the impresario of the Teatro di San Carlo, paid d. 60 as a completion of d. 75 for the efforts of the Conservatory's sons in the three Dramas titled L'Arbace, l'Armida and Amore e Psiche staged during the previous year's Carnival. The same Montalto paid another d. 25 for participation in the drama l'Antigone. In September 1784, Giuseppe Coletta, perhaps another impresario, paid d. 14.40 as compensation for the nine evenings (d. 1.6 per evening) in which eight sons had served in the Choirs of the Teatro dei Fiorentini, in the cantata titled I filosofi immaginari. Giuseppe Lucchesi paid, in April 1785, 80 ducats for the boys who had sung in the choirs of the Teatro del Fondo in the staging of the Drama titled La figlia di Gefte. On that occasion, the conservatory student Ranieri Delpino, for having played a part in that drama, earned 9 ducats. The same student then received 12 ducats from Antonia Rubinaccio, for having replaced her in the 8 performances of the opera L'Antigone. In September 1786, Diomede Carafa de' Duchi di Maddaloni paid a total of d. 16.95 for the services rendered at the Teatro Nuovo by four singing sons for sixteen evenings in the reruns of the opera Il Credulo given during the Carnival season (A.P.T., Giornali d'introito ed esito del Rettore, nn. 28, 31, 32, years 1781, 1784, 1785). Evidently, the same need for cash suggested to the Conservatory's rector to overlook, even if "unofficially," the prohibition of musical performances by the sons at the theaters.↑

229. "Whenever a church or a group wants to put on a musical performance (which often happens in Italy), a letter is sent to the rector asking for the service of 20, thirty or more boys for a modest but established price. This benefits the institution, contributes to its maintenance, and multiplies the number of artistic performances in the city," Josse de Villeneuve, Letter on the mechanism of Italian opera, 1756, p. 108.

230. Proposals for the census of two properties of the Conservatory date back to 1793, which would have given the institute about 30 ducats more than the income from the rents collected on those houses (A.P.T., volume of Cautele ed Istrumenti, I.3.16).

231. It was precisely to provide the conservatorists with the sources of tradition that, after the royal approval of the memorandum presented to the Court by Mattei, a vast collection of different music was arranged, which constituted the basic core of that bibliographic musical treasure that, even today, is in the Library of the San Pietro a Majella Conservatory (M. Amato, The Library of the "San Pietro a macella" Conservatory in Naples: From the Original Core to the Donations of Private Nineteenth-Century Funds, in M. Marino, R. Cafiero (eds.), *Francesco Florido and the Musical Nineteenth Century*, cit., pp. 645–669).

232. The first "obligations," a sort of public act stipulated between two people, were signed by the clarinet teacher Demetrio Pellegrino, who accompanied his group of students for the music of the SS. Maria Vergine della Concezione and for the Octave of the same festivity. The price of that service was 30 ducats, which would have been paid according to predetermined methods: 10 ducats in advance in "sounding money," another 10 ducats in a policy to be stipulated on the day of his return to Naples. The earnings of that service would then have been divided equally between the teacher and his students. 10 ducats were given to him before departure. The hunting horn professor, Gaetano Coluzzi, for the same type of service, would have had to collect 40 ducats: 15 in advance in cash, another 15 upon return, always in cash, and the remaining in the form of a 10 ducat policy. The clarinet professor, Domenico Briscoli, accompanied his group of students on November 15 of the same year, first to Maratea, by land, then to Catanzaro where he would have arrived by boat, for the "price and value" of 70 ducats, of which 40 in actual currency, 30 in policies before leaving and the remaining upon return. He would have received 24 ducats before setting off on his journey. The last obligation was that destined for the bassoon teacher, Nunziante Rava. He too would have passed through Maratea where he would have embarked for Catanzaro, for the price of 40 ducats: 30 in cash, 10 in policy. He was given 15 ducats in advance at the time of departure (A.P.T., SectionAlunni e Convittori).

233. A.P.T., Libro Maggiore II, 2, 29, f. 130.

234. A.P.T., Bilanci mensuali, 1798.

235. During the period 1753–1779, expenses for the provisioned at the Pietà dei Turchini ranged between 608 d. and 1009.40 d.

(A.P.T., Monthly budgets 1753–1779). If we consider the 893 d. of 1797 and the increased number of paid employees, it is clear that we are facing a rather low figure.

236. A.P.T., I, 3, 17.

237. The ledgers that attest to these expenses are all from the Banco dello Spirito Santo and provide details of the repairs, the names of the workers, the Royal Engineer, and the various payments (Historical Archive of the Banco di Napoli,Banco dello Spirito Santo, vol. of ledgers, 26 November 1805; 4 December 1805; 10 December 1805).↑

238. G. Pannain, *The Royal Conservatory of Music in Naples*, Florence 1952, supplemented by very useful appendices with laws and various documents from 1883 to 1941. On the establishment of the Royal College of Music, see also R. Cafiero, The Royal College of Music in Naples in 1812: A Balance Sheet, in *Analecta musicologica*, 30 and Id., Musical Education in Naples: The "College of Music for Young Ladies" (1806–1832), in *Francesco Florimo and the Nineteenth-Century Music*, cit., pp. 753–826.

239. In the report sent by the President of the board of the new conservatory to the Minister of the Interior, in January 1814, there are among other suggestions for a "judicious" administration of the assets of the ancient conservatories, also instructions for the teachers who at that time served in the Royal College of Music: they were required to provide their service for both administrations "for the same money" (Archive of the Royal College, n. 210, f. 2, in R. Cafiero, The Royal College of Music in Naples in 1812, cit.).

240. R. Cafiero, *Istruzione musicale a Napoli*, cit., p. 756.

The Entrepreneurial Adventure of Music in the 1800s: The Places, the Protagonists, the System of Production and Fruition, Publishing

1 CULTURE ON THE AGENDA OF THE MINISTERS OF UNITED ITALY

The cause of civilization is dearer to me than to anyone else. I would gladly devote my whole life to advancing it one step.

So wrote, in March 1829, Camillo Benso Count of Cavour, politician and statesman, minister of the Kingdom of Sardinia, head of the government and, in 1861, with the proclamation of the Kingdom of Italy, first president of the Council of Ministers. And suppose it is true that theater was considered a means of civilization, representation and social control, we should be able to assume that Cavour devoted some attention to it. Certainly, he was a regular attendee of it, as well as of salons, that is, of those places that were the epitome of a rising bourgeoisie that carved out its spaces among those of the aristocracy.

The concept of "middle class" and then the somewhat later concept of "borghesia" dominated the history of municipal, urban, and manufacturing Italy. The interweaving of behaviors, social realities differing in modes of economic investment, wealth and family strategies, defined the middle class and the national and local bourgeoisie in the long Italian and European nineteenth century.[1] The theater, like the salon, retained an

© The Author(s), under exclusive license to Springer Nature
Switzerland AG 2024
R. Del Prete, *The Neapolitan Creative Economy*, Palgrave Studies in
Economic History, https://doi.org/10.1007/978-3-031-55903-7_5

exquisitely worldly character and constituted at the same time a surrogate of political associationism at the forbidden time, a place of confrontation often time very different opinions; "it was by its very nature a cosmopolitan place, with open features, where the local *elite* that constituted its core (the *habitués*) mingled with a supra-regional *elite* [...]. An eclectic and worldly place, then, the salon [like the theater] also had the specificity of mixing within it men and women, young and old",[2] aristocrats, members of the financial and productive bourgeoisie, students, and military personnel.

The theater, in particular, reflected the different hierarchies and social classes, discernible in the way spectators were distributed among the stalls, boxes and gallery. The authorities' control over the theaters was strictly exercised and enforced in compliance with regulations and rules that governed the behavior of the audience in the auditorium, although it was very difficult to contain the enthusiasm, criticism, and strong emotional participation, especially during the 1840s, when, circumventing censorship, Giuseppe Verdi's music acted as a soundtrack to patriotic ferment, sending out allusive political messages and incitements to war against the foreigner.[3] Thus, it was in this way that in the first half of the nineteenth-century opera, also and above all thanks to Giuseppe Verdi's political commitment, acquired a patriotic and nationalistic value, defining its space, scenic and social, in the multiplied and revitalized theaters. The attention of the unified state to theaters, however debatable, as we shall see later, intersected with an ever-increasing attention to the dissemination of culture: the new Italian municipalities tried, despite a thousand economic difficulties, to finance the construction or expansion of municipal theaters as well as the opening of libraries and museums. The long and complex process of unification brought with it a growing demand for information, scientific, and political knowledge, literary and artistic consumption, and in the municipal rhetoric that was reserved for investment in infrastructure and public works, the theater became a monument to decorum and civilization.[4] The 1861 census noted an illiteracy rate of 78 percent among the Italian population; the remaining 22 percent were only able to write their names. In such a social framework it was inevitable that literature would have a small number of users. Melodrama, on the contrary, presented itself as a kind of "popular novel," easy to enjoy even at low levels of social understanding, because it was based on a universal language, the melodramatic one, capable of interpreting the instances of independence and freedom. At that time, the opera audience included all social classes and participated with a certain awareness in an era of radical changes: Verdi and the Risorgimento became one, and the *Rigoletto*—*Trovatore*—*Traviata* trilogy represented the highest and most passionate moment of nineteenth-century melodrama, while also marking its conclusion. Musical theater was increasingly destined to become, after Unification, a luxury good reserved for the *elites*.

The spread of opera had begun in the mid-seventeenth century and continued in an immediately extraordinary way until well into the nineteenth century. Its theatrical system, although not regulated and supported by any established legislative discipline, in the preunification period could count on constant subsidies from the governments and municipalities of the various Italian states, which considered the spectacle—in its highest forms—as an activity of education and instruction for the people and a source of "luster" for the government.[5] The Italian Decurionate, therefore, recognized the theater's function as a *public service* and endeavored to guarantee its survival and educational purposes through the granting of subsidies, as was the case for hospitals, fine arts and the university. But the debate was heated and there were also those who attributed a private nature to theatrical activity and would have wanted it regulated by the Commercial Code. In fact, between 1825 and 1846, the number of opera seasons increased from 128 to 270 per year, with a growth in stagings from 388 to 798 per year[6] a true economic *boom in* Italian theater.

The Statuto Albertino, issued in 1848 and later extended to the unified state, made no mention of entertainments activities.[7] It was only after unification that thought was given to establishing a "modern" national theater system, but, paradoxically, the moment an attempt was made to give it a new structure, the whole system went into crisis. Between 1859 and 1861 the former court or government theaters, including La Scala in Milan and the San Carlo in Naples, became part of the public domain and thus the responsibility of the Ministry of the Interior. The historical moment that followed was not the best for their fortunes: between the dismantling of the courts, that of the garrisons and the departure of entire diplomatic corps, the audience of *habitués*, which had guaranteed for years, along with government subsidies, a large part of the revenue, was greatly reduced.

In 1862, during the Ricasoli Ministry, a Commission for the Improvement of the National Theater was appointed to find "means to promote the increase of dramatic art." Considering Italy's ethnographic diversity, it envisioned a circuit of state theaters located in five cities, to which would be attached schools for actors and drama competitions, as well as five companies. The desirability of a General Directorate of Theaters, which would bring together supervisory and promotional powers, was evaluated; a qualified network of public acting schools and the formation of a number of stable companies to encourage the sector were envisioned; finally, the system of annual competitions for the best plays was expanded. But the project failed: there was still a lack of an institutional body in charge, and state expenditures for financing theaters fell under the budget of the Ministry of the Interior, which at that time had quite different priorities.[8] The issue was debated for a long time in Parliament, which, in 1863, voted for the abolition of the state subsidy (*dowry*) to theaters: the expenditure was eliminated from the ordinary budget of the Ministry of the Interior and was authorized, on a transitional basis, in the extraordinary budget. In that year the state allocated more than a million liras to a dozen of the theaters with the greatest opera traditions (Milan, Naples, Turin, Parma, Piacenza and on those in Modena, Pontremoli, Borgo S. Donnino, Borgotaro, and Massa) (Table 1).

The parliamentary process was long and complex. In 1865 the first royalty law was enacted (No. 2337 of June 25). In the same year another law stipulated that municipal expenditures for theaters were no longer obligatory, and in 1866, state-owned theaters were transferred to the municipalities, which continued to be under no obligation to finance theaters (Table 2).

Table 1   Budget of the Ministry of the Interior of 1863—Expenditure Chapters 10–15—Distribution of subsidies to theaters

Chapter	Detail	Lire
10	Personnel to review plays	16,776.80
11	Staff of theaters	175,136.11
12	Office expenses	3323.83
13	Endowments	776,012.42
14	Miscellaneous expenses	48,871.35
15	Premises maintenance	116,491.47
Total		1,136,611.98

Source E. Rosmini, *Legislazione e giurisprudenza dei teatri,* Hoepli, Milan 1893, p. 191

Table 2 Allocation of subsidies to theaters according to the 1866 bill

Year	Total sum (in lira)	Breakdown			
		Turin	Milan	Rome	Naples
1867	600,000	35,000	215,000	50,000	300,000
1868	450,000	27,000	160,000	38,000	225,000
1869	300,000	17,500	107,500	25,000	150,000
1870	150,000	8800	53,700	12,500	75,000

Source E. Rosmini, *Legislazione e giurisprudenza dei teatri*, Hoepli, Milan 1893, p. 191

The issue, officially raised by the bill advanced by Interior Minister Chiaves (he was the one who proposed the transfer of state-owned theaters to municipalities), concerned the debated consideration of the theater as a pastime for the few, burdening the shoulders of all contributors, or as a high public value, with important cultural and economic spillover effects on society. Two opposing fronts were created that debated for a long time what value to place on the theater; at first, as we have seen, it was decided, mainly for pragmatic reasons, to transfer funds from the ordinary budget to extraordinary expenditures (Table 2); but, in the spring of 1866, the transfer of the capital to Florence, the suppression of religious guilds and the reorganization of the ecclesiastical axis, roads and railroads, public education, and other major legislative works, together with the heralded winds of war and the urgency of related financial and military measures for defense and internal security, absorbed the government's efforts, leaving the theaters' question in abeyance.

It was resumed at the June 17, 1867, session, when on the budget of the interior, "the committee proposed that for the future it should have to cut all governmental expenditures for theaters."[9] In vain the minister pleaded the need for transitional solutions between the previous system and that of the absolute abolition of all theatrical subsidies, proposing a moderate figure provisionally for the endowment of the San Carlo di Napoli, the Scala di Milano and the Teatro di Parma; in vain some parliamentarians "advocated the cause of the fine arts and the Italian primacy of the same; but, economic and financial considerations [...] obtained the majority of the votes, and the subsidy to the theaters was cancelled."[10] The new state had other priorities, and those were years of strong economies and high taxes, such as the dreaded one on the millstone.[11]

From then on, all state expenditures on theaters were permanently abolished. An implementing regulation to the '65 law on royalties was enacted that specified the percentages to be paid to authors, according to the category of the theater in which the performance took place; to the town halls went the responsibility of controlling the income of the shows from which to take the fees for authors, keeping 5 percent for themselves. The political and popular debate did not stop: "Attempts were made to prove how the theater benefited the cities and generated wealth as well as repute among foreigners," and it is curious to think that even today, a century and a half later, the debate is still on to affirm the same principle.[12]

After the Law of 1867 was passed, the government initiated a series of practices with the municipalities in the territories where the state-owned theaters were located to cede their ownership. Rights and obligations of the ceding municipalities were dealt with on a case-by-case basis, without organic deliberation, sticking to the common law if there were no special conditions of fact or contract. Many municipalities already owned theaters and thus were already included in the system of subsidies, or endowments, which they bestowed in exchange for direct intervention in the management and supervision of the theaters.[13] On July 19, 1868, another law instituted a 10 percent tax on the gross receipts from all theatrical performances.[14]

After the splendor and economic *boom* of the first half of the century, following Unification, while Italy was actually "progressing," theater and any other form of live performance increasingly took on the characteristics of any other commercial activity, becoming a product that the artist proposed on the market, measuring himself against the laws of supply and demand and gradually losing any kind of protection by the public administration. Under free competition, both for authors and for actors and impresarios "there must be no exclusive privilege to delight, as there is not to exercise any other industry or any art."[15] And so, amid the mistrust and disengagement of the post-unification political class, relying on scarce local resources, many theaters were forced to close, either temporarily or permanently.[16]

The climate of discontent against the state was rampant, and some pointed out how France, despite the serious economic situation after the war with Prussia, had not failed to subsidize the top Parisian opera house with 800,000 francs. "Since the establishment of the Kingdom of Italy nothing has been done for music," lamented the Milan "Gazzetta musicale" in '83, echoed by the "Nuova Antologia," which, contradicting

Verdi's judgment of the illustrious statesman, accused Cavour of having been responsible for the governor's artistic absenteeism.[17] The same one who, commenting on that bursting phenomenon of "commercialization" of entertainment which exploded in the first half of the century, had called Opera "a real and great industry with ramifications all over the world," helping to spread the consideration that theater, especially musical theater, of "melodrama," stimulated commerce, tourism, circulation of currency, giving work not only to "theater people," but also to the employees of the theater's induced industries.[18] And in retrospect, we cannot blame them.

2 THE PLACES OF LIVE PERFORMANCE AND MUSIC PRODUCTION

The city is what contains all possibilities, all senses; it is the place of presence. [...] the city is also a continuous succession of scenes and stalls, places to be looked at and from which one looks and which overturn each other, continuously.[19]

Theaters have always had a strong connection with the city, in which they feel their physical presence (because of the grandeur of the buildings) and symbolic presence (because of their social role).

The European capitals of the nineteenth century were marked by the expansion of their theatrical spaces, and in Risorgimento Italy, the multiplication and expansion of theaters resulted in a substantial investment, on the part of local authorities and *elites*, that followed the directives of broader project of modernization of the urban apparatus aimed, at the same time, at performing an act of affirmation of their cultural specificity.[20]

Central places of cultural life, capable of registering the smallest changes in the taste and customs of a people, theaters have characterized every phase of the development of Western civilization, and Italy, in this particular cultural process, has played a very prominent role. The spread throughout Europe of the Italian-style theater, with its typical horseshoe layout, surrounded by several tiers of boxes, simulating windows and balconies, defines a symbolic space, a public place par excellence, which establishes with its architecture a relationship of osmosis: the theater is the elegant staging of an idealized reality, in which the portico, typical of "Italian-style" theatrical buildings, projects outward its image as a temple of "high culture," to which it attributes an "aura of sacredness" that marks its separateness from everyday existence.[21]

What is also charged with a profound symbolic value is the location of the theater building in the urban layout: near the Magistral Streets, the historical centers, the busiest squares, or close to royal palaces. The intended site of the theater building's insertion into the urban structure is both constitutive of a theater's identity and determinant in the audience's attitude: to the point of defining the type of attendance at the theater and that same urban space.[22]

Thus, from the sixteenth to the nineteenth century, the predominant performance building in European culture was that of the "Italian-style" theater, which has strongly characterized the contemporary urban environment,[23] which, while losing the significance of the building-institution, it has recovered a new cultural dimension that continues to interact powerfully with the urban landscape, but making use of totally different architectural and symbolic languages.[24]

U.S. director and anthropologist Richard Schechner, referring to the spatial arrangement derived from the Italian-style theater, structured internally by the elements that define and separate hall and stage, speaks of theaters "with the proscenium."[25] As for the interior, in fact, the first difference between traditional and alternative spaces lies precisely in this architectural, rigid, and identifiable separation that starts from the atrium, connected to the portico, which in turn starts from the street in front of the theater. This type of theater is often a focal point of the city center, characterized by mechanisms that channel much of the most important social and cultural activity toward it.[26]

Between the end of the Empire and the first two decades of the Restoration in the entire peninsula the fashion for opera spread, and every city, every municipality, large or small, built its own monument to decorum and civilization. Expensive, elaborately decorated buildings, modeled after the great eighteenth-century royal theaters (La Scala, Il San Carlo, the Regio in Turin) were erected with the concurrence of local *elites*, public interventions, or the courts, in a wild race for the most beautiful theater that prompted many municipalities to deliberate on expenditures and investments often well above their financial capacities in order to endow their city with the most fashionable ornament.

Between 1806 and 1807, Milan redecorated and restored the grand Teatro alla Scala and the Canobbiana theater, which were joined by at least seven others, all opened between 1803 and 1806: the number of seats for Milanese spectators increased from 5600 to 9400. In 1814 the new Scala stage was completed and large chandeliers were purchased to improve the lighting. In 1816 the San Carlo theater in Naples, which had been completely destroyed by fire, was rebuilt: only seven months were needed for its rebuilding entrusted to the Tuscan architect Antonio Niccolini, with an expenditure of 241,000 ducats.[27]

Care for performance venues was deeply rooted in the fabric of urban society and posed as a central element in the production of imagery and social life for the aristocratic, patrician, and upper middle-class merchant and financial classes, as well as the intellectual and artisan classes.

Dramas in verse, prose, comic operas, melodramas, dances, and puppet shows were staged in the halls, and the participation of the always diverse public was broad in all performances.

Between 1868 and 1869, the conduct of a census of active tea-rooms counted 942 of them on Italian territory (from which Latium, Trentino, and Venezia Giulia were then excluded and would later join), distributed in 650 municipalities. Almost two-thirds of them had been built or renovated after 1815. In the 1990s, a new topographic map of Italian theaters: 1,055 theaters surveyed (prose and opera) distributed in 775 municipalities, of which only 11 were first-class and reserved for opera.[28]

But theaters were already an important presence in the great eighteenth-century Italian cities,[29] and what happened from the end of the century and throughout the first half of the nineteenth century was a very peculiar and typically Italian phenomenon. In urban centers throughout the peninsula, the construction of the new theaters exactly reproduced, in their facades as in their architecture and internal artic-ulation, the country's major eighteenth-century theaters, although they offered different importance and capacity: large halls such as the Carlo Felice in Genoa (1825) or the Ducale in Parma (1829), which re-proposed the traditional model of the court theater and could hold more than 2,000 spectators, to very small theaters for 2–300 people, scattered in smaller towns or halls of medium dimensions, from 800 to 1,500 seats, built in many other cities. The principle of emulation between cities thus triggered a theater "fever" that considerably multiplied the number of theaters in the preunification territory, all, despite the diversity of local contexts, with the same symbolic centrality and the same financing mech-anism.[30] The latter proved particularly ingenious and allowed for the surprising growth of theatrical spaces in a country poor in the capital, as

Italy certainly was in the early nineteenth century. Indeed, the construction of a hall took place with the help of the so-called "monopoly of the theatre boxes." Local notables would purchase the boxes that they used as private lounges and as a place of representation that displayed their social status. Theater, especially musical theater, represented, then as now, one of the most coveted consumptions for city *elites*, who were careful to take good care of appearances. Having a reserved box at the theater was thus a necessity for an aristocracy and a bourgeoisie forced to defend their role of power in the city. The Englishman W.J.A. Stamer, in 1878 wrote how important it was to "show up four days out of seven." Those who could not afford the expense of a subscription would be able to rent or sublet the box together with friends to whom they might even borrow it from time to time.[31] In Naples, in the '70s, an aristocratic family, "after having squandered in revelry a property," entertained relations with "affluent young people" for the sole purpose of having as gifts from them, invitations to the opera and "theater boxes."[32] Those at the San Carlo, given in concession to influential families since the theater's founding, had now become "a kind of real estate that is transmitted[va] by inheritance."[33]

Much of the social life of the upper classes took place in those boxes, the ladies received friends and admirers there informally, showing off their best *mises* while the gentlemen even used it to do business (political or economic).[34]

The system of boxes privatization thus consisted of a singular dissociation between the ownership of the building as a whole (which could be of the state, the city hall, an academy, or a shareholder company) and that of the individual boxes. In nineteenth-century buildings, in particular, new spaces were introduced where audience members gathered to discuss, take coffee, or play games and in this way theaters became self-sufficient venues for city *loisir*.

The spread of theaters was favored even by local political authorities, as these were more controllable meeting places than other meeting places such as circles, cafes, or drawing rooms; therefore, the opening of a theater was not subject to any restrictions by public authorities. Unlike in France and England, in Italy there were no limits on the number of theaters, nor were there any particular requirements regarding the genres represented in them: anyone, companies or private individuals, could open a new theater, with only the approval of the public security authorities, who had to guarantee order inside the theaters, while censor offices would regulate and control what happened on the stages.

The theater thus assumed both a public and private role, and, as the new gravitation pole of city life, became the symbolic building of the period. Equally monumental, and with similar symbolic functions, would be the buildings of the second half of the century, such as those of the railway stations, the Stock Exchange, or the large banks, all with neoclassical façades and a prospectively good position in the urban layout, which referred back to the model of the theater-temple.

From the accounts of foreign travelers of the period, we learn that to get to know the essence of a community, it was necessary to go to the theater, in small as well as large cities, because it was in the theaters that the most important part of society life was played out, without running the risk of promiscuity, given the strict hierarchical distribution of seats.

3 THE PRODUCTION SYSTEM

[...] the identification of the theater company with the productive commercial enterprise, did not lead to the expansion of theatrical life because, inevitably, the company went to operate where there was already an active market, a strong demand, thus predominantly in the large urban concentrations, precisely in the capitals of bourgeois theater. The theatre company, as a productive commercial enterprise, guaranteed only by market demand, did not have the strength to change the demand itself, and in this way it was deprived of a specific quality of intellectual work: to contribute to the transformation of cultural demand. Therefore, the autonomy of the theater 'in form and content' that the most modern sections of the intellectual class claimed was undermined. [...] In fact there was a great contradiction because the theater as a productive organization enjoyed the freedom of enterprise, but as a cultural product placed on the market it was constrained by the bonds and ties of government intervention through censorship regulations.[35]

In this system the role of the impresario was decisive. He was often a former singer, former dancer, noble amateur, or pure businessman.[36] Setting up a theatre Company or Agency meant taking up the risk of an entrepreneurial activity with dubious, yet extraordinary economic implications. The theatrical impresario was a key figure among theater owners, often the municipality, the "contracted" artists and the "paying" public. Municipalities, in particular, following a practice already known to governments that had "ceded" (i.e., contracted out) the tax collection because their own administrative apparatus was in deficit, preferred to contract out the management of the theater to a professional impresario, taken on as a sort of administrator rather than a speculator, and, just as it was the case with other monopolies, the granting of licenses or so-called "privatization" to competing impresarios almost always contemplated the issuance of a bribe.

However, it is necessary to better define roles.

The figure of the theatrical agent was born in Italy in the late eighteenth century but was not defined as a profession until the following century, coinciding with the economic *boom* of theaters. Theatrical agencies were responsible for an early, relevant form of economic and productive organization of entertainment, both drama and music. However, the first professional agents appeared in the musical field and only in a second moment they started to be active even in the drama sector.[37] The agent has a mediation and communication function and plays a role of primary importance especially in the negotiations between the impresario and the individual artist. Mediation or, as it was then called, "theatrical correspondence,"[38] is also a predominantly nineteenth-century phenomenon, although it has older origins. In particular, the spread of operatic performances outside the courts and the establishment of a tour system in the peninsula intensified and stabilized the relations between artists and patrons. For this reason, princes, diplomats, aristocrats, court officials, prelates, and wealthy merchants began to facilitate the exchange of information and set up a network of relations between them, artists, impresarios, and theater managers. Gradually, with very different purposes, those early "theatrical agents" ended up conducting real negotiations, taking full advantage of the benefits of holding public office and wide and high-level social contacts.[39]

Since the very beginning, the work of impresario attracted mainly merchants and members of the city's petty bourgeoisie or men already belonging to the world of show business, drawn by the "prospect of financial gain from the investment of capital in a promising commercial operation, but also aristocrats, induced, often for pleasure, to invest, even at a loss, their personal wealth and become involved in the commercial adventure of show business."[40]

The economic *boom* of theaters imposed the "principle of speculative efficiency," and early nineteenth century impresarios, acquiring a new economic *status*, were able to implement it: the theatrical organization thus lost "its old character of service, of performance due to the powerful," to acquire a more complete autonomy. Indeed, the theater impresario in the early nineteenth century acquired a new, more and autonomous stature. Between the emergence of money, the consequent release from an aristocratic and patronage regime that saw the traditional meddling of patrons in the organization of the show—with the increasingly rarer implication of clients in the production of the show—and a temporary inclusion of the functions of theatrical correspondence within the duties of the oldest theater organizers, the first professional theatrical agents also emerged: the impresario and for prose, the head-comedians.

As much as the operation of regular theatrical circuits fostered a widespread diffusion of opera performances in the peninsula and in many European countries, as long as the market was governed by preindustrial criteria and limited distribution needs, impresarios personally managed their own trades, dealing directly with singers, dancers, librettists, and musicians, procuring contracts, organizing seasons and forming companies. So did the head-comedians within their prose theater circuits, albeit more limited in size and resources.[41]

As the theatrical production system became more complex and articulated, the impresario had the need to interfere with the operatic theater agency. The two roles thus tended to blur, and the agent, like the impresario, was always attracted by the possibility of exercising in parallel and intermittently the more perilous path of contracting. Such behavior, typical of the first half of the century, characterized the entire category of mediators, from minor agents to the best-known merchants of the time, who succeeded in combining agency and enterprise very profitably.

The three most famous and original impresarios of the century were Domenico Barbaja, Alessandro Lanari, and Bartolomeo Merelli, who, with unusual skill, experimented with different forms of contamination between the two professions.[42] Their solid management of the Scala theater was characterized by a combination of culture, art, and gambling: Barbaja, for example, introduced *roulette tables* in the *foyer of* La Scala in 1805 and then moved to Naples, where he built a large empire between gambling, theaters, army supplies, and building contracts.[43]

The theatrical enterprise as expertly described by John Rosselli, was thus a contract that in some situations could even turn into a monopoly. But in order to exploit it, usually the entire theater facility was not delivered to the impresario, nor was it regarded as a single economic entity to be employed in order to derive maximum profit. The boxes, just as they were separated in a material and social sense from the rest of the facility, also in an economic sense might not figure in the proceeds.

The revenue of Italian theaters was constituted in a fairly complex way. Everyone (with the exception, in some periods, of stagehands) paid an entrance fee, either time by time or by a subscription for the entire season. Since the theater was the center of society life, someone could very well pay admission for the sole purpose of making visits or playing in the entrance hall. [...] The contribution of the boxes varied according to the type of ownership and the business contract. Stage owners were not part of the regular paying audience. In many theaters they were allowed to sublet their boxes making a profit, and thus competing with the impresario [...]. According to the idea in force in Italy between the eighteenth and nineteenth centuries, each theater season contracted out to an impresario involved a dowry. This could consist of a cash sum, a privilege (generally that of holding jousts or lotteries), or the right to resell the boxes.[44]

However, theater, especially musical theater, had very high costs that the bourgeoisie and aristocracy, despite its wide enjoyment for "social," purposes they could not cover. The very high production costs turned opera into an assisted industry, continually in need of economic coverages offered, once again, by the prince or by groups of the city's noble or economic power. In other words, opera theaters never fully emancipated themselves acquiring a complete professional autonomy (as happened later with prose theater), and the function originally exercised by the courts passed, in different forms according to time and place, to the hegemonic class, whose action oscillated between magnifying its social role and financial investment, sometimes extending even to the stage organization of the performance. The decisive intervention of certain musical publishing giants, as will be seen below, did the rest Musical opera, then, was (and is) certainly a very expensive product, and the geography of its venues was composite: its areas of production and those of consumption fell within a system of imperfect relations among many small, medium and large centers, none truly self-sufficient and none entirely "superfluous" to the smooth functioning of the system as a whole. This justified the different geographical origins of the many companies applying for contract theaters. The attractiveness of the product related, therefore, to the ways in which exchanges and knowledge were transmitted, and the opera house became the most important of the organizational forms on which musical production and consumption were based.

In Italy, theaters belonged either to the state (such as the ancient court theaters of Naples and Turin) or to individual families (this is the case of several Roman theaters), or, more often, to societies of aristocrats and landowners (such as the Fenice of Venice and most small provincial theaters). Almost never, however, did the owners allow themselves to be directly involved in the management of the theater, preferring to delegate it to professionals operating in the cultural sector of business. The engine of the complex organization needed to feed the opera circuit was therefore the impresario, a picturesque figure straddling the seventeenth-eighteenth-century adventurer and the modern entrepreneur. Like the latter, the impresario invested his own capital in the theater, but unlike the latter, his earning potential was linked not only to caution and initiative, since opera was (and is) a constitutionally loss-making enterprise, whose expenses regularly exceeded (and exceed) its revenues. And today, more than ever, its survival could not be guaranteed, without state incentives independent of the performances income from.[45]

The basic coordinates of the growth of the role of theater in the civic life of Italians (production, circulation, and enjoyment of texts) gave rise to an unprecedented experience of cultural consumption, offering us today an important exemplification of how to make a socio-economic history of cultural practices understood as communication practices, as well as consumption practices.[46]

4 MILAN AND THE RISE OF MUSIC PUBLISHING

Milan, unlike other Italian cities, in the early nineteenth century was a wealthy and "modern" city, characterized by a solid alliance between the large agricultural aristocratic estate and the urban merchant class, by important patrician families and those of the upper merchant bourgeoisie, freed from dynastic and conservative restraints by a long process of capital accumulation. The first stock exchange was established in Milan, followed by the Savings Bank; factories experimented with new technologies, and workers organized for their claims. An intellectual class developed in Milan that reasoned about economics and Europe, as well as United Italy. In 1748, Italy's largest theater, La Scala, was founded in Milan and between 1806 and 1807 it recovered its splendor and glitter, amid new colors, new decorations, new furnishings, and above all, new chandeliers, because of that care that Italian governments in those years reserved for theaters, monuments to decorum and civilization.

Economic development, political centrality, European-influenced industrial and financial initiatives, participation in cultural and economic life more intense and varied than elsewhere, and finally the exceptional growth of the city's printing and publishing industry had a direct effect on the theater, too which, like and more than in other Italian cities, experienced its *golden age* in the first half of the nineteenth century.[47]

The first traces of busy theatrical agents in Milan date back to the Napoleonic era, although at that time, any private activity in the theatrical field was, at least in intentions, hampered. Between 1811 and 1823, the first real theatrical agencies were those of Antonio Cuniberti and Pietro Camuri, who then decided to move their business elsewhere. These were the 1830s and 1840s, and Milan was in the hands of one of the greatest theater merchants of preunification Italy, Bartolomeo Merelli.[48]

It was also in Milan that in the early nineteenth century a young music copyist at the Carcano Theater, Giovanni Ricordi, turned his work around by acquiring ownership of the books of music he transcribed. Like almost all copyists, Ricordi was also a musician, thus able to distinguish a score copied from memory from an autograph transcription. His business grew in a short time and his interest shifted from sheet music to operas and their staging: in addition to printing the scores, Ricordi became a kind of guarantor of the quality of the performance and the intellectual property of the music. With Bellini and Donizetti he began his entrepreneurial adventure and his battle for the recognition of copyright. Giovanni Ricordi gave birth to a new profile, that of publisher-mediator, the creator of the radical transformation process that the musical and theatrical system would undergo.[49]

Between 1830 and 1870, the most important transformation of Italian opera took place: its protagonists, their intentions in the compositions, the system of production and fruition, and its social and cultural significance changed.

Music meets the publishing industry, opera knows a new season of international success and seeks new ways to secure its economies. It is the leap into modernity, a passage that bequeaths the most relevant opera repertoire in history, the recognized core of a cultural heritage that shapes the ideology of the Risorgimento.

The helmsmen are Giulio Ricordi and Giuseppe Verdi, who formed a kind of symbiotic association. Ricordi needs Verdi's genius, Verdi needs Giulio's industry, together they become great. They will be joined by Puccini and Giulio's son, Tito Ricordi, [who will be] the man of the twentieth century.[50]

Meanwhile, on the theatrical agency front, around the '50s there was a similar leavening process: Milan was swarming with aspiring opera agents, lured by the mirage of easy earnings. There were two main reasons: the country's liberalist turn and the surplus of artistic labor. On the one hand, in fact, the new rulers were no longer so concerned about controlling the opera market, making it easier to open new agencies. On the other, a surplus of artistic workforce poured into the Italian theaters, which, for sheer survival, was forced to abandon the more uncertain and competitive artistic professions and turn toward journalism and theatrical correspondence, apparently more remunerative.[51] Even more interesting is the result of the Italian population censuses that showed the numerical growth of theatrical impresarios and agents, especially in the Milanese area; a phenomenon that fits in with that, of much wider scope, of the increased demand, in the theatrical organization, for technical- logistical roles and an early development of the tertiary sector.[52]

In short, after the Unification Milan, despite the end of the expansive phase of Italian opera, was still a particularly active city on the side of cultural production, management, and enjoyment. By this time, the spread of Opera had created a ramification of productive and professional activities that were difficult to halt and that, despite the ups and downs of various economic and political conjunctures, had now laid a solid foundation for a modern and complex live performance production system and its not insignificant economic spin-off.

The second half of the nineteenth century saw another important phenomenon: the influence of music publishing houses on the opera market. Two major opera publishers from Milan, Ricordi, and Lucca, consolidated and imposed their dominance throughout the country. Italian music publishing actually had older origins and, until the 1770s, had dealt essentially with manual reproductions of orchestral or vocal parts used in theaters or conservatories.[53] Already in those years, the music press tried its hand at early forms of industrial production, in Naples and Venice, but evidently, the time was not ripe and the demand was not yet such to sustain a real publishing market.[54] In the last years of the century, the polarization among the big publishers became more pronounced: Lucca, Ricordi, and Sonzogno, by offering a large catalogue, increasingly open to all kinds of music, became the arbiters of Italian and foreign opera activity. Alongside them, a large number of musical publishing houses, mainly local in character, engaged in the printing of low-cost music or characterized by a clear specialization of repertoire.[55] In particular, from 1888 the opera market was firmly in the hands of Ricordi, which also absorbed the Lucca publishing house, and in those of the younger Sonzogno house: two score giants capable of conditioning the stylistic choices of authors and especially of Italian and foreign theaters. Thus, Milan was the city richest in entrepreneurial initiatives in the field of music publishing: in particular, from the late '60s, there was a proliferation of publishing houses that, taking advantage of the change in taste and consumption, put into the market a large number of romances, ballads and piano pieces, destined mostly for "domestic" uses, but without disdaining pieces of religious music, patriotic and school choirs, and methods for voices and instrumentalists.

In Milan, moreover, books were printed and, in the first thirty-five years of the nineteenth century, the most important publishing center of the Peninsula was defined: as a small book production district located close to La Scala, and regularly visited by officials and intellectuals who fed the activity of an entrepreneurial nucleus of printers and booksellers, the foundations were laid for the consolidation of music publishers.[56]

In no other European musical context did the development of music publishing take place—at least in the nineteenth century—in such a concentrated and oligopolistic manner as in Milan, and in no other case, to the best of our knowledge from research to date, did the advance of publishers play as decisive and far-reaching a role.

In contrast, Neapolitan publishing, which had also reaped important early results, often competing with northern publishing, declined progressively.[57]

Many publishing houses also equipped themselves with their own music magazines, with essays, reviews, and correspondence, to meet another need appearing on the Italian cultural market: that of information and culture. Much more often, however, the primary purpose of those journals was to support the publishing house's editorial policy, thus further conditioning the market, the theaters' stylistic choices, and the public's taste. Economically, it remained customary for the author to be paid a one-time sum for printing rights and a percentage on rentals and sales to theaters (for a limited period of time). The custom of paying the initial sum in monthly installments during the composition of the music became established. In addition, Italian publishers tended to establish an exclusive relationship with successful composers, preventing them from simultaneously writing for competing publishers. But the publisher's interference in composition became even more evident when the major music publishers (the case of Giulio Ricordi is emblematic), in their claim to share the gestation of an opera, began to propose subjects to be set to music, to discuss with composers and librettists the setting of the dramaturgy, even intervening in the specific musical solutions adopted by the composer.

Equally important was the role of the publisher in supporting the author once the time for staging had come: through control of the various elements of the performance (choice of conductor, singers) and through the organization of mighty publicitarian campaigns. The power that in the last decades of the nineteenth century and the early years of the twentieth century was concentrated in the hands of publishers was enormous. Then again, for many musicians in the late nineteenth century, feeling free from practical preoccupations that were all taken care of by the organizational machine that the large publishing houses put at their disposal was still a positive thing. In fact, however, many of them found themselves living and producing in a state of strong psychological dependence on their publishers, the only true arbiters of the fate of their theatrical creations.

Among the various activities of Italian music publishers was the organization of concerts, although a minority. In some cases, these were auditions organized occasionally for publicity purposes, often at the publisher's premises. Between the '30s and '40s, on Spring Sundays, Giovanni Ricordi used to organize some vocal and instrumental academies. They alternated between a large number of pieces: works in vogue, transcriptions of opera symphonies for piano for 4 or 8 hands, variations and fantasies on opera themes. The performers were often young singers, sometimes fresh out of the Milan Conservatory, seeking affirmation, but also celebrated virtuosi passing through Milan. Among the music performed, of course, were mostly those published by Ricordi.

To get an idea of the productivity of the house of Ricordi, in the fifty-year period from the end of Giovanni's era, the direction of Tito I and the initial period of Giulio Ricordi, it may be useful to mention the number of contracts that the house entered into. A total of 169 contracts with 96 different authors were registered in those years, of which 153 involved the publishing of operas; 9 the printing of librettos, and 8 that of musical compositions. What mattered the most in those negotiations, more than the number of editions derived, was the management of performance rights that on the one hand, implied a revenue on each performance of an opera (net of other rights or duties to the author), and on the other hand, it gave the publisher the right to control the manner of performances, the directions, and the staging, attributing to him, in fact, the quality criteria necessary for their success.

Income derived from rentals for performances constituted the largest income for publishers, far exceeding that from retail sales of sheet music. That was therefore the most difficult and risky time in an entrepreneurial activity that had to be conducted with resourcefulness, shrewdness, and luck.[58]

A final mention of the relationship between Ricordi and Verdi seems extremely necessary to us: in the preunification period, from '39 to '60, 36 operatic compositions were negotiated by the house of Ricordi. Of these, only 27 were remunerated, providing for a predetermined payment and a capital investment; the remaining 9, on the other hand, were contracted without fixed commitment and were therefore free of editorial risk. Among the 27 remunerated compositions, as many as 19 were by Verdi for a total amount of 282,000 lire. The contractual risks that the House took on in that 20-year period amounted to 322,724 Austrian lire, of which more than 87 percent was concentrated on Verdi's operas. This was a particularly extraordinary concentration of risk and was also the result of an upward game: Verdi became more and more expensive, but Ricordi accepted the price and, even before the Unification, secured all the maestro's major productions.[59] That of music, connected to theater, was thus a peculiar and complex entrepreneurial adventure that lasted for the long nineteenth century.

Musicians, librettists, and publishers were confronted with a highly articulated urban, legal, and economic structure, in a varied artistic system that grew, changed, flourished, and finally entered into a crisis.

In the second half of the century, the entertainment industry, by then well-articulated in its various segments, began to experiment with new

musical practices, both at the amateur level (with the explosion of the
phenomenon of philharmonic and philodramatic societies) and at the
professional and artistic level. A complex and diverse world was defined,
in which the presence of agents, impresarios, critics, and specialized magazines was felt. The debate on the issue of public promotion of the
performing arts has never died down and is still alive and intense today.
Italy also became the homeland of the resident companies that sprang
up, at the local level, thanks to forms of agreement between municipalities and private individuals (the first was, in 1877, the Dramatic Company
of the City of Turin). On the institutional terrain, the Consolidated Act of
1882 redefined copyright law and, in the same year, after a long gestation
and a serious delay compared to the French, English, and German situation, the Società italiana degli autori (SIA then SIAE) was created, with
the task of supervising effective compliance with the regulations. Finally,
the most important turning point: in the same year, Minister of Education Guido Baccelli established the first permanent Council for Dramatic
and Musical Art. At last, a permanent institutional space for reflection and
proposal on the key issues of the nation's musical and theatrical life.[60]

5   NAPLES, CITY OF LOISIR

The tradition of live entertainment—as has been said from the very first
pages of this volume—has very ancient origins in Naples. Without going
too far back in time, to recall its social, religious, political, and financial value, it will suffice to recall the Baroque festivals, the festivities on
the water of the Viceroy d'Onātte, up to those of the historic cuccagna
tree mounted in Piazza del Plebiscito. The information we glean from
the manuscript *notices*, with which *notaries, leaflets* or *gazetteers* spread
the news, laying the foundations of modern journalism, describes the
many public occasions for making music: in addition to the opera house,
which has also already been mentioned, there were indeed many occasions
for *partying* in Naples: sacred music, which responded to the demand
coming from the many Neapolitan churches, oratories, congregations,
and academies; music in homes, for festivities, weddings, or baptisms;
music intended for celebratory occasions of political power, religious
festivals, and much more.[61]

   The Neapolitan musical background, particularly the one developed
throughout the seventeenth century, preceded the systematic introduction of opera theater in the city, laying the groundwork for the creation

of a live performance market that would diversify its cultural offers and spaces and modes of performance over time, supporting variations in domanda.[62]

Naples, the city of *loisir*, which by the end of the eighteenth century was already a praised destination of the *Grand Tour*, drawing artists and intellectuals from all over Europe in search of inspiration, built or perhaps only modified, in the nineteenth century, its system of live performance.[63] Certainly, at the beginning of the new century, the artistic fervor that had characterized Neapolitan theater and music experienced the waning of an era that had seen Naples as a European musical center in which certain stylistic aspects, characteristic of opera, cantata, and, more generally, vocal solo style, had been defined and spread throughout Europe.

In the early nineteenth century the music schools that had constituted an early example of structured music education designed to create the professionals of the music market (singers, instrumentalists, copyists, masters...), under the impetus of French reorganization, were merged into a single music conservatory, first the Real Collegio di San Sebastiano, then the Conservatorio S. Pietro a Majella.[64] The institute, although while maintaining its own administrative autonomy, lost many of the musicians who had given birth to the Neapolitan School of Music and experienced the crisis of a system that now had to contend with the difficulties of theaters in securing subsidies and funding necessary for the survival of their theater seasons and that prevented them from "hiring" singers, copyists or musicians that the Conservatories had provided them with throughout the eighteenth century. Moreover, public tastes changed, and the so-called cultured music that by that time represented exclusively the social *elites*, started to lose its *appeal*. The publishing industry, which in Milan had managed to dominate the stylistic choices of composers and the playbills of most Italian theaters, was unable to find the same spaces in Naples, but it was not as active.[65]

It was foreseeable that with the Unification of Italy, in the music world life, which was an obvious part of artistic and cultural life but in some ways governed by its own laws, the relations between the various Italian regions and cities, already quite active and effective even when there was division and plurality of states, expanded into more vigorous currents in as much as they were more freely circulating and thus propitious to that general renewal of art and culture of which clear signs had already appeared, and to which circumstances and events of various kinds contributed with increasing force.

During the nineteenth century, Naples took on the full connotation of the "city of theaters": to the royal ones (San Carlo and Fondo) were added the Teatro de' Fiorentini, the Teatro Nuovo, and later the San Ferdinando and the San Carlino.[66] But there were many other places of entertainment and leisure in the *city of loisir*: public and private places, aristocratic and bourgeois residences, salons, clubs and, later, *café chantants*.

The Teatro San Carlo, founded by Charles III in 1737, was destroyed by fire in 1816: only the wall structure delimiting its perimeter remained intact. Its reconstruction was entrusted to the Tuscan architect Antonio Niccolini, who in just seven months, with a total expenditure of 241,000 ducats, succeeded in returning its monument to art and decorum to the city. Two days after the theater's reopening, a letter from the Minister of the Interior manifested "the sovereign's approval."[67]

Responsible for the fortunes of the San Carlo was, from 1809 to 1840, the impresario Domenico Barbaja who came from La Scala Theater in Milan, where, in 1805 he had already experimented with the introduction of gambling in the *foyer of* the theater (in Milan he had inserted roulette tables, in Naples he went from dice to cards).[68]

It was Charles of Bourbon who first built a real live entertainment system, giving it a balanced organization later undermined by the interference of all kinds that, over the years, could not fail to take into account the thickening gears of the system. The definitive structure was later achieved with the intervention of the French. The spectacular organization of the capital, in fact, has been over the centuries the object of governmental attention: the abundance of regulations, laws, decrees, and norms, that characterized the French decade, also invaded the world of entertainment, which, thanks to special attention, benefited from quite a good number of improvements projected in a modern and efficient vision.[69]

French intervention in the complex Neapolitan performance machine took the form, first of all, of a legislative framework, the construction of which began, with various attempts at artistic reorganization, between the end of 1806 and 1807 and found its final shape in the decree of November 7, 1811, which, in 39 articles, organically and definitively regulated theatrical matters, intervening in the programming and management of the halls, reprogramming the increasingly hectic musical life of the palace, and confirming the Royal Chapel and the Royal Theater as the propulsive centers of power.[70] Daily entertainment for the Neapolitan aristocracy and the new bourgeoisie was assured, but the involvement of the more popular classes was not lacking: dance parties, musical academies, theatrical shows, and food and wine appointments of various kinds ensured that leisure time was always used in the spirit of merriment and good music.[71]

The bourgeois salons of nineteenth-century Naples, in particular, became the promoters of their own musical activity on a weekly basis, often offering launch opportunities for young local talent. The ritual of "periodiches," salon appointments in which new musical or literary compositions were launched and, at the same time, repertoire pieces, particularly pieces of early music,[72] were re-proposed, was inaugurated. These were regular gatherings in which people were pleasantly and lightly entertained by singing, acting, and dancing. A text by Raffaele Viviani, *Fatto di cronaca*, in 1922, enacts one of the most widespread customs among the Neapolitan petty bourgeoisie that mimicked the customs of patrician and upper middle-class families. A well-established practice at that time that, starting with the most catchy arias of the official musical culture, triggers a strong interest in popular music. The repertoire in vogue in private halls, in fact, was particularly varied and reused mainly in the operatic genre, in different variants: transcriptions, variations, and paraphrases that immediately met the needs of the local publishing market, forced by circumstances to shift its attention to the most favored pieces of the melodramatic repertoire, varying the composition of its catalogues and publishing a conspicuous heritage of author sheets (some decidedly authoritative such as Rossini, Ricci, Donizetti) that had widespread circulation and fruition. This was a very effective editorial choice that would find its most authoritative affirmation only by the end of the century.[73]

What is most striking, in nineteenth-century Neapolitan theater culture, is the close and persistent relationship between the eighteenth century, highbrow theatrical and musical tradition and the encroaching popular scene of the *pulcinellate*, with its farces, parodies, and comedy. The social change to which post-Revolution Naples of 1799 was subject was becoming increasingly evident, and the theater was picking up on the signs: audiences were changing and were increasingly eager for novelty. For its part, the entertainment industry was now well articulated in its

various segments and, increasingly free from the constraints of constituted power, was able to experiment with new musical practices, both at
the amateur level (with the explosion of philharmonic and philodramatic
societies) and at the professional and artistic level.

A complex and diverse world was defined, in which the need for
agents, impresarios, critics, and specialized journals was felt, and the
debate on the issue of public promotion of the performing arts began,
never dormant and still alive and intense. Naples, like Venice, were the
Italian cities in which more than elsewhere the new medium repertoire
was becoming established. The quantity of audiences and the theaters
they had at their disposal became strong elements of attraction for the
itinerant companies, which were forced by the demands of the market to
adapt themes, repertoires, and scenic forms, to the taste of the paying
spectators.[74]

The economic boom in theaters had imposed the principles of speculative efficiency, and the impresarios of the early nineteenth century were
able to implement it. The seasons that enlivened the artistic life of the
Teatro San Carlo until the 1860s demonstrate this. On the contrary,
the two decades that followed Italian Unification were not among the
happiest in the life of the maximum Neapolitan theater: moments of
increasingly rare prosperity were succeeded by moments of increasing
crises and depressions, such as those that forced the "silent seasons" of
1875 and 1876, and the interrupted and laboriously conducted one in
1893. In the second half of the century, Europe's first Opera House,
experienced an obvious and perhaps inevitable period of decline: in those
years the city's musical life lived its best seasons in a few minor theaters
that, thanks to their intense activity and, above all, to a new proactive
dynamism, were able to cope with the fatigued and jammed progress of
the serious Sancarlian mole. Accounts and chronicles of the time cannot
help but note the feeling of frustration of a city that appeared downgraded
from its rank as the European capital of music. But Naples was able to
react to the melodrama crisis, and the real turning point came around the
years 1860–1870, when, while in almost all the major Italian theatrical
centers, interest in theaters began to wane except for its paramount function of disseminating national and international operas in an ever-wider
area, in Naples, the city of *loisir* par excellence, alternative channels of
spectacular enjoyment were spontaneously organized.

And so, although the scarcity and propulsion of original musical energies and directions were felt, the importance of the Conservatories remained fundamental, with the growing importance also of the circles where other musical domains besides opera were being cultivated, and among them in particular that of instrumental music: initiatives for concert societies increased and progressed, and with them, interest in music criticism and historiography.

These are the aspects and centers of activity that will need to be reflected upon, without neglecting other lateral ones, but of some importance.

With Barbaja's death and the thinning of subsidies (250,000 francs in 1869–1873, 214,243 in 1889–1891 [820 million vs. 650], the San Carlo's activity was discontinuous with interrupted performances before the end of the season, quarrels between impresarios and political authority, and strikes by the masses.[75]

A colorful, controversial, and disputed figure in San Carlo history, was, in the 1970s Don Antonio Musella. The impresario was distinguished by roughness of character and a very bad reputation: he used to interrupt the cycle of performances and often defaulted on the artists, to whom he did not pay the agreed *caches*. His *gaffes* toward influential and famous singers were numerous, and equally notorious was the indignation he suscitated in Verdi. In the summer of '72, he provoked the strike of the orchestra members left without salaries and bitterly polemicized with the mayor, who was forced, in an absolutely unprecedented manner to resign. A perhaps unpleasant man, but endowed with uncommon resources, he managed the fortunes of the Neapolitan Massimo for at least a decade.[76]

Those were the years when the financial difficulties of theaters often forced the temporary or permanent closure of many of them.

The situation of the San Carlo was no different, as the theater's budgets for the seasons between 1861 and 1881 show. It is not an easy thing to reconstruct the performance of the budgets of a historical theater, first because of the scarcity of documentation and, secondly, because of the difficulty of comparing different geographical situations: there are too many elements that complicate a historical economic research on Italian opera, and they range from the difficulty of comparing quantitative data by homogeneous categories (impresarios and theaters did not limit themselves to representing a single genre, what is more, the same impresario could also work in different places, using different currencies and criteria), to problems of method (no two theaters ever

existed equal in size, fame, the possibility of invasion, relationship with
city society). In the case of the San Carlo then, it seems that these are the
only "historical" financial statements preserved and that we found casually
thirty years ago at the Historical Archives of the Conservatorio S. Pietro a
Majella in Naples. It may not be much, but enough to get an idea of the
magnitude of the income and expenditures of one of the greatest theaters
in Europe in the years immediately following the Unification (Table 3).

The details of expenditure and income items will better clarify the
financial performance of the Theater (Table 4).

Details of costs have been divided into ordinary, artist, and extraordinary costs. Ordinary costs include general, lighting, theatrical costs
(props, set design, costumes, stage machinery, sheet music rental, etc.),
and those for salaried and clerical staff (i.e., those who had a continuous
and long-term relationship with the theatrical enterprise: ushers, porters,
sweepers). Artists' costs refer exclusively to dancers, singers, musicians,
orchestras, bands, choreographers, directors, etc., personnel contracted
from time to time and with often different criteria.

The revenue detail shows the amount of subsidies, which could
be different, such as state or municipal "encouragements," superintendence reimbursements, or special subsidies to different typologies
of artists. Ordinary income includes receipts from ticket sales (sold

Table 3 Income and Expenses of the San Carlo Theater of Naples in relation
to the seasons of 1861–1881 (in lire)

Seasons	Revenue	Outputs	Profits/Losses
1861–62	432,791.20	582,767.87	−149,976.68
1864–65	1,054,568.72	1,070,150.00	−15,581.28
1865–66	775,259.42	829,347.65	−59,057.23
1866–67	761,815.02	579,901.75	+181,913.27
1867–68	–	–	–
1868–69	–	–	–
1869 70	1,220,749.12	1,029,535.25	+191,213.86
1879–80	772,326.47	673,431.49	+98,894 98
1880–81	707,177.44	664,786.00	+42,391.44

Notes The accounts for the first season (1861–62) were in ducats and have been translated into lire.
Because some artists preferred to be paid in French francs, the accounts often report payments with
a dual currency of account, in francs and in lire
Source Archives of the S.Pietro a Majella Conservatory of Naples—*Newspaper Books—Teatro San
Carlo*—years 1861–1881, without cataloging

Table 4 Operating costs of the San Carlo Theater in Naples in relation to the 1861–1881 seasons

Season	Ordinary costs	Artists	Extraordinary costs	Total
1861–62	155,891.23	373,153.32	53,723.32	582,767.87
1864–65	399,682.24	657,139.39	13,238.37	1,070,150.00
1865–66	358,693.54	433,974.30	36,679.71	829,347.65
1866–67	300,288.62	260,981.23	18,631.90	579,901.75
1867–68	–	–	–	–
1868–69	–	–	–	–
1869–70	533,197.86	477,503.31	18,834.08	1,029,535.25
1879–80	202,589.54	463,436.45	7,405.50	673,431.49
1880–81	246,152.52	394,420.60	24,213.15	664,786.00

Source Archives of the S.Pietro a Majella Conservatory of Naples—*Newspaper Books—Teatro San Carlo—years 1861–1881*, without cataloging

outside of subscriptions), revenue from mediations, and revenue from daytime performances. Extraordinary income refers to various extraordinary receipts and those for dance parties. Subscription income, covers all subscription income, whether in the stalls or boxes (Table 5).

This is not the place to dwell further on the financial situation and production system of the San Carlo Theater. The data reported is only

Table 5 Revenue of the San Carlo Theater of Naples in relation to the Seasons 1861–1881

Season	Grants	Ordinary proceeds	Extraordinary proceeds	Subscriptions	Total
1861–62	191,745.98	91,660.73	46,417.83	102,966.66	432,791.20
1864–65	392,346.94	183,969.74	98,628.20	379,623.84	1,054,568.72
1865–66	390,705.31	155,133.56	4,969.00	224,451.55	775,259.42
1866–67	211,774.42	218,129.52	52,538.68	279,372.40	761,815.02
1867–68	–	–	–	–	–
1868–69	–	–	–	–	–
1869–70	326,189.79	167,161.28	264,640.42	462,757.63	1,220,749.12
1879–80	385,883.00	90,400.00	296,043.47	0.00	772,326.47
1880–81	180,000.00	197,704.14	329,473.30	0.00	707,177.44

Source Archives of the S.Pietro a Majella Conservatory of Naples—*Newspaper Books—Teatro San Carlo*—years 1861–1881, without cataloging intended to draw attention to the importance of the accounting sources of theatrical enterprises, in order to reconstruct not only the economic-financial structure of the theater, but to trace back to so much other information about the number and type of performances, the way in which artists and stage personnel are recruited, the costs of staging an opera, and the revenues from the sale of tickets and subscriptions.[77]

The fact remains that opera was and is a very expensive entertainment and that regardless of the budget surpluses, the revenues were not and never will be able to fully cover the expenses of its stage settings.[78] An absolutely inconstant trend emerges from the tables, which should be better explained by referring to the typology of performances staged in those years, the number and fame of the artists employed, and the conditions that the city found itself experiencing in that particular contingency of Italian opera theater.

As mentioned above, the increasingly rare production and performance of new operas, and the difficulties in the debut of new talents, were obvious phenomena of a theatrical activity now in crisis after the splendors of the first half of the nineteenth century. The post-unification period profoundly challenged the basic features of the opera system, which was seeing its social, economic, and productive frame of reference change. The press of the time reported the discontents of the moment and often proposed institutional reforms and strenuous remedies to what appeared to be the most alarming epochal decline for the country: "a humiliating abdication of Italy to its perhaps brightest glory, at the very moment when it could finally assert itself in the concert of European nations."[79]

However, the inexhaustible demand for musical occasions did not subside, despite the decline of theaters. In Naples, in particular, it took the form of the emergence of numerous private associations, often supported by patronage initiatives, which encouraged the creation of cenacles open to young amateurs. In a little more than three decades, from the late 1860s to the early 1900s, the number of organizations (together with a small number of private houses) reached nearly 200, including circles, associations, societies, halls, theaters, lounges, and churches.[80] Some of them had no small size and roles such as the Orchestral Society at the Circolo Mandolinisti Partenopeo, the Filarmonica Bellini, or the Circolo Bonamici, which, in 1864, organized the First Italian Musical Congress to encourage young composers and debate the role that the state and municipalities should have in promoting theaters and providing financial support.[81] Among the participants in the Congress were the five music publishers active in Naples, Cottrau, Del Monaco, Girard, Orlando, and Clausetti. The only one to be proactive was Guillaume Cottrau, then owner of, among other things, the "Gazzetta Musicale di Napoli," who proposed the project for the protection of copyright formulated by the special committee and subsequently approved by the Congress; his were also the proposals to endow each municipality with a popular music library, and to establish an annual prize of 2,000 lire, which for the first year he undertook to disburse, for the composition—words and music—of choral songs.[82]

On the institutional ground, in 1882 the Minister of Public Education Guido Baccelli established the first permanent Council for Art Drama and Music. At last a permanent institutional space for reflection and proposal on the key issues of the nation's musical and theatrical life.[83] In the same year the Consolidated Act of 1882 redefined copyright legislation and, in the same year, after a long gestation and a serious delay compared to the French, English, and German situations, the Società Italiana degli Autori (SIA, later SIAE) was created, with the task of supervising effective compliance with the regulations. In Naples, the SIAE was born in 1883 thanks to Marco Praga, a successful playwright, an influential theater critic, and a point of reference for everyone, especially for Neapolitans.

6   THE ECONOMIC AND PRODUCTIVE SPIN-OFF OF MUSIC: PUBLISHING AND COMMERCE IN NAPLES

One of the problems common to all arts organizations, public or private, was, inevitably, the chronic economic hardship and the absence of public intervention.

During the nineteenth century, at the same time as the rise of theaters and melodrama, there was an important phenomenon of a more purely economic-productive nature: the birth of numerous music publishing houses that exerted a decisive influence on the Opera market. Milan was the city's richest in entrepreneurial initiatives in music publishing with its two national giants, Ricordi and Lucca. In no other European musical context did the development of music publishing take place—at least in the nineteenth century—in such a concentrated and oligopolistic way as in Milan, and in no other case, to the best of our knowledge from the research carried out so far, did the advance of publishers play such a decisive and far-reaching role.[84]

When, in the late 1860s, audience tastes began to change, slowly setting the opera system on its way to its "relative decline," there was a proliferation of publishing houses that, taking advantage of that change and the new consumption, put out a large number of romances, ballads, and piano pieces, mostly intended for "domestic" uses, but not disdaining pieces of religious music, patriotic and school choirs, and methods for voices and instruments.

This particular change was well taken advantage of by the Neapolitan publishing industry, which, from the very beginning, although being an underdog in the race with the northern ones, was always particularly attentive to novelty and inclined to investment.

The publishing industry, which in Milan had managed to dominate the stylistic choices of composers and the playbills of most Italian theaters, failed to find the same spaces in Naples, but was no less productive for that. It was to be expected that, with the Unification of Italy, in the musical sector which was an obvious part of artistic and cultural life although in some ways governed by its own laws, the relations between the various Italian regions and cities, already quite active and effective even when there was division and plurality of states, expanded into more vigorous currents in as much as they were more freely circulating and thus propitious to that general renewal of art and culture of which clear signs had already appeared, and to which circumstances and events of various kinds contributed with increasing force. Since the second half of the eighteenth century, Naples had distinguished itself as a center of publishing production of considerable magnitude,[85] specializing in the *clandestine* publication of Goldonian texts: this was an intense production of abusive reprints of countless Goldonian originals that in Naples, but not only there, found a good market. Undoubtedly, Neapolitan publishers distinguished themselves by promptness, entrepreneurial timing and the usual Neapolitan "ability to make do," seizing the opportunities of the moment. At the same time, strong demand for music was constantly coming from both high and professional circles (instrumentalists and composers) and medium and petit-bourgeoisie, where the use of music, while taking on a more domestic characterization, in the inexhaustible demand for opportunities for musical entertainment, fueled a sustained demand for sheets, sheet music, and theatrical or song lyrics, which the numerous copyshops scattered throughout the city tried to cope with first, then the print shops attached to the first publishing houses.

The demand for texts and scores for ballroom dances, chamber operas, and vernacular songs increased as "periodicals" and "pulcinellate" intensified. Appointments that became the most frequent and crowded occasions, at least until the first two decades of the twentieth century, in which official and traditional culture met the more popular, oral-tradition culture, which resulted in one of the most important publishing events for the Neapolitan music market: the publication, in 1827, of *Passatempi musicali* edited by Guillaume Cottrau, an anthology that, for the first time, collected, in a more functional, usable and absolutely original editorial format, endless production of leaflets distributed up to that time on the numerous stalls that animated commerce in the alleys of the city center and that reproduced that flourishing of salon entertainment works that would give real impetus to nineteenth-century music publishing.[86]

The main purchasers of Cottrau's editorial products—who in the meantime had become a partner in the Girard publishing house—sheet music, lithographs, collections, and popular ditties, were precisely those who attended the salons who, by then in the grip of the globalization movement that was beginning at that time—as Maria Luisa Stazio put it—were forced to recover their identity by restructuring their horizons from a global and bourgeois perspective:

> We find ourselves, I believe, at the roots of the glocal character of future Neapolitan song. What we call glocalization today indicates the double movement of culture that, while opening up and homogenizing, at the same time enhances certain aspects of the local, both to ensure the necessary dinamics, as well as to exploit them economically. The latter possibility depends essentially on the possibilities and capacities of integration of local dominant groups into the broader economic and cultural system. But also on the capacities for differentiation and local image creation generated by cultural activities. This causes a partial deconstruction of the cultural dynamic in relation to its anthropological and aesthetic dimensions, and a restructuring - also partial - operated from an economic logic. The relationship between valorization of aspects of local identity and image - with what of them is linked to tangible and intangible cultural heritages - with a view to economic exploitation in global markets is therefore of strategic importance. It seems that Ferdinand IV (later, from 1816, Ferdinand I, King of the Two Sicilies) had already sensed this.[87]

But the Neapolitan publishing industry did not stop at Cottrau's resourcefulness and foresight and, thanks to the circulation of poetics and currents of thought that had arrived from beyond the Alps, began to engage in the dissemination of new books and the identification of emerging texts and authors.

The editorial production of those years, even when it was specifically musical, was embedded in contexts of innovation and transformation that affected society and the urban context of reference on many levels. We recall, among many others, the exceptional event of the inauguration of the Naples-Portici railroad, which provided the cue for one of Altavilla's comedies, *Na juta a Castiellammare per la strada de fierro, with Punchinello as cook for a fake German and third-class traveler.*[88]

The "Neapolitan song" boom had not yet exploded, but the link of Neapolitan publishing with the national-popular Opera production system, dominated primarily by the Milanese Casa Ricordi, was just as productive.

The first outpost of Casa Ricordi in the Kingdom of the Two Sicilies was created by the publishing activity of Pietro Clausetti, who at the age of eighteen was hired by the Ricordi Company as an engraver. In those years, a full-fledged school of musical engraving was being started at Casa Ricordi. The young Clausetti exercised his apprenticeship there and soon after, in 1841, moved to Naples where, with his brother Lorenzo, he founded a music publishing house just "rimpetto il Regio Teatro S. Carlo," while the intaglio was located in Via Nunziatella.

Clausetti's publications "stood out for their elegance, graceful text, and other new and beautiful qualities of type that had not yet been seen here. The most striking parts were the frontispieces, some of which could still present themselves today as excellent models of industrial art."[89] The first Catalogue of the Stabilimento musicale di Pietro e Lorenzo Clausetti was published in 1860 and collected a variety of works, from Rossini, Bellini, Donizetti and Verdi to Meyerbeer, Weber, Auber and Mendelssohn.[90]

Meanwhile, Casa Ricordi was consolidating its publishing power by absorbing numerous other music publishers, and interest in the Neapolitan area was growing: as early as 1834 G. Ricordi had entered into a contract for the ownership of new operas written for Naples, and decade later he personally went there to make arrangements with the impresario of the Royal Neapolitan theaters. After 1860, Casa Ricordi's expansionist policy in the direction of Naples became more explicit: first, it formed a trading company with the Clausettis (under the name of "Tito di Gio. Ricordi e fratelli Clausetti"), then, in August 1864, Tito Ricordi permanently purchased the Neapolitan establishment upon payment of 70,000 lira for the store and the intaglio plant, holding as many as 33,354 plates.[91]

This was the birth of the first Italian branch of the Casa Ricordi, the direction of which was entrusted, because of the bonds of long-standing friendship and collaboration, to Pietro; Lorenzo was appointed director of the chalcographic plant, but in 1867 he abandoned that position to move to South America, where he established himself as a theatrical impresario. In July 1887 Pietro signed, on behalf of Tito Ricordi, the contract to absorb the Neapolitan publishing house Dal Monaco, whose management he retained until his death in Naples on December 3, 1892.

The new course of joint Ricordi-Clausetti management was immediately evident: numerous publications among those offered by the Clausetti catalogue to Neapolitan customers traced some of the main editorial choices conceived by Ricordi and, conversely, the Ricordi catalogue drew heavily on Clausetti's. Numerous collections of Neapolitan songs were thus borrowed that effectively met the needs of the new market.

Casa Ricordi's control over the country became increasingly widespread, implementing policies to absorb other establishments. Certainly, the acquisition of the Clausetti Catalogue helped consolidate the influence of the national music publishing giant and brought new life to an already diverse range of publishing proposals.[92]

The many music publishers in Naples still include Francesco Azzolino with print shop at vico Gerolamini 10, himself an author of canzonette; Salvatore De Marco, at vico San Niccolò alla Carità; Francesco Migliaccio, Giuseppe Colavita, Gaetano Romeo, Ferdinando Cinque at vico Cinque in Montesanto; Gaetano Rusconi at via Sant'Anna dei Lombardi; an Ariosto at largo Pentite in Pignasecca.[93]

It seems more interesting to us, however, for the purposes of our reflection, to mention another form of musical production that exploded precisely during the two decades under consideration. This was a musical phenomenon with a popular character that, reacting, perhaps unconsciously, to the decline of the opera system, created a new expansive phase for Neapolitan music, but also for the Italian image and economy. We are talking about the *boom* of *Neapolitan song*, which succeeded in giving new vigor to the urban economy, projecting the city of Napoli, in a totally unexpected way, on the international scene.

For the first time, in 1894, the Naples Merchants' Association, in collaboration with the municipal authorities and the Bank of Naples, gave rise to one of the many *summer festivals* in vogue at the time, especially at bathing and spa establishments, but also at the many *café-chantants*, which by then had also opened in Naples under the influence of French fashion. The feast in question was that of Piedigrotta, whose origins actually dated back to the 1880s, but which at the end of the century took on the characteristics of a particular richness. This type of celebration, which certainly revived the ancient splendor of Baroque festivals and those on the water, profoundly modified the territorial, economic, and organizational articulation of the city and its way of "consuming." The feast of Piedigrotta involved the entire population and constituted a moment in which the city staged itself, its characteristics, and potential. The summer entertainments found their most important sponsorships among commercial merchants, but also among the Società Nazionale delle Strade Ferrate and the Navigazione Generale d'Italia, which used them as advertising opportunities for goods and new consumption. In 1895, the Piedigrotta feast had for the first time an original dissemination tool: the "Official Program Guide for Summer Feasts," which collected not only all the initiatives scheduled but, facilitated the participation of the public, local and otherwise, provided a series of indications on train and boat schedules and other useful information. A tourist guide in full swing. That summer saw exhibitions of agricultural and industrial products, the festival of women's folk costumes, fireworks competitions, fishermen's and boatmen's regattas on the Gulf, parades of floats, newsagents, and the great Fantasmagorica Torchlight Procession, enlivened by numerous marching bands, which passed through the city's busiest streets. It was a kind of *Excelsior* Street *Ball* that mixed flowers, fruits, animals, minerals, and cameras, with special lighting effects, scenic and choreography. But, as every year, the most anticipated event was the song contest. A true "cultural industry" that, between the late nineteenth and the early twentieth century, put in place all its apparatus, a wealth of initiatives, talents, and knowledge, an articulation, complexity, and maturity, which still awaits to be explored, especially in its more exquisitely economic aspects.

In particular, the Neapolitan song in competition at Piedigrotta attracted the attention of the highest-rated music publishers on the market: publishers such as Giulio Ricordi or the local Casa Bideri (the most innovative and long-standing publisher of Neapolitan songs) found in the Neapolitan song an important opportunity for profit. What the Piedigrotta festival managed to become was something unexpected, in an era such as the one in which the phenomenon exploded: it became a highly original showcase for the city of Naples and its productive activities, in which the city's commercial, touristic, and economic forces found a multiplicity of business opportunities, but also communication, promotion, and publicity by financing initiatives, shows, parades, sheet music, albums, and *copielle*, understanding their economic returns (commercial, tourist and productive).

The printing of sheet music for example, dedicated primarily to the small- and middle-class domestic groups that were open to the sociality and easy consumption of melodrama, romance, and song, served as an underground and private channel certainly connected with the other channels of dissemination among the public, from concerts to pianini, from the street to the café. Another very useful tool for spreading the notes and myth of song was the dissemination of *copielle*, a new version of those flyers that had been the most common means of circulation of popular literature for centuries. These were pamphlets, almost always illustrated, that contained the text or score of the song. Sometimes it even offered an original transcription of the music in a numerical system referring to the four strings of the mandolin, so that even those who were ignorant of reading the musical staff could perform it. The sales of these flyers, accessible even to the less affluent, was exceptional, and revenues reached staggering figures. But the *copielle* were not printed only as a "cheap edition" of the songs, very often they were distributed free of charge, during the Piedigrotta for public purposes: increasingly, in addition to the lyrics of the songs, the sheets also carried printed advertisements of city firms and industries that in different ways had helped "sponsor" the event.[94]

Countless were the men devoted to music publishing and commerce in Naples. From the *Registers of Business Complaints*, kept at the Naples Chamber of Commerce, we have inferred other names, to which we can trace musical publishing activity in the late nineteenth and early twentieth centuries.[95] First and foremost is the well-known Ferdinando Bideri, who recorded the start of its publishing activity in the form of an individual firm in 1876. The Ferdinando Bideri Publishing House qualified as a "journalistic sector with related editions" and was based at first in Via Università Vecchia, then, from 1883, in Via S. Pietro a Majella, 17. In 1930 the firm ceased its activities due to the death of the owner, but the termination report was not officially registered until 1938.[96]

Her early publications included several volumes on the history of entertainment, including Salvatore Di Giacomo's *Storia del Teatro San Carlo*, but soon Bideri devoted herself to publishing songs, putting under contract all the major protagonists of the revival of Neapolitan song at the turn of the century.[97] Many of the songs from that period toured the world: the most famous, '*O sole mio*, would also be sung by Elvis Presley and Bill Haley, but how can we not remember *I' te vurria vasà*, *O marenariello*, *Voce 'e notte*, *Io 'na chitarra e 'a luna*....

Upon Ferdinando's death, the management of the publishing house passed to his daughter, Valentina Bideri, a shy and very discreet woman who rarely participated in public life. She took charge of the publishing house together with her sister Flavia, who succeeded her in ownership in 1964.[98] Other successful Neapolitan songs published by Bideri date back to the 1950s (*Scapricciatiello, Accarezzame, Serenatella sciuè sciuè, Tuppe tuppe mariscià*), and in the course of a particularly successful business, the company acquired other houses with an important past but in the process of demobilization, such as Edizioni musicali Santa Lucia, Edizioni musicali Santojanni and Poliphon Music Editions.

The 1970s saw the transition of the management of the publishing house to the third generation of the Bideri family: grandsons Luciano and Paolo Villevieille Bideri. It was with them that the publishing group decided to experiment in the recording sector as well, for which the label *Edibi* was founded, later deciding to move all activities to Rome, based in Via Teulada. In the 1980s Casa Bideri passed to Luciano Bideri and then to his daughter Silvia.[99]

In the same year that Casa Bideri was founded, 1876, the Casa Musicale named after Giuseppe Santojanni, a "music publisher," had also sprung up in Naples, establishing its headquarters at Via Paolo Imbriani,

6. In 1935 the firm, founded as an individual firm, was sold in favor of Mario Cosentino's firm and later, as noted above, was taken over by the Bideri group.[100] The business reporting records in Naples also inform us about the Casa Editrice Musicale Raffaele Izzo, which was established as a general partnership in 1879 and qualified as "publishers, music printers and shopkeepers" and was based at Via Posillipo.[101] In 1925, the same firm was registered as a "de facto company" and qualified as "wholesale and detail import and export of music." Transformed into a limited partnership, it moved to Dante Square, 32–33, and will cease operation in 1931.[102]

In 1890 "Gaetano Pisano's Music Publishing," opened its doors at 391 Via Roma, to deal with "music papers."[103]

In a particularly lively editorial context, already projected toward the publication of popular songs, a new activity of Casa Ricordi was inserted, after it had already taken over the Clausetti firm in 1864. In 1887, in fact, the report of a new business named after G. Ricordi & C., as "music publishers," located at Via Chiaia, 20–28, whose final transfer of business dates back to 1991.[104]

In 1916, the E.A. Mario Music Publishing House, named after Giovanni Gaeta, produced "canzonette" and opened its headquarters at Via Vittorio Emanuele Orlando, 9. The cessation seems to date back to 1928.[105]

Also invested in the production of canzonette was La Sorgente Musicale, registered in the name of Emilio Maestrale, which set its registered office at Via Milano, 40, but, in registering with the Naples Chamber of Commerce, qualified as "publications of canzonette (verse and music) without a sales store." The business of this sole proprietorship was registered in 1924. In 1927 it would be sold in favor of the publishing house "L'Artistica."[106]

In about the same years (1922–1930), Salvatore Panzetta's "La Canzonetta napoletana," "Editions of music songs and articles of optics," located in Via Oronzio di Massa 23, carried out its publishing activities. In 1961 the ceasing of activities was registered.[107]

The publishing or music engraving houses were then flanked by an elevated number of printing houses, printers, chalcographies, or lithographies (more than one hundred) and several stores, pure and simple businesses, but, also workshops for repairing or manufacturing musical instruments that reported the beginning of their activity in the last thirty years of the nineteenth century. The number noted in the chamber sources consulted so far is already remarkable, despite the fact that the state of research is just beginning.[108]

In particular, the name of the Loveri Brothers, who are still known especially among instrument dealers, stands out among the owners of the establishments of Neapolitan musical instruments in historic Via San Sebastiano. The first of the dynasty seems to be Giuseppe Loveri who, in 1885, opened his individual firm of "musical instruments and pianos" in Via S. Sebastiano, 68. The business was interrupted by the death of the owner in 1930.[109] In 1923 Gennaro Loveri opened his musical instrument store on Carrera Street, 46[110] and the following year the firm "Loveri Fratelli," named after Enrico, opened another on Constantinople Street, 77.[111] In 1935, due to economic difficulties, the cessation of operation was recorded. Isolita, on the other hand, is the individual firm named after a woman, Marcellina Ropa, who dealt in piano repair work, at 25 Bari Street, since 1904.

As time passed, and with the spread of the first "talking machines," manufacturers and dealers of sheet music, books, and musical instruments were joined by record and gramophone dealers. Among those taken over were Fratelli Loreto, a de facto company based at Piazza Borsa, 27, between 1900 and 1936[112]; the individual firm Giuseppe Rossi, which dealt in "building materials, gramophones and records," at 1Via Marinelli[113]; the one named after Pietro Gennarelli di Emilio who sold "gramophones and radio items" at 13 Via Guglielmo Sanfelice between 1924 and 1933[114]; and the oldest, the one named after R. Jaforte who traded in "gramophones, records and accessories" between 1897 and 1932, at 31 Via Chiaia.[115]

An economic and productive spin-off of a certain magnitude, if we consider that the data reported here is absolutely partial, and that it detects a city music market all but concentrated in the urban center, in the area bounded by the main theaters and the historic S. Pietro a Majella Conservatory of Music.

The problem now is to rebuild in more purely economic terms, the productive activity and the profits of these musical activities spurred by customs and traditions now marked by the consumption of music at various levels. And here the chamber sources at our disposal, unfortunately, do not help us. The research will therefore have to be broadened to diverse documentary types that cannot neglect those of the newspapers and periodicals of the time, or the often-indirect evidence on the costs of this particular artistic product (instruments, sheet music, strings, repairs…).

For example, we know that at the Clausetti Music Establishment it was possible to subscribe to "the eight ducats" (for every purchase in the amount of 8 ducats there was a free gift worth 3 ducats) and a subscription to "the reading of Music both of one's own fund and abroad." With this second type of subscription, by paying 1 ducat and 29 grana, it was possible to "read all Music (except the Etudes), with due security, with the faculty of taking four pieces at a time or one score."[116] Just as we know from printed sources, although not entirely reliable, that

> [...] There is no writing in the Kingdom of which copies are printed and sold in such numbers, as happens daily of such songs. Of the song - Io te voglio bene assaje - 180,000 copies were printed.
> La Luisella, 45,000
> D. Ciccillo alle fanfare, 100,000
> Alla finestra affacciati, 40,000
> Il Bivacco, 12,000
> La Palombella, 30.000[117]

This is the greatest difficulty for those of us who want to conduct a study of the economic history of art and culture: finding of economic and accounting sources that allow the reconstruction of costs and revenues of public or private productive activity, often entrepreneurial in nature, which conditioned social and professional life for centuries and is still the subject of much attention today.

With music publishing, the daily and periodical press also developed, whose action was instrumental in creating vehicles and channels of penetration designed to multiply sales. Then, from the early twentieth century, the recording industries also came to the fore, which—from the Neapolitan *Phonotype*, to the German *Polyphon*—recorded and distributed, all over the world, recordings of the songs. The Neapolitan song market thrived on an ever-increasing demand at least until the early sixties to seventies of the twentieth century. Today, demand has certainly declined, but that Neapolitan song is a musical *topos that* endures and should perhaps be better protected and enhanced, as a component of an Italian cultural heritage that is very difficult to ignore.

This type of consumption was addressed by the journals that the most important publishers—or those aspiring to become so—in the late nineteenth century, following the example of Ricordi and his "Gazzetta musicale di Milano." "La Tavola rotonda," published by the historic Casa Bideri, was the long-lived, best-edited, and best-preserved among these publications. It was Bideri himself who described its beginnings:

> [The magazine was born] with exclusively literary and artistic criteria of severity and elegance, and it was a complete economic disaster. But later we adapted to what the public demanded: a bit of entertainment and no boring disquisitions and spiels. So by degrees, little by little, we managed to guarantee a long-lasting life by popularizing our musical production.[118]

A production that numbered more than 60 songs per year, published weekly, and that in the annual Piedigrotta contests named after the newspaper collected from a minimum of 80 and a maximum of 300 songs per contest.

This impressive and complex Neapolitan cultural industry based all its strength on Neapolitan songs, which, in addition to representing a not insignificant share of a self-representation in which the city to a large extent still empathizes, became a key component of an image that the rest of the world still like to recognize.

The *boom* of the Neapolitan songs was not simply a musical phenomenon, a pure song genre, but was the explosion (and to some extent still is) "of a great collective myth, one of the places where Naples staged, spectacularized, mourned, and sold its eternal de- cline, the splendors and miseries of a capital both noble and ragged."[119]

Neapolitan song also experienced its own entrepreneurial adventure, embedded in that larger phenomenon of the Italian music industry.

From melodrama to Neapolitan songs, we are left with an immense tangible and intangible cultural heritage and a lot of good music. The survival of both is in the hands of those who, today, are in a position to claim, on the one hand, an increasingly indispensable balance between art and economics, and on the other hand, an ethical-professional commit-ment to work for the dissemination of their knowledge (Tables 6 and 7).

Table 6 Neapolitan publishers between business reports and business closures. Years 1876–1991

N.	Type	Name	Holder	VIA	Start	End
1,882	Sole proprietorship	Music Editor	Joseph Santojanni	P. Imbriani, 6	1876	1935
3,570	Sole proprietorship	Music Publishing	Gaetano Pisano	Rome, 391	1890	1935
4,337	Society accom Simple	Music Publishers	G. Memories & C	Chiaja, 20–28	1887	1991
5,180	Sole proprietorship	Music Publishing House E.A.Mario	John Gaeta	V. E. Orlando, 9	1916	1928
9,356	Sole Proprietorship	The Musical Source	Emilio Maestrale	Milan, 40	1924	1927
10,686	Sole Proprietorship	The Song Neapolitan	Salvatore Panzetta	Orontius of Mass, 23	1922	1961
12,297	Sole Proprietorship	Publishing House Musical Bixio	Caesar Andrew Bixio	Rome, 85	1921	1961
16,782	De facto society/S.a.s	Music Publishing House	Raphael Izzo	Dante Square, 32–33	1925	1932
3,317	Sole Proprietorship	Publishing House F. Bideri	Ferdinand Bideri	S.Pietro a Majella, 17	1876	1938
14,030	Sole Proprietorship	Postcard Editions, photographs	Joseph Clement	S. George Arcoleo, 6	1922	1941
1,928	Sole Proprietorship	Art editions	Eduardo Donvito	Rome, 373	1921	1935
2,070	Sole Proprietorship	Paper Editions	Alberto Morano	Capitals, 26	1921	1958
460	De facto society	La Canzonetta Publishers	Capolongo-Feola	T. Carovita, 8	1912	–
358	De facto society	Editiones populaires	Meiermann & C	S. Lucia, 31	1901	1912
473	Sole Proprietorship	Bookseller Publisher	Augustus Regina was Gabriel	Piazza Cavour, 34	1870	–

N.	Type	Name	Holder	VLA	Start	End
143	Sole Proprietorship	News agency	Valentino Ceccoli was Gaetano	N. Monteoliveto,19	1900	–
273	Company name Collective	Music Publishing House	Raphael Izzo	V. Posillipo, 375	1879	–

Source Naples Chamber of Commerce Historical Archives, *Economic Registry, Registers of business reports and terminations*, nos. 1–80

Table 7 Musical business activities between business reports and activity terminations. Years 1800–1967

N.	Type	Name	Holder	VIA	Start	End
1,715	Sole proprietorship	Musical items	Alfredo Curatoli	S. Sebastian, 48	1913	1931
1,716	Sole proprietorship	Pianos and Musical instruments	Luigi Ricci and Sons was Pasquale	Piazza Cavour, 65	1885	1926
2,692	Sole Proprietorship	Musical instruments wind and string	Ugo and Giulio De Feo	N. Pizzofalcone, 14	1925	1951
2,778	Sole proprietorship	Musical instruments	Diego Loveri	Port'Alba, 7	1922	1930
2,791	Sole Proprietorship	Instruments Resale musical	Michael Ussano	Corso Umberto I, 270	1910	1950
2,796	Sole Proprietorship	Musical instruments	Joseph Tarantino	Wisdom, 18	1922	1928
4,820	Sole Proprietorship	Object repairer musical	Alfredo Contini	Umberto I Gallery, 50	1923	1932
5,611	Sole Proprietorship	Instrument emporium musical	Vincenzo Cappiello	Corso Garibaldi	–	1933
6,471	Sole Proprietorship	Musical instruments	Joseph Dell'Anno	Vico 2° Casanova, 14	1925	1946
7,048	Sole Proprietorship	Repair and sale musical instruments	Carmine Ussano	Cathedral, 182	1870	1958
9,955	Sole Proprietorship	Musical instruments and pianos	Joseph Loveri	S. Sebastian, 68	1885	1937
12,122	Sole Proprietorship	Representative musical instruments	Peter Piana	National Square	–	1961
12,704	Sole Proprietorship	Repairs of musical instruments	John Coppola	Corso Garibaldi, 100	1919	1930
12,802	Sole Proprietorship	Music and Books Buying and selling used books	Teresa Cacciapuoto	Port'Alba, 21	1916	1954
13,310	Sole Proprietorship	Musical instruments	Gennaro Loveri	Correra, 46	1923	1925
14,561	Sole Proprietorship	Musical instruments Loveri Brothers	Enrico Loveri	Constantinople, 77	1924	1935

N.	Type	Name	Holder	VIA	Start	End
15,386	De facto society	Engraving and printing of the musics	De Marino Brothers	Porch -12 S. Francesco de Paola, 11	1920	1961
17,512	De facto society	Musical instruments	Caesar Ruggiero	Corso Garibaldi, 35	–	1951
18,456	Sole Proprietorship	Music Store	Francis Accountant	Torre del Greco, Avernana Street, 16	1924	1936
18,804	De facto society	Instrument lab musical strings	Commendatore Professor Raffaele Calace and Son	E. Pizzofalcone, 75	1925	1934
13,679	Sole Proprietorship	Stringed instruments and accordions	Joseph Quail	Corso Garibaldi, 345	1909	1937
18,921	Sole Proprietorship	Manufacture of stringed and bowed instruments Vinaccia Brothers & C	Gaetano Vinaccia fu Pasquale	Chiatamone, 32	1912	1967
2,104	Sole Proprietorship	Resale of instruments stringed	Vincenzo Gagliano	Monteoliveto, 48	1800	1930
2,654	Sole Proprietorship	Musical instruments	Xavier Germano	Nino Bixio, 413	1922	1939
2,692	Sole Proprietorship	Musical instruments wind and string	Ugo and Giulio De Feo	N. Pizzofalcone, 14	1925	1951
3,503	Sole Proprietorship	Instrument repairer harmonic and mechanical	Vincenzo Cioffi	S. Sebastian, 18	1895	1926
18,167	Sole Proprietorship	Talking machines and Neapolitan song	Emilio Knight Gennarelli & C	Monteoliveto, 39	1912	1957
19,550	Sole Proprietorship	Talking machines and discs	Francis Esposito by Raphael	Rome, 392	1925	1936
6,292	Sole Proprietorship	Construction materials, gramophones and records	Joseph Rossi	Marinella, 1	–	1958

(continued)

Table 7 (continued)

N.	Type	Name	Holder	VIA	Start	End
12,722	Sole Proprietorship	Gramophones, records, accessories	R. Jaforte	Chiaia, 31	1897	1932
18,068	Sole Proprietorship	Gramophones and radio articles	Peter Gennarelli by Emilio	Gugl. Sanfelice, 13	1924	1933
19,455	Sole proprietorship	Phonographs and records	Vincenzo Esposito by Raphael	Rome, 132	1917	1936
185	Sole proprietorship	Piano workshop	Charles Frigatti	Monteoliveto, 12	1909	–
495	Sole Proprietorship	Factory and sale musical instruments	Salvatore De Falco	S. Sebastian, 40	1912	–
8	Sole proprietorship	Piano dealer	John D'Avena was Francis	Rome, 368	1886	–
470	Sole proprietorship	Buying and selling used books	Thomas Rome was John	S. Blaise, 9	1890	–
481	Sole Proprietorship	Piano repairs	Marcellina Ropa	Bari, 25	1904	–
493	Sole Proprietorship	Musical instruments	Luigi Ricci	Piazza Cavour, 65	1904	–
606	Indivual Firm	Mandolin factory	Louis Salsedo	Formal Road, 35	1882	–
102	Sole Proprietorship	Harmonic instruments	Vincenzo Cioffi	S. Sebastian, 18	1896	–
351	Sole proprietorship	Gramophones	Raphael Esposito	Rome, 392	1908	–

Source Naples Chamber of Commerce Historical Archives, *Economic Registry, Registers of business reports and terminations*, nos. 1–80.

NOTES

1. P. Macry, *Premessa*, in «Quaderni Storici», n.s. 56, *Borghesie urbane dell'800*, no. 2, August 1984, pp. 333–338.
2. A vivid description of the Risorgimento salons is in T. Mori, *Figlie d'Italia.Poetesse patriote nel Risorgimento (1821–1861)*, Carocci, Rome 2011.
3. C. Sorba, *Musica e Teatro*, in *L'Unificazione Italiana*, Istituto per l'enciclopedia italiana Treccani, 2011, pp. 533–549; p. 533.
4. C. Sorba, *Theaters. L'Italia del melodramma nell'età del Risorgimento*, Il Mulino, Bologna 2001, pp. 61–68.
5. A. Di Lascio, S. Ortolani, *Instituzioni di diritto e legislazione dello spettacolo*, Franco Angeli, Milan 2010, p. 55.
6. C. Sorba, *Musica e Teatro*, cit. p. 536.
7. Article 32 regulated freedom of assembly, but excluded shows, which, as "to gatherings in public places, or open to the public" remained subject to police laws. (I. Piazzoni, *Spettacolo, Instituzioni e Società nell'Italia post-unitaria (1860–1882)*, Archivio Guido Izzi, Rome 2001, p. 66).
8. Ibid.
9. E. Rosmini, *Legislazione e giurisprudenza dei teatri*, Hoepli, Milan 1893, p. 198.
10. Ibid., p. 199.
11. Ibid.
12. Finance Minister Tremonti's quip a few years ago, "with Culture you can't eat", will go down in history as the most unfortunate expression a democratic government could ever have. Unfortunately, despite the fact that statistics and official data continue to show that the cultural sector is, first of all, a productive sector, we are still forced to defend it, as best we can, but above all by invoking attention, awareness and pro-fessionality.
13. C. Sorba, *Teatri*, cit. p. 245.
14. A. Di Lascio, S. Ortolani, *Instituzioni di diritto*, cit. p. 55.
15. F. Bettini, *Giurisprudenza degli Stati sardi*, 1856, p. 223.
16. The Carlo Felice in Genoa remained inactive from 1879 to 1883; the Fenice in Venice remained closed even from 1872 to 1897; the Comunale in Bologna in 1898; even La Scala in Milan, Italy's largest theater, remained closed in 1897–1898 [F. Nicolodi, *Il sistema produttivo*, cit. p. 170].

17. Ibid.
18. J. Rosselli, *Il Sistema produttivo, 1780–1880*, cit. pp. 77–165.
19. V. Fiore, *Luoghi per lo spettacolo: recupero e valorizzazione tra flessibilità e contaminazione*, in «Techne», 3/2011, Florence University Press.
20. C. Sorba, *Musica e Teatro*, cit. pp. 533–549.
21. W. Griswold, *Sociologia della Cultura*, Il Mulino, Bologna 2005, p. 20.
22. M. Gallina, Organizzare teatro. Produzione, distribuzione, gestione nel sistema italiano, Franco Angeli, Milan 2007, p. 277.
23. F. Cruciani, *Lo spazio del teatro*, Laterza, Roma-Bari 2005, pp. 90–91.
24. We mention, among others, the Sydney Opera House (1973), located in Sydney Bay, equipped with an amusement park and a large parking lot, well connected and close to the huge Sydney Harbour Bridge. The spherical shells are reminiscent of a flotilla of ships. In 2007 it became a World Heritage Site under the auspices of UNESCO. Or the Valencia Opera House (1996–2006), which reproduces the shape of a huge warrior helmet. Or the new Opera House (2008), which overlooks Copenhagen Bay and stands on an island created by building a new section of canal. The intervention is part of an urban development plan for a large area whose goal was to create a new cultural center whose unifying elements were water and the Bay. The huge floating roof and the auditorium, whose shape is reminiscent of a seashell, characterize the intervention [R. Pasqualetti, Editoriale, in *Il teatro nella città contemporanea*, Collana Architetture Pisane (20), Edizioni ETS, Pisa 2010, pp. 7–15].
25. R. Schechner, *Verso una poetica della performance,* in Idem, *La teoria della performance 1970–1983,* Bulzoni, Roma 1984, pp. 121–123.
26. M. Serino, *Spazio urbano e spazio teatrale nell'organizzazione dello spettacolo dal vivo,* in Metropolis, July 26, 2011—Tafter Journal—http://www.tafterjournal.it.
27. S. Baia Curioni, *Mercanti d'Opera. Storie di Case Ricordi,* Il Saggiatore, Milan 2011, p. 27 (vedi nota 447 sul libro, non risulta tradotta, ma sostituita da questa.
28. The Comunale (Bologna), Bellini (Catania), Pergola (Florence), Carlo Felice (Genoa), La Scala (Milan), S. Carlo (Naples), Bellini

(Palermo), Argentina and Costanzi (Rome), Regio (Turin), La Fenice (Venice) [F. Nicolodi, The production system, cit. pp. 171–172].

29. The construction site of the San Carlo in Naples had begun in 1735 (although the theater was later rebuilt in 1816 after a fire), that of the Pergola in Florence in 1738, the Regio in Turin was built from 1741, the Comunale in Bologna from 1763, La Scala from 1778, while the opening of the Venetian Fenice was in 1791.

30. C. Sorba, *Musica e Teatro*, cit. pp. 533–549.

31. W.J.A. Stamer, *Dolce Napoli. Naples: its streets, people, fêtes, pilgrimages, environs* etc. etc., London 1878, p. 65.

32. P. Macry, *Borghesie, città e Stato. Appunti e impressioni su Napoli, 1860–1880*, «Quaderni storici», *Borghesie urbane dell'800*, cit. pp. 338–383; pp. 340–341.

33. J. Chalon, *Naples. 1874–1886*, Mons, 1886, p. 23.

34. W.J.A. Stamer, *Sweet Naples*, cit. p. 66.

35. V. Monaco, *Le capitali del teatro borghese*, in *Teatro dell'Italia Unita*, edited by Siro Ferrone, Il Saggiatore, Milan 1980, p. 102.

36. Cf. again J. Rosselli, *L'impresario d'opera*, cit.

37. L. Cavaglieri, *Tra arte e mercato. Agenti e agenzie teatrali nel XIX secolo*, Bulzoni Editore, Rome 2006, p. 14.

38. The expression "theatrical agency", now in use, does not appear until the second half of the 1800s, close to Unification. Before that date, the most common expressions were correspondent, matchmaker, commission agent, theatre procurer, agent (ibid., p. 27).

39. Ibid., p. 28.

40. Ibid.

41. Ibid., pp. 28–30.

42. J. Rosselli, *L'impresario d'opera*, cit. p. 146.

43. M.R. Pelizzari, *Dalle caserme ai salotti: gioco d'azzardo, teatro e loisir a Napoli tra fine Settecento e Decennio francese*, in R. De Lorenzo (ed.), *Ordine e disordine. Amministrazione e mondo militare nel Decennio francese*, Giannini, Napoli 2012, pp. 381–408.

44. J. Rosselli, *Il Sistema produttivo*, cit. pp. 87–90.

45. A.F. Leon-M. Ruggeri, *Il costo del melodramma*, «Quaderno della rivista Economia della Cultura», Il Mulino, Bologna 2004.

46. C. Sorba, *Teatri*, cit. pp. 20–21.

47. G. Canella, *Il sistema teatrale a Milano*, Dedalo libri, Bari 1966, p. 61.
48. L. Cavaglieri, *Tra Arte e Mercato*, cit. pp. 231–235.
49. S. Baia Curioni, *Mercanti d'Opera*, cit. pp. 9–24.
50. Ibid., p. I.
51. L. Cavaglieri, *Tra Arte e Mercato*, cit. pp. 247–248.
52. In 1871, out of 18 agents and impresarios surveyed in the city of Milan, 15 reside permanently in the city and 3 reside there temporarily. In 1881, out of the 44 census takers, 31 were born outside the city of Milan and 3 were considered occasional residents; in 1901, out of the 151 census takers, 20 occasionally resided in Milan and only 43 were born there (L. Cavaglieri, *Tra arte e mercato*, cit. p. 246).
53. As mentioned in the preceding pages, from the ancient Neapolitan music conservatories, there came out, along with instrumentalists, singers and chapel masters, a large number of copyists. The activity of copying was used in the Conservatory as a form of "paid" engagement of students that contributed to the reduction of tuition.
54. B.M. Antolini, *Editori, copisti, commercio della musica in Italia: 1700–1800*, In «Studi Musicali», XVII, 2, 1989, pp. 273–375.
55. B.M. Antolini, *Nuove acquisizioni sull'editoria musicale in Italia (1800–1920)*, in L. Sirch, ed, *Canoni Bibliografici. Contributi italiani al convegno internazionale LAML-LASA*, international conference, Perugia September 1–6, 1996, LIM, Lucca, pp. 95–130; p. 101.
56. S. Baia Curioni, *Mercanti d'Opera*, cit. p. 45.
57. Clausetti ceded his catalogue to Ricordi, Cottrau narrowed his activities from the mid-1970s [R. Cafiero, *Un capitolo di storia dell'editoria musicale fra Milano e Napoli: lo Stabilimento musicale Clausetti (1847–1864)*, in S. Martinotti (ed.), *La musica a Milano*, in *Lombardia e oltre*, II, Vita & Pensiero, Milan 2000, pp. 321–330].
58. S. Baia Curioni, *Mercanti d'Opera*, cit. p. 99.
59. Ibid., pp. 101–102.
60. C. Sorba, *Musica e Teatro*, cit. p. 548.
61. The bibliography on these topics is today very articulate and vast. We cite as the last monumental work of research, that conducted by Francesco Cotticelli and Paologiovanni Maione,

which converged in the first two volumes, both in two tomes, of an important publishing project of Turchini edizioni: *History of Music and Performance in Naples. The Seventeenth Century* (Naples, 2019) and *The Eighteenth Century* (Naples 2009), extensively cited in this volume.

62. R. Del Prete, *Arts&Business: cultural institutions and artistic market in the Italian history in support of cultural tourism*, in A. Morvillo (ed.), Competition and Innovation in Tourism: New Challenges in an Uncertain Environment, Enzo Albano Editore, Naples 2012, pp. 521–539.

63. On music tourism and its connections with the Grand Tour, particularly in Naples see D. Fabris (2015), Italian Soundscapes: Souvenirs from the Grand Tour, cit.; Rice J.A. (2013), *Music and the Grand Tour in the Eighteenth Century*, cit; N. Dubowy (2016), *Musician Travels. Sources of Musicians' Tours and Migrations in the Seventeenth and Eighteenth Centuries*, cit.; M Calella (2102), *Musik und imaginative Geographie: Franz Liszts Années de pèlerinage und die kulturelle Konstruktion der Schweiz*, cit.; R. Cafiero et al. (2020), *Music tourism: history, geography, didactics*, cit.

64. Over the past two decades, research on Neapolitan music conservatories has acquired new information, and the reconstruction of the long process of consolidation of the music education system, in Naples and in Italy, has engaged authoritative scholars of music history. We cite some of them: R. Cafiero, *Il Real Collegio di Musica di Napoli nel 1812: un bilancio*, in «Analecta Musicologica», Band 30/I-II, Laaber Verlag, 1998, pp. 635–659; L. Sirch, M. G. Sità, M. Vaccarini (eds.), *L'insegnamento dei conservatorii, la composizione e la vita musicale nell'Europa dell'Ottocento*, Lim, Lucca 2012; L. Aversano, *La musica nella scuola tra Cavour e l'Italia unita*, in E. Careri, E. Donisi (eds.), *Prima e dopo Cavour. La musica tra Stato Sabaudo e Italia unita (1848–1870)*, Clio-Press, Naples 2015, pp. 67–88; F. Seller, A. Caroccia, *Il Collegio di musica negli anni francesi*, in P. Maione (ed.), *Musica e spettacolo a Napoli durante il decennio francese (1806–1815)*, Turchini edizioni, Naples 2016, pp. 393–415; E. Donisi, *Istruzione musicale in Italia nel secolo XIX: le scuole di violoncello*, in R. Del Prete, *Saperi, parole e mondi. La scuola italiana tra permanenze*

e mutazioni (secc. XIX–XXI), Kinetès edizioni, Benevento 2002, pp. 221–239.

65. An expert on music publishing in Naples is Francesca Seller who has published several essays on the subject. We mention only a few of them: F. Seller, *Lo Stabilimento Musicale Partenopeo*, in R. Cafiero, M. Marino (1999), *Francesco Florimo e l'Ottocento musicale*, Atti del convegno (Morcone April 19–21, 1990), Jason, Reggio Calabria 1999, pp. 469–497; Ead., *Copisti e stampatori teatrali a Napoli nel diciottesimo secolo*, in F. Cotticelli, P. Maione (eds.), *Storia della musica e dello spettacolo a Napoli. The Eighteenth Century*, cit. pp. 805–822; Ead., *Verdi and Music Publishing in Naples in the Nineteenth Century*, in *Verdi in Naples. Verdi at the San Carlo*, Skira, Naples 2016, pp. 75–80; Ead., Music publishing in Naples, in *Storia della musica e dello spettacolo a Napoli. The Seventeenth Century*, cit. pp. 1815–1824.

66. To list them all would be very long, but we still remember the Partenope theater, that of the Pietà dei Turchini, Donna Marianna, Donna Michela, Donna Peppa, the San Severino, the Darsena theater, the Bellini, the Sannazzaro, the Metastasio and many, many others. For the Naples theater system in the early nineteenth century see P. Maione, F. Seller, *I Reali Teatri di Napoli nella prima metà dell'Ottocento*, Caserta, Santagata-Istituto Italiano per gli Studi Filosofici, 1994.

67. F. Mancini, *Teatro di San Carlo. 1737–1987*, The history, the structure, cit.

68. On gambling see again M. R. Pelizzari, *Dalle caserme ai salotti: gioco d'azzardo, teatro e loisir a Napoli tra fine Settecento e Decennio francese*, cit. On Barbaja's impresario in Naples cf. F. Seller, P. Maione, *L'ultima stagione napoletana di Domenico Barbaja (1836–1840): e spettacolo*, in «Rivista Italiana di Musicologia», vol. XXVII, Olschki, nn. 1–2, Florence 1992, pp. 257–235; Idd, *Gioco d'azzardo e teatro a Napoli dall'età Napoleonica alla Restaurazione Borbonica*, in «Musica/Realtà», April 1994, pp. 23–40; Idd., *Domenico Barbaja in Naples (1809–1840): meccanismi di gestione teatrale*, in P. Fabbri (ed.), *Gioachino Rossini. Il testo e la scena*, Fondazione Rossini Pesaro, Urbino 1994, pp. 403–429; Idd., *Da Napoli a Vienna: Barbaja e l'esportazione di un nuovo modello impresariale*, in R. Angermüller, E. Biggi Parodi (eds.), Antonio Salieri (1750–1825) e il teatro

musicale a Vienna. Convenzioni, innovazioni, contaminazioni stilistiche, LIM, Lucca 2012, pp. 405–420; Idd., *Uno spettacolo a misura dei tempi: Barbaja reinventa il teatro*, in A. Caroccia, F. Cotticelli, P. Maione (eds.), *Napoli&Rossini. Di questa luce un raggio*, Edizioni S. Pietro a Majella, Naples 2020, pp. 64–72.

69. M. Traversier, *Gouverner l'opera: une histoire politique de la musique à Naples, 1767–1815*, Ecole Française de Rome, Rome 2009; see also the bulky bibliography given in P. Maione, F. Seller, *Scene musicali a Napoli nel primo Ottocento*, in P. Scialò, F. Seller (eds.), *Passatempi musicali. Giullaume Cottrau e la canzone napoletana di primo '800*, pp. 87–98.

70. The spectacular life in Murat's time is outlined in P. Maione, *La clemenza di Gioacchino*, in A. Scirocco (ed.), *Protagonisti nella Storia di Napoli: Gioacchino Murat*, Elio De Rosa editore, Naples 1994, pp. 50–59. The legislative decree of 1811 is reported in full in P. Maione, F. Seller, *I Reali Teatri di Napoli*, cit. pp. 115–121.

71. On the theme of food connected to the trinomial we considered strategically music, sea and feast, see M. Sirago, *Il mare in festa. Musica, balli e cibi nella Napoli viceregnale (1503–1734)*, Kinetès edizioni, Benevento 2022.

72. F. Seller, *Il recupero della musica "antica" nell'editoria musicale napoletana dall'Unità d'Italia alla Grande Guerra*, in G. Feroleto, A. Pugliese (eds.), *Alessandro Longo: l'uomo, il suo tempo, l'opera*, Istituto di Bibliografia Musicale Calabrese, Vibo Valentia 2001, pp. 391–400.

73. P. Scialò, La canzone napoletana dalle origini ai giorni nostri, NewtonCompton, Rome 1995.

74. S. Ferrone, *Introduzione a Il Teatro italiano. La commedia e il dramma dell'Ottocento*, edited by S. Ferrone tomo I, V, Einaudi, Turin 1979, p. XX.

75. J. Rosselli, *Materiali per la storia socio-economica del San Carlo nell'Ottocento*, in L. Bianconi, R. Bossa, *Musica e Cultura a Napoli*, cit. pp. 369–381.

76. F. Nicolodi, Il Sistema produttivo, cit. pp. 177–178.

77. The information available to us, is now substantial and allows us to reconstruct the economy and producty of the San Carlo's theatrical enterprise at least throughout the nineteenth century, including the costs incurred for the establishment of the Scuola Governativa di Ballo, on which an important and unpublished

research project is underway, conducted by Roberta Albano and Maria Venuso, which will be part of a larger editorial project of Kinetès edizioni, in the Pagine di Danza Series, directed by Elena Randi.

78. This is the unresolved dilemma discussed by W. Baumol in Performing Arts: the Economic Dilemma, cit.

79. R. Di Benedetto, *Il Circolo Bonamici e il "Primo Congresso Musicale Italiano"*, in Francesco Florimo e l'Ottocento musicale, cit. pp. 417–440; p. 417.

80. A. Tarallo, *Ancora sui circoli musicali e mecenati nella Napoli postunitaria*, in *Francesco Florimo e l'Ottocento musicale*, cit. pp. 441–468.

81. R. Di Benedetto, *Il Circolo Bonamici e il "Primo Congresso Musicale Italiano"*, cit.

82. Ibid., p. 425.

83. C. Sorba, *Musica e Teatro*, cit. p. 548.

84. S. Baia Curioni, *Casa Ricordi*, cit.

85. A. Scannapieco, *Vicende della fortuna goldoniana nella Napoli del secondo Settecento*, in Antonia Lezza, A. Scannapieco (eds.), *Oltre la Serenissima. Goldoni, Napoli e la cultura meridionale*, Liguori, Naples 2012, pp. 11–25.

86. P. Scialò, F. Seller (eds.), *Passatempi musicali*, cit., passim.

87. M.L. Stazio, Back to the Future. Giullaume Cottrau. Viaggio temporale fra «Divertimenti per Pianoforte» e canzone napoletana, ovvero la storia ricostruita dai suoi esiti, in P. Scialò, F.Seller (eds.), *Passatempi musicali*, pp. 209–246; p. 212.

88. The play was staged 5 years later in the presence of Ferdinand II at the Teatro del Fondo on the evening of November 28, 1844 [A. Lezza, *La cultura teatrale di primo Ottocento. Intersezioni e Interferenze*, in *Passatempi musicali*, cit. pp. 99–118; p. 113].

89. E. De Mura, *Enciclopedia della canzone napoletana*, Naples 1969, entry *Clausetti, ad Indicem*, vol. I, p. 448.

90. R. Cafiero, *Un capitolo di storia dell'editoria musicale fra Milano e Napoli: lo stabilimento musicale Clausetti (1847–1864)*, in S. Martinotti (ed.), *La musica a Milano, in Lombardia e oltre*, II, Vita e Pensiero, Milan 2000, pp. 321–330.

91. Ibid.

92. Ibid.

93. Max Vajro, *La canzone napoletana dalle origini all'Ottocento. Saggi di folklore musicale*, Vajro, Naples 1957, pp. 105–107.
94. The mechanism in short was reversed in the songs-rèclame (of the Miccio Stores, the Diodato or Pizzicato Café, the Cordial Campari or the Ferrenosio Favara) distributed, precisely on copielle (M.L. Stazio, *La fabbrica della festa*, in M.L. Stazio (ed.) *Catalogo Piedigrotta 1895–1995*, Progetti museali editore, Rome 1995).
95. The Historical Archives of the Naples Chamber of Commerce, was subjected years ago to a cataloguing project, which was then discontinued [see Guida all'Archivio Storico della Camera di Commercio Industria Artigianato e Agricoltura di Napoli (1808–1944), edited by Tommasina Boccia and Concetta Damiani, Napoli, Giannini, 2008]. At the time of our consultation, the Chamber's conspicuous documentary patrimony was not kept on the premises, for a number of reasons due to the new layout of the rooms used for the Historical Archives. It was 2013 and, thanks to a research project shared with the Napoli Confesercenti, we had permission to consult the scarce material left on site. Among them, the most homogeneous documents available to us were the "Registers of Business Complaints" attributable to the archival section of the Economic Registry. This is one of the most representative series of chamber archives, launched with Law No. 121 of 1910 by which the "Register of Companies," also known as the "Economic Registry," was formally established at the Chambers of Commerce. The series is divided according to a chronological distribution in two periods: the post-unification period (65 archival units produced between 1911 and 1924) and the fascist period (46,104 archival units produced in the years 1925 and 1945). Our consultation and work on census and filing of the recorded establishments was limited, to the first 80 volumes (all 65 units of the first period and part of the second). For convenience, we report in the two summary tables, the registration numbers of the firms, since quoting individual records would often be misleading.
96. Naples Chamber of Commerce Historical Archives, (henceforth ASC.CIAA.Na), no. 317.
97. Among the lyricists the names of Libero Bovio, E.A. Mario, Ernesto Murolo, Salvatore Di Giacomo, Ferdinando Russo,

Rocco Galdieri, Pasquale Cinquegrana, and Edoardo Nicolardi return; while among the composers those of Mario Costa, Eduardo Di Capua, Vincenzo Valente, Salvatore Gambardella, Ernesto De Curtis, Vincenzo De Crescenzo, Francesco Buongiovanni, and again E.A. Mario

98. We have no documented news about Valentina Bideri, except for the description and account we received from a fruitful conversation with one of her grandchildren, Ferdinando Bideri, currently at the head of one of the subsidiaries of the Bideri publishing group, whom we thank for receiving us, in the course of our research.

99. Bideri entry, by Enzo Giannelli in Dictionary of Italian Song, edited by Gino Castaldo, ed. Curcio, 1990, pp. 171–172.

100. ASC.CIAA.Na, no. 1,882.

101. ASC.CIAA.Na, no. 273.

102. ASC.CIAA.Na, no. 16,782.

103. ASC.CIAA.Na, no. 3,570.

104. ASC.CIAA.Na, no. 4,337. The file also preserves the Chamber of Commerce Visas.

105. ASC.CIAA.Na, no. 5,180.

106. ASC.CIAA.Na, no. 9,356.

107. ASC.CIAA.Na, no. 10,686.

108. On the production of pianos in Naples see F. Seller, P. Maione, First archival reconnaissances on piano makers in Naples in the nineteenth century, in «Liuteria Musica e Cultura», 1997, pp. 21–41; Idd., Le fabbriche di pianoforti nel regno delle due Sicilie, in «Napoli Nobilissima», vol. VII, fasc. I-II, January-April 2006, pp. 47–56; Ead., I pianoforti a Napoli nell'Ottocento, in «Fonti Musicali Italiane», 14/2009, pp. 171–199.

109. ASC.CIAA.Na, no. 9,955.

110. ASC.CIAA.Na, no. 13,310.

111. ASC.CIAA.Na, no. 481.

112. ASC.CIAA.Na, no. 2,350.

113. ASC.CIAA.Na, no. 6,292.

114. ASC.CIAA.Na, no. 18,068.

115. ASC.CIAA.Na, no. 12,722.

116. *Catalogue of music published by the publishers Clausetti and C. in Naples, Stabilimento del Poliorama Pittoresco*, Naples, 1852, in R. Cafiero, *Un capitol di storia dell'editoria musicale*, cit.

117. G. Regaldi, *I canti popolari in Napoli*, in M.L. Stazio, *Back to the Future*, cit, p. 217.
118. Ibid.
119. M.L. Stazio, *La fabbrica della festa*, cit. A more recent and important contribution on Neapolitan song is that of R. Perrotta, Fonti per la storia della canzone napoletana: hla «Collezione Ettore De Mura» del Comune di Napoli, in A. Bini, T. Grande, F. Riva (eds.), *Scripta Sonant: Contributions on Italian Musical Heritage*, IAML Italia, Milan 2018.

CONCLUSIONS

With this volume, in which we have resumed and expanded studies to which we have been devoting ourselves for a long time, we intend to recover and clarify some important conceptual categories that help us investigate some of the most fascinating aspects of the forms of musical production in Naples in the modern age, starting with the methods of assistance to abandoned children and social inclusion that construct, without a precise initial economic strategy, forms of cultural entertainment shared by the broadest strata of the population—street festivals, games in the piazzas, around the "*cuccagna* trees," etc.—and ending with the performances intended for the most select aristocratic circles, as well as the organization of the profession of musician and the forms of musical and theatrical offerings.—up to the performances intended for the inner circles of the most select aristocracy, as well as the organization of the musician's profession and the forms of musical and theatrical offerings.

The Neapolitan experience six centuries ago anticipates, in deed and in words, the concept of the creative economy. The debate on creativity, culture, and economy is very recent and they are considered fertile areas for innovation and inclusive and sustainable growth. The city of Naples, starting from the organization of a welfare system based on the work and education of orphaned children abandoned to the street and poverty, became a model of educational and vocational training provision that, responding to a very strong social demand for shelter and survival, succeeded in creating real social enterprises that very quickly took

R. Del Prete, *The Neapolitan Creative Economy*, Palgrave Studies in Economic History, https://doi.org/10.1007/978-3-031-55903-7

on the characteristics of cultural and creative industries: the four ancient Conservatories.

On this historical basis, eighteenth-century Naples established itself as the capital of music and culture. Naples was, in the second half of the century, one of the main centers of opera production in music, and a place where a not inconsiderable number of renowned European composers were concentrated. The theater is the very symbol of the city's cosmopolitan projection, a practice invested with significance by an aristocracy that was fascinated by European models, a symbol of power, and the hub of the circuits that, through the grand tour, Masonic affiliations, and the circulation of composers, transmitted works and musical tastes.

At the beginning of the eighteenth century, it was home to four theaters, which became six at the end of the century. Conservatories' musical education and production and the frequent and numerous theatrical performances are common practice in both religious institutions and the private salons of the aristocracy. The theater and music industry fed a highly articulated "creative" labor market (composers, chapel masters, librettists, actors and singers, set designers, theatrical architects, and music copyists) and nourished a not inconsiderable induced industry, from suppliers of textiles and costumes, stage materials, construction, music teachers, called upon for private education, to the publishing market (represented by the trade in theater texts, opera librettos, lyrics and musical scores). Public performances spread operas and music that the private salons consecrated as successful works, reproducing them in the festivities and rituals of courtly sociability, fueling an industry of handicraft reproduction and copying.

Eighteenth-century Naples became, in short, the seat of an extended "creative class," a place where the cultural market provided opportunities for the social ascent, and absorbed many of the surplus demographic resources of the great human aggregate. A significant part of this "creative class" produces styles and formal novelties, exports its works, and succeeds in conquering the European theater market. Naples exports to Europe not only its operas but also singers and musicians and the very characters born from the centuries-old gestation of the improvised «commedia dell'arte», which survived its crisis, sanctioned precisely in the eighteenth century by the advance of musical comedy and «opera buffa», by taking on new characters and meanings. It also exports singers, musicians, and scores.

This explosion of liveliness of the cultural market and the creative class, certainly driven by the new power structures and the political role of the theater, can only be understood in relation to the city's historical heritage, which makes it a collector of human resources and generator of artistic skills, and to the complex relationship between the regulatory system connected to the new political order and the dynamics of the market.

Although the reference to eighteenth-century Naples refers to those musical personalities who have left their mark on the history of music, innovation can only be understood as a social phenomenon. In this case, primarily the result of a widespread and structured system of "production of intellectual/artistic capital," constituted by the conservatories.

Founded as brephotrophs that used music as a means of re-education and salvation of the soul, at the beginning of the eighteenth century, their transformation into music schools was brought about by two factors: the need for alternative sources to cover the costs of care and the growing demand for musical services, both religious and secular.

This definition of the conservatoires as producers of knowledge and know-how, as well as "music factories," passes through the definition of selective admission rules that are functional to the music market, and of "guarantees" for compliance with contracts. Music teaching is based on an internal exchange of expertise. The relationship with the conservatoire is based on a contract that provides for a course of education and work for which patronage is required.

The students of the conservatories, among whom were many children from the hinterland, immigrants, and children of the middle and lower classes, satisfied the widespread demand for "musical services," and while in the seventeenth-century patronage was mainly religious, there was a growing secular demand from merchants, bankers and government officials, who hired musicians as house musicians, teachers of singing and musical instruments, or as occasional performers of music.

In the collective imagination, the eighteenth century undoubtedly remains the most shining segment in the history of Neapolitan conservatories. However, they do not exhaust the picture of Neapolitan music education. There exists, alongside this educational system, an entirely private market of musical education, constituted mainly by singing masters with whom pupils enter into special contracts. And a third system of professional training is that at the music workshops, true harmony workshops in which the most established chapel masters surround themselves with promising apprentices and professionals through a recruitment system based on trust.

The system of musical education structured in this way created a substratum of knowledge and skills that gradually consolidated: in the eighteenth century, real dynasties of musicians operated in Naples. The Neapolitan School of Music produced music that was appreciated far beyond the borders of the Kingdom. The professionalization of the musician is also expressed in the widespread organization of associations that perform a mutualistic function but also one of "regulation" of the market. Gradually this abundant supply of musical services is increasingly oriented toward the growing demand of theaters, which increasingly draw on conservatories.

The creative city is, in short, the result of both power and market dynamics, but above all of a system of training and circulation of artistic knowledge produced by the city's attractiveness, by an underlying system of education originally oriented to perform another function, that of poverty relief, and by the progressive affirmation of a cultural institution, which grows to the extent that it is able to support widespread cultural consumption, in an overcoming of the elitist and "political" characterization that the absolutist eighteenth century tried to impose on the theater as an institution of power.

Rarely have economic historians dealt with theater, music, and live performance, and many of them still find it difficult to recognize the scientific nature and relevance of the subject to their own disciplinary field. The only "cultural industry" studied turns out to be the film or publishing industry, perhaps because in that case, establishing prices and production processes of films and books is easier.

Thus, the cases of study of the economic history of art and culture appear very limited, perhaps due to the difficulty of integrating quantitative and serial analyses with qualitative ones linked to other historiographic categories, judged too humanistic. And yet, as we have tried to highlight in this book, the issues to be assessed are those of production, patronage, and the art market, relating to a sector that today, as in the past, is embedded in a complex global system of cultural and economic exchanges.

In the first part of the volume, to explain our historical-economic approach to art and culture, we referred to the words of C. M. Cipolla and those of Luigi De Rosa, two fathers of Italian economic history. We feel it is absolutely necessary to reflect on the fact that, in the academic sphere, the Economics of Art and Culture has by now gained scientific recognition and autonomy as a discipline, while the Economic History of Art and Culture is still searching for affirmation.

We have always been concerned with tangible and intangible cultural heritage, and with great conviction, over the years, we have continued to look with particular interest at the variegated world of the performing arts (theater, music, opera, dance) as the central element of a cultural industry whose history is still to be retraced because its most appropriate field of study is still to be invented: the economic and financial history of art and culture, precisely.

The interest in economic analysis in the cultural sector has increased significantly since the 1960s, corresponding to the growth of cultural consumption. There are several reasons for this. First of all, there is the growing role played by the demand and production of cultural goods and activities in more advanced economies. This growth is also linked to the use of cultural goods and activities as a means of production of other market and nonmarket goods (production of information, entertainment, audiovisual, content for the multimedia industry, input for education and training processes; resources for tourism attractiveness, etc.). Secondly, the cultural sector is, in whole or in part, a beneficiary of public expenditure, and therefore, as it has grown, it has become relevant in terms of collective choices.

Theater agents and impresarios are the cornerstones of a world in which some not untalented business leaders stand out. It is to them that we owe, in addition to the theatrical and operatic activity proper, the publication of a number of agency journals which, although within a commercial and business logic, provide valuable and first-hand information, not only on the life and production activity of many artists and their companies but also on the destinies of many dramatic texts, another cultural product on which many investments were made.

In short, it is our intention to offer a further reflection on a cultural industry that has its deepest roots in the construction of a music market that intersected from the very beginning with the theatrical market and, even earlier, with the welfare market. In a multiform and plural production context, products, producers, and distributors were defined, on which it is necessary today to channel the energies of historical-economic research.

At the beginning of this volume, we posed questions that we promised to answer. How the demand and supply of music was defined in the period from the seventeenth century to the Risorgimento, we have seen by reconstructing practices and traditions and attempting to intercept an ever-increasing demand for musical and theatrical goods and services. The case study, among the four conservatories of Santa Maria della Pietà de' Turchini, accurately reconstructed, using original sources, the characteristics of the music market.

The geography of Italian music venues led our reflections to talk not only about Naples, Venice, Rome, and Milan but also about other types of conservatories, impresario theaters, and royal theaters. We then reconstructed the professional and production roles defined by the music market and, when possible, reported on the amount of remuneration received. The role first of the various governments, then of the Italian State, in the development of musical culture was defined through the various provisions and legislative references. On the costs of stage sets, on the public and private funding received by theaters or conservatories, we reported whenever possible, as well as on the strategies artists used to secure major commissions. But the subject matter is vast and needs to be compared with other studies of economic history carried out in different periods and places in order to construct long-term time series or average prices of cultural goods and services.

Our intention was to tell a complex, ancient yet topical story: that of a prototype cultural and creative industry which, starting from a private initiative of a charitable and welfare nature, encouraged in various forms by the Bourbon viceroys, created a special human capital protagonist of a cultural market, music and theater above all, which laid the foundations for the development of the CCI—Cultural and Creative Industries in Italy and Europe. A sector that today is growing strongly in terms of employment, production, and consumption, with a highly significant socio-economic impact on people's well-being.

SOURCES AND REFERENCES

This volume collects, enlarging and interpreting them in the light of new knowledge, all the essays I have published as articles in scientific journals or as contributions in volumes from 1999 to the present, as well as, of course, recovering all the material collected in my research first on the occasion of my Degree Thesis at the Federico II University in Naples in History of Music, under the guidance of Prof. Agostino Ziino, and then on the occasion of my PhD Thesis in Economic History (X cycle), under the guidance of Prof. Luigi De Rosa, discussed at the Bocconi University in Milan.

SOURCES

BIBLIOTECA NAZIONALE DI NAPOLI (I-NN)
I. Fuidoro, Giornali di Napoli dal 1660 al 1680, ms. X.B.14–19
ARCHIVIO DI STATO DI NAPOLI (A.S.N.)
Fondo Cappellano Maggiore, Cantori e musici, Statuti Fasci Teatrali 1759–60.
ARCHIVIO STORICO BANCO DI NAPOLI (ASBN)
Banco dello Spirito Santo, vol. di bancali
Banco di San Giacomo, libri giornali
Banco dell'Annunziata, libri giornali
ARCHIVIO STORICO PIETÀ DEI TURCHINI (A.P.T.)
Sezione Patrimonio – (Platee, Libri Maggiori)
Sezione Contabilità e Bilanci (Bilanci mensuali, bilanci annuali, libri del tesoriere, entrate e uscite)
Sezione Corrispondenze, Suppliche e Memoriali
Sezione Assistenza, Beneficenza, Culto e Maritaggi

© The Editor(s) (if applicable) and The Author(s), under exclusive license to Springer Nature Switzerland AG 2024
R. Del Prete, *The Neapolitan Creative Economy*, Palgrave Studies in Economic History, https://doi.org/10.1007/978-3-031-55903-7

Sezione Alunni e Convittori
Sezione Cautele ed Istrumenti Regole a stampa del 1769
ARCHIVIO DEL CONSERVATORIO DI S. MARIA DI LORETO (A.S.M.L.)
Sezione Patrimonio – (Platee, Libri Maggiori)
Sezione Contabilità e Bilanci (Bilanci mensuali, bilanci annuali, libri del tesoriere, entrate e uscite)
Sezione Corrispondenze, Suppliche e Memoriali Sezione Alunni e Convittori
ARCHIVIO STORICO DELLA CAMERA DI COMMERCIO DI NAPOLI
Sezione Anagrafe economica - «Registri delle Denuncie di Esercizio»
[This is one of the most representative series of Chamber of Commerce archives, started with Law No. 121 of 1910 with which the 'Register of Companies', also known as the 'economic registry', was formally established at the Chambers of Commerce. The series is divided chronologically into two periods: the post-unification period (65 archival units produced between 1911 and 1924) and the fascist period (46,104 archival units produced in the years 1925–1945). Our consultation and work on the census and filing of the registered businesses was limited to the first 80 volumes (all 65 units from the first period and part of the second]

References

(1991), Banchi pubblici, banchi privati e monti di pietà nell'Europa preindustriale, vol. II, Genova.

(1991), Enfance abandonnée et société en Europe, XIX–XX siécle, «Collection de l'école Francaise de Rome», 140, Roma.

Ago R., Raggio O., a cura di, (2004), Consumi culturali nell'Italia moderna, in «Quaderni storici», 115/1, numero monografico.

Alberigo G. (1960), Contributi alla storia delle confraternite dei disciplinati e della spiritualità laicale nei secoli XV e XVI, in Il Movimento dei Disciplinati nel settimo centenario del suo inizio, Perugia, pp. 156–252.

Amato M. (1999), La biblioteca del conservatorio «San Pietro a macella» di Napoli: dal nucleo originale alle donazioni di fondi privati ottocenteschi, in Cafiero R., Marino M., a cura di, Francesco Florimo e l'Ottocento musicale, Jason. Reggio Calabria, pp. 645–669.

Amin A., N Thrift (2007), Cultural economy and cities, «Progress in Human Geography», 31 (2), pp. 143–161.

Antolini B. M. (1989), Editori, copisti, commercio della musica in Italia: 17001800, in «Studi musicali», XVII, 2, pp. 273–375.

Antolini B. M. (2001), Nuove acquisizioni sull'editoria musicale in Italia (18001920), in L. Sirch, a cura di, Canoni bibliografici. Contributi italiani al convegno internazionale LAML-LASA, Perugia 1–6 settembre 1996, LIM, Lucca, pp. 95130.

Arrighi G., Emeljanov V. (Eds), (2014), Entertaining Children. The Participation of Youth in the Entertainment Industry, Palgrave Macmillan, United States, New York.

Assante F. (1999), I profeti della previdenza: monti e conservatori nelle corporazioni napoletane in età moderna, in A. Guenzi, P. Massa, A. Moioli, a cura di, Corporazioni e gruppi professionali nell'Italia moderna, FrancoAngeli, Milano, pp. 601–612.

Avallone P. (1995), Stato e banchi pubblici a Napoli a metà del 700. Il Banco dei Poveri: una svolta, Napoli.

Avallone P. (1999), I banchi pubblici napoletani tra XVII e XVIII secolo: strategie e gestione, in «Sintesi», n. 1.

Avallone P., Salvemini R. (1999), Dall'assistenza al credito. L'esperienza dei Monti di Pietà e delle Case Sante nel Regno di Napoli tra XVI e XVIII secolo, in «Nuova Rivista Storica», Anno LXXXIII, Fasc. I, Roma, pp. 21–54.

Aversano L. (2004), La scuola di musica dell'Orfanotrofio Provinciale di Salerno nel XIX secolo, in A. Carlini, a cura di, Accademie Società Filarmoniche in Italia. Studi e ricerche, Società Filarmonica Trento, Trento, pp. 9–56.

Aversano L. (2015), La musica nella scuola tra Cavour e l'Italia unita, in E. Careri, E. Donisi, a cura di, Prima e dopo Cavoru. La musica tra Stato Sabaudo e Italia unita (1848–1870), ClioPress, Napoli, pp. 67–88.

Badolato N. (2018), Amazzoni e sovrani, la festa e il teatro, in S. Cappelletto (a cura di), Il contributo italiano alla storia del pensiero. Musica, Istituto della Enciclopedia Italiana fondata da Giovanni Treccani S.p.A., Roma, pp. 156–163.

Baia Curioni S. (2011), Mercanti dell'Opera. Storie di Casa Ricordi, Il Saggiatore, Milano.

Baldauf-Berdes (1993), Women Musicians of Venice. Musical Foundation. 15251855, Clarendon Press, Oxford.

Barbier P. (1991), Gli evirati cantori, Rizzoli, Milano.

Barbieri G. (1961), Origini ed evoluzione dei Monti di Pietà in Italia, in «Economia e Credito», Palermo.

Barletta L. (1981), Il Carnevale del 1764 a Napoli Protesta e integrazione in uno spazio urbano, Società Editrice Napoletana, Napoli.

Baumol W. J., Bowen W. G. (1966), Performing Arts: The Economic Dilemma, Twentieth Century Fund, New York.

Besutti P. (2007), Note e monete. Strategie economiche di musicisti nella prima Età moderna, in R. Morselli, a cura di, Vivere d'arte. Carriere e finanze nell'Italia moderna, Carocci, Roma, pp. 167–204.

Bianconi L. (1989), Storia della musica. Il Seicento, EDT, Torino.

Bianconi L., Bossa R., a cura di, (1983), Musica e Cultura a Napoli dal XV al XIX sec., Olschki, Firenze.

Bianconi L., Bossa R., a cura di, (1983), Musica e Cultura a Napoli dal XV al XIX sec., Olschki, Firenze.

Bianconi L., G. Pestelli, a cura di, (1987), Il sistema produttivo e le sue competenze, EDT, Torino.

Bianconi L. (1987), Music in the seventeenth century, Cambridge University Press.

Bianconi L., Walker T. (1975), Dalla finta pazza alla veremonda: storie di Febiarmonici, «Rivista Italiana di Musicologia», X, pp. 379–454.

Bizzarini M. (2018), La versione di Burney. Modalità esecutive della musica sacra in Italia al tempo di Mozart, in R. Cafiero et al., a cura di, «La nostra musica di chiesa è assai differente...». Mozart e la musica sacra italiana, Atti del Convegno internazionale di studi (Pavia, Collegio Ghislieri, 9–10 ottobre 2015), Società Editrice di Musicologia, Roma, pp. 9–23.

Black C. (1992), Le confraternite italiane del Cinquecento, Torino.

Boccadamo G. (1988), L'antico ospedale napoletano di San Nicola a Molo, in «Campania Sacra», 19/2, pp. 311–340.

Borsay P. (2008), Invention, Innovation, and the "creative milieu" in urban Britain: The Long Eighteenth Century and the Birth of the Modern Cultural Economy. In Hessler, M. and Zimmermann, C. eds, 2008. Creative Urban Milieu: Historical Perspectives on Culture, Economy, and the City. Frankfurth and New York: Campus Verlag, pp. 77–100.

Boswell J. (1991), L'abbandono dei bambini in Europa occidentale, Milano.

Burney C. (1771), The present state of music in France and Italy, or The Journal of a Tour through those Countries, undertaken to collect Materials for a General History of Music, T. Becket and Co., London (trad. It. Viaggio musicale in Italia, a cura di E. Fubini, Torino, EdT/Musica 1979, p. 294).

Cafiero R. (1998), Il Real Collegio di Musica di Napoli nel 1812: un bilancio, in «Analecta Musicologica», Band 30/I-II, Laaber Verlag, pp. 635–659.

Cafiero R. (1999), Istruzione musicale a Napoli tra decennio francese e restaurazione borbonica: il «collegio di musica delle donzelle» (1806–1832), in Cafiero R. (2000), Un capitolo di storia dell'editoria musicale fra Milano e Napoli: lo Stabilimento musicale Clausetti (1847–1864), in S. Martinotti, a cura di, La musica a Milano, in Lombardia e oltre, II, Vita e Pensiero, Milano, pp. 321–330

Cafiero R., G. Lucarno, R. G. Rizzo, G. Onorato, a cura di, (2020), Turismo musicale: storia, geografia, didattica, Pàtron Editore, Bologna.

Cafiero R., Marino M., a cura di, Francesco Florimo e l'Ottocento musicale, Jason, Reggio Calabria, pp. 753–825.

Calella M. (2012), Musik und imaginative Geographie: Franz Liszts Années de pèlerinage und die kulturelle Konstruktion der Schweiz, in «Die Musikforschung», 65, pp. 211–230.

Canella G. (1966), Il sistema teatrale a Milano, Dedalo libri, Bari.

Capasso B. (1879), Catalogo ragionato dei libri o registri esistenti nella sezione antica o prima serie dell'archivio Municipale di Napoli, Napoli.

Cappellieri A. (2000), Il Teatro di San Bartolomeo da Scarlatti a Pergolesi, «Studi pergolesiani», 4, pp. 131–156.

Carocci, Roma, pp. 131–187.

Caroccia A. (2015), Scelte editoriali al tempo di Carlo Gesualdo: le fonti a stampa della biblioteca del Conservatorio «San Pietro a Majella» e dell'Archivio Musicale dei Gerolamini di Napoli, in A. Caroccia, M. Columbro, a cura di, Giornata Gesualdiana. Atti della giornata di studio (Castello di Gesualdo, 7 dicembre 2015), ilCimarosa, Avellino, pp. 105–145.

Carpitella D. (1973), Musica e tradizione orale, Palermo.

Carpitella D. (1976), Folklore e analisi differenziale di cultura, Roma. Cavaciocchi S., a cura di, (1995), Il tempo libero. Economia e Società. Secc. XIIIXVIII, Le Monnier, Firenze.

Cavaglieri L. (2006), Tra arte e mercato. Agenti e agenzie teatrali nel XIX secolo, Bulzoni Editore, Roma.

Cavallo S. (1980), Assistenza femminile e tutela dell'onore nella Torino del XVIII secolo, «Annali della fondazione L. Einaudi», v. 14, Torino, pp. 127–156.

Cavallo S. (1995), Charity and power in early modern Italy, Cambridge. Ceci G. (1970), Un mercante mecenate nel secolo XVII, Gaspare Roomer, in «Napoli Nobilissima», vol. XVI.

Cenedella C., G. Fumi, a cura di, (2015), Oltre l'assistenza. Lavoro e formazione professionale negli istituti per l'infanzia irregolare in Italia tra Sette e Novecento, Vita e Pensiero, Milano.

Ceriello G. R. (1920), Comedias de santos a Napoli, nel '600, «Bulletin Hispanique», XXII/2, pp. 77–100.

Chalon J. (1886), Naples. 1874–1886, Mons.

Charle C. (2002), Les theâtre et leurs publics à Paris, Berlin et Vienne 1860–1914, in C. Charle, D. Roche, a cura di, Capitales culturelles, Paris, Publ. de la Sorbonne, pp. 403–420.

Chirico T. (1988), La scuola di musica del Real Orfanotrofio provinciale di Reggio Calabria e le istituzioni musicali napoletane, «Nuova Rivista Musicale Italiana», n. 3, luglio/Settembre, ERIRAI, pp. 462–491.

Chirico T. (1999), La scuola musicale nel Reale Albergo dei Poveri di Napoli e negli istituti dipendenti (1817–1861), in R. Cafiero, M. Marino, a cura di, Francesco Florimo e l'Ottocento musicale, Jason editrice, Reggio Calabria, pp. 827860.

Ciapparelli P. L. (1987), I luoghi del teatro a Napoli nel Seicento. Le Sale "private", in D.A. D'Alessandro, A. Ziino, a cura di, La musica a Napoli durante il Seicento, Roma, Torre d'Orfeo, pp. 379–412.

Ciapparelli P. L. (1999), Due secoli di teatri in Campania (1694–1896). Teorie, progetti e realizzazioni, Electa, Napoli.

Ciapparelli P. L. (2009), I luoghi del teatri e dell'effimero. Scenografia e scenotecnica, in F. Cotticelli, P. Maione, Storia della musica e dello Spettacolo a Napoli, Vol. II, Il Settecento, tomo I, Turchini Edizioni, Napoli, pp. 223–329.

Cipolla C. M. (2003), Tra due Culture. Introduzione alla Storia economica, il Mulino, Bologna.

Clemente A., Del Prete R. (2017), Cultural Creativity and Symbolic Economy in Early Modern Naples: Music and Theatre as Cultural Industries, in I. Van Damme, B. De Munck, A. Miles (eds), Cities and Creativity from Renaissanse to the Present, Routledge, Taylor & Francis New York and London, pp.107126.

Codignola F. (2010), Globalizzazione e mercato dell'arte culturale, «Tafter Journal», www.tafterjournal.it n. 24, giugno.

Coen P. (2010), Il mercato dei quadri a Roma nel sec. XVIII. La domanda, l'offerta e la circolazione delle opere in un grande centro artistico europeo, L. Olschki, Firenze.

Columbro M. (2000), Considerazioni sulla condizione sociale e lavorativa del musicista napoletano nel Sei e Settecento, in M. Columbro, P. Maione, a cura di, Pietro Metastasio. Il testo e il contesto, Altrastampa, Napoli, pp. 17–27

Columbro M., Intini E. (1998), Congregazioni e corporazioni di musici a Napoli tra Sei e Settecento, «Rivista italiana di musicologia», XXXIII, pp. 41–76.

Columbro M., Maione P. (2008), La Cappella musicale del Tesoro di San Gennaro di Napoli tra Sei e Settecento, Turchini Edizioni, Napoli. Conte C. (1884), Gli stabilimenti di beneficenza di Napoli, Napoli.

Cordella E. (1857), Sulla storia della beneficenza nei domini continentali del Regno, in «Annali civili del Regno di Napoli», fs. CXXII, pp. 113–126.

Cotticelli F., Maione P. (1999), Per una storia della vita teatrale napoletana nel primo Settecento: ricerche e documenti d'archivio, «Studi pergolesiani», 3, pp. 31–116.

Cotticelli F., Maione P., a cura di (2006), Le carte degli antichi banchi e il panorama musicale e teatrale della Napoli di primo Settecento 1732–33, «Studi pergolesiani», 5, pp. 21–54, con cd-rom allegato (Spoglio delle polizze bancarie di interesse teatrale e musicale reperite nei giornali di cassa dell'Archivio del Banco di Napoli per gli anni 1732–1734).

Cotticelli F., P. Maione (1996), Onesto divertimento ed allegria de' popoli. Materiali per una storia dello spettacolo a Napoli nel primo Settecento, Ricordi, Milano.

Cotticelli F., P. Maione, a cura di, (2009), Storia della musica e dello spettacolo a Napoli. Il Settecento, in due tomi, Turchini edizioni, Napoli.

Cotticelli F., P. Maione, a cura di, (2019), Storia della musica e dello spettacolo a Napoli. Il Seicento, in due tomi, Turchini edizioni, Napoli.

Creativity, Culture & Capital (2021), Impact investing in the global creative economy, gennaio, https://www.creativityculturecapital.org/wpcontent/upl oads/2021/01/Creativity-Culture-and-Capital-Impact-investing-inthe-glo bal-creative-economy-English.pdf.

Croce B. (1891), I Teatri di Napoli (secoli XV–XVII), Napoli, Pierro 1891, [rist. Berisio 1968].

Cruciani F. (2005), Lo spazio del teatro, Laterza, Roma-Bari.

D'Addosio G. (1883), Origine e vicende storiche e progressi della Real S. Casa dell'Annunziata di Napoli, Napoli.

D'Alessandro D. A. (2019), Mecenati e mecenatismo nella vita musicale napole-tana del Seicento e condizione sociale del musicista. I casi di Giovanni Maria Trabaci e Francesco Provenzale, in F. Cotticelli, P. Maione, a cura di, Storia della musica e dello spettacolo a Napoli, Il Seicento, vol. I, Turchini edizioni, Napoli, pp. 71–603.

D'Alessandro D. A., Ziino A., a cura di, (1987), La musica a Napoli durante il Seicento, Edizioni Torre d'Orfeo, Roma.

D'Aloe S. (1882), Storia dell'Augustissima Compagnia della Santa Croce, Napoli.

D'Arienzo V. (1996), L'arrendamento del sale dei Quattro Fondaci, Salerno.

D'Ario C., Gli esposti a Napoli nel XVIII sceolo, in Chiesa, Assistenza e Società nel Mezzogiorno moderno, cit., pp. 515–567;

D'Engenio C. (1624), Napoli Sacra, I ed. di Ottavio Beltrano, Napoli. Da Molin G. (1993), Nati e abbandonati Aspetti demografici e sociali dell'infanzia abbandonata in Italia nell'età moderna, Cacucci Editore, Bari.

Da Molin G., a cura di, (1994), Trovatelli e balie in Italia, secc. XVI-XIX, Bari.

Da Molin G., Carbone A. (2000), Un mondo al maschile: il Real Ospizio di Giovinazzo nell'Ottocento, in G. Da Molin, a cura di, Senza famiglia. Modelli demografici e sociali dell'infanzia abbandonata e dell'assistenza in Italia (secc. XV-XX), Cacucci, Bari, pp. 407–440.

Da Molin G., CarboneA. (2009), Gli artigiani nel Mezzogiorno d'Italia nel XVIII secolo: modelli differenti delle famiglie, del matrimonio e del controllo degli assetti produttivi, in S. Cavaciocchi, a cura di, La famiglia nell'e-conomia europea dei secoli XIII-XVIII, Fondazione Internazionale di Storia Economica "F. Datini", Prato, pp. 305–324.

De DOMINICI B. (1742), Vita de' pittori, scidtori ed architetti napoletani, 3 tt., Francesco e Cristoforo Ricciardi, Napoli.

De Lellis C. (1893), I sunti di Carlo d'Angiò, Caserta.

De Maio R. (1971), Società e vita religiosa a Napoli nell'età moderna, 16561799, Napoli.

De Maio R. (1992), L'Ospedale dell'Annunziata il «migliore e più segnalato di tutta Italia», in Riforma e miti nella Chiesa del '500, Napoli, 2° ed., pp. 241249.

De Matteo L. (1998), Tra "arte" e industria. L'editoria napoletana nella seconda metà del Settecento, in «Storia Economica», anno I, fase. I, Edizioni Scientifiche Italiane, Napoli, pp. 7–26.

De Mura E. (1968), Enciclopedia della canzone napoletana, Napoli 1969, voce Clausetti, ad Indicem, vol. I, p. 448.

De Renzi E. (1863), Sull'alimentazione del popolo minuto di Napoli, Napoli.

De Rosa L. (1958), Studi sugli Arrendamenti del Regno di Napoli. Aspetti della distribuzione della ricchezza mobiliare nel Mezzogiorno continentale (1649–1806), L'Arte tipografica, Napoli.

De Rosa L. (1968), Navi, merci, nazionalità, itinerari in un porto dell'età industriale. Il porto di Napoli nel 1760, in Saggi e Ricerche sul Settecento, Napoli.

De Rosa L. (1990), L'avventura della storia economica in Italia, Laterza, RomaBari.

De Rosa L. (1991), Le corporazioni nel Sud della Penisola: problemi interpretativi, «Studi storici Luigi Simeoni», XLI, pp. 49–68.

De Rosa L. (1987), Il Mezzogiorno spagnolo tra crescita e decadenza, Mondadori, Milano.

De Simone (1977), Case e botteghe a Napoli nei secoli XVII e XVIII, Droz, Genéve 1977.

De Simone (1987), Il Banco della Pietà di Napoli, 1734–1806, Napoli. DE Simone E. (1985), Storia della Banca. Dalle origini ai nostri giorni, Arte Tipografica, Napoli.

De Simone E. (1996), Il Monte di Pietà di Cusano. Origini e funzioni (17971811), in «Annali della Facoltà di Economia di Benevento», Napoli, pp. 6197.

Degrada F. (1977), L'opera napoletana, in G. Barblan, A. Basso, a cura di, Storia dell'opera, I, Utet, Torino, pp. 237 - 332.

Del Donna A. (2016), Opera, theatrical culture and society in late eighteenth-century Naples, Routledge.

Del Donna A. (2020), Instrumental Music in Late Eighteenth.century Naples: Politics, Patronage and Artistic Culture, Cambridge University Press.

Del Giudice F., a cura di, (1992), Dizionario Giuridico, Edizioni Simone, Napoli 1992.

Del Prete R. (1999), La trasformazione di un istituto benefico-assistenziale in Scuola di Musica: una lettura dei libri contabili del Conservatorio di S. Maria di Loreto in Napoli (1586–1703), in R. Cafiero, M. Marino, a cura di, Francesco Florimo e L'Ottocento musicale, Jason Editrice, Reggio Calabria, pp. 671–715.

Del Prete R. (1999), Un'azienda musicale a Napoli tra Cinquecento e Settecento: il Conservatorio della Pietà dei Turchini, «Storia Economica», n. 3, pp. 413464.

Del Prete R. (2002), Il musicista a Napoli nei secoli XVI–XVIII: storia di una professione, in S. Zaninelli, M. Taccolini, a cura di, Il lavoro come fattore produttivo e come risorsa nella storia economica italiana, Vita e Pensiero, Milano, pp. 325–335.

Del Prete R. (2008), Universo Teatro, in R. Resciniti, G. Maggiore, a cura di, Event experience. Progettare e gestire eventi da ricordare, Napoli, ESI, pp. 85–108.

Del Prete R. (2010), Un teatro per la nuova borghesia. Il «Vittorio Emanuele» di Benevento, in R. Matarazzo, a cura di, Risorgimento e Questione meridionale. La vicenda beneventana, Vereja, Benevento, pp. 431–464.

Del Prete R. (2011), Tra botteghe, cappelle e teatri: l'articolazione socio-professionale della famiglia dei musicisti a Napoli in età moderna, in G. Da Molin, a cura di, Ritratti di famiglia e infanzia. Modelli differenziali nella società del passato, Cacucci, Bari, pp. 51–71.

Del Prete R. (2012), Arts & Business: cultural institutions and artistic market in the Italian history in support of cultural tourism, in A. Morvillo (a cura di), Competition and Innovation in Tourism: New Challenges in an Uncertain Environment, Morvillo, Napoli, pp. 521–539.

Del Prete R. (2012), Cultural and Artistic Institutions can meet the needs of young generation also in the "hinterland": the case of Benevento (Italy), in Proceedings of 15 Years European Network Culture and Management, Görlitz University Studienewoche, 28. Mai-1. Juni, Görlitz, www.kultur.org, pp. 65–75.

Del Prete R. (2012), Il Teatro nell'industria culturale e creativa italiana, in «Amaltea». Trimestrale di cultura on line- Anno VII, n. 3.

Del Prete R. (2013), «che i suoni divengano visibili e che l'orecchio veda». Savinio e la musica, in T. Iermano, P. Sabbatino, Passione Savinio. Letteratura, Arte, Politica (1952–2012), Napoli, Edizioni Scientifiche Italiane, pp. 121–148.

Del Prete R. (2013), La città del loisir. Il sistema produttivo dello spettacolo dal vivo a Napoli tra '800 e '900, in A. Pesce, M. L. Stazio, a cura di, La canzone napoletana tra memoria e innovazione, CNR Issm, Napoli, pp. 121–164, http://www.issm.cnr.it/pubblicazioni/ebook/canzone_napoletana/canzone_napoletana.pdf.

Del Prete R. (2014), Musical Education and the Job Market: the employment of children and young people in the Neapolitan music industry with particular reference to the period 1650 to 1806, in G. Arrighi, V. Emeljanov (Eds), Entertaining Children. The Participation of Youth in the Entertainment Industry, Palgrave Macmillan, United States, New York, pp. 15–32.

Del Prete R. (2015), Gli archivi storici locali come strumento di promozione territoriale. L'Archivio dell'Istituto «San Filippo Neri» di Benevento (secoli XVIIXX), in C. Cenedella, a cura di, Istituti di assistenza, biblioteche e archivi:

un trinomio caratteristico, virtuoso e previdente. Conservare e promuovere, Vita e Pensiero, Milano, pp. 3–39.

Del Prete R. (2015), L'avventura imprenditoriale della musica nell'Ottocento: i luoghi, i protagonisti, il sistema di produzione e di fruizione, l'editoria, in E. Careri, E. Donisi, a cura di, Prima e dopo Cavour: la musica tra stato sabaudo e Italia unita (1848–1870), ClioPress, Napoli, pp.17–66.

Del Prete R. (2016), I grandi tesori negli archivi degli antichi Conservatori musicali di Napoli, in P. A. Toma, a cura di, Napoli in love, Compagnia dei Trovatori, Napoli, pp. 67–70.

Del Prete R. (2017), La musica come rinnovamento sociale e professionale: dagli antichi Conservatori italiani ai Nuclei de El Sistema Abreu, in A. Carbone, a cura di, Popolazione, famiglia e società in età moderna, Scritti in onore di Giovanna Da Molin, Cacucci, Bari, pp. 173–192.

Del Prete R. (2018), Le imprese culturali e creative in Italia: un settore produttivo in crescita, tra occupazione e sistemi di governance, in M. Vetis Zaganelli, L. Síveres, M. C. da Silva Gonçalves, R. Del Prete, (Organizadores), GESTÃO PÚBLICA: responsabilidades e desafios contemporâneos - estudos interdisciplinares, CENBEC-FINOM, Paracatu, pp. 22–47.

Del Prete R. (2019), L'industria creativa: creazione, regolazione e dinamiche del mercato musicale a Napoli nel Seicento, in F. Cotticelli, P. Maione, a cura di, Storia della Musica e dello Spettacolo a Napoli. Il Seicento, Turchini Edizioni, Napoli, tomo II, pp. 1715-1766.

Del Prete R. (2020), Istruzione, sviluppo economico e capitale umano: l'economia della conoscenza in Italia nei secc. XIX–XXI, in R. Del Prete, a cura di, Saperi, parole e mondi. La scuola italiana tra permanenze e mutazioni (secc. XIX–XXI), Kinetès edizioni, Benevento, pp. 607–674.

Del Prete R., Clemente A. (2017), Cultural Creativity and Symbolic Economy in Early Modern Naples: Music and Theatre as Cultural Industries, in I. Van Damme, B. De Munck, A. Miles (eds), Cities and Creativity from Renaissanse to the Present, Routledge, Taylor & Francis New York and London, pp.107126.

Del Prete R., Leone A., Nardone C., a cura di, (2018), La Bellezza del Paesaggio Rurale. Sostenibilità e buone prassi per la valorizzazione delle infrastrutture rurali, Napoli, Regione Campania.

Del Prete R. (2002), Legati, patronati e maritaggi del Conservatorio della Pietà dei Turchini di Napoli in età moderna, in « Rivista di Storia Finanziaria», Luglio-Dicembre 2001, n. 7, Napoli, pp. 7–32.

Del Tufo G. B. (1609), Historia della religione de' Padri Clerici Regolari, Roma. DEUMM, Utet, Torino 1988, Le biografie, voi. VII.

Di Benedetto R., Il Circolo Bonamici e il «Primo Congresso Musicale Italiano», in R. Cafiero, M. Marino, a cura di, Francesco Florimo e l'Ottocento musicale, Jason editrice, Reggio Calabria, pp. 417–440.

Di Benedetto R., Maione P., Seller F. (1998), Napoli Itinerari Armonici, Napoli, Electa.

Di Giacomo S. (1924), Il Conservatorio di Sant'Onofrio a Capuana e quello di S. Maria della Pietà dei Turchini, Sandron, Palermo.

Di Giacomo S. (1928), Il Conservatorio dei Poveri di Gesù Cristo e quello di S. M. di Loreto, Sandron, Palermo.

Di Lascio A., Ortolani S. (2010), Istituzioni di diritto e legislazione dello spettacolo, FrancoAngeli, Milano.

Divenuto F., a cura di, (1990), Napoli sacra del XVI secolo. Repertorio delle fabbriche religiose napoletane nella Cronaca del Gesuita Giovan Francesco Araldo, Napoli.

Domìnguez J. M. (2011), Danza y baile en las celebraciones festivas de la corte virreinal de Nàpoles a finales del siglo XVII, in M. P. Barrios Manzano, M. Serrano Gil, a cura di, Danzas ituales en los paìses iberoamericanos: maestra del patrimonio compartio: entre la tradiciòn y la historia. Estudios e informes, Consejerìa de Educaciòn y Cultura. Junta de Extremadura, Madrid, pp. 323–334.

Dominguez J. M. (2019), L'opera durante il primo periodo napoletano di Alessandro Scarlatti, in F. Cotticelli, P. Maione, a cura di, Storia della musica e dello spettacolo. Il Seicento, tomo I, Turchini edizioni, Napoli, pp. 653–710.

Dominguez J. M. (2019), Napoli e l'opera italiana nel Seicento, in F. Cotticelli, P. Maione, a cura di, Storia della musica e dello spettacolo. Il Seicento, tomo I, Turchini edizioni, Napoli, pp. 605–651.

Donisi E. (2012), Le scuole musicali dell'Orfanotrofio di S. Lorenzo di Aversa, Città di Aversa, Assessorato alla Cultura, Aversa 2012.

Donisi E. (2020), L'istruzione musicale in Italia nel sec. XIX: le scuole di violoncello, in R. Del Prete, Saperi, parole e mondi. La scuola italiana tra permanenze e mutazioni (secc. XIX–XXI), Kinetès edizioni, Benevento, pp. 221–239.

Dubini P. (1999), Economia delle aziende culturali, Etas, Milano.

Dubini P. (2018), «Con la cultura non si mangia». Falso, Laterza, Bari-Roma.

Dubowy N. (2016), Musician Travels. Sources of Musicians' Tours and Migrations in the Seventeenth and Eighteenth Century, in zur Nieden G., Over B. (eds.), Musicians' Mobilities and Music Migrations in Early Modern Europe. Biographical Patterns and Cultural Exchanges, transcript Verlag, Bielefeld (Mainz Historical Cultural Sciences, 33), pp. 207–226.

Esch A. (2002), Prolusione. Economia ed arte: la dinamica del rapporto nella prospettiva dello storico, in S. Cavaciocchi, a cura di, Economia e arte secc. XIIIXVIII, Atti della «Trentaseiesima Settimana di Studi» 30 aprile-4 maggio 2001, Firenze, pp. 21–49.

Fabris D. (1983), Strumenti di corde, musici e congregazioni a Napoli alla metà del Seicento, «Note d'archivio per la storia musicale», n.s. I, pp. 63–110.

Fabris D. (1994), Istituzioni assistenziali e congregazioni di musici a Napoli e nell'Italia meridionale durante il viceregno spagnolo, in L. Bertoldi Lenoci, a cura di, Confraternite, Chiesa e società. Aspetti e problemi dell'associazionismo laicale europeo in età moderna e contemporanea, Schena, Fasano (Br), pp. 779–800.

Fabris D. (2001), La Capilla Real en las etiquetas de la corte virreinal de Nàpoles durante el siglio XVII, in B. J. Garcìa Garcìa, J. J. Carreras, a cura di, La Capilla Real de los Austrias. Mùsica y ritual de corte en la Europa moderna, Fundaciòn Carlos de Amberes, Madrid, pp. 235–250.

Fabris D. (2014), Spettacoli e opera in musica ala corte di Napoli fino all'arrivo di Alessandro Scarlatti (1649–1683), in P. Di Maggio, P. Maione, a cura d), La scena del Re. Il Teatro di Corte del Palazzo Reale di Napoli, Clean edizioni, Napoli, pp. 100–115.

Fabris D. (2105), Italian Soundscapes: Souvenirs from the Grand Tour, in D. Fabris, M. Murata, a cura di, Passaggio in Italia. Music on the Grand Tour in the Seventeenth Century, Brepols, Turnhout, pp. 23–32.

Farolfi B., Melandri V., a cura di, (2008), Il fund raising in Italia. Storia e prospettive, il Mulino, Bologna.

Faverzani, a cura di, Les capitales méditerrranénnes de la culture, Naples lieu de convergences: circulation des langue set des arts en Meditérranéee, Peter Lang, Bern, pp. 29–40.

Ferrone S. (1979), Introduzione a, S. Ferrone, a cura di, Il Teatro italiano. La commedia e il dramma dell'Ottocento, Einaudi, Torino.

Filangieri R. (1940), I banchi di Napoli dalle origini alla costituzione del Banco delle Due Sicilie, 1539–1808, Napoli.

Fiore V. (2011), Luoghi per lo spettacolo: recupero e valorizzazione tra flessibilità e contaminazione, in «Techne», 3/2011, Firenze University Press.

Florida R. (2000), The Rise of the Creative Class and How It's Transforming Work, Leisure, Community and Everyday Life, New York: Basic Books.

Florimo F. (1881–83), La scuola musicale di Napoli e i suoi Conservatori, Morano, Napoli 1881–83, 4 voll. [rist. anastatica Forni, Bologna 1969].

Frey B., Pommerehne W. W. (1991), Muse e mercati. Indagine sull'economia dell'arte, il Mulino, Bologna.

Friedman W. A., Jones G. (2011), Creative industries in history, «Business History Review», 85, pp. 237–244.

Galan Vivas M. C., J. Bonmariage (1969), Signification démographique de la nuptialité, «Recherches économique de Louvrain», n. 4.

Galanti G. M. (1780), Della descrizione geografica e politica delle Sicilie, Napoli [nuova edizione a cura di F. Assante e D. Demarco, Napoli 1969].

Galasso G. (1972), Napoli spagnola dopo Masaniello, Napoli.

Galasso G. (1978), Intervista sulla storia di Napoli, Bari.

Galasso G. (1983), Breve premessa alla storia civile e sociale di Napoli, in L. Bianconi, R. Bossa, a cura di, Musica e cultura a Napoli dal XV al XIX secolo, Olschki editore, Firenze, pp. 13–27.

Galasso G. (2005), Napoli spagnola dopo Masaniello: politica, cultura, società, Edizioni di Storia e Letteratura, Roma [1° edizione Sansoni, Firenze 1982].

Galasso G., Russo C. (1982), Per la storia sociale e religiosa del Mezzogiorno d'Italia, Guida Editore, Napoli.

Gallina M. (2007), Organizzare teatro. Produzione, distribuzione, gestione nel sistema italiano, Franco Angeli, Milano.

Garrani (1957), Il carattere bancario e l'evoluzione strutturale dei primigeni monti di pietà, Milano.

Geremek B. (1973), Il pauperismo nell'età preindustriale (sec. XIV–XVIII), in Stona d'Italia, Einaudi, Torino, vol. V, pp. 669–698.

Geremek B. (1973), Renfermement des pauvres en Italie (XIV-XVII siécle). Remarques préliminaires, in Melanges en l'honneur de Femand Braudel, Toulose, vol I, pp. 205-217.

Geremek B. (1991), La pietà e la forca, Bari-Napoli.

Giannelli E. (1990), Voce Bideri, in G. Castaldo, a cura di, Dizionario della canzone italiana, ed. Curcio, luogo, pp. 171–172.

Giura Longo R. (1961), I beni ecclesiastici nella storia economica di Matera, Matera.

Giustiniani L. (1793), Saggio storico-critico sulla tipografia nel Regno di Napoli, Orsini, Napoli.

Giustiniani L. (1808), Nuova collezione delle prammatiche del Regno di Napoli, t. XV, Napoli.

Gjerdingen R. O. (2020), *Child Composers in the Old Conservatories: how Orphans became elite musicians*, Oxford University Press.

Glixon B. (2017), *Studies in seventeenth-century Opera*, Routledge.

Goldthwaite R. A. (1995), Ricchezza e domanda d'arte in Italia dal Trecento al Seicento. La cultura materiale e le origini del consumismo, Unicopli, Milano.

Goldthwaite R. A. (2003), Economic Parameters of the Italian Art Market (15th–17th Centuries), in M. Fantoni, L. Matthew, S. Matthews Grieco, The Art Market in Italy (15th-17th Centuries), Panini, Modena, pp. 423–444.

Golini A. (1961), Omogamia secondo il luogo di origine in Italia, «Atti della XXI Riunione della Società Italiana di Statistica», Roma.

Grassi P. (1946), Teatro, pubblico servizio, in «Avanti!», 25 aprile.

Griswold W. (2005), Sociologia della cultura, il Mulino, Bologna.

Guerzoni G. (2006), Apollo e Vulcano. I mercati artistici in Italia (1400–1700), Marsilio, Venezia.

Gutton J. P. (1970), La societé et les pauvres. L'exemple de la généralité de Lion, Paris.

Gutton J. P. (1974), La société et les pauvres en Europe, Paris.

Haskell F. (1966), Mecenati e Pittori: studio sui rapporti tra arte e società italiana nell'età barocca, Sansoni, Firenze.

Holzappel P. M. (1905), Le origini del Monte di Pietà (1462–1515), Rocca San Casciano.

Howkins J. (2103), The creative economy: How people make money from ideas, Penguin Books Ltd.

Hunecke J. (1989), I trovatelli di Milano, Bologna.

Karmel P. H. (1948), The relations between male and female nuptiality in a stable population, «Population studies», vol. I, P.4.

Keynes J. M. (1936), Art and State, in «The Listener», 26 august, 1936, in Pennella G., Trimarchi M. (1993), L'Arte e lo Stato, in «Quaderni di Problemi di Amministrazione Pubblica», il Mulino, Bologna.

King M. L. (1991), Le donne nel Rinascimento, Editori Laterza, Roma-Bari.

Larson K. A. (1983), Condizione sociale dei musicisti e dei loro committenti nella Napoli del Cinque e del Seicento, in L. Bianconi, R. Bossa, a cura di, Musica e Cultura a Napoli dal XV al XIX sec., Olschki, Firenze, pp. 61–77.

Lauria G: A. (1877), Napoli alla fine del XVIII sec, Napoli.

Lazarevich G. (1971), The Neapolitan Intermezzo and its Influence on the Symphonic Idiom, «The Musical Quarterly».

Leon A. F., Ruggeri M. (2004), Il costo del melodramma, «Quaderno della rivista Economia della Cultura», il Mulino, Bologna.

Leon P. (1991), Beni culturali: il dilemma fra Stato e mercato, in «Economia della Cultura», n. 1.

Lepre A. (1970), Rendite di monasteri nel Napoletano e crisi economica del '600, in «Quaderni storici» n. 15, pp. 844–865.

Lezza A. (2013), La cultura teatrale del primo Ottocento. Intersezioni e interferenze, in P. Scialò, F. Seller, a cura di, Passatempi musicali. Guillaume Cottrau e la canzone napoletana di primo '800, Guida, Napoli, pp. 99–118.

Lombardi G. (2000), Tra le pagine di San Biagio. L'economia della stampa a Napoli in età moderna, ESI, Napoli.

Lombardi G. (1998), L'attività carto-libraria a Napoli tra fine '600 e primo '700, in A. M. Rao, a cura di, Editoria e cultura a Napoli nel XVIII secolo, Liguori, Napoli.

Macry P. (1984), Borghesie, città e Stato. Appunti e impressioni su Napoli, 18601880, «Quaderni storici», Borghesie urbane dell'800, n. 2, agosto, pp. 338–383. Macry P. (1984), Premessa, in «Quaderni storici», Borghesie urbane dell'800, n. 2, agosto, pp. 333–338.

Maione P. (1994), La clemenza di Gioacchino, in A. Scirocco, a cura di, Protagonisti nella Storia di Napoli: Gioacchino Murat, Elio De Rosa editore, Napoli, pp. 50–59.

Maione P. (1997), Giulia de Caro «seu Ciulla» da commediante a canta-rina. Osservazioni sulla condizione degli «armonici» nella seconda metà del Seicento, «Rivista italiana di musicologia», XXXII, pp. 61–80.

Maione P. (2003), Le metamorfosi della scienza tra generi e imprenditoria nella seconda metà del Seicento a Napoli, in A. Lattanzi, P. Maione, a cura di, Commedia dell'arte e spettacolo in musica tra Sei e Settecento, a cura di Napoli, Editoriale Scientifica, Napoli, pp. 295–328.

Maione P., Cotticelli F., a cura di, (2000–2015), «Studi Pergolesiani/Pergolesi Studies » [IV (2000); V (2006); IX (2015)].

Maione P., Seller F. (1992), L'ultima stagione napoletana di Domenico Barbaja (1836–1840): organizzazione e spettacolo, in «Rivista Italiana di Musicolo-gia», vol. XXVII, Olschki, nn. 1–2, Firenze, pp. 257–223.

Maione P., Seller F. (1994), Domenico Barbaja a Napoli (1809–1840): meccan-ismi di gestione teatrale, in P. Fabbri, a cura di, Gioachino Rossini. Il testo e la scena, Urbino, Fondazione Rossini Pesaro, pp. 403–429.

Maione P., Seller F. (1994), Domenico Barbaja a Napoli (1809–1840): meccan-ismi di gestione teatrale, in P. Fabbri, a cura di, Gioachino Rossini. Il testo e la scena, Fondazione Rossini Pesaro, Urbino, pp. 403–429.

Maione P., Seller F. (1994), Gioco d'azzardo e teatro a Napoli dall'età napoleonica alla Restaurazione borbonica, in «Musica/Realtà», aprile, pp. 23–40.

Maione P., Seller F. (1997), Prime ricognizioni archivistiche sui costruttori di pianoforti a Napoli nell'Ottocento, in «Liuteria Musica e Cultura», pp. 21–41.

Maione P., Seller F. (2002), Da Napoli a Vienna: Barbaja e l'esportazione di un nuovo modello impresariale, in «Römische Historische Mitterlungen», 44, pp. 493–508.

Maione P., Seller F. (2006), Le fabbriche di pianoforti nel regno delle due Sicilie, in «Napoli Nobilissima», vol. VII, fasc. I-II, gennaio-aprile, pp. 47–56. Maione P., Seller F. (2006), Le fabbriche di pianoforti nel regno delle due Sicilie, in «Napoli Nobilissima», vol. VII, fasc. I-II, gennaio-aprile, pp. 47–56.

Maione P., Seller F. (2013), Scene musicali a Napoli nel primo Ottocento, in P. Scialò, F. Seller, a cura di, Passatempi musicali. Giullaume Cottrau e la canzone napoletana di primo '800, Guida, Napoli, pp. 87–98.

Maione P., Seller F. (2020), Uno spettacolo a misura dei tempi: Barbaja reinventa il teatro, in A. Caroccia, F. Cotticelli, P. Maione, a cura di, Napoli&Rossini. Di questa luce un raggio, Edizioni S. Pietro a Majellia, Napoli, pp. 64–72.

Maione P., Seller F. (2015), Artigiani e mercanti: l'industria degli strumenti musi-cali a Napoli nell'Ottocento, in M. Vaccarini, M. G. Sità, A. Estero, a cura di, Musica come pensiero e come azione. Studi in onore di Guido Salvetti, Lim, Lucca, pp. 363–401.

Maione P., Seller. F. (2012), Da Napoli a Vienna: Barbaja e l'esportazione di un nuovo modello impresariale, in R. Angermüller, E. Biggi Parodi, a cura di, Antonio Salieri (1750–1825) e il teatro musicale a Vienna. Convenzioni, innovazioni, contaminazioni stilistiche, LIM, Lucca, pp. 405–420.

Maione, F. Seller (1994), I Reali Teatri di Napoli nella prima metà dell'Ottocento, Caserta, Santagata-Istituto Italiano per gli Studi Filosofici.

Majarelli S., Nicolini U. (1962), Il Monte dei Poveri di Perugia. Le origini (14621474), Perugia.

Mamczarz I. (1972), Les Intermedes comiques italiens au XVIIIe Siècle en France et en Italie, Paris.

Mancini F. (1968), Feste ed apparati civili e religiosi in Napoli dal Viceregno alla Capitale, Edizioni Scientifiche Italiane, Napoli.

Mancini F. (1984), «L'immaginario di regime». Apparati e scenografie alla corte del Viceré, in Civiltà del Seicento a Napoli (catalogo della mostra di Napoli 1984), Electa, Napoli.

Mancini F. (1997), Capolavori in festa. Effimero barocco a Largo di Palazzo (1683–1759), Electa, Napoli.

Maragi M. (1956), Cenni sulla natura e sullo svolgimento storico dei Monti di Pietà, in «Archivi storici delle aziende di credito», Roma, vol. I, pp. 291-314.

Mascilli Migliorini L. (1992), Il sistema delle arti: corporazioni annonarie e di mestiere a Napoli nel Settecento, A. Guida, Napoli.

Mastrodonato A. (2013), La norma inefficace: conflitti e negoziazioni nelle Arti napoletane (secc. XVI-XVIII), «Mediterranea-ricerche storiche», Anno X, Aprile, n. 27, pp. 65-92.

Merli C. (2007), Il teatro a iniziativa pubblica, Led-edizioni, Milano. Monaco M. (1971), La questione dei Monti di Pietà al V concilio lateranense, in «Studi Salernitani», gennaio-giugno, n. 7.

Monaco V. (1980), Le capitali del teatro borghese, in S. Ferrone,a cura di, Teatro dell'Italia Unita, Il Saggiatore, Milano.

Mori T. (2011), Figlie d'Italia.Poetesse patriote nel Risorgimento (1821–1861), Carocci, Roma.

Moricola G. (1994), L'industria della carità. L'Albergo dei Poveri nell'economia e nella società napoletana tra '700 e '800, Napoli, Liguori editore.

Moulin R. (2000), Mercato dell'arte contemporanea e globalizzazione, «Economia della cultura», X, 3, pp. 273–284.

Musi A. (1982), Pauperismo e pensiero giuridico a Napoli nella prima metà del secolo XVII, in G. Politi, M. Rosa, F. Della Peruta, a cura di, Timore e carità. I poveri nell'Italia Moderna, Cremona, pp. 259–274.

Musi A. (1990), Medici e istituzioni a Napoli nell'età moderna, in P. Frascani, a cura di, Sanità e società, Bologna, vol. V, pp. 19–66.

Muto G (1982), Forme e contenuti economici dell'assistenza nel Mezzogiorno Moderno: il caso di Napoli, in G. Politi, M. Rosa, F. Della Peruta, a cura di, Timore e carità. I poveri nell'Italia Moderna, Cremona, pp. 237–258.

Muto G. (1985), Gestione politica e controllo sociale nella Napoli spagnola, in C. De Seta, Le città capitali, Roma-Bari-Laterza.

Muto G. (1998), La crisi del Seicento, in Storia moderna, Roma, Donzelli, pp. 249–272.

Muto G. (2019), La Napoli spagnola, in F. Cotticelli, P. Maione, a cura di, Storia della musica e dello spettacolo a Napoli, Il Seicento, vol. I, pp. 19–70, Turchini edizioni, Napoli.

Nicolini N., a cura di, (1930), Domenico Confuorto, Giornali di Napoli da MDCLXXIX al MDCIC, L. Lubrano, Napoli.

Nicolodi F. (1987), Il sistema produttivo dall'Unità a oggi, in L. Bianconi, G. Pestelli, a cura di, Storia dell'Opera italiana, EdT, Torino, pp. 167–229.

Nicolodi F. (1993), Il teatro lirico e il suo pubblico, in S. Soldani, G. Turi, a cura di, Fare gli Italiani. Scuola e cultura nell'Italia contemporanea, 1° vol., La nascita dello Stato nazionale, il Mulino, Bologna, pp. 257–304.

Olivieri G., Aggiunte a La scuola musicale di Napoli di F. Florimo: i contratti dei figlioli della Pietà dei Turchini nei protocolli notarili (1667–1713), in R. Cafiero, M. Marino, a cura di, Francesco Florimo e l'ottocento musicale, Jason editrice, Reggio Calabria, pp. 717–752.

Pannain G. (1914), Le origini della scuola musicale di Napoli, Napoli.

Pannain G. (1952), Il Regio Conservatorio di Musica di Napoli, Firenze.

Pardi G. (1924), Napoli attraverso i secoli, Napoli.

Pasqualetti R. (2000), Editoriale, in Il teatro nella città contemporanea, Collana Architetture Pisane (20), Edizioni ETS, Pisa, pp. 7–15.

Pelizzari M. R. (2012), Dalle caserme ai salotti: gioco d'azzardo, teatro e loisir a Napoli tra fine Settecento e Decennio francese, in R. De Lorenzo, a cura di, Ordine e disordine. Amministrazione e mondo militare nel Decennio francese, Giannini, Napoli, pp. 381- 408.

Pennella G., Trimarchi M. (1993), L'Arte e lo Stato, in «Quaderni di Problemi di Amministrazione Pubblica», il Mulino, Bologna.

Perrotta R. (2018), Fonti per la storia della canzone napoletana: la «Collezione Ettore De Mura» del Comune di Napoli, in A. Bini, T. Grande, F. Riva, a cura di, Scripta sonant: contributi sul patrimonio musicale italiano, IAML Italia, Milano. Petraccone C. (1981), Napoli moderna e contemporanea, Guida Editore, Napoli.

Piazzoni I. (2001), Spettacolo, istituzioni e società nell'Italia post-unitaria (18601882), Archivio Guido Izzi, Roma.

Pinchera V. (2006), Arte ed economia. Una lettura interdisciplinare, «Rivista di Storia economica», il Mulino, n. 2, agosto, pp. 241–266.

Placanica A. (1972), Il patrimonio ecclesiastico calabrese nell'età moderna, Chiaravalle.

Placanica A. (1982), Moneta, prestiti, usure nel Mezzogiorno moderno, Napoli.

Pompilio A. (1982), Editoria musicale a Napoli e in Italia nel Cinque-Seicento, in Musica e Cultura a Napoli dal XV al XIX secolo, pp. 79–139.

Pompilio A., Vassalli A. (1983), Il madrigale a Napoli nel Cinque-Seicento, in D. A. D'Alessandro, A. Ziino, a cura di, La musica a Napoli durante il Seicento, pp. 9–16.

Pontieri E. (1972), Sulle origini della Compagnia dei Bianchi della Giustizia in Napoli e sui suoi statuti nel 1525, in «Campania sacra», n. 3.

Pozzi R. (1990), Vita musicale e committenza nei conservatori napoletani nel Seicento. Il S. Onofrio e i Poveri di Gesù Cristo, in A. Pompilio, D. Restani, L. Bianconi, F. A. Gallo, a cura di, Trasmissione e ricezione delle forme di cultura musicale, III, Atti del XIV Congresso della Società Internazionale di Musicologia, Torino, pp. 915–924.

Preston K. (1993), Opera on the Road. Traveling Opera troupes in the United States, 1825–60, Urbana & Chicago, University of Illinois Press.

Prota-Giurleo U. (1958), Francesco Provenzale, «Archivisti d'Italia e Rassegna internazionale degli archivi», S. II, 25.

Pullan B. (1996), Povertà, carità e nuove forme di assistenza nell'Europa moderna, in D. Zardin, a cura di, La città dei poveri, Milano.

Pullan B., S. J. Wolf (...), Plebi urbane e plebi rurali: da poveri a proletari, in «Storia d'Italia, Annali», vol. I, Einaudi, Torino, p. 1021.

Rak M., Conforti M., Lombardi C., a cura di, (2000–2005), Lezioni dell'Accademia di Palazzo del Duca di Medinaceli. Napoli 1698–1701, voll. I-V, Istituto Italiano per gli Studi Filosofici, Napoli.

Rao, A.M. (2009), Una capitale del pensiero. In F. Cotticelli and P. Maione eds, Storia della musica, Naples: Turchini Edizioni, pp. 1–32.

Rescigno G. (2016), Lo «Stato dell'Arte». Le corporazioni nel Regno di Napoli dal XV al XVIII secolo, X, coll. «Alle origini di Minerva trionfante», Ministero per i Beni e le Attività Culturali, Roma.

Rice J. A. (2013), Music and the Grand Tour in the Eighteenth Century, Hollander Distinguished Lecture in Musicology, Michigan State University, 15 March 2013, DOI: https://sites.google.com/site/johnaricecv/music-and-the-grandtour (data u.c.: 10.07.2020).

Rienzo M. G. (1982), Nobili e attività caritativa a Napoli nell'età moderna. L'esempio dell'Oratorio del SS. Crocefisso dei Cavalieri in S. Paolo Maggiore, in G. Galasso, C. Russo, a cura di, Per la storia sociale e religiosa del Mezzogiorno d'Italia, Napoli.

Rivero Rodrìguez M. (2012), El mundo desordenado: el cambio de dinastìa en el reino de Nàapoles (1707), in Immaculada Arias de Saavedra Alìas (ed), Vida cotidiana en la Espana de la Illustraciòn, Universidad de Granada, pp. 463–486.

Robinson M. F. (1972), Naples and Neapolitan Opera, Clarendon Press, Oxford.

Romano R. (1962), Tra XVI e XVII secolo. Una crisi economica: 1619–1622, «Rivista Storica Italiana», 3, pp. 480–531.

Robinson M. (1990), A late 18th century account book of the San Carlo Theater, Naples, Early music, 18 (1), pp. 73–82.

Romano R. (1965), Prezzi, salari e servizi a Napoli nei secoli XVII e XVIII, Milano.

Romano R. (1976), Napoli dal Viceregno al Regno, Einaudi, Torino.

Rosmini E. (1893), Legislazione e giurisprudenza dei teatri, Hoepli, Milano.

Rosselli J. (1908), The Castrati as a Professional Group and a Social Phenomenon, 1550–1850, Brighton.

Rosselli J. (1982), Agenti teatrali nel mondo dell'opera lirica italiana dell'Ottocento, Olschki, Firenze.

Rosselli J. (1982), Materiali per la storia socio-economica del San Carlo nell'Ottocento, in L. Bianconi, R. Bossa, Musica e Cultura a Napoli, Olschki, Firenze, pp. 369–381.

Rosselli J. (1983), Elenco provvisorio degli impresari e agenti teatrali italiani dal 1770 al 1890.

Rosselli J. (1984), The opera industry in Italy from Cimarosa to Verdi: the role of the impresario, Cambridge University Press.

Rosselli J. (1989), L'apprendistato del cantante italiano: i rapporti contrattuali fra allievi e insegnanti dal '500 al '900, Olschky, Firenze.

Rosselli J. (1991), Music & musicians in nineteenth century Italy, Batsford.

Rosselli J. (1992), La musica sul palcoscenico, in V. Castronovo, a cura di, Il trionfo della borghesia, Electa, Milano.

Rosselli J. (1992), Sulle ali dorate: il mondo musicale italiano dell'Ottocento, il Mulino, Bologna.

Rosselli J. (1993), Il cantante d'opera: storia di una professione (1600–1990), il Mulino, Bologna.

Rosselli, J. (1981), Governi, appaltatori e giochi d'azzardo nell'Italia napoleonica, «Rivista Storica Italiana».

Russo C. (1970), I monasteri femminili di clausura a Napoli nel secolo XVII, Napoli.

Russo C. (1976), La storiografia socio-religiosa e i suoi problemi, in C. Russo, a cura di, Società, Chiesa e vita religiosa nell'Ancien Régime, Napoli.

Russo C., a cura di, (1994), Chiesa, Assistenza e Società nel Mezzogiorno Moderno, Lecce.

Russo G. (1976), Vita popolare napoletana dal 1860 a oggi, in Storia di Napoli, vol. X ESI, Napoli, pp. 645-715.

Salvemini R. (1997), La asistencia en la ciudad de Nàpoles en los ss. XVI-XVII, in Ciudad y Mundo urbano en la Epoca Moderna, Madrid, pp. 271–299.

Salvemini R. (1998), La difficile combinazione tra assistenza e credito in età moderna, in «Rassegna Storica Salernitana», n. 29, pp. 29-67.

Saracino E. (1995), Imprenditori del teatro e della musica, in S. Cavaciocchi, a cura di, Il tempo libero. Economia e Società. Secc. XIII-XVIII, Le Monnier, Firenze 1995, pp. 751-763.

Sasportes J., a cura di, (2011), Storia della danza italiana dalle origini ai giorni nostri, EdT, Torino.

Sbordone S. (1990), Editori e tipografi a Napoli nel '600, Accademia Pontaniana, Napoli.

Scannapieco A. (2012), Vicende della fortuna goldoniana nella Napoli del secondo Settecento, in A. Lezza, A. Scannapieco, a cura di, Oltre la Serenissima. Goldoni, Napoli e la cultura meridionale, Liguori, Napoli, pp. 11-25.

Schechner R. (1984), Verso una poetica della performance, in R. Schechner, a cura di, La teoria della performance 1970-1983, Bulzoni, Roma.

Schiattarella F. (1969), Maritaggi di cuccagna, Napoli.

Schifa M. (1923), Il regno di Napoli al tempo di Carlo Borbone, Milano-RomaNapoli.

Scialò P. (1995), La canzone napoletana dalle origini ai giorni nostri, Newton Compton, Roma.

Scialò P., Seller F. (2013), a cura di, Passatempi musicali. Giullaume Cottrau e la canzone napoletana di primo '800, Guida, Napoli.

Seller F. (1999), Lo Stabilimento Musicale Partenopeo, in R. Cafiero, M. Marino, a cura di, Francesco Florimo e l'Ottocento musicale, Atti del convegno (Morcone 19-21 aprile 1990), Jason editrice, Reggio Calabria, pp. 469-497.

Seller F. (2001), Il recupero della musica «antica» nell'editoria napoletana dall'Unità d'Italia alla Grande Guerra, in G. Feroleto, A. Pugliese, a cura di, Alessandro Longo: l'uomo,il suo tempo, l'opera, Istituto di Bibliografia Musicale Calabrese, Vibo Valentia, pp. 391-400.

Seller F. (2004), Editoria verdiana a Napoli nell'Ottocento, in «Studi verdiani», n. 18, pp. 148-230.

Seller F. (2009), Copisti e stampatori teatrali a Napoli nel diciottesimo secolo, in F. Cotticelli, P. Maione, a cura di, Storia della musica e dello spettacolo a Napoli. Il Settecento, Turchini edizioni, Napoli, pp. 805-822.

Seller F. (2009), I pianoforti a Napoli nell'Ottocento, in «Fonti Musicali Italiane», 14, pp. 171-199.

Seller F. (2016), Verdi e l'editoria musicale a Napoli nell'Ottocento, in Verdi a Napoli. Verdi al San Carlo, Skira, Napoli, pp. 75-80.

Seller F. (2019), L'editoria musicale a Napoli, in F. Cotticelli, P. Maione, a cura di, Storia della musica e dello spettacolo a Napoli. Il Seicento, tomo II, Turchini edizioni, Napoli, pp. 1815-1824.

Seller F., A. Caroccia (2016), Il Collegio di musica negli anni francesi, in P. Maione (a cura di), Musica e spettacolo a Napoli durante il decennio francese (18061815), Turchini edizioni, Napoli, pp. 393–415.

Serino M. (2011), Spazio urbano e spazio teatrale nell'organizzazione dello spettacolo dal vivo, in Metropolis, 26 luglio – Tafter Journal - http://www.tafter journal.it

Silvestri A. (1951), Sui banchieri pubblici napoletani nella prima metà del '500. Notizie e documenti, in «Bollettino dell'Archivio Storico del Banco di Napoli», tomo II.

Silvestri A. (1952), Sui banchieri pubblici napoletani dall'avvento di Filippo II al trono della costituzione del monopolio. Notizie e documenti, «Bollettino dell'Archivio Storico del Banco di Napoli», tomo IV.

Sirago M., Il mare in festa, musica balli e cibi nella Napoli viceregnale (15031734), Kinetès edizioni, Benevento 2022.

Sirch L., M. G. Sità, M. Vaccarini, a cura di, (2012), L'insegnamento dei conservatorî, la composizione e la vita musicale nell'Europa dell'Ottocento, Lim, Lucca.

Smith A. (1776), An Inquiry into the Nature and Causes of the Wealth of Nations, 1776, libri I e II, cap. 3, edited by R. H. Campbell and A. S. Skinner, William B. Todd, Textual Editor.

Sorba C (2001), Teatri. L'Italia del melodramma nell'età del Risorgimento, il Mulino, Bologna.

Sorba C. (2011), Musica e Teatro, in L'Unificazione Italiana, Istituto per l'enciclopedia italiana Treccani, pp. 533–549.

Sorbe C. (2012), Per una nuova storia sociale e culturale della musica, in «Contemporanea», vol. 15, No. 3 (luglio-settembre 2012), pp. 493–497, Il Mulino.

Spezzaferro L., a cura di, (2004), Mercanti di quadri, in «Quaderni storici»», 116/2, numero monografico.

Staffieri G. (2017), «Versi, macchine e canto»: il teatro in musica del Seicento, in A. Chegai et al., a cura di, Musiche nella storia,

Stamer W. J. A. (1878), Dolce Napoli. Naples: its streets, people, fêtes, pilgrimages, environs etc. etc., London.

Stazio M. L. (1995), La fabbrica della festa, in M. L. Stazio, a cura di, Catalogo Piedigrotta 1895–1995, Progetti museali editore, Roma.

Stazio M. L. (2013), Back to the Future. Giullaume Cottrau. Viaggio temporale fra «Divertimenti per Pianoforte» e canzone napoletana, ovvero: la storia ricostruita dai suoi esiti, in P. Scialò, F.Seller, a cura di, Passatempi musicali, Guida, Napoli, pp. 209–246.

Stefani G. (1974), Musica Barocca. Poetica e Ideologia, Bompiani, Milano.

Stiffoni G. (2001), Il Teatro San Carlo dal 1747 al 1753: Documenti d'archivio per un'indagine sulla gestione dell'impresario Diego Tufarelli. In: P. Maione,

Ed. Fonti d'Archivio per la storia della musica e dello spettacolo a Napoli tra XVI e XVIII secolo. Napoli: Editoriale Scientifica, pp. 271–374.

Summonte A. (1675), Historia della città e regno di Napoli, Napoli, vol. I.

Symbola (2021), Io sono Cultura, Rapporto, https://www.symbola.net/ricerca/io-sono-cultura-2021/.

Tarallo A. (1999), Ancora sui circoli musicali e mecenati nella Napoli postunitaria, in R. Cafiero, M. Marino, a cura di, Francesco Florimo e l'Ottocento musicale, Jason editrice, Reggio Calabria, pp. 441–468.

Tenenti A. (1977), Il senso della morte e l'amore della vita nel Rinascimento, Einaudi, Torino, pp. 62-111.

Thorsby D. (2001). Economics and Culture. Cambridge: Cambridge University Press.

Tortora E. (1882), Raccolta di documenti storici e delle leggi e regole concernenti il Banco di Napoli, Giannini, Napoli.

Tortora S. (2005), La nascita di un modello per l'architettura dei teatri partenopei: il Teatro Nuovo a Montecalvario, in B. Gravagnuolo, F. Adriani, a cura di, Domenico Antonio Vaccaro sintesi delle arti, Guida, Napoli, pp. 251-264.

Traversier M. (2009a), Gouverner l'opéra: una histoire politique de la musique à Naples, 1767–1815, Ecole Française de Rome, Roma.

Traversier M. (2009b). L'impresario d'opera nel decennio francese tra libertà economia e tutela politica: Il caso di Domenico Barbaja. In A.M. Rao and L. Mascilli Migliorini eds. Cultura e lavoro intellettuale: istituzioni, saperi, professioni nel Decennio francese. Napoli, Giannini, pp. 65–109.

Tufano L. (2009), Il mestiere del musicista: formazione, mercato, consapevolezza, immagine. In : F. Cotticelli and P. Maione eds. Storia della Musica. Naples: Turchini Edizioni, pp. 733–771.

Vajro M. (1957), La canzone napoletana dalle origini all'Ottocento. Saggi di folklore musicale, Vajro, Napoli.

Van Damme I., B.De Munck, A. Miles (Eds), (2017), Cities and Creativity from Renaissanse to the Present, Routledge, Taylor & Francis New York and London.

Vecchione E., Genovesi E. (1908), Le istituzioni di beneficenza nella città di Napoli, Napoli.

Veneziano G. A. R. (2013), «Napoli è tutto il mondo»: la cappella musicale del Pio Monte della Misericordia (1616-1749), in C.

Villani P. (1972), Note sullo sviluppo economico e sociale del Regno di Napoli nel Settecento, in «Rassegna economica», 1.

Yamada T. (2004), L'attività e la strategia di Gennaro Bianchi, impresario dei teatri napoletani nella seconda metà del Settecento: Interpretazione del suo sistema di gestione dalle scritture dell'Archivio Storico dell'Istituto Banco di Napoli – Fondazione. Quaderni dell'Archivio storico, pp. 95–116.

Zamagni V. (a cura di), Povertà e innovazioni istituzionali in Italia dal Medioevo ad oggi, Il Mulino Bologna 2000.

Zeithaml V. A., M. J. Bitner (2000), Il marketing dei servizi, McGraw-Hill, Milano.

Zilli I. (2001), «El arbol de la cucana»: Ocio y tiempo libre en la Napoles del XVIII, in L. Ribot, L. De Rosa (dir. por), Trabajo y ocio en la Epoca Moderna, Editorial Actas, Madrid, pp. 267–294.

INDEX